TEXTS *AND* CONTEXTS

P9-CEN-495

TEXTS *AND* CONTEXTS

Seventh Edition

William S. Robinson
Emeritus, San Francisco State University

Stephanie Tucker
California State University, Sacramento

With the assistance of Cynthia G. Hicks
Chabot College

WADSWORTH
CENGAGE Learning™

Australia • Brazil • Japan • Korea • Mexico • Singapore • Spain • United Kingdom • United States

Texts and Contexts, Seventh Edition
William S. Robinson

Publisher: Lyn Uhl

Acquisitions Editor: Annie Todd

Development Editor: Cathy Richard Dodson

Director of Marketing: Annie Mitchell

Marketing Assistant: Kathleen Remsberg

Advertising Project Manager: Stacey Purviance

Senior Content Project Manager: Karen Stocz

Creative Director: Rob Hugel

Art Director: Linda Helcher

Print Buyer: Susan Carroll

Permissions Editor: Bob Kauser

Cover Designer: Kathleen Kemp

Compositor: Integra Software Services

© 2009, 2006 Wadsworth Cengage Learning

ALL RIGHTS RESERVED. No part of this work covered by the copyright herein may be reproduced, transmitted, stored, or used in any form or by any means graphic, electronic, or mechanical, including but not limited to photocopying, recording, scanning, digitizing, taping, Web distribution, information networks, or information storage and retrieval systems, except as permitted under Section 107 or 108 of the 1976 United States Copyright Act, without the prior written permission of the publisher.

For product information and technology assistance, contact us at
Cengage Learning Academic Resource Center, 1-800-423-0563
For permission to use material from this text or product, submit all requests online at
www.cengage.com/permissions.
Further permissions questions can be e-mailed to **permissionrequest@cengage.com.**

Library of Congress Control Number: 2007942028

ISBN-13: 978-1-4130-3345-8
ISBN-10: 1-4130-3345-8

Wadsworth Cengage Learning
25 Thomson Place
Boston, MA 02210
USA

Cengage Learning products are represented in Canada by Nelson Education, Ltd.

For your course and learning solutions, visit
academic.cengage.com.
Purchase any of our products at your local college store or at our preferred online store
www.ichapters.com.

Printed in the United States of America.
1 2 3 4 5 6 7 12 11 10 09 08

This book is dedicated to the memory of
Susan Skov, Steve Stedman, and Jim Whearty
Their students never had better teachers.

Contents

Part I   Writing from the Top Down   1

Practice in developing the ability to read critically and to summarize; learning the fundamentals of the academic writing process through writing a short report; shaping texts and sentences.

CHAPTER 1   THE WRITING PROCESS   3

P*reface: To the Student*

OR, WHAT YOU'VE GOTTEN YOURSELF INTO AND HOW TO GET OUT OF IT

Here you are, after twelve years of school, and you're in still *another* English class, and you're probably thinking, "Now what?"

Meanwhile, your new English teacher is going to look at your first paper, which you are probably going to put a lot of work into and which you'll probably think is pretty good, and he or she is going to think, "How could anyone who's gone to school for twelve years write like this?"

And to make matters worse, the first time you and your fellow students hand in an essay test or a paper for some other college class, *that* teacher is going to groan, "Why don't they teach them to write anymore?"

On the one hand, the students are saying, "What's wrong with my writing anyway? Its always been okay before." And on the other hand, the teachers are saying, "This stuff is terrible. They can't even write a sentence."

What do we have here, a failure of communication?

I don't know whether it's going to make you feel any better about this or not, but college teachers have been complaining about their students' writing since people were dipping quill pens into little bottles of ink. And colleges have been running special writing classes for their weaker writers since long before you (or I) were born.

There are probably numerous reasons why college students don't write as well as their teachers think they ought to, but the main point is that for the most part they don't, and there are a few things you ought to know about this.

One is that the teachers are right; most students don't write as well as they should be able to.

Another is that if you think poor writing won't hold you back, you may be right, but there is a good chance that you're wrong. You can cast this proposition in the form of a bet, if you want. You can bet against needing to write fairly well; you can say, "Learning English is a pain, and I probably won't need it anyway, so why bother?" In this case, if you turn out to be wrong, you've lost the bet and suffered major financial and career disadvantages. Your poor writing has held you back from promotion or, in some cases, even employment in the first place.

Or you can bet the other way; you can say, "Learning English is a pain, but I might need it, so I better do it." In this case, if you turn out to be wrong (you didn't need to learn to write well after all), you haven't lost anything. But if you turn out to be right, you've gained a lot. So which bet makes more sense?

One of the mildly amusing things about all this from an English teacher's point of view is that in precisely the fields where the majority of students think writing is unimportant—business and engineering—the people who do the hiring think it's extremely important.

Anyway, regardless of how you bet, you still have to pass this course, so you might as well know what you're in for and why. This book is designed to help you improve your writing in certain very specific ways, for certain very specific reasons, and here's what they are.

First, the most important thing about writing is to be able to get your ideas across. Obviously. But that isn't always so easy. Someone once said, "Writing is God's way of showing you how sloppy your thinking is." So the main part of this book is a series of writing assignments like the ones you'll have to do in college, assignments in which you gather information either from personal observation or from readings, decide what you think the information means or shows, and then organize an essay to explain the issue and your ideas on it. You'll be working on summarizing, analyzing, classifying, comparing, and arguing, and you'll be working on organizing your ideas into coherent papers that will get them across. It is, literally, easier said than done.

Second, you'll be working on developing your sentences. A famous study of the writing of fourth graders, eighth graders, twelfth graders, and published writers showed a number of interesting differences among them. One difference was that as the writers got older and more experienced, their sentences got longer. The fourth graders wrote sentences averaging 13.5 words long, the eighth graders 15.9 words, the twelfth graders 16.9 words, and the published writers 24.7 words. (You might count the words in the sentences in a page of your writing and see where you come out.)

This doesn't mean that a long sentence is automatically better than a short one or that you should never write short sentences. It does mean that more capable writers are able to say more in each sentence and have more different ways of doing so. In other words, better writers have more tools.

Besides that, writing that averages seventeen words a sentence is so childish and monotonous that it would drive you, as a reader, crazy in fifteen minutes. You do want mainly to communicate, but you also want someone else to be able to read it.

So a major part of this book consists of what are called "sentence combining" exercises, which are designed not just to enable you to get more into your sentences, as professional writers do, but also to begin using certain kinds of structures that most inexperienced writers tend to use very infrequently. If you apply what you learn in these exercises to your own writing, you will start sounding on the page like an intelligent human being.

Finally, and most uninterestingly, if you are still making mistakes in matters that you should have learned by the seventh grade—stuff like using apostrophes correctly—this book provides the usual explanations and exercises. For God's sake, learn it.

No book or workbook, no explanations or exercises, can make anyone into a good, or even capable, writer. You can no more learn how to write by reading a book than you can learn how to ride a bicycle, water-ski, or fly a jet fighter by reading a book. Learning *how to do* anything requires someone there to help you, to show you the right techniques and correct you when you do something wrong. That's the teacher's job. It also requires a learner who wants to learn, who is willing to learn both from the teacher and from his or her own mistakes, someone who will try to make active use of the lessons given. That's your job. This is your big chance.

WSR

Preface: To the Instructor

TOP-DOWN AND BOTTOM-UP

What do we do when we write? We think about what we want to say, for-mulate some sort of plan or goal, and get at it. In the process, we employ what we know about English in general and written English in particular. Seeing flawed and inexpert written texts, writing teachers used to think that the writer's main, or only, problem was error, and that the solution to that problem was to teach the writer grammar and the correction of errors. Of course, many writing teachers still advocate this approach.

But researchers in composition, linguistics, and psycholinguistics have found that this approach—which is now called the "bottom-up" approach—does not correspond with, to rephrase the question above, what we do when we write and so does not address the most basic difficulties writers have or the *sources* of their errors.

At least three sources of the writing problems that students encounter have been identified. One is the knowledge source—not knowing certain rules (and thus producing errors). A corollary of this is not using certain syntactic structures with the frequency competent writers use them (and thus producing choppy, monotonous, undeveloped sentences). A second is the process source—the writer's not understanding how capable writers work and therefore trying to write in unproductive ways, usually trying to produce perfect first drafts. Much has been written about these two sources, but somewhat less has been written about the third source, what we might call the text source.

Under one circumstance every basic writer faces, the text itself may be the source of numerous writing problems—everything from disorganized, undeveloped essays to errors of usage. That circumstance is *when the writer doesn't understand the characteristics of the text he or she is being asked to write.*

Students who have been put through drills in sentence structure, usage, and paragraph organization will still be completely at sea when asked to write an essay if they have no idea what an essay looks like—what its structural and substantive features are. Students who learn to write personal essays with competence characteristically fail at every level, from text to word, when required to write a piece of literary analysis. How can they not? They don't know what those texts look like.

The traditional solution to this problem has been the infamous five-paragraph essay, but the five-paragraph essay is not an example of academic, professional, or any other kind of writing, nor even a stepping stone to them, but merely a formula for getting words on paper.

Because doing exercises that do not involve communication is stultifying, because learning rules in a vacuum is fruitless, and because the text itself is a major source of problems for the inexperienced writer, it has become an axiom of current composition theory—as found, for instance, in Theresa Enos' *A Sourcebook for Basic Writing Teachers*—that we should tackle the job of teaching inexperienced writers in the same way writers write—from the top down—working on building meaning as a primary goal rather than attempting to extirpate errors first.

Yet most composition texts for basic writers still work from the contrary idea—that you can't write an essay until you can write a paragraph and that you can't write a paragraph until you can write certain esteemed kinds of sentences and that you can't even write those sentences until you have learned a lot of grammar. Thus, we find a bottom-up approach to a top-down activity.

An assumption of this book is, then, that if inexperienced writers are to learn to write essays, they must begin writing essays as soon as possible—that is, immediately—and that the part of the writing process most central to their learning is the one involving shaping the whole text. That is not to say that they won't need help at the lower levels; they will. And this text provides that help. It is to say that the traditional order of priorities has been reversed here.

GETTING PERSONAL

A second assumption behind this book is that students in developmental writing courses are still college students. That means that they are being assigned college-level readings and college-level writing tasks right away, depending to a limited extent on their majors and other curriculum requirements. What, then, are they to do in these other classes if their English curriculum defers until some later date their preparation for this work? Poorly prepared students need immediate help in doing college-level reading and writing.

A growing number of teachers has come to realize that we give these students the most effective help if we assign them not the traditional personal-experience essay, a form derived from the belletristic tradition, but essays more nearly of the kind they will be assigned in their other courses. There, characteristically, they must read and then write about their readings. They may have to summarize, analyze, synthesize, compare or contrast, figure out what they think and argue for it, discuss implications. They will be asked to make discoveries in fields alien to them and think about what those discoveries mean. In short, they will be asked to join the educational enterprise as the academic world defines it (not write five-paragraph essays).

And so the assignments in this book are based on readings or other data from which the student writers are asked to extract meanings and implications as the basis for their essays.

That does not mean that students must not draw on their own experience. It is surely a crucial part of their educations that students look at their own lives in the light of what they are learning, and so most assignments begin by asking them to think about questions related to the assignment that bear on their own experience. Additionally, some assignments require students to use what they know and can observe as an important part of their essays. The assignments vary considerably in this respect. But all emphasize making valid inferences about both the readings and the students' experiences.

WRITING TO WRITE OR WRITING TO LEARN

Another salient characteristic of the writing assignments is that they involve writing to learn rather than merely writing for writing's sake. Too many textbooks suggest, for instance, "classification" assignments in which the writer categorizes students into types (always three) or describes three different kinds of friends—in one classic case, "best friends," "good friends," and "hi and bye friends." Never is there an indication of why one would want to do such a thing nor what one would learn from doing it, and so the result is invariably vacuous and formulaic, the counterfeit of writing.

In the assignments in this text, students use common thinking strategies—classifying, comparing, arguing, discussing—for genuine purposes.

- They may classify a typical list of contemporary jobs in order to find out what kinds of skills, training, and education the job market today and tomorrow will be asking for, or they may set up their own research project to investigate ethnic or gender representation in Saturday morning children's television.

- They may compare American and Asian educational methods in order to learn the strengths and weaknesses of different approaches to education and thus to look at their own experiences in school, or they may compare the health-care systems of the United States and France.

- They may examine the arguments for and against handgun control or whether high school students should work in order to decide for themselves on an informed basis how they stand.

There is always a reason for the writing assignment and something to be learned by doing it.

CHALLENGE AND CONFIDENCE

It is a truism that the initial work in basic writing courses should, among other things, promote the confidence of student writers. No one performs well when he or she feels doomed to failure. The easy way to promote such confidence is to assign work that the student already knows how to do. Unhappily, such assignments do not promote learning.

Assignments must push students toward what Lev Vygotsky calls their "zone of proximal development"—that is, the next stage at which they can succeed *with help*. In short, from the very beginning, a skills course should work to edge the students' skill level ever higher. Consequently, this text includes enough assignments of every kind—both essay and sentence—that students can solidify in their new skill levels before they advance.

Some classes may need to spend more time in solidifying skills than others and so may not move as far through the book. In one of the courses we teach, the students take two full semesters to work through Chapter 5, while in another, many sections get into Chapter 6 in one semester. With the right pacing, all students begin to develop a strong sense that they can do college-level work.

ERROR'S ENDLESS TRAIN

Linguists have known for many decades that native speakers of English have mastered pretty much the entire grammar of English by the time they are four years old. This grammar is, of course, the grammar of speech rather than that of writing, but while the two differ in ways that may seem more or less obtrusive, depending on the spoken dialect, these grammars are, for all practical purposes—such as communication—virtually identical. If they weren't, we wouldn't be able to understand one another.

As we noted earlier, inexperienced writers face the problem that because the cognitive demands of written communication are so great, they may have difficulty using the grammar they know and so produce ungrammatical structures. A second problem is that they may use structures grammatical in speech but not in writing. And finally, and much more frequently and obtrusively, they usually demonstrate degrees of unfamiliarity with written usages, the kinds of things covered in handbooks and workbooks (and covered in Part III of this book). These elements, however, should not be confused with grammar.

In writing there are "errors" of omission as well as errors of commission, the kind of "error" represented by choppy, childish syntax. As Kellogg Hunt noted many years ago, while inexperienced writers use the same syntactic structures used by experienced writers, they don't use them as frequently. Even a fourth grader will turn up with an occasional appositive phrase, but the frequency of appositives in published writing will be scores of times greater.

Sentence combining, though no panacea, is helpful in dealing with many of the difficulties outlined above, and research strongly suggests that it is particularly effective with developmental writers. A consistent program of sentence combining, one in which the students do exercises one or more times a week, helps develop fluency and consequently a greater ability to produce grammatical structures. If properly designed, it can also promote the use of structures—such as concessive clauses, appositives, and verbal phrases—that inexperienced writers rarely use, structures that not only add texture to writing but also tend to promote more mature thinking.

Usage errors are another matter, and that is what the workbook section is for, though again it is important for the teacher to distinguish between usage errors that crop up as production problems and those that are truly knowledge problems. For knowledge errors, explanations and exercises are essential. For process errors, only practice and help in proofreading will do. (For a complete discussion of the different kinds and sources of error, see my article "Towards a Theory of Error" in the September 1998 *Teaching English in the Two-Year College,* reprinted in the Instructor's Manual.)

WRITING PROCESS, TEACHING PROCESS

As a result of the work of Nancy Sommers and others, we now understand that "the writing process" is not a linear, step-by-step affair, beginning, say, with invention activities, proceeding to an outline, moving on through various drafts, and winding up with proofreading, each step discrete and individual. We know that writers actually work in a much messier and more recursive fashion, one that involves these activities but tends to conflate them.

While this knowledge is very important to us as writing teachers, it is not necessarily very helpful to us as *basic* writing teachers. Learning specialists have also shown us that when we learn a new activity we go through (among others) three basic stages:

1. Ignorance of how to perform the activity
2. Ability to perform it only by closely following rules or directions
3. Ability to perform it without reference to rules or directions

Moreover, it is impossible to go directly from stage 1 to stage 3. Inexperienced writers, writers who may think, for example, that the way writers write is to sit down and produce polished, finished articles and stories, must have guidance, "rules" even, to help them achieve workable composing processes. Both Chapter 1 and the writing assignments in Chapters 3 through 6 attempt to give that guidance without being excessively prescriptive and linear. Still, carefully taking classes through recognizable steps in the process helps students to begin finding themselves as writers.

EXAMPLES OF STUDENT WRITING

There are a number of examples of student writing in the text. They are used to demonstrate key points and as readings. You will find these examples in:

- Chapter 2 (Student Writers at Work)
- Chapter 3 "We've Come a Long Way, but Magazines Stayed Behind"
- Chapter 4 "School Here in the United States and There in Vietnam"

In addition, the revised Instructor's Manual includes more examples of student writing, should you wish to use them in the course.

TEACHING AIDS

Print Supplements

- **Instructor's Manual** (1413010466). This edition has been revised to provide additional help, particularly to new users. It includes more examples of student writing, background and information on the elements of the text and how to use them, a sample course outline, a journal article on the approach of this text, chapter-by-chapter strategies for teaching the writing assignments, and teaching tips for using the Workbook.

Electronic and Online Supplements

- **Texts and Contexts with Writer's Resources CD-ROM 2.0.** The Writer's Resources CD-ROM Version 2.0 is an interactive multimedia program that use audio, animation, auto-graded exercises, and a course management system to teach all aspects of grammar and writing. This CD-ROM is available for a reduced price when packaged with new copies of *Texts and Contexts,* Seventh Edition.

ACKNOWLEDGMENTS

The materials in this book are the result of a number of years of development and revision, trial and error and retrial, and we would like to express our obligations and thanks to the many instructors at San Francisco State University and California State University, Sacramento, who have used them and made suggestions for improvements. We are also in debt to Shelley Circle for the hours she spent in gathering publishers' and writers' permissions and helping us with library research and to Randall Roorda, whose comments on the penultimate manuscript were of the greatest value.

Reviewers for the Seventh Edition

Doug Rice, *Sacramento State College*
Dave Sullivan, *Chabot College*
Lourdes Villarreal, *Hartnell Community College*
Mark Fuzie, *Yakima Valley Community College*
Gary Enns, *Cerro Coso Community College*
Gordon Dossett, *Santa Monica College*

Ken Kottka, *Chabot College*

Chris Doyen, *Bakersfield College*

Christine Swiridoff, *Cerro Coso Community College*

Teeka James, *College of San Mateo*

Robin Calitri, *Merced College*

Tracy Schneider, *Solano Community College*

Lanka Sunita Vijay, *Hartnell and Monterey Peninsula college*

Barbara Jones, *College of San Mateo*

Kathy Rodgers, *American River College*

Michelle O'Dell, *Shasta College*

Dana Morgan, *Santa Monica College*

Ursula Irwin, *Mt.Hood Community College*

Amanda Field, *Chabot College*

Sera Hirasuna, *Hartnell College*

Elli England, *Orange Coast College*

Gary Zacharias, *Palomar College*

Merle Cutler, *College of San Mateo*

Denise Albright, *Pasadena City College*

Norman Stephens, *Cerro Coso Community College*

Reviewers for the Sixth Edition

Pam Altman, *San Francisco State University*

Erwin C. Barron, *Chabot College*

Candace Boeck, *San Diego State University*

Shirley Guthrie, *California State University, Long Beach*

Cynthia G. Hicks, *Chabot College*

Bonnie Lenore Kyburz, *Utah Valley State College*

Thank you also to Anne Stafford, *College of San Mateo,* for her suggestions for the new edition.

Reviewers for the Fifth Edition

William Sweigart, *Indiana University, Southeast*

Gary Zacharias, *Palomar College*

Fourth Edition

Thanks are very much in order to Cindy Hicks of Chabot College and Pam Altman of San Francisco State for invaluable help with the fourth edition of this book.

Reviewers for the Fourth Edition

Nancy M. Anter, *Wayne State University*

Nora Bacon, *University of Nebraska at Omaha*

Elizabeth Jones, *Fontbonne College*

Laura Knight, *Mercer County Community College*

Michael Lomax, *Hartnell College*

Janet Madden, *El Camino College*

Ken McLaurin, *Central Piedmont Community College*

William Sweigart, *Indiana University, Southeast*

Third Edition

And for contributions to the third edition, I would like to add my thanks to Elizabeth Sommers, Karen Wong, and Susan Zimmerman of San Francisco State and Jim Bowsher of College of Marin. Thanks also to reviewers for this third edition: Donna Alden, Dona Ana Community College; Sandra Blakeman, Hood College; Natalie S. Daley, Linn-Benton Community College; Cindy Hicks, Chabot College; Pamela McDonough, Palomar College; and Robert T. Mundhenk, Northampton Community College.

Second Edition

For help with the second edition thanks are owing to Pam Altman, whose generosity with her time and energy have been exceptional and gratefully received, and to Juanita Alunan, Doreen Deicke, Michael Martin, and Lisa Metge, all of San Francisco State, and to Marc Kemp of Fullerton College and Bill Sweigart of Indiana University, Southeast. I wish this edition were as good as they would have made it.

First Edition

We would like to thank the following people for their help in reviewing the manuscript; we are grateful for the teaching wisdom they brought to the task and for the resulting suggestions and criticisms, which have improved this text immeasurably: Barbara Baxter, State Technical Institute at Memphis; Judith Boschult, Phoenix College; Barbara Carpenter, Marist College; Linda Daigle, Houston Community College; Laura Knight, Mercer County Community College; John C. Lovas, De Anza College; Milla McConnell-Tuite, College of San Mateo; Randall Popken, Tarleton University; Claudia Questo, Green River Community College; and Penny O. Smith, Gannon University.

We also want to thank Angela Gantner, our former editor at Wadsworth, for her faith in this project, her determination that we would do the job right whether we wanted to or not, and her unfailing good nature through even the most trying of times.

Writing from the Top Down

Writing is a lot like inflating a blimp with a bicycle pump. Anybody can do it. All it takes is time.

Kurt Vonnegut, Jr.

CHAPTER *1*

The Writing Process

In college, most of the writing you do will be based on other writing—on books and articles you dig up in the library or on the internet. In this class, you will be doing the same thing except that you won't have to find the materials you write about; they are provided for you. In both cases, your writing process, like that of scholars, businesspeople, and professional writers, will start not with writing but with reading. And how well you manage to write will start with how well you read.

One can make two mistakes in reading done for writing. The first is just to read the stuff, whatever it is, assuming that you will remember it all. You won't. Nobody can. The second is to try to remember everything. You won't do that, either. Some students buy highlighters and go through their textbooks highlighting everything, page after page, figuring that now they will remember it all. But when everything is highlighted, nothing is highlighted. The only difference is that the page is yellow instead of white.

READING ACTIVELY AND EFFICIENTLY

The first step in the writing process is reading actively. To read actively, you need to find the main points in what you read and work out a way of recording them so that you will be able to find them easily later on.

How do we know what the main points in a written text are? We first need to realize that all expository writing—the kind that explains something or argues a position—has a special shape. You can even draw it; it looks something like the chart (Figure 1.1) on the following page. The dark areas represent general statements, ones that serve to introduce the reader to what's coming next. The first paragraph or so is, of course, the introduction, telling the reader what the whole essay or article will be about. The following paragraphs (however many there are) usually begin with their own general statements, a sentence or two called the topic sentence, which tells the reader what to expect in the paragraph.

Why do writers use topic sentences? Read the following sentence and ask yourself if you know what it's supposed to mean.

She was really annoyed, but she decided she had to go.

Obviously, you don't know who "she" is or why she was annoyed, or where she was supposed to go. Now read the same sentence with another one preceding it:

Joanne received an invitation to her ex-boyfriend's wedding. She was really annoyed, but she decided she had to go.

Now we *can* understand the second sentence (though we would have to read further to learn why she decided she had to go). Linguists call this issue "text coherence"—that is, what makes pieces of writing understandable. The same text coherence issue that works between sentences also works in paragraphs. Read the following paragraph:

The spectators enjoy the sun or the evening, chat, drink beer or soda, cheer or boo as the occasion demands, and hope for a victory by the home team. The analysts keep score, watch each pitch intently, note the strengths and weaknesses of the players, and follow managerial strategy with microscopic attention.

You may or may not have been able to figure out what this paragraph is supposed to be about. The problem is that it isn't coherent. Making a reader guess about a paragraph's meaning is not what writers want to do, because their readers will get irritated at having to do all that guessing and stop reading. (Or, in college, they may read it and give it a D or F.) Readers don't want to

Figure 1.1

have to figure out each paragraph. That's why we use topic sentences; they make paragraphs more coherent, easier to read. Here's the incoherent paragraph again, but this time with a topic sentence:

> At every baseball game, there are basically two kinds of fan—the spectators and the analysts. The spectators enjoy the sun or the evening, chat, drink beer or soda, cheer or boo as the occasion demands, and hope for a victory by the home team. The analysts keep score, watch each pitch intently, note the strengths and weaknesses of the players, and follow managerial strategy with microscopic attention.

This is how most informational paragraphs work; they usually begin with a general statement telling us what's coming up and then get into the specifics of their subject.

Here is another example. Which sentences contain the general point of the paragraph, which the specifics?

> We [students] were forever being organized into activities that, I suspect, looked good on paper and in school board reports. New programs took over and disappeared as approaches to child education changed. One year we would go without marks, on the theory that marks were a "poor motivating factor," "an unnatural pressure." . . . Another year every activity became a competition, with posters tacked up on the walls showing who was ahead that week, our failures and our glories bared to all the class. Our days were filled with electrical gimmicks, film strips and movies and overhead projectors and tapes and supplementary TV shows, and in junior high, when we went audio-visual, a power failure would have been reason enough to close down the school.
>
> Joyce Maynard, *Looking Back: A Chronicle of Growing Up Old in the Sixties*

In this case, the first two sentences are the general introductory ones, and the rest are specific. The point of most paragraphs lies in a combination of their general and specific statements. Joyce Maynard's general sentences (the first two) introduce us to the idea that child education in the sixties didn't follow any set principles, and her specific sentences then give us illustrations of that idea, showing us that education was governed by gimmicks. If we summarized this paragraph for someone, we would include its main point, without going into its details. (If we covered all the details, we'd just be recopying the paragraph, not summarizing it.) We might write our summary this way:

> Education in the 60s was ruled by gimmicks that looked good on paper rather than real principles.

As the two example paragraphs indicate, one clue as to which points are most important lies in the way in which most paragraphs are organized; their general sentences usually come first and their specifics follow them. Sometimes it will almost be possible to make an outline of a text just by noting the first two or three sentences of each of its paragraphs. It is important to remember, however, that not every paragraph works this way. The main exception is the paragraph in which all the sentences are about specifics; in these cases, the generalization covering them may be in a previous paragraph or the specifics may be so important that each one should be noted.

EXERCISE

Following are three paragraphs. Underline or highlight the general statements (the introductory sentences), write an S in front of the specific statements (the sentences giving details) in each of them, and write a one- or two-sentence summary of what each paragraph means.

In the presidential election of 1868, the first one to be held after the Civil War, there was no question who would win, General Ulysses Grant. For one thing, he was the biggest hero of that war, the general who defeated Robert E. Lee, the Confederacy's greatest general, and forced the South to surrender. People forgot the enormous casualties in Grant's army. The other thing Grant had going for him was that he was a charming and modest man, and people usually like that.

Summary: _____

_____

_____

Of course, population growth is not occurring uniformly over the face of the Earth. Indeed, countries are divided rather neatly into two groups: those with rapid growth rates, and those with relatively slow growth rates. The first group, making up about two-thirds of the world population, coincides closely with what are known as the "undeveloped countries" (UDCs). The UDCs are not industrialized, tend to have inefficient agriculture, very small gross national products, high illiteracy rates and related problems. That's what UDCs are technically, but a short definition of undeveloped is "starving." Most Latin American,

African, and Asian countries fall into this category. The second group consists, in essence, of the "developed countries" (DCs). DCs are modern, industrial nations, such as the United States, Canada, most European countries, Israel, Russia, Japan, and Australia. Most people in these countries are adequately nourished.

Paul R. Erlich, The Population Bomb

Summary: _____

_____

_____

Comic books had been criticized in print since 1940 or so; because most of the readers were children, some people worried that comic books—crude and violent as many of them were—might be damaging young minds. The crime and horror comic books were found especially alarming, and a storm of **indignation** finally struck the industry with full force in 1954. Comic books were dumped on bonfires; comic books were denounced in Congress; comic books were solemnly condemned by psychiatrists as the root of a host of social evils. (And, more important for business, distributors started refusing to accept some comic books from the publishers.) As the movie producers had done twenty years earlier, the comic-book publishers responded to charges of immorality by drawing up an extremely strict code and entrusting its enforcement to a panel recruited from outside the industry. Only one major publisher—Dell, whose comic books starred such licensed characters as Donald Duck and the Lone Ranger and had attracted little criticism—could afford to **shun** the new Comics Code.

Michael Barrier and Martin Williams, Introduction to
A Smithsonian Book of Comic-Book Comics

Summary: _____

_____

_____

---

indignation: anger caused by an injustice;   **shun:** avoid, keep away from

Following is a passage from a sociology textbook. Although not an essay in itself, it is organized like one—except without the introduction and conclusion. Read the passage, underlining or highlighting the general, introductory statements of each paragraph:

What age is viewed as old depends, in part, on the age of the viewer.   1
A teenager may feel old in relation to a brother still in grammar school, but young in relation to a sister who already has a career and children. Forty may seem over the hill until we have reached that age. And a ninety-year-old may regard a retired person of seventy as a mere youngster.

More objectively, what age is old depends on the average life   2
expectancy in a particular society. This, in turn, is related to the society's overall standard of living and its technological ability to control disease and other threats to human life. Throughout most of human history, people's lives were quite short by current American standards. Teenagers married and had children, those in their twenties were middle-aged, and people became old by about thirty. Reaching the age of forty was rare in most societies until the late Middle Ages, when the rising standard of living and technological advances began to provide the means to control **infectious** diseases that were common killers of people of all ages.

Although elderly Americans experience less physical disability   3
than the cultural stereotype suggests, physical decline is indeed an important part of old age and can cause considerable emotional stress. Human beings at all stages of life are familiar with the problems caused by illness and physical injury. Pain, loss of activity, dependence on others, and reminders of our mortality can be sources of frustration, self-doubt, and depression. Since American culture so highly values youth, physical vitality, and good looks, changes in physical capabilities and physical appearance can threaten the self-esteem of older people. Unlike the young, however, the elderly must face the fact that their physical decline has no cure and is a prelude to ultimate death.

Psychologist Erik Erikson has described old age as a stage of life   4
in which individuals experience the tension of "**integrity** versus despair." However much they may still be learning and achieving,

---

infectious: transmittable;   **integrity:** commitment to personal values

the elderly must face the fact that their lives are nearing an end. Thus old age involves reflection about one's past, which brings a variable degree of satisfaction and regret. Erikson claims that people who are able to maintain high self-esteem in the face of physical and social decline, accepting their mistakes as well as their successes, are likely to experience old age as a time of personal integrity. For those who find little worth in their lives, however, old age may be a time of despair—a dead end that lacks positive meaning.

John J. Macionis, "Aging and the Elderly," *Sociology*

Besides improving your reading comprehension, active reading can improve your writing by revealing the role of structure, as these questions illustrate:

1. Look back at the diagram at the beginning of this chapter showing how essays and paragraphs are organized. How does your underlining or high-lighting compare with the shaded areas of the paragraphs in the diagram?

2. Go over the first two or three paragraphs again, this time reading them without reading your underlined or highlighted sentences. How does the passage read now?

3. What does this show you about how you should try to write your own paragraphs?

While most paragraphs in most informative writing (such as textbooks) are organized like the ones above, not every single one necessarily is. Though writers do carefully follow the principle of starting with general, introductory statements and following up with specifics, they don't always do so in such clear and highly organized ways.

Let's look now at a section of a text in which things aren't organized so neatly paragraph by paragraph. Which are the general and which the specific statements in this text? Again, write a short summary of what the *whole text* means.

Why do I think network TV does a better job of informing than [the   1 newspapers]? Well, let's get the **partisan** bit over with. Television lives on advertising to an even greater extent than newspapers, and since advertising is big business, advertising is by nature Republican. Yet nowhere in network newscasts or network commentaries on current

----

partisan: supports a particular idea

events have I encountered the intense partisanship, the often **rabid** bias that colors the editorial pages of the majority of newspapers in this country. Douglass Cater, in his book *The Fourth Branch of Government,* confines himself to only one **pungent** footnote on this subject. "I have deliberately avoided," he writes, "getting into the predominantly one-party nature of newspaper ownership. It is a fact of life." This particular fact of life is a shameful one: that newspapers whose duty it is to inform the American public give them only one side of the issues that affect them profoundly—the Republican side. This is shameful not only for Democrats—they have survived it before and will survive it again—but for the maturity of our people. Some of the same papers which loudly **extol** the virtues of free enterprise and a free press are consistently failing to print the facts on which a people can form a balanced and independent opinion. That balanced and independent opinion is our only real security as a nation.

Now, very often, television coverage of news is superficial and inadequate. Very often the picture takes precedence over the point. But by and large the news reports and commentaries on CBS and NBC and ABC make every effort to present viewers with more than one aspect of an issue, either by letting opposing spokesmen have their say, or by outlining the positions held by both major parties on the subject involved.   2

Television also provides a wide range of opinion by setting up four or five experts and letting them knock each other down. What has the local press of this nature? Is it discharging its duty to diversity by printing snippets of opinion from unqualified readers? Is this exploring an issue?   3

Marya Mannes, But Will It Sell?

Summary: _____

_____

_____

_____

_____

------

rabid: fanatical, biased;   **pungent:** sharp, biting;   **extol:** give high praise

In addition to paragraph organization, the organization of whole texts also provides clues you can use in deciding which points to write down for easy reference. The introduction of an essay or article will tell you what it's going to be about, and that, of course, is the most important point of all. The conclusion of an essay or chapter often highlights for the reader the material the writer feels is most important. And sometimes texts will contain section headings to make it easy for the reader to see when a new point is coming up.

The active reader, then, sorts out the main general points from the text and writes them down *in his or her own words.* It is most important to use your own words rather than copying the author's, because trying to put the ideas into your own words forces you to think about them closely, and thus helps you remember them. Finally, when you make your notes, be sure to put page references after each idea you have jotted down so that when you later begin to use the information, you will be able to find again the specifics or quotations you may want to use.

WRITING SUMMARIES

A summary is a concise restatement, in one's own words, of another, longer document, usually an article or a report. Summaries are often used in business and academic settings in which a committee or a small group of teachers or students needs to grasp a great deal of material very quickly. In such cases, the group will often assign two or three articles or reports to each of its members to read and summarize for the group as a whole, so every person won't have to read every single document. Needless to say, in such cases, the summaries must be accurate as well as brief.

Summaries are also handy study tools for students, particularly those facing essay tests. Summarizing the chapters in a textbook or the articles assigned to be read can help in reviewing the material and is a great help in remembering the material. Moreover, once you have written down the information, writing it again under the pressure of time, as during an essay test, becomes much, much easier.

A summary written for a committee or similar group should be as carefully composed as an essay and have all of an essay's usual characteristics, including paragraphs with topic sentences. A working summary that you write for yourself need not be so formal; it may even be all one paragraph if that suits you.

A good working summary is written in your own words, though you may want to borrow key phrases from the original. It *must* have the following characteristics:

- Above all, it must maintain and communicate the meaning of the original.
- It must *not* contain your opinions or views on the original.

- It must stick strictly to what the original writer had to say.
- It must contain all the main points of the original.
- Usually it will not contain the supporting points, unless one or more of them is of unusual importance.

You can see that to write a good summary, you need to exercise a great deal of judgment about what is important and what isn't.

A good working summary should answer these questions:

1. What is the subject of the original? What problem or situation is the writer addressing? (You might want to set this off as a separate paragraph, like an introduction, to make it stand out.)
2. What are the main points of the original? The summary may or may not stick to the same order as the original. Normally summaries will cover the most important points first, although articles and reports often do not do that. If the original involves discussion of some pro/con issue or compares two things, the summary will usually give all the pro points together and all the con points together or keep the various points of the comparison together, even though the original might not be organized that way. (If the original covers many main points, you might want to set them in separate paragraphs for clarity's sake.)
3. What conclusions does the original reach?

STEPS IN WRITING A SUMMARY

How do you go about writing a good working summary? If you follow the steps below, you will have an excellent chance of producing a useful and accurate summary.

1. Read through the entire original to get an understanding of the whole piece. On a piece of scratch paper, write in your own words the *point* of the piece, which you will usually find in the introduction, and its conclusion.
2. Reread and underline or highlight the important ideas. Carefully check the beginnings of paragraphs for topic sentences that announce new points. Normally, you will not want to highlight supporting facts, but some may be so striking or otherwise important that you will want to include them in your summary.

3. Now write the introductory statement of your summary, explaining what the original is about. Try to confine yourself to one sentence—two at the most.

4. Decide on the order in which you want to present the main points of the original; you will probably need to do some scribbling on scratch paper to do this. Review the materials you have highlighted to make sure you cover everything.

5. Write the body of your summary, using your own words and making sure to cover all the key points.

6. Write your last part, in which you explain what the original author's conclusions were. Be sure to keep your own opinions out of this part.

7. Proofread for spelling, typographical errors, and the conventions of usage. In particular, compare the spelling of titles, authors, and other names and key terms with that in the original document.

AN EXPERIENCED WRITER WRITES A SUMMARY

Following is a short essay about one element in the history of the English language. It has been marked up by a person preparing to write a summary of it. Although each person will mark up a text somewhat differently, this kind of work will have some features in common regardless of who does it. For one thing, the words indicating the subject and main points are sure to be noted. Examine the essay to see how the reader marked it—what was noted, and what was not. Following the essay is the summary written from the notes. Compare the two to see how the notes led to the summary.

Point: *Because of Wm. the Cong., English, now heavily influenced by* *— originally Germanic language* *French*

HOW ENGLISH BECAME FRENCH

There is a question you won't find in the game "Trivial Pursuit" that will stump your audience every time: "Name the one person who had the greatest effect on the English language." You will get answers like "Shakespeare," "Samuel Johnson," and "Webster," but none of those men had any effect at all compared to a man who didn't even speak English— William the Conqueror. *— subject had greatest effect on English*

before William Prior to 1066, in the land we now call Great Britain lived peoples belonging to two major language groups. In the west-central region lived the Welsh, who spoke a Celtic language, and in the north lived the Scots, whose language, though not the same as Welsh, was also Celtic.

The rest of the country was inhabited by the dominant Saxons, actually a mixture of Angles, Saxons, and other Germanic and Nordic peoples, <u>who spoke what we now call Anglo-Saxon (or Old English), a Germanic language.</u> If this state of affairs had lasted, English (which comes from *Engle,* the Angles) today would be close to German.

when it changed

But this state of affairs didn't last because a <u>Norman Duke</u>, William,   3 living in the part of France called Normandy, decided to extend his domain over England. In <u>1066</u> the Normans under Duke William met the Saxons under King Harold in battle at a place called Hastings.

effects

There the French-speaking Normans defeated the Saxons and began their rule over England, establishing not only their political dominance but <u>their linguistic dominance as well.</u>

For about a century, French became the official language of   4 England while Old English became the language of peasants and outcasts. As a result <u>our current vocabulary of politics and the law comes</u> from French rather than German. Such words as *nation, state, realm, capital, senate, president, legal, court, appeal*—even *politics* and *law*—as well as many others, come from French. On the other hand, words like *field, road, plow, bread, milk, water,* and *steal* come from Old English.

① *examples*

effects

②
③

In some cases, <u>modern English even shows a distinction between</u>   5 <u>upper-class French and lower-class Anglo-Saxon</u> in its vocabulary. *examples* Which is higher-class, *car* (from French) or *wagon* (from German)? What about *people* (French) and *folk* (German)? Or *chair* (French) and *stool* (German)? <u>We even hace different words for some foods,</u> <u>meat in particular</u>, depending on whether it's still out in the fields or *examples* at home ready to be cooked. The words *cow, sheep,* and *lamb* are, not surprisingly, all German, reflecting the fact that the Saxon peasants were doing the farming. But the words *beef, mutton,* and *veal* are French, perhaps indicating that the Norman nobility were doing most of the eating.

When Americans visit Europe for the first time, they usually find   6 Germany more "foreign" than France because the German they see on signs, posters, and advertisements seems much more different from English than French does. Few realize that our language is actually Germanic in its origins and that the <u>French influences are all the result of one man's ambition.</u>

Summary

Because of a Norman duke, William the Conqueror, English, which is actually a Germanic language, is now heavily influenced by French.

The dominant people in England were the Saxons, who spoke Anglo-Saxon or Old English. When they were defeated in 1066 by the Normans, French became the official language of England. We can see three big results of that. One is that today many of our words in politics and law are from French rather than German. A second is that we even have upper-class words from French and lower-class words from German. Finally, we use French words for meat on the table but German words for the animal sources of the meat.

No other person ever had such a major effect on English as William the Conqueror.

EXERCISES

Mark up the following three essays and write summaries of them as indicated by your instructor.

Pre-reading

Some articles, particularly ones in the sciences and social sciences, and many textbooks will show you how they are organized or what their main points are through subtitles in the articles. Before you start reading Jane Brody's article on fatigue, look over the article to see what its subtitles are. Even before you begin writing your summary, you can see what the main points of Brody's article are. Next look to see whether one of the sections of the article is longer than the others. If it is, look at the topic sentences of its paragraphs to see whether this section contains a major point or example so important that it should be part of your summary.

FATIGUE
Jane Brody

Fatigue is one of the most common complaints brought to doctors,   1
friends, and relatives. You'd think in this era of labor-saving devices
and convenient transportation that few people would have reason
to be so tired. But probably more people complain of fatigue today

than in the days when hay was baled by hand and laundry scrubbed on a washboard. Witness these typical complaints:

"It doesn't seem to matter how long I sleep—I'm more tired 2 when I wake up than when I went to bed."

"Some of my friends come home from work and jog for several 3 miles or swim laps. I don't know how they do it. I'm completely exhausted at the end of a day at the office."

"I thought I was weary because of the holidays, but now that 4 they're over, I'm even worse. I can barely get through this week, and on the weekend I don't even have the strength to get dressed. I wonder if I'm **anemic** or something."

"I don't know what's wrong with me lately, but I've been so col- 5 lapsed that I haven't made a proper meal for the family in weeks. We've been living on TV dinners and packaged mixes. I was finally forced to do a laundry because the kids ran out of underwear."

The causes of modern-day fatigue are diverse and only rarely 6 related to excessive physical exertion. The relatively few people who do heavy labor all day long almost never complain about being tired, perhaps because they expect to be. Today, physicians report, tiredness is more likely a consequence of underexertion than of wearing yourself down with overactivity. In fact, increased physical activity is often prescribed as a cure for sagging energy.

Kinds of Fatigue

There are three main categories of fatigue. These are physical fatigue, 7 **pathological** fatigue, and psychological fatigue.

Physical. This is a well-known result of overworking your muscles 8 to the point where metabolic waste products—carbon dioxide and lactic acid—accumulate in your blood and sap your strength. Your muscles can't continue to work efficiently in a bath of these chemicals. Physical fatigue is usually a pleasant tiredness, such as that which you might experience after playing a hard set of tennis, chopping wood, or climbing a mountain. The cure is simple and fast. You rest, giving your body a chance to get rid of accumulated wastes and restore muscle fuel.

Pathological. Here fatigue is a warning sign or consequence of 9 some underlying physical disorder, perhaps the common cold or flu

---

anemic: weak, listless;   **pathological:** caused by disease or something more serious like diabetes or cancer. Usually other symptoms besides fatigue are present that suggest the true cause.

Even after an illness has passed, you're likely to feel dragged out   10
for a week or more. Take your fatigue as a signal to go slow while your body has a chance to recover fully even if all you had was a cold. Pushing yourself to resume full activity too soon could precipitate a relapse and almost certainly will prolong your period of fatigue.

Even though illness is not a frequent cause of prolonged fatigue,   11
it's very important that it not be overlooked. Therefore, anyone who feels drained of energy for weeks on end should have a thorough physical checkup. But even if nothing shows up as a result of the various medical tests, that doesn't mean there's nothing wrong with you.

Unfortunately too often a medical work-up ends with a **battery**   12
of negative results, the patient is dismissed, and the true cause of serious fatigue goes undetected. As Dr. John Bulette, a psychiatrist at the Medical College of Pennsylvania Hospital in Philadelphia, tells it, this is what happened to a Pennsylvania woman who had lost nearly fifty pounds and was "almost dead—so tired she could hardly lift her head up." The doctors who first examined the woman were sure she had cancer. But no matter how hard they looked, they could find no sign of malignancy or of any other disease that could account for her wasting away. Finally, she was brought to the college hospital, where doctors noted that she was severely depressed.

They questioned her about her life and discovered that her trou-   13
bles had begun two years earlier, after her husband died. Once treated for depression, the woman quickly perked up, gained ten pounds in just a few weeks, then returned home to continue her recovery with the aid of psychotherapy.

Psychological. Emotional problems and conflicts, especially   14
depression and anxiety, are by far the most common causes of pro- longed fatigue. Fatigue may represent a defense mechanism that prevents you from having to face the true cause of your depression, such as the fact that you hate your job. It is also your body's safety valve for expressing repressed emotional conflicts, such as feeling trapped in an ungratifying role or an unhappy marriage. When such feelings are not expressed openly, they often come out as physical

---

battery: a large number, a series

symptoms, with fatigue as one of the most common **manifestations.** "Many people who are extremely fatigued don't even know they're depressed," Dr. Bulette says. "They're so busy distracting themselves or just worrying about being tired that they don't recognize their depression."

One of these situations is so common it's been given a name— tired housewife syndrome. The victims are commonly young mothers who day in and day out face the predictable tedium of caring for a home and small children, fixing meals, dealing with repairmen, and generally having no one interesting to talk to and nothing enjoyable to look forward to at the end of their boring and unrewarding day. The tired housewife may be inwardly resentful, envious of her husband's job, and guilty about her feelings. But rather than face them head-on, she becomes extremely fatigued.   15

Today, with nearly half the mothers of young children working outside the home, the tired housewife syndrome has taken a new twist, that of conflicting roles and responsibilities and guilt over leaving the children, often with an overlay of genuine physical exhaustion from trying to be all things to all people.   16

Emotionally **induced** fatigue may be compounded by sleep disturbance that results from the underlying psychological conflict. A person may develop insomnia or may sleep the **requisite** number of hours but fitfully, tossing and turning all night, having disturbing dreams, and awakening, as one woman put it, feeling as if she "had been run over by a truck."   17

Understanding the underlying emotional problem is the **crucial** first step toward curing psychological fatigue and by itself often results in considerable lessening of the tiredness. Professional psychological help or career or marriage counseling may be needed.   18

Pre-reading

As you have learned, topic sentences may be one sentence or they may be more than one, though not usually more than two. It is also true that what makes a sentence a topic sentence may be no more than one key word in that

---

manifestations: signs; **induced:** caused; **requisite:** needed, required; **crucial:** of supreme importance

sentence. Before reading all of the following essay, read only the first three paragraphs—these are the introduction—and then underline or highlight or jot
down in the margin the kinds of violence McGrath says he is going to cover.

After you have done that, go through the essay looking only at the first
sentence of each paragraph. In that sentence find the word (or words) that tell
the reader what the paragraph will be about. Write down these words in order,
paragraph by paragraph, along with the number of each paragraph. For example, in paragraph 4, the topic word in the first sentence is "robbery," one of the
forms of violence McGrath notes in his introduction. So for the first entry in
your outline you should write

robbery (4)

When you have written down these words and their paragraph numbers,
you will have an outline of McGrath's essay, and this can serve as the basis for
your summary.

THE MYTH OF VIOLENCE IN THE OLD WEST
Roger D. McGrath

It is commonly assumed that violence is part of our frontier heritage.   1
But the historical record shows that frontier violence was very different
from violence today. Robbery and burglary, two of our most common
crimes, were of no great significance in the frontier towns of the Old
West, and rape was seemingly nonexistent.

Bodie, one of the principal towns on the trans-Sierra frontier,   2
illustrates the point. Nestled high in the mountains of eastern
California, Bodie, which boomed in the late 1870s and early 1880s,
ranked among the most **notorious** frontier towns of the Old West.
It was, as one prospector put it, the last of the old-time mining
camps.

Like the trans-Sierra frontier in general, Bodie was indisputably   3
violent and lawless, yet most people were not affected. Fistfights and
gunfights among willing **combatants**—gamblers, miners, and the
like—were regular events, and stagecoach holdups were not unusual.
But the old, the young, the weak, and the female—so often the
victims of crime today—were generally not harmed.

---

notorious: widely and unfavorably;   **combatants:** fighters

Robbery was more often aimed at stagecoaches than at individ-   4
uals. Highwaymen usually took only the express box and left the
passengers alone. There were eleven stagecoach robberies in Bodie
between 1878 and 1882, and in only two instances were passengers
robbed. (In one instance, the highwaymen later apologized for their
conduct.)

There were only ten robberies and three attempted robberies of   5
individuals in Bodie during its boom years, and in nearly every case
the circumstances were the same: the victim had spent the evening
in a gambling den, saloon, or brothel; he had revealed that he had
on his person a significant sum of money; and he was staggering
home drunk when the attack occurred.

Bodie's total of twenty-one robberies—eleven of stages and ten   6
of individuals—over a five-year period converts to a rate of eighty-
four robberies per 100,000 inhabitants per year. On this scale—the
same scale used by the FBI to index crime—New York City's robbery
rate in 1980 was 1,140, Miami's was 995, and Los Angeles's was 628.
The rate for the United States as a whole was 243. Thus Bodie's robbery rate was significantly below the national average in 1980.

Between 1878 and 1882, there were only thirty-two burglaries—   7
seventeen of homes and fifteen of businesses—in Bodie. At least a
half-dozen burglaries were **thwarted** by the presence of armed citizens. The newspapers regularly advocated shooting burglars on
sight, and several burglars were, in fact, shot at.

Using the FBI scale, Bodie's burglary rate for those five years was   8
128. Miami's rate in 1980 was 3,282, New York's was 2,661, and Los
Angeles's was 2,602. The rate of the United States as a whole was
1,668, thirteen times that of Bodie.

Bodie's law enforcement institutions were certainly not responsi-   9
ble for these low rates. Rarely were robbers or burglars arrested, and
even less often were they convicted. Moreover, many law enforcement officers operated on both sides of the law. Perhaps the greatest
deterrent to crime in Bodie was the fact that so many people were
armed. Armed guards prevented bank robberies and holdups of
stagecoaches carrying shipments of **bullion,** and armed homeowners and merchants discouraged burglary.

---

thwarted: prevented;   **deterrent:** prevention;   **bullion:** pure gold or silver

It was the armed citizens themselves who were the most   10
potent—though not the only—deterrent to **larcenous** crime.
Another was the threat of **vigilantism.** Highwaymen, for example,
understood that while they could take the express box from a stagecoach without arousing the citizens, they risked inciting the entire
populace to action if they robbed the passengers.

There is considerable evidence that women in Bodie were rarely   11
the victims of crime. Between 1878 and 1882 only one woman, a
prostitute, was robbed, and there were no reported cases of rape.
(There is no evidence that rapes occurred but were not reported.)

Finally, juvenile crime, which accounts for a significant portion   12
of the violent crime in the United States today, was limited in Bodie
to pranks and malicious mischief.

If robbery, burglary, crimes against women, and juvenile crime   13
were relatively rare on the trans-Sierra frontier, homicide was not:
thirty-one Bodieites were shot, stabbed, or beaten to death during
the boom years, for a homicide rate of 116. No U.S. city today comes
close to this rate. In 1980, Miami led the nation with a homicide rate
of 32.7; Las Vegas was a distant second at 23.4. A half-dozen cities
had rates of zero. The rate for the United States as a whole in that
year was a mere 10.2.

Several factors contributed to Bodie's high homicide rate.   14
A majority of the town's residents were young, adventurous, single
males who adhered to a code of conduct that frequently required
them to fight even if, or perhaps especially if, it could mean death.
Courage was admired above all else. Alcohol also played a major role
in **fostering** the settlement of disputes by violence.

If the men's code of conduct and their consumption of alcohol   15
made fighting inevitable, their **sidearms** often made it fatal. While
the carrying of guns probably reduced the incidence of robbery and
burglary, it undoubtedly increased the number of homicides.

For the most part, the citizens of Bodie were not troubled by the   16
great number of killings; nor were they troubled that only one man was
ever convicted of murder. They accepted the killings and the lack of
convictions because most of those killed had been willing combatants.

---

larcenous: having to do with theft;   **vigilantism:** people taking the law
into their own hands;   **fostering:** encouraging;   **sidearms:** small weapons
carried at the side

Thus the violence and lawlessness of the trans-Sierra frontier bear   17
little relation to the violence and lawlessness that **pervade** American
society today. If Bodie is at all representative of frontier towns, there
is little justification for blaming contemporary American violence on
our frontier heritage.

Pre-reading

The following essay will be more difficult to summarize than the preceding
ones because the signals that Heilbroner gives at the beginnings of his paragraphs are quite subtle. But if you skim the first few lines of each paragraph,
you will begin to see that the essay has distinct sections. Notice that the title of
the essay is a warning to us about a problem. So it will make sense to think of
this essay as setting forth a problem (that would be one section), showing us
how the problem comes about (that would be another), and offering us possible solutions to the problem (that would be a third).

DON'T LET STEREOTYPES WARP YOUR JUDGMENT
Robert L. Heilbroner

Is a girl called Gloria apt to be better-looking than one called Bertha?   1
Are criminals more likely to be dark than blond? Can you tell a good
deal about someone's personality from hearing his voice briefly over
the phone? Can a person's nationality be pretty accurately guessed
from his photograph? Does the fact that someone wears glasses
imply that he is intelligent?

The answer to all these questions is obviously, "No."   2

Yet, from all the evidence at hand, most of us believe these   3
things. Ask any college boy if he'd rather take his chances with a
Gloria or a Bertha, or ask a college girl if she'd rather blind-date a
Richard or a Cuthbert. In fact, you don't have to ask: College students
in questionnaires have revealed that names **conjure up** the same
images in their minds as they do in yours—and for as little reason.

Look into the favorite suspects of persons who report   4
"suspicious characters" and you will find a large percentage of them
to be "swarthy" or "dark and foreign-looking"—despite the
testimony of criminologists that criminals do not tend to be dark,

---

pervade: spread through;   **conjure up:** call up as by magic foreign or "wild-eyed." **Delve** into the main asset of a telephone stock swindler and you will find it to be a marvelously confidence-inspiring telephone "personality." And whereas we all think we know what an Italian or a Swede looks like, it is the sad fact that when a group of Nebraska students sought to match faces and nationalities of 15 European countries, they were scored wrong in 93 percent of their identifications. Finally, for all the fact that horn-rimmed glasses have now become the standard television sign of an "intellectual," optometrists know that the main thing that distinguishes people with glasses is just bad eyes.

Stereotypes are a kind of gossip about the world, a gossip that makes us prejudge people before we ever lay eyes on them. Hence it is not surprising that stereotypes have something to do with the dark world of prejudice. Explore most prejudices (note that the word means prejudgment) and you will find a cruel stereotype at the core of each one.   5

For it is the extraordinary fact that once we have typecast the world, we tend to see people in terms of our standardized pictures. In another demonstration of the power of stereotypes to affect our vision, a number of Columbia and Barnard students were shown 30 photographs of pretty but unidentified girls, and asked to rate each in terms of "general liking," "intelligence," "beauty" and so on. Two months later, the same group were shown the same photographs, this time with fictitious Irish, Italian, Jewish and "American" names attached to the pictures. Right away the ratings changed. Faces which were now seen as representing a national group went down in looks and still farther down in likeability, while the "American" girls suddenly looked decidedly prettier and nicer.   6

Why is it that we stereotype the world in such irrational and harmful fashion? In part, we begin to type-cast people in our childhood years. Early in life, as every parent whose child has watched a TV Western knows, we learn to spot the Good Guys from the Bad Guys. Some years ago, a social psychologist showed very clearly how powerful these stereotypes of childhood vision are. He secretly asked the most popular youngsters in an elementary school to make errors in their morning gym exercises. Afterwards, he asked the class if anyone had noticed any mistakes during gym period. Oh, yes, said the   7

---

delve: dig

children. But it was the unpopular members of the class—the "bad guys"—they remembered as being out of step.

We not only grow up with standardized pictures forming inside   8
of us, but as grown-ups we are constantly having them thrust upon us. Some of them, like the half-joking, half-serious stereotypes of mothers-in-law, or country yokels, or psychiatrists, are dinned into us by the stock jokes we hear and repeat. In fact, without such stereotypes, there would be a lot fewer jokes. Still other stereotypes are **perpetuated** by the advertisements we read, the movies we see, the books we read.

And finally, we tend to stereotype because it helps us make sense   9
out of a highly confusing world, a world which William James once described as "one great, blooming, buzzing confusion." It is a curious fact that if we don't know what we're looking at, we are often quite literally unable to see what we're looking at. People who recover their sight after a lifetime of blindness actually cannot at first tell a triangle from a square. A visitor to a factory sees only noisy chaos where the superintendent sees a perfectly **synchronized** flow of work. As Walter Lippmann has said, "For the most part we do not first see, and then define; we define first, and then we see."

Stereotypes are one way in which we "define" the world in or-   10
der to see it. They classify the infinite variety of human beings into a convenient handful of "types" towards whom we learn to act in stereotyped fashion. Life would be a wearing process if we had to start from scratch with each and every human contact. Stereotypes economize on our mental effort by covering up the blooming, buzzing confusion with big recognizable cutouts. They save us the "trouble" of finding out what the world is like—they give it its accustomed look.

Thus the trouble is that stereotypes make us mentally lazy. As   11
S. I. Hayakawa, the authority on **semantics,** has written: "The danger of stereotypes lies not in their existence, but in the fact that they become for all people some of the time, and for some people all the time, substitutes for observation." Worse yet, stereotypes get in the way of our judgment, even when we do observe the world. Someone who has formed rigid preconceptions of all Latins as "excitable,"

---

perpetuated: made to last longer;   **synchronized:** operated together;
semantics: the study of the meaning of language

or all teenagers as "wild," doesn't alter his point of view when he meets a calm and deliberate **Genoese**, or a serious-minded high school student. He brushes them aside as "exceptions that proved the rule." And, of course, if he meets someone true to type, he stands triumphantly **vindicated**. "They're all like that," he proclaims, having encountered an excited Latin, an ill-behaved adolescent.

Hence, quite aside from the injustice which stereotypes do to   12
others, they impoverish ourselves. A person who lumps the world into simple categories, who type-casts all labor leaders as "racketeers," all businessmen as "reactionaries," all Harvard men as "snobs," and all Frenchmen as "sexy," is in danger of becoming a stereotype himself. He loses his capacity to be himself—which is to say, to see the world in his own absolutely unique, **inimitable** and independent fashion.

Instead, he votes for the man who fits his standardized picture   13
of what a candidate "should" look like or sound like, buys the goods that someone in his "situation" in life "should" own, lives the life that others define for him. The mark of the stereotyped person is that he never surprises us, that we do indeed have him "typed." And no one fits this strait-jacket so perfectly as someone whose opinions about other people are fixed and inflexible.

Nor do we suddenly drop our standardized pictures for a blind-   14
ing vision of the Truth. Sharp swings of ideas about people often just substitute one stereotype for another. The true process of change is a slow one that adds bits and pieces of reality to the pictures in our heads, until gradually they take on some of the blurriness of life itself. Little by little, we learn not that Jews and Negroes and Catholics and Puerto Ricans are "just like everybody else"—for that, too, is a stereotype—but that each and every one of them is unique, special, different and individual. Often we do not even know that we have let a stereotype lapse until we hear someone saying, "all so-and-so's are like such-and-such," and we hear ourselves saying, "Well—maybe."

Can we speed the process along? Of course we can.   15

First, we can become aware of the standardized pictures in our   16
heads, in other people's heads, in the world around us.

Genoese: a person from Genoa, Italy;   **vindicated:** shown to be correct;
inimitable: unable to be imitated

Second, we can become suspicious of all judgments that we 17 allow exceptions to "prove." There is no more chastening thought than that in the vast intellectual adventure of science, it takes but one tiny exception to topple a whole **edifice** of ideas.

Third, we can learn to be **chary** of generalizations about people. 18 As F. Scott Fitzgerald once wrote: "Begin with an individual, and before you know it you have created a type; begin with a type, and you find you have created—nothing."

Most of the time, when we type-cast the world, we are not 19 in fact generalizing about people at all. We are only revealing the embarrassing facts about the pictures that hang in the gallery of stereotypes in our own heads.

ANALYZING AND EVALUATING YOUR INFORMATION

When most people think about writers, if they ever do, they probably imagine someone sitting at a typewriter and writing. If writers aren't people who write, who are they? Actually, people who write usually spend a lot more time getting ready to write than they do writing. The writing process starts long before the actual writing does.

Many people think that writers know something others don't know, have some secret about writing that makes them good writers. They do. In fact, they have two secrets. We're going to save one secret to tell you later, but here's the first secret: *The more carefully you think about what you are going to write, the easier it will be to write it. And conversely, the less you think and prepare ahead of time, the harder the writing will be.*

In reading preparatory to writing summaries, you have already engaged in reading actively. But when you read in preparation for writing your own essay, rather than merely summarizing someone else's, you need to take active reading one small step further. Sometimes in doing your first reading—but more often when you reread—you will find yourself getting ideas about what you've read, seeing connections or contradictions, often finding material relevant to your own experience. When you are making your notes, be sure to write down the ideas or questions that come to you, perhaps putting them in the margin or in parentheses so that you don't confuse them with your notes. These materials, the results of your own thinking, will help you enormously in the next crucial step, analyzing what you have been reading.

---

edifice: structure; **chary:** careful, wary

For the most part, your analysis of each item of information should cover three points:

1. What is the *relevance* of this item to what you're going to be writing about? For instance, if you were doing a paper on rates of Chinese immigration to the United States in the nineteenth century, you might come across some fascinating material on social life in west coast Chinese communities. However, you would realize that this material had no bearing on immigration rates, and so you would discard it (or save it for another paper).

2. Closely related to relevance is *importance*—that is, given that a particular item is relevant, how important is it? Writers will often put asterisks or stars alongside materials they think are especially important.

3. Finally, what is the *relationship* of each item to other items? If some items support each other, you will want to know that before you start writing. If an item contradicts or proves another item wrong, you will again need to know that. The important point here is that you won't know what your information means until you get it organized. *This is not the same as organizing your essay.* That comes later.

ORGANIZING AND FINDING YOUR POINT

In some of your college writing, including some of the assignments for this course, you will be asked to explain something, to show what a group of data means. In other assignments, you will have to argue a position, to make up your mind which side seems to you to have the stronger points on a particular issue and argue for that side.

In both cases, you have to decide what your point is before you can start. If you have analyzed and organized your information, you will have little trouble deciding on your point.

The single biggest mistake a writer can make is to decide on his or her point without having gone carefully over the available information. It is unfortunately true that most people form opinions on important matters without carefully investigating them first. If challenged, they then say, "Well, I'm entitled to my opinion." That's true. They are. But the opinion is probably worthless if they haven't analyzed and organized their information.

Even so, it is important for a writer to draw on the knowledge he or she does possess as a way of *beginning* to think about a topic. Although you may not realize it, you bring an enormous amount of knowledge and information into this course, the result of your age, experience, and education. Although you may not be an expert in every topic assigned (who is?), you probably know something about each one and therefore have an opinion about it. One way to find out what you already know about a topic is to ask yourself general questions before you start examining the available information—not as a way of arriving at definitive answers, but as a way of beginning to think about a topic. We call this *pre-reading*.

WRITING A REPORT

Following are two short essays on the same subject, a problem in male-female relationships that often has serious effects: how men and women verbally communicate with each other.

Imagine that you are serving as a consultant to a marriage guidance class. The instructor of the class gives you the following task:

> ### *Writing Assignment*
>
> Write a report indicating which of the following two essays you think newly married couples attending the marriage guidance class should read. Your report should consist of three parts: a short introduction about the general problem of male-female communication, summaries of each of the two essays, and a concluding recommendation about which one you think should be required reading. The recommendation section should compare the strengths and weaknesses of the two essays to show *why* you recommend one over the other.

Before you read the two essays, spend a few moments on *pre-reading*—that is, thinking in a fairly organized way about the subject you are going to tackle.

Pre-reading

Ask yourself the following questions (or ones like them):

- Have you ever noticed—on a date for example—that you and the opposite sex don't always want to talk about exactly the same things—that sometimes you have to listen to your partner talk about something that doesn't really interest you at all?

- Who spends more time on the phone—your women friends (or sister) or your men friends (or brother)?

- What do women use the phone for, primarily? How about men?

- If you have a sibling of the opposite sex, have you noticed that he or she talks with friends about different things than you like to talk about with your friends?

- On social occasions, have you noticed that married couples often split up, with the women getting in one group and the men in another?

- Do your mother and father tend to want to talk about different topics? Do they have different conversational styles? Does one tend to talk more than the other?

After you've given this subject some thought from your own experience, you're ready to read what others think about it. Keep an open mind as you read; you may learn something new.

Reading

Read the following essays, underlining or highlighting and making notes on their main points and anything else you think is particularly important. (If a piece of information is something that *you* didn't know before and are glad you learned, that's a sign that it's important.) As you did in writing your previous summaries, first skim these two essays, looking for their introductions and indications of what their main sections are, what main points they cover. Notice, however, that the first essay, by Joyce Maynard, is organized in a completely different way from the essays you've previously worked on and from the second essay, by Sherman and Haas. Maynard's is a very informal essay written for a newspaper column and so she doesn't use a conventional introduction but instead drifts into her main subject. Sherman and Haas write the kind of standard introduction your teachers in college will expect you to write.

HIS TALK, HER TALK
Joyce Maynard

It can be risky these days to suggest that there are any **innate** differ- 1
ences between men and women, other than those of anatomy. Out
the window go the old notions about man and aggression, woman

---

innate: possessed at birth

and submission (don't even say the word), man and intellect, woman and instinct. If I observe that my infant son prefers pushing a block along the floor while making car noises to cradling a doll in his arms and singing lullabies (and he does)—well, I can only conclude that, despite all our earnest attempts at nonsexist childrearing, he has already suffered environmental contamination. Some of it, no doubt unwittingly, came from my husband and me, **reared** in the days when nobody **winced** if you recited that old **saw** about what little girls and little boys are made of.

I do not believe, of course, that men are smarter, steadier, more   2
high-minded than women. But one or two notions are harder to shake—such as the idea that there is such a thing as "men's talk" or "women's talk." And that it's a natural instinct to seek out, on occasion, the company of one's own sex, exclude members of the other sex and not feel guilty about it.

Oh, but we do. At a party I attended the other night, for instance,   3
it suddenly became apparent that all the women were in one room and all the men were in the other. Immediately we redistributed ourselves, which was a shame. No one had suggested we segregate. The talk in the kitchen was simply, all the women felt, more interesting.

I think I know my husband very well, but I have no idea what   4
goes on when he and his male friends get together. Neither can he picture what can keep a woman friend and me occupied for three hours over a single pot of coffee.

The other day, after a long day of work, my husband Steve and   5
his friend Dave stopped at a bar for a few beers. When he got home, I asked what they had talked about. "Oh, the usual." Like what? "Firewood. Central America. Trucks. The Celtics. Religion. You know."

No, not really. I had only recently met with my friend Ann and   6
her friend Sally at a coffee shop nearby, and what we talked about was the workshop Sally would be holding that weekend concerning women's attitudes toward their bodies, Ann's 11-year-old daughter's upcoming slumber party, how hard it is to buy jeans, and the recent dissolution of a friend's five-year marriage. Asked to **capsulize** our afternoon's discussion, in a form similar to my husband's outline of his night out, I would say we talked about life, love, happiness and heartbreak. Larry Bird's name never came up.

reared: brought up, raised;   **winced:** flinched;   **saw:** saying;
capsulize: summarize

I don't want to reinforce old stereotypes of bubble-headed   7
women (Lucy and Ethel), clinking their coffee cups over talk of clothes
and diets while the men remove themselves to lean on mantels, puff
on cigars and **muse** about world politics, machines and philosophy. A
group of women talking, it seems to me, is likely to concern itself with
matters just as pressing as those broached by my husband and
friends. It might be said, in fact, that we're really talking about the
same eternal conflicts. Our styles are just different.

When Steve tells a story, the point is, as a rule, the ending, and   8
getting there by the most direct route. It may be a good story, told
with beautiful precision, but he tells it the way he eats a banana: in
three efficient chews, while I cut mine up and savor it. He can (although
this is rare) spend 20 minutes on the telephone with one of his brothers, tantalizing me with occasional exclamations of amazement or
shock, and then after hanging up, reduce the whole conversation for
me to a one-sentence summary. I, on the other hand, may take three
quarters of an hour describing some figure from my past while he
waits—with thinly veiled impatience—for the point to emerge. Did this
fellow just get elected to the House of Representatives? Did he die and
leave me his fortune?

In fairness to Steve, I must say that, for him, not talking about   9
something doesn't necessarily mean not dealing with it. And he
does listen to what I have to say. He likes a good story, too. It's just
that, given a choice, he'd rather hear about quantum mechanics
or the history of the Ford Mustang. Better yet, he'd rather play
ball.

MAN TO MAN, WOMAN TO WOMAN
Mark A. Sherman and Adelaide Haas

When it comes to conversation, husbands and wives often have   1
problems that close friends of the same sex don't have. First, they
may not have much to talk about, and second, when they do talk,
misunderstandings often develop that lead to major fights. Our
research concludes that these problems are particularly resistant to
solution. Not only do men and women like to talk about different
topics, spoken language serves different functions for the sexes.

---

muse: think about

Our findings are based on responses to a nationally distributed   2
questionnaire, in-depth interviews and observation of same-sex
conversations. We found much variation within each gender and
no verbal absolutes to differentiate the sexes. But whether we look
at topics of conversation or at the role language plays for each gender, we see enough difference to explain why men and women are,
to use Lillian Rubin's book title, "intimate strangers."

One hundred sixty-six women and 110 men, ranging in age from   3
17 to 80, returned a questionnaire asking how often they discussed
each of 22 topics with friends of the same sex. For some topics there
is little difference—work, movies and television are, in that order, frequent topics of conversation for both sexes. On the other hand
female friends report more talk than do men about relationship problems, family, health and reproductive concerns, weight, food and
clothing. Men's talk is more likely than women's to be about music,
current events and sports. Women's topics tend to be closer to the
self and more emotional than men's (in another questionnaire item,
60 percent of the women but only 27 percent of the men said that
their same-sex conversations were often on emotional topics). A common topic, and one generally reserved for one's own sex, is the other
sex and sexuality. Interestingly, women talk about other women
much more than men talk about other men (excluding sports heroes
and public figures). This includes "cattiness," a feature of conversation that many women wished to see eliminated. "Keep the gossip
but get rid of the cattiness" is how one put it.

Of course, there are men who are eager to talk about family   4
matters and women who love to talk about sports, but for a typical
couple, there will be areas of personal importance that the other
partner is simply not interested in and, in fact, may **deride.** "Trivial"
is a term used often by both sexes to describe topics of obvious significance to the other.

But the difference in topics is not so damaging to intimate male-   5
female relationships as are the differences in the style and function of
conversation. For men, talks with friends are enjoyed primarily for
their freedom, playfulness and **camaraderie.** When we asked men
what they liked best about their all-male talk, the most frequent
answer had to do with its ease. "You don't have to watch what you

deride: make fun of;   **camaraderie:** friendship

say" is how one young man put it. Some men commented on enjoying the fast pace of all-male conversation, and several specifically
mentioned humor. A number of men said that they liked the practical
aspects of these talks. As one wrote, "We teach each other practical
ways to solve everyday problems: New cars, tax handling, etc."

A different picture emerged when we asked women what they   6
liked best about talking with other women. While many mentioned
ease and camaraderie, the feature mentioned most often was empa-
thy or understanding, which involves careful listening as well as talking. "To know that you're not alone." "The feeling of sharing and
being understood without a sexual connotation." "Sensitivity to
emotions that men feel are unimportant." In questionnaire responses
and interviews, women spoke of their same-sex conversations not as
something they merely liked, but truly needed.

Women's greater need for same-sex conversation was shown by   7
responses to other questions. When we asked how important such
conversations were, 63 percent of the women, but only 43 percent
of the men, called them important or necessary. Women are also far
likelier than men to call up a friend just to talk. Nearly half the
women in our sample said they made such calls at least once a week,
whereas less than one man in five said he did. In fact, 40 percent of
the men said they never called another man just to talk (versus 14
percent of the women). Men use the phone a great deal for business, and in the context of a business call they may have friendly
conversation. But a call just to "check in" is a rare event.

Consider then the marriage of a man who has had most of his   8
conversations with other men, to a woman who has had most of hers
with other women, probably the typical situation. He is used to fast-
paced conversations that typically stay on the surface with respect to
emotions, that often enable him to get practical tips or offer them to
others and that are usually **pragmatic** or fun. She is used to conversations that, while practical and fun too, are also a major source of
emotional support, self-understanding and the understanding of
others. Becoming intimate with a man, the woman may finally start
expressing her concerns to him as she might a close friend. But she
may find, to her dismay, that his responses are all wrong. Instead of
making her feel better, he makes her feel worse. The problem is that

---

pragmatic: practical, useful

he tends to be direct and practical, whereas what she wants more than anything else is an **empathetic** listener. Used to years of such responses from close friends, a woman is likely to be surprised and angered by her husband's immediate "Here's what ya do . . ." Adding to her anger may be her belief, as expressed by many women in our survey, that men don't credit her with good sense and intelligence, and that perhaps that is why he is advising her. The fact is, he does the same with male friends.

Men can be good listeners, of course, and women can give direct advice. But just as women read books and take courses on how to be assertive, men take courses on how to become better listeners. Indeed, whether it was Shakespeare—"Give every man thine ear but few thy voice"—or Dale Carnegie—"Be a good listener"—men have impressed on each other the value of good listening. The advice, however, must often fall on deaf ears. Women continue to be seen as better listeners. 9

Many books and articles have been written on how language discriminates against women, and there is no doubt that it does. Attempts have been made to change this—in the last couple of years, for example, we have heard men say "he or she" instead of the generic "he" in all-male conversation—but as long as boys play with boys, and girls with girls the sexes will use language in different ways and for different purposes. Whether it is for the feeling of freedom that comes from not having to watch what you say, or the feeling of relief and joy that comes from another human being truly understanding you, we will continue to seek out those of our own sex to talk to. There is no reason each must adopt the other's style. What is necessary is to recognize and respect it. 10

Post-reading

Your assignment here is to prepare the following in order to write a first, or *idea,* draft of the report.

- Notes on the two articles, legibly written, with comments of your own about the importance of the points noted
- A rough outline of the report with the main points written under each section

————

empathetic: understanding

Remember that you are both summarizing the articles and writing a recommendation and that your recommendation should cover both the strong and the weak points of each of the two essays.

THE IDEA DRAFT

A lot of people think that when writers actually begin to write, the words flow out of them the way they will appear in the book or newspaper or magazine article that eventually gets published. That is far, far from being the case. In fact, it almost never happens that way. On the next page, for instance, is a page from a piece of writing by one of the authors of this book.

This is the place where we get to tell you the second secret professional writers have. Here it is:

* *Nobody gets it right the first time. Everybody has to rewrite.* Kurt Vonnegut, Jr., a well-known and successful American novelist, said this about himself and his fellow writers: "Our power is patience. We have discovered that writing allows even a stupid person to seem halfway intelligent, if only that person will write the same thought over and over again, improving it just a little bit each time. It is a lot like inflating a blimp with a bicycle pump. Anybody can do it. All it takes is time."

There are two pieces of good news here, and one other bit of news that you may find surprising. The good news is

1. you have an edge; because you aren't stupid (or you wouldn't be in college), you have a head start on the writing process, and
2. hard as it is, writing is a lot easier than filling a blimp with a bicycle pump.

The (perhaps) surprising news is what Vonnegut is saying about rewriting. Notice that he doesn't talk about rewriting as going back to look for spelling mistakes or other kinds of errors; he talks about rewriting as improving the *ideas.*

Your first draft is not one in which you try to get everything right—try to get all the words spelled correctly, all the apostrophes in the right places, all the sentences correct. Not at all. If you try to do all that stuff, you won't be able to concentrate on your ideas. The human mind can only do so much work at one time. Ever try to drive in heavy traffic and hold a serious or intense conversation at the same time? Or talk on the phone when someone in the room is

Life, as we all know, is ~~fu~~yll of unan~~w~~serable questions. In the area
of food, I can easily understand how someone discovered ~~how to get~~x the the way
skin off the garlic clove. He, or (I)more likely, she got fed up one day
trying to peel the stupid stuff off, ~~and just~~ whacked the clove with her
fist in a fit of temper, and lo! off it came. But how did mayonnaise
ever get invented? ~~What made the~~ woman from Mayonne say to herself,   *Dida*
"Let's see. If I put an egg yoke, some mustard, and some vinegar in a
bowl, whip them up, then add oil slowly until the whole thing ~~forms a~~   *though,*
thick emulsion, that ought to taste pretty good~~?~~.*I know, why American*
chemical companies decided to make phoney mayonnaise.
~~In the same~~ way, I have trouble understanding why the ~~very~~ first ~~people~~   *But my*
~~to live where Sacramento~~ now is thought it would be a ~~good idea. to~~   *speculations*   *one*
~~settle there.~~ It's ~~very~~ hard for me to ~~imagine~~ the following going   *lately been*   *#*
through someone's mind: "Okay, ~~here's a~~ place where it's over a 100 ~~all~~   *have been*
~~the time~~ during the ~~summer,~~ where it rains ~~like hell~~ and floods during   *occasioned*
the winter, ~~and~~ where various vicious (r)attack pollen ~~thrive~~ in b~~e~~tween   *not by*
so the ~~few~~ people who can breathe are always coughing or sn~~eezi~~ng their   *food or*
h~~eads~~ off. ~~I think I'll live here.~~" This seems like a good place ~~to~~   *chemicals,*
~~live."~~   *but by*
~~But the questions bothering me lately have been occasioned by~~
~~But this is just background to my real subject, which is~~ (the 90 mile(s)
of Interstate 80 between San Francisco and Sacramento, ~~90 miles of~~
~~heavy, often stop-and-go traffic~~ ~~90 miles of traffic congestion~~ 90
miles of heavy traffic and crappy scenery. ~~(And speaking of~~
~~unanswerable questions, how does one explain Vacaville? At least~~
~~Sacramento has rivers.)~~ In my view of the thing, I80 falls ~~into three~~
~~parts~~: going east, these are the part from San Francisco to the
Carquinez ~~Bridge~~, a 25 minutes drive if you ~~do it~~ at midnight but an
hour or more under ~~all other~~ conditions; the section from Vallejo to
Vacaville, a transition zone ~~that gets~~ you ready for the horrors still
ahead; and finally, ~~when~~ you cross one last ~~ridge~~ line, the last 30
miles, a dead ~~flat~~, dead straight shot to our glorious state capital,
farmland ~~on~~ which little or nothing seems to grow seething under ~~a clear~~
sky ~~turned~~ slate blue with heat and haze.

                    does answer a
Interstate 80 ~~answers one~~ question ~~many people have, particularly~~
visitors from other states: namely, (W)hy can't ~~your~~ Highway Patrol use   *like*
radar? The answer is that our state legislators want to ~~be able to~~   *everyone*
speed as fast as they can from Sacramento to San Francisco, and they   *else?*
don't want to get caught doing it. But even though I-80 an~~s~~wers th~~i~~s
question, it raises a number of others.
A big one has to do with the drivers you see.
~~While~~ most drivers on I-80 out in the wilds beyond Vallejo are content
to poke along at a sedate and conservative 65 to 70 miles per hour,
there are a few, the mad dogs, who regard this as an impediment to the
natural order of things and infringement on their rights. These ~~folks~~ *people*
barrel through the traffic, or try to, at speeds in the 90's, changing
lanes without signalling (they probably don't have ti~~me~~ to, actually),
viciously tailgating anyone in their way. Then there are the uncon~~ci~~ous
tailgaters, ~~Maybe they don't have adequate~~ depth perception, ~~In any~~ *Whatever,*
~~case,~~ *maybe people with inadequate*
                                        maybe just morons.

talking to you? That's what you ask your mind to do if you try to get your ideas down *and* get all the mechanics correct too.

Your first draft is your *idea draft*. That's when you just get your ideas on paper. In the idea draft you try to say *what* you want to say (not *how* you want to say it) and get things in the order you want them. It's a draft that's a total mess. It looks horrible. But in many ways, the worse it looks, the better it is, because lots of changes and written-in stuff and crossed-out stuff all means that you are getting your ideas—the most important part of the paper—in shape.

Although the first draft is an idea draft, it's also the time to try to get the ideas in the order you want them, and part of that process is grouping them in paragraphs. You will learn more about paragraphs later, but you've already learned a lot. If you remember the diagram of an essay at the beginning of this chapter and all the paragraph examples you've seen, you will remember that paragraphs tend to be written in one way: with an introductory sentence or two telling what the paragraph will be about and then specific sentences that give the details.

In getting ready to write your first draft, group your ideas as you think you will write them in paragraphs. Organize the groups in the order you think you will want them. Write introductory (topic) sentences that seem to you to cover each of the groups. You might change your mind about the groupings or the order or what you have written as topic sentences later. That's not a problem. But you do have to start somewhere, and this is the place.

Idea Draft Assignment

Using your notes, write an idea draft of your report. Remember: This draft is *only* for getting your ideas on paper and in the order you want them. Many people like to double-space this draft so that when it becomes a mess, they can still read it. Others feel that single spacing makes it easier for them to see the whole thing. If you write your draft by hand, you may want to leave yourself wide margins for making changes.

LATER DRAFTS

Many college professors and many businesspeople have to write for professional audiences, people in their own fields. Papers explaining new ideas or giving critiques of old ones, discussing new theories or discoveries, reporting on matters assigned by the firm, and so on are the bread and butter of professional life. When a professional person works on a paper or report, he or she will almost always try to write a pretty good draft—usually the second or third draft—and then show it to a trusted colleague, someone he or she knows will offer constructive criticism. All professional people realize that no matter how good their ideas are, other people will always find weaknesses that can be corrected or see ways their ideas could be expressed better. People who write for professional reasons never write alone. When they have got things about as good as they think they can get them, and often well before, they always try to get extra help from others.

After you have completed the idea draft, the one that's a total mess, you should rewrite it, again concentrating mostly on its content rather than on mechanics, and then get a friend to read it. But here you need a friend who will really read it critically, looking for problems of logic or other weaknesses in the content and giving specific suggestions.

After this part of the process, when the content is as good as you can get it, you are usually prepared to start working on the mechanics of the paper, cleaning it up for "publication," even though in college, publication may mean just handing it in to a teacher.

The very last step, after you have produced the final neat version, is to proofread it carefully, word by word and line by line. Proofreading is a difficult skill; few people enjoy it. But even the most carefully typed text will contain surprising numbers of errors, and so proofreading is an absolute necessity. An otherwise intelligent, well-written essay full of spelling errors or other mistakes that a reader would consider stupid creates so bad an impression that most readers simply won't bother reading the whole piece. And in the professional world, that's a killer.

Final Draft Assignment

Turn the first draft of your report into a final draft. First, write the first draft out in good form and then get together with at least one other student in the class to go over each other's drafts, making suggestions about content and organization.

Concentrate on the ideas and their order in this draft. If something in the other student's report doesn't make sense, sounds confusing, or doesn't seem to belong where it is (or in the report at all), speak up. Even if you can't *label* what the problem is, trust your instincts. By the same token, *listen* to what the reader of your report says about your ideas and organization. Pay attention to his or her questions. Remember: *A report is written to be read by other people, and if they have questions or don't understand it, the report fails at its job.*

If time permits, you may be able to do this in class, but if not, get together at the student center or library to share drafts. Remember: *There is not necessarily one right way to organize your material or one right conclusion to come to.* You and your colleague may find that you differ in various ways, but as long as you back up your general points with good specific ones, you may both produce excellent papers.

After you have discussed your report with another student or students, revise it, taking into consideration the constructive criticism you have received. When you've written this draft, you're ready to look at sentence-level or mechanical issues. Read your draft aloud, listening for any places that seem "wrong," even if you're not sure what's "wrong" with it. If this happens, ask yourself: "What do I want to say here?" Answer yourself aloud and quickly write down what you've said. If you can't answer that question, you need to do more thinking about it in order to be able to say or write what you mean. You may have to write one or two additional drafts before you are satisfied with your essay. (Remember Kurt Vonnegut's point about blowing up a blimp with a bicycle pump.)

Now write a final draft—one ready for "publication." Finally, proofread your report as carefully as you can. If you have done everything this assignment has called for, you have worked hard on this report. Therefore, make sure that, by being as professional looking as possible, your final draft reflects the care and effort you have expended. You may want to exchange your report with another student's—even right before you submit it—and each of you proof the other's, marking the following *with a pencil:* typos, words you think are misspelled, or possible punctuation errors.

USING QUOTATIONS

Quoting the words of an author you are referring to is a very good and very convenient way of helping to back up a point you are making. Here is part of a paragraph written by a student on a writing assignment that comes later in this book. Notice how she has incorporated quotations into her paragraph:

> Working long hours under stressful conditions, especially in fast-food restaurants, appears to promote some forms of delinquent behavior. Lou DeRosa, a 29-year-old manager of a McDonald's, said, "This is a survival job. A lot of people can't handle it." In addition to low wages and a hot, high-speed work environment, some employees complain of poor treatment by managers. Through Mark Kershaw's own experience as a manager he agrees that "there are some managers who treat them like slaves."

You can incorporate quotations into your report on men's and women's talk too, and you will certainly want to do it both in later assignments and in papers you write for your other courses. Fortunately, it is both easy and effective.

Punctuating Quotations

As in the paragraph above, when you want to introduce a quotation with words like "she said" or "he wrote," you put a comma after your introductory phrase and capitalize the first word in your quotation:

Lou DeRosa said, "This is a survival job."

If you want to incorporate the quoted words right into your own sentence, you use the word *that* instead of the comma, and you don't capitalize the first quoted word:

Mark Kershaw agrees that "there are some managers who treat them like slaves."

Punctuating Titles of Works

The general rule is that we underline (in print, as in this book, underlining is turned into italicizing) the titles of long works and put quotation marks around the titles of short works. So the names of books, movies, magazines, newspapers, and record albums get underlined:

The Great Gatsby
Citizen Kane
Cosmopolitan
The Atlanta Constitution

But we put quotation marks around the titles of essays or articles, short stories, songs, and so on.

Introducing Quotations

Let us suppose we are going to quote from an article by Leon Cheung and Marlene Johnson. The article is entitled "Three Issues in AIDS Research," and it appeared in *Current Social Issues,* a magazine. In our first reference to this article, we would give the names of the authors, the complete title of the article, and the name of the magazine. Here are three ways of doing this:

> In their article, "Three Issues in AIDS Research" in *Current Social Issues,* Leon Cheung and Marlene Johnson write, "Now that we have . . ."
>
> In "Three Issues in AIDS Research" in *Current Social Issues,* Leon Cheung and Marlene Johnson write, "Now that we have . . ."
>
> According to Leon Cheung and Marlene Johnson in "Three Issues in AIDS Research" (*Current Social Issues*), "Now that we have . . ."

Note that these three sentences are based on two simple patterns. The first two follow this pattern:

> In + title, + authors *write,* + quotation

The third uses a different pattern:

> *According to* + authors *&* title, + quotation

In later references, we would simply use the last names of the two authors with no further mention of the title of the article or the name of the journal:

> Cheung and Johnson write, "The evidence shows . . ."
>
> According to Cheung and Johnson, "The evidence shows . . ."

EXERCISE

Following are exercises in using quotations. Here are the quotations you will use:

A. Although the breakup of the Soviet Union marked the end of the Cold War, in Eastern Europe Communism has been replaced by new ethnic strife.
    Mario Cuellar, *The More Things Change*

B. It is difficult to defend free speech when groups exploit it, as is done in some popular music, to foment racial and sexual prejudices.
    Sarah Murray, "The Aesthetics of Injustice," in *Current Social Issues*

1. Referring back to the sections "Punctuating Quotations," "Punctuating Titles of Works," and "Introducing Quotations," write four sentences using quotation A. Each time, you should introduce the quotation in a

different way. In your first sentence, assume that you are quoting this author for the first time. In the next three sentences, assume that you have already quoted him before.

2. Referring back to the sections "Punctuating Quotations," "Punctuating Titles of Works," and "Introducing Quotations," write four sentences using quotation B. Each time, you should introduce the quotation in a different way. In your first sentence, assume that you are quoting this author for the first time. In the next three sentences, assume that you have already quoted her.

PARAPHRASING

One of the meanings of the prefix *para-* is "alongside" or "near." We use it with this meaning in terms like "paralegal," a legal worker who is not actually a lawyer, one who works with or alongside lawyers, and "paramilitary," armed forces that are not actually members of armies. A *paraphrase,* then, is a phrasing or wording of an original meaning that is not quite the same as the original wording. It is the same thing in different words. Usually a paraphrase is a shorter, more condensed version of a much longer original. Writers often paraphrase other writers in order to get their meaning on paper without having to quote the entire original. You will often find this to be a useful tool when you are writing about an article you've read in this book, but you don't want to spend a page or most of it just copying the original words. Paraphrasing is frequently very close to summarizing.

There are three important steps to paraphrasing.

- *First,* make sure you've really understood the original passage; a paraphrase has to be an accurate account of the original.
- *Second,* write your paraphrase using your own words; you can, of course, use key terms from the original, and you may often find it helpful even to quote short phrases because you can't think of a better way to write them, but a good paraphrase is someone else's idea expressed in your words.
- *Third,* compare your completed paraphrase with the original to make sure you haven't changed the meaning.

A good method for writing a paraphrase is to read the original passage, jotting down the key points, the ones you know you'll want to include in your paraphrase. (That's point 1 above.) The best thing to do is to write these points in short phrases rather than complete sentences. Make them reminders of what's in the original rather than copies of what's there. When you've done that, put the original aside and, just using your notes, write out your paraphrase. (That's point 2.) Then compare your version with the original to make sure what you've written is accurate. (That's point 3.)

Here is a paragraph from the essay "Man to Man, Woman to Woman," which appears earlier in this chapter:

> A different picture emerged when we asked women what they liked best about talking with other women. While many mentioned ease and camaraderie, the feature mentioned most often was empathy or under-standing, which involves careful listening as well as talking. "To know that you're not alone." "The feeling of sharing and being understood without a sexual connotation." "Sensitivity to emotions that men feel are unimportant." In questionnaire responses and interviews, women spoke of their same-sex conversations not as something they merely liked, but truly needed.

Here is one possible paraphrase of this paragraph:

> The women who were surveyed tended to use same-sex talk for different rea-sons than men. They especially liked it for "empathy or understanding" and for sharing their feelings. Unlike men, they didn't just like this kind of talk but felt they needed it.

IMPORTANT! Remember that when you paraphrase another writer's ideas, you must *always* give the original writer credit. Not doing so is just as bad as copying the original writer's words without giving credit. It's called plagiarism, and most colleges will expel students caught doing it.

A Problem

Sometimes students start a sentence with a prepositional phrase, particularly one beginning with *in,* and then get stuck for how to continue. Introductory prepositional phrases are very handy for referring the reader to a document you previously mentioned, as in these cases:

In this article
In this book
In the essay I previously mentioned

In such cases, remember that the word after the *in* (*article, book, essay*) cannot be the subject of the sentence. In other words, the following sentence is incorrect:

> In this article stated that Ethiopia is once again facing a famine.

Students sometimes try to solve this problem by putting the word *it* in as the subject, but this is again incorrect. *Do not use the word* it *as the subject when* it *refers to a noun immediately preceding it.* In other words, the following sentence is incorrect:

> In this article, it stated that Ethiopia is once again facing a famine.

How do you handle such a situation? If you know the name of the author, use that as the subject:

> In this article, Fernandez stated that Ethiopia is once again facing a famine.

If you don't know the author, then don't start the sentence with the *in* phrase. (If you've already started it, go back and scratch it out.) Use the word *article* itself as the subject:

> This article stated that Ethiopia is once again facing a famine.

EXERCISE

Correct the following sentences:

1. In an article from a Seattle newspaper stated that a study revealed that of gun-shot deaths in a white, urban county in Washington State, 53 percent took place in the home.
2. Over the sixteen-year survey of Cuyahoga County's accidental firearm fatalities, it showed that during four consecutive years, the number of deaths tripled the average rate of the first ten years.
3. In a pamphlet called "It Could Happen to You" by the National Rifle Association, it stated that "firearms in the hands of law-abiding citizens can and do produce a chilling effect on criminal behavior."
4. In another study of gun-shot deaths in a white, urban county in Washington revealed that over half of the killings took place in the homes where guns were kept.

5. Recently from a study of firearm fatalities in one Washington State county, it showed that 53 percent of homicides took place in gun-protected homes.

6. When looking at the pros and cons of owning a gun, it tells me that a gun is not the right answer for protection.

7. After reading the reasons for owning a gun and the results of having one, it changed my point of view.

8. In a survey done by two major women's magazines unveiled that a fast-growing number of women see firearms as a possible means of self-defense.

Sentence Combining

SHAPING SENTENCES

One of the problems with improving one's sentences is that understanding sentences means understanding at least some grammar, but at the same time studies have shown that very few people remember the grammar they study. And even more studies have shown that no one ever learned to write better by studying grammar. What to do?

One solution to the problem is called *sentence combining.* One of the signs of improved writing is longer, more varied, better shaped sentences. Studies have shown that the sentences of sixth graders are longer and more varied than those of fourth graders, those of eighth graders are longer and more varied than those of sixth graders, and so on. Professional writers write the longest and most varied sentences of all, and they go to a lot of trouble to shape them well.

Actually, there are good reasons why the sentences of less experienced writers tend to be shorter and more monotonous than those of more experienced writers. We can't get into all of these here, but we can tell you that knowing or not knowing grammar has nothing to do with it. And we can follow that up with two more reassuring points:

1. If you were born in this country or have lived here since you were very young, you probably know as much English grammar as any professional writer in America.

2. Professional writers don't use any grammatical structures than fourth graders—or you—don't also use.

So how do their sentences become longer and more varied? There are two primary reasons. One reason is that they make their sentence length and construction follow their ideas. That's what we mean when we talk about *shaping* sentences. That in turn means they don't chop up a single idea into several little sentences. The other reason is that although they don't use any constructions you don't know about and use, they do use some of them far more often than you probably do.

Let's look at an example of these two principles in action. Following is a passage about how the staff of President Reagan got him to help George Bush's campaign to become the next president. Here is that passage as an inexperienced writer might handle it:

> The Reagan White House cooperated with the Bush campaign to an unprecedented extent. It had the President sign or veto bills. These bills were judged helpful to Bush. It had him make appointments. It had him put off unpleasant business until after the election.

This passage doesn't read too badly—until you imagine trying to read ten or twelve pages of writing like it. You would drop dead from boredom. The thing is that while there are five sentences here, there aren't five ideas; there's only one idea, the idea that the White House helped the Bush campaign in a variety of ways. Here is what was actually written:

> The Reagan White House cooperated with the Bush campaign to an unprecedented extent—in having the President sign or veto bills as deemed helpful to Bush, in making appointments, in putting off unpleasant business until after the election.

The writer, Elizabeth Drew, used structures here called verbal phrases. (As you will shortly learn, *-ing* words—*having, making, putting off*—are verbals.) Instead of new sentences, she used verbals to keep all the parts of her idea together, to shape her sentence. You use verbals yourself all the time, but in writing an idea like the example just given, you might not think of using them as Drew did. That's where sentence combining comes in.

Sentence combining concentrates on the structures that experienced writers are most likely to use a lot and inexperienced writers are most likely to use very little, and it gives you practice in using them. It gives you the feel of using those structures frequently, and it tries to get you to remember to do so.

To help you remember what you learn in your sentence-combining work, we will give you reminders of it with each one of your writing assignments. But don't worry about combining your sentences when you are working out your idea draft. That's a time for concentrating on the ideas, not the writing. When you have all your ideas in place and your first draft completed, *then* go over your sentences to see whether you can combine some of them—or even add further information—using the sentence-combining techniques you have learned. Shaping sentences—and this is true for professional writers as well as those of us with less experience—is mainly a *second draft* operation.

And finally, don't worry that your sentences will get too long. There is really no such thing as a too-long sentence. And don't worry about mistakes. That's the way we learn.

The sentence-combining lessons in Chapter One are designed primarily to familiarize you with how sentence combining works. The first lesson, "Recognizing Verb Forms," will help you eliminate a verb problem that often crops up in student writing, and it will prepare you to do the next sentence-combining lessons. The next two lessons in Chapter One will show you easy ways to make crucial parts of your sentences say more. The lessons in Chapters Three through Six will give you practice with key structures found frequently in the work of experienced writers, ones that will make your writing more effective and more mature.

RECOGNIZING VERB FORMS FOR WRITING AND SENTENCE COMBINING

Have you ever been stumped about whether to write "we had swam in the pool" or "we had swum in the pool"? Or "she has run for president twice" or "she has ran for president twice"? This lesson will give you a brief overview of the basic verb forms in English to help you solve such problems in the future as well as to prepare you for work in sentence combining that you will shortly be doing.

In addition to having forms that make the present, past, future, and other tenses, all English verbs have three forms that do not make tenses; these three forms together are called *verbals* to distinguish them from the normal verbs. The three verbal forms are the *base* form, the *-ing* form, and the *-ed* or *have* form.

The base form of a verb is the one you find in the dictionary when you look up the verb. If you were to look up the verbs *walk, sing, think,* and *abolish,* those words would be the base forms of those verbs. If you were to look up a verb form that was not the base form—say, *is* or *has*—the dictionary would tell you that they were forms of the verbs *be* and *have.* So base forms are easy to spot. Base forms may also have the word *to* in front of them, as *to walk, to sing, to think, to abolish, to be,* and *to have.*

Every English verb has an *-ing* form also, and the *-ing* form always consists of the base form with *-ing* added. Thus, the verbs above all have the following forms: *walking, singing, thinking, abolishing, being,* and *having.* If the base form of the verb ends in *e*, as *give*, drop the *e* before adding the *-ing* (*giving*); if the base form of the verb ends in a single consonant (a letter other than *a, e, i, o*, or *u*), like the verb *get*, usually you should double the consonant (*getting*).

And finally, all verbs have a *have* form. We call this form the *have* form because it is the verb form that follows the word *have*, as in these cases:

I have *walked*
I have *sung*
I have *thought*
I have *abolished*

The *have* form of most verbs consists of the base form with *-ed* added, and in most cases the *have* form of the verb and its past-tense form are spelled in exactly the same way:

Base	**Past Tense**	***Have* Form**
walk	walked	walked
abolish	abolished	abolished
pause	paused	paused
open	opened	opened

But a great many of our verbs—the ones we use most frequently—have *have* forms that do not end in *-ed*. Again, however, their past-tense and *have* forms are identical:

Base	**Past Tense**	***Have* Form**
find	found	found
think	thought	thought
feel	felt	felt
have	had	had

Still another group has *have* forms that are spelled differently from the past-tense forms:

Base	**Past Tense**	***Have* Form**
sing	sang	sung
drive	drove	driven
swim	swam	swum
be	was/were	been

Usually we can easily think of any verb's *have* form simply by asking ourselves what form of the verb we would use after *have*, but in cases of doubt, look up the verb in the dictionary. All dictionaries list verb forms in the same way. First they give the base form, then the past-tense form, then the *have* form, then the *-ing* form. If the past-tense and *have* forms are spelled the same way, the dictionary will list only the past-tense form.

EXERCISE

To ensure that you can spell the common have *forms correctly and to enable you to do future exercises in this book, you will need to get a little practice in finding past-tense and have forms of verbs. Using your dictionary, find the past-tense and* have *forms of the following verbs:*

advance	eat	ride
become	fly	see
blur	lead	sink
buy	mark	suppose
choose	pay	teach
deplore	play	use

Following is a short passage to be written in the past tense. Most of the verbs are given in parentheses in their base forms. Write out the passage completely on a sheet of paper, putting the verbs in their proper forms. The verbs following *was, had,* and *grew* should be put into their *have* forms:

Martin was a person who (dislike) Christmas. He knew that he was (suppose) to see it as a happy, festive time, but he (see) only the commercialization. As a child, he had (know) happy Christmases and he (use) to look forward to them, but as he (grow) up, he grew (disgust) by the pressures to buy and buy. He (learn) that the suicide rate always rose on Christmas, and he (see) this as a sign that it was an unhappy rather than a happy time. Every December 1, he (post) above his desk his Christmas motto, which he (steal) from a writer named Quentin Crisp: "I try at Christmas time to carry on as though nothing unpleasant were happening."

SHAPING SENTENCES WITH ADJECTIVES AND VERB FORMS

A *modifier* is a word or group of words that adds to the meaning of another word or group of words. You may once have learned that a noun is a word naming a person, place, or thing. That is true, but nouns have many other functions as well. In doing the exercises in this section, you will, by good fortune, not have to worry about identifying nouns; they will be identified for you. Soon you will have a good feel for what nouns are, if you don't already, but more importantly, you will have learned something about how writers write that you can use whether you know what a noun is or not.

In the following exercises, you will be given one sentence such as this one in which the nouns are underlined:

The car drove down the road.

It will be followed by one or more short sentences containing the underlined words along with other words telling something about them—modifiers, in other words. You will add these modifiers to the original sentence to make one longer sentence. Here are three examples:

1.   The car drove down the road.
     The car was old.

     Solution: The old car drove down the road.

2.   The car drove down the road.
     The road was bumpy.

     Solution: The car drove down the bumpy road.

3.   The monster arose from the swamp.
     The monster was huge.
     The monster was ugly.
     The swamp was smelly.

     Solution: The huge, ugly monster arose from the smelly swamp.

Several different kinds of words can modify nouns. In the preceding examples, all the modifiers—*old, bumpy, huge, ugly,* and *smelly*—are adjectives. In addition to adjectives, verb forms, in particular the *-ing* and *have* forms, can modify nouns. When one of these forms all by itself modifies a noun, we put it in front of the noun:

1.   A monster arose from the swamp.
     A monster was groaning.

     Solution: A groaning monster arose from the swamp.

2.   A <u>monster</u> arose from the swamp.

A monster was <u>bored</u>.

Solution: A bored monster arose from the swamp.

However, if the *-ing* or *have* form has other words attached behind it or begins a phrase, then we must put it behind the noun we want it to modify:

1.   A <u>monster</u> arose from the swamp.

A monster was <u>groaning loudly</u>.

Solution: A monster groaning loudly arose from the swamp.

2.   A <u>monster</u> arose from the swamp.

A monster was <u>bored by the company of frogs</u>.

Solution: A monster bored by the company of frogs arose from the swamp.

EXERCISE

Witchcraft 101

1. A <u>student</u> is strolling to class.
   The student is tall.
   The student is good-looking.

2. The student is walking with a <u>friend</u>.
   The friend is pretty.
   The friend is well dressed.

3. The two <u>students</u> seem to be relaxed and enjoying each other's company.
   The two students are walking along together.

4. The <u>student</u> is thinking about asking his friend for a date.
   The student is tall.
   The student is walking with his friend.
   His friend is attractive.

5. The attractive <u>student</u> thinks her friend is a <u>dope</u>.
   The student is known for her high standards.
   The dope is hopeless.
   The dope is simple-minded.

6. The <u>students</u> walked into the <u>classroom</u>.
   The students were laughing.
   The students were happy.
   The classroom was bright.
   The classroom was sunny.

7. They were greeted by their <u>witchcraft instructor</u>.
   Their witchcraft instructor was ancient.
   Their witchcraft instructor was ugly.
   Their witchcraft instructor was staring at them from the front of the room.

8. Switching his tail, the <u>instructor</u> spoke in a <u>voice</u>.
   The instructor was frowning.
   His voice was deep.
   His voice was menacing.

9. On their midterm exams, almost half of them had changed their <u>frogs</u> into <u>real-estate brokers</u> instead of into <u>princes</u> or <u>princesses</u>.
   Their frogs were harmless.
   Their frogs were little.
   The real-estate brokers were aggressive.
   The princes were handsome.
   The princesses were beautiful.
   The princesses were charming.

10. While going over these <u>midterms</u>, the <u>instructor</u> was talked into buying a <u>condominium</u>.
    The midterms were wretched.
    The instructor was furious.
    The condominium was extremely expensive.
    The condominium was located at the edge of a swamp in Florida.

REVIEW

Since you probably are able to recognize nouns by this time and understand how to do this kind of exercise, the nouns in the review exercises are not underlined.

The Sounds of Music

1. Four music students hoped to find work.
   The music students were young.

The music students were talented.

The music students were graduating from college.

The work was playing classical music.

2. They formed a group called the Family Rat Quartet, but no one wanted to hear quartets played by musicians.

   The quartets were famous.

   The musicians were unknown.

   The musicians were scruffy.

   The musicians were wearing faded jeans.

3. So they changed their appearance; now they had hair, suits, neckties, and shoes.

   The hair was short.

   The hair was neatly trimmed.

   The suits were dark blue.

   The neckties were red.

   The shoes were polished.

4. They looked like funeral directors.

   The funeral directors were unemployed.

   The funeral directors were soliciting new business.

5. They found that audiences would not pay to hear musicians.

   The audiences were middle-aged.

   The audiences were attracted to string quartets.

   The musicians were young.

   The musicians were neatly dressed.

   The musicians were unknown.

   The musicians were wearing blue suits.

6. The concerts were those by string quartets.

   The concerts were well attended.

   The string quartets were established.

   The string quartets were made up of well-known players.

7. So the Family Rat changed its name to the Franz Joseph Haydn String Quartet and adopted hair, leotards, tennis shoes, and instruments.

   The hair was wild.

   The hair was Day-Glo orange.

The leotards were grass green.

The leotards were skin tight.

The tennis shoes were worn out.

The instruments were amplified.

8. They played music that killed insects, made dogs howl, and made bodies walk around.

The insects were flying and crawling.

The dogs were deaf.

The bodies were unburied.

The bodies were dead.

9. They gave concerts, made bundles of money, and, according to the critics, wrote music.

The concerts were jammed with admirers.

The music was grotesque.

The music was reflecting the death of Western civilization.

10. Between their concerts, during which their fans almost destroyed themselves, they gathered quietly in warehouses, got out their original instruments, and played the quartets.

The concerts were frantic.

The concerts were orgiastic.

Their fans were churning.

Their fans were writhing.

The warehouses were isolated.

The quartets were beautiful.

The quartets were intricate.

The quartets were written by the composers they loved.

SHAPING SENTENCES WITH PREPOSITIONAL PHRASES

Another noun modifier that we commonly use is the *prepositional phrase.* A prepositional phrase consists of a preposition followed by a noun (and any modifiers that noun may have). Prepositions are among the most common words in the language; you've seen and used them millions of times. They are little function words, like these: *in, on, up, down, across, from, to, of,* and *at.*

Prepositional phrases serve a wide variety of purposes. Here is a sentence with all its prepositional phrases underlined:

Without a doubt, the horse in the lead at the end of the second turn will finish in front of the field.

Prepositional phrases often tell location:

on the water	up the street
in the water	down the street
across the river	inside the box
over the river	beside the box

Sometimes they indicate time:

in a minute	at the moment

But they perform a variety of other functions as well:

of the dog	for a friend
about George	with her mother

In the following exercises, you will use prepositional phrases to modify—add meaning to—nouns, as in these examples. The prepositional phrases are underlined to help you spot them.

1. A bird is worth two.

    The bird is in the hand.

    The two are in the bush.

    Solution: A bird in the hand is worth two in the bush.

2. A stone gathers moss.

    The stone is in a swamp.

    The moss is on its surface.

    Solution: A stone in a swamp gathers moss on its surface.

3. A flight is a beautiful sight.

    The flight is of pelicans.

    The pelicans are over the water.

    The sight is in the late afternoon.

    Solution: A flight of pelicans over the water is a beautiful sight in the late afternoon.

In the last example, note that the second prepositional phrase—*over the water*—modifies a noun in the prepositional phrase preceding it. Prepositional phrases frequently work this way, coming in a series with each modifying the noun of the phrase before it:

the people / with a canoe / on a lake / in Canada

However, long strings of prepositional phrases generally don't sound good and are usually considered bad style.

In the following exercises, the prepositional phrases are underlined to aid you in locating them.

EXERCISE

Buying a Bathing Suit

1. A sale attracted a crowd.
   The sale was at the local shopping center.
   The crowd was of bargain hunters.

2. A friend wanted to find a new swimsuit.
   The friend was of mine.
   The swimsuit was in the latest style.

3. The store was mobbed with people.
   The store was with the biggest sale.
   The people were of every age.

4. The bathing suit always looks better than the one, but we found a promising one.
   The bathing suit is on the rack.
   The one is on the body.
   The one was on the sale table.

5. People were standing in a long line.
   The people were with all kinds of clothes.
   The line was for the dressing rooms.

6. The person was a woman who didn't seem to have any clothes to try on.
   The person was in front of us.
   The woman was in her thirties.
   The clothes were in her hands.

7. Finally, we noticed a small piece, a swimsuit.

   The piece was <u>of nylon</u>.

   The nylon was <u>in her hand</u>.

   The swimsuit was <u>of a truly astounding size</u>.

8. It was a tiny garment.

   The garment was <u>from a collection</u>.

   The collection was <u>by a Brazilian designer</u>.

9. When we found the racks, we saw other tiny pieces.

   The racks were <u>of designer swimsuits</u>.

   The racks were <u>down another aisle</u>.

   The pieces were <u>of nylon</u>.

   The pieces were <u>in violent reds, bright blues, blazing yellows</u>.

10. The tiny pieces of nylon bore large cardboard tags; when we reached the
    parking lot, we agreed that since the swimsuits were about the size, it was
    appropriate that they bore the price.

    The tags were <u>with prices of astronomical size</u>.

    The parking lot was <u>outside the store</u>.

    The size was <u>of diamonds</u>.

    The price was <u>of diamonds</u>.

REVIEW

*In the following exercises, you will practice using all the modifiers you have worked
with so far.*

Round-Trip

1. The student waited at a bus stop in the rain.

   The student was shivering.

   The student was suffering from a cold.

   The bus stop was on a wind-swept corner.

   The rain was pouring.

2. When the bus arrived, it was jammed with people.

   The bus was overcrowded.

   The people were depressed.

   The people were dripping water on each other.

3. At that moment, the student decided it was time to buy a car.
   The student was disgusted.
   The student was standing between two people.
   The two people were sneezing on her.
   The car was nice.
   The car was clean.
   The car was convenient.
   The car was for the commute.
   The commute was to school.

4. Several days later, she went to a dealer and selected a car.
   The dealer was reputable.
   The car was attractive.
   The car was used.
   The car was apparently in good condition.

5. The student loved her car, which kept her out of buses.
   Her car was new.
   Her car was used.
   The buses were crowded.
   The buses were full of people.
   The people were miserable.
   The people were suffering from colds.

6. The student gave her car a name, Fritz.
   The student was happy.
   The car was friendly.

7. One morning, Fritz the car showed some symptoms.
   The morning was gloomy.
   The morning was threatening.
   The symptoms were alarming.
   The symptoms were of trouble.

8. Fritz developed a disposition, so she took him to a garage.
   The disposition was surly.
   The disposition was uncooperative.
   The garage was recommended by a friend.
   The friend was trustworthy.

9. The mechanic said that Fritz was suffering from old age in many of his parts.

   The mechanic was sympathetic.

   The mechanic was at the garage.

   His parts were most essential.

10. In particular he pointed out Fritz's oil pump, his radiator, his cylinders, and others.

    His oil pump was ailing.

    His radiator was leaking.

    His cylinders were worn out.

    The others were of equal importance.

11. The student waited at a bus stop in the rain.

    The student was shivering.

    The student was remembering her car.

    Her car was cozy.

    Her car was warm.

    Her car was named Fritz.

    The bus stop was on a wind-swept corner.

    The rain was pouring.

CHAPTER *2*

The Shape of Texts

In Chapter 1 you began, through your work in analyzing essays and writing summaries, to see how texts are shaped. In this chapter, we will look closely at four key elements of texts: introductions, paragraphs, topic sentences, and conclusions.

INTRODUCTIONS AND THESIS STATEMENTS

Introductions are an essential part of life. How would we ever get to know one another if it weren't for introductions? How would we bring up an item of conversation or change the subject? It would be an odd class if, at the first meeting of the semester, the instructor walked in and just plunged into the material of the course without first introducing himself or herself and the subject to be studied. Unconsciously, you use or hear some form of introduction every day, probably many times a day.

Essay introductions, like other kinds of introductions, are nothing more than a way of telling the reader what's coming up. Along with the title, they help the reader find out whether this is a piece he or she is going to enjoy or be interested in or learn from.

The kinds of introductions we encounter in life tend to follow standard forms:

"John, I'd like you to meet Mary. Mary, this is John."

"You know that movie we saw last Friday? Well, . . ."

"Hello, class. My name is Professor Burpsmith, and I'd like to welcome you to English 565, a course in which we'll cover the American novel from Melville through Twain."

Essay introductions also follow formats, but you have a fair amount of leeway in how you handle the opening paragraph of your essays.

Basically, essay introductions take two different forms. One is the form used by most articles in popular magazines, the other the form used in academic work and in many articles in more intellectual magazines. The popular—or "Wowee!"—introduction is often, for reasons that are ill understood, taught in high school and even some college English classes. This introduction is supposed to *grab* the reader in some way or other. Here is one by a well-known American writer:

Thirty-nine years old! A recluse! Bonafide! Doesn't go out, doesn't see the light of day, doesn't put his hide out in God's own unconditioned Chicago air for months on end; *years.* Right this minute, one supposes, he is somewhere there in the innards of those forty-eight rooms, under layers and layers of white wall-to-wall, crimson wall-to-wall, Count Basie—lounge leather, muffled, baffled, swaddled, shrouded, closed in, blacked out, shielded by curtains, drapes, wall-to-wall, blond wood, screens, cords, doors, buzzers, dials, Nubians—he's down in there, the living Hugh Hefner, 150 pounds, like the tender-tympany green heart of an artichoke.

What on earth is that all about? It's by a writer named Tom Wolfe, and it's the introduction to an essay ("King of the Status Dropouts") about Hugh Hefner, founder and publisher of *Playboy* magazine. Sometimes grabber introductions get a little far out. Here's another, more conservative one:

As it happens I am in Death Valley, in a room at the Enterprise Motel and Trailer Park, and it is July, and it is hot. In fact it is 119 degrees. I cannot seem to make the air conditioner work, but there is a small refrigerator, and I can wrap ice cubes in a towel and hold them against the small of my back. With the help of the ice cubes I have been trying to think, because *The American Scholar* asked me to, in some abstract way about "morality," a word I distrust more every day, but my mind veers inflexibly toward the particular.

Like Wolfe's introduction, this one by Joan Didion hints at its subject (the title of the essay is "On Morality"), but it certainly does not explain what the essay will be about. Rather, it tries to engage readers so that they will be intrigued to continue. That's fine, but grabber introductions are not in great demand in academic work or in the business world. The last thing you want to do is begin a paper for a history or sociology or business class with an introduction like Tom Wolfe's. In these contexts, your teachers expect you to get to the point with a minimum of fuss. Here is a fairly typical academic introduction:

When we talk about history, there is always the danger of oversimplifying. In reflecting upon recent times we often focus on their uniqueness and turbulence, ignoring what they have in common with previous eras. When we consider the more distant past, we tend to think of a more serene age; the sharp edges of controversy and uncertainty become blunted by the passage of time. Yet even in acknowledging these tendencies, I think we can also acknowledge that the past two decades of our profession's history have been extraordinary.

As is often, but not always, the case, the last sentence of this introduction states the point of the essay—to review the "extraordinary" events of the past twenty years of "our profession's history." There it is, no bones about it, no guessing what's going on. A sentence like this one in an introduction, one that states the point of the whole essay, is often called a *thesis sentence.* Strictly speaking, the thesis part of this thesis sentence is only the part underlined:

> Yet even in acknowledging these tendencies, I think we can also acknowledge that the past two decades of our profession's history have been extraordinary.

Just as the thesis sentence of an introduction might be less than a complete sentence, so it may sometimes be more than one sentence. There are no rules involved here; writers just do what makes the most sense in the circumstances.

Here are the introductions from the two essays on male and female talk that are reprinted in Chapter 1 of this book. One of the essays first appeared as a newspaper column, the other in *Psychology Today.* Reread them and answer the questions following them:

It can be risky these days to suggest that there are any innate differences between men and women, other than those of anatomy. Out the window go the old notions about man and aggression, woman and submission (don't even say the word), man and intellect, woman and instinct. If I observe that my infant son prefers pushing a block along the floor while making car noises to cradling a doll in his arms and singing lullabies (and he does)—well, I can only conclude that, despite all our earnest attempts at nonsexist child-rearing, he has already suffered environmental contamination. Some of it, no doubt unwittingly, came from my husband and me, reared in the days when nobody winced if you recited that old saw about what little girls and little boys are made of.

I do not believe, of course, that men are smarter, steadier, more high-minded than women. But one or two notions are harder to shake—such as the idea that there is such a thing as "men's talk" or "women's talk." And that it's a natural instinct to seek out, on occasion, the company of one's own sex, exclude members of the other sex and not feel guilty about it.

Joyce Maynard, "His Talk, Her Talk"

When it comes to conversation, husbands and wives often have problems that close friends of the same sex don't have. First, they may not have much to talk about, and second, when they do talk, misunderstandings often develop that lead to major fights. Our research concludes that these problems are particularly resistant to solution. Not only do men and women like to talk about different topics, spoken language serves different functions for the sexes.

Mark A. Sherman and Adelaide Haas,
"Man to Man, Woman to Woman"

- Which introduction seems to be aimed at a popular audience (that is, is more of a "grabber" introduction) and which seems to be aimed at a more academic audience?
- What seems to be the thesis sentence (or sentences) of the first introduction?
- What is the thesis sentence of the second introduction?
- Where in their introductions do these writers put their thesis sentences?

In popular writing, the writer wants to lure you into reading the piece. In academic writing, the writer wants to give you enough information so that you can decide whether you want to read the piece or not. In the school writing you do, your teachers will expect you to follow the academic model, even though they have no choice about whether to read your work. They will, however, evaluate your introduction for its accuracy in setting up the problem you are going to be dealing with or stating your intentions, and they will usually expect to see a thesis sentence or sentences—a very clear and direct indication of what your essay will be about.

In your next writing assignments, it will be best if you use the following form in your introductions:

- First, a sentence or two of background on why (theoretically) you are writing the essay; the introduction by Sherman and Haas is a good model here.

- Second, a simple statement of what you intend to do, what you have been assigned to do (your thesis sentence).

For instance, suppose you were assigned in a business class, or even in a real job, to survey computer programs concerning the organization of personnel files. Your task would be to find out what types of programs existed within the general category outlined by your teacher or boss and describe the characteristics of those in each category. Your introduction might read something like this:

> The number of programs available for use in helping organize personnel files is fairly limited, but they do fall into four recognizable types. In the following report, *I will describe these types and the chief characteristics of each.*

STUDENTS AT WORK: INTRODUCTIONS

In Chapter 3 there is a writing assignment in which students read two essays about gender and ethnic representation in 1987 Saturday morning television programs and advertisements for children. Students are then asked to conduct their own study of *either* the programs *or* the advertisements today to see whether there seems to be a problem in one or more of the following areas:

- more or less equal representation of both boys and girls
- fair representation of the different ethnic groups in our society
- presence or absence of sexual stereotyping in the ways boys and girls are portrayed

Students are not asked to compare the 1987 studies with today's programing, though they may do so if they wish. Nor do students have to cover all three of the points above. Students are, however, expected to discuss the meaning of their findings. Following are four student introductions to essays on this topic. Read them and then consider the questions in the introduction checklist.

Commercials in general are detrimental to society. After viewing many commercials aimed at children, I saw many incidents of racism and sexism. When our population views these commercials it reinforces the sexist and racist behaviors in each of us.

In the United States every Saturday morning, young children begin watching their programs on television. Many people wonder if the commercials will affect their children. Are the programs showing or teaching good or bad values? In this essay, I will discuss the commercials in 1987 and in 1992. Then I will give my opinion about the commercials.

There haven't been many improvements in television ads shown to children today compared to 1987, although certain changes have taken place. Certain stereotypes in gender and also in race still seem to exist. Most of the commercials on Saturday mornings today are still about sugary cereals, sweet drinks, fruit-flavored candies, toys, etc. Besides all of the exploitative products that they're trying to sell to children, language, attitudes, and values are also being sold.

The 1980s was a time when the commercials showed little or no ethnicity and only males were present in the commercials. Children's commercials consisted of cereals loaded with sugar, drinks that clogged your throat, fruity candies, and of course, who could forget those wonderful blue-eyed, blond-haired dolls with a great figure. Those were the days when boys played with rough, masculine toys, and the girls played with dolls.

For each of the introductions above, answer the following questions. Note that you probably won't always be able to give a simple yes or no answer to each question. Some of the introductions will be stronger in some ways and weaker in others.

Introduction Checklist

1. Is it clear what the subject of the essay is—what it's about, why it's being written?
2. Is it clear what *specific* aspects of that subject this essay will discuss? (To judge this point, see the paragraph preceding the introductions, in which the different aspects of the assignment are explained.)

3. Does the introduction make clear that the essay will discuss both the nature of either the programs or the advertisements and what that means for children and for society?

4. Does the introduction contain a clear, specific thesis statement? (Note that the thesis statement doesn't have to give the writer's conclusions about the subject; those can come at the end of the essay.)

5. Is there anything in the introduction that seems irrelevant or pointless as far as the assignment is concerned?

6. What do you feel are the strong and weak points of these introductions? What did you like or dislike about each one? What did each teach you about what you'd like to do or not do in your own introductions?

Writing Your Introduction

Using the checklist above or one of your own making, decide on the points you want to put in your introduction *before* you start writing it.

Some writers prefer to wait until they have finished at least the idea draft of their essays before they write an introduction. They feel that it's better to know ahead of time what the introduction is going to introduce.

Others, however, use the introduction as a way of getting the essay going, of getting into it. If you like to write your introduction first, that's okay, but be sure that it doesn't limit you in what you want to say. Consider it a draft, subject to revision. You may even change your mind entirely about what you want to say as you write your essay, and if you do that, you'll want to go back and change your introduction. That's what happened in the case of Vanessa Thai, a student writing on the question of whether high school students should take part-time jobs. Here is the first version of her introduction:

Nowadays, teenagers are very anxious about having a job. As a student who worked during high school, I believed that the major reason why teenagers work is because they want to have more work experience and they can also make extra money for their own spending. However, working while in high school is quite stressful. It has both advantages and disadvantages, as I discovered from reading three articles, "Part-Time Work Ethic: Should Teens Go For It?" by Dennis McLellan, "McJobs," by Ben Wildavsky, and "Why Fast-Food Joints Don't Serve Up Good Jobs for Kids," by Amitai Etzioni.

Nevertheless, I truly recommend that high school students should look
for a part-time job because there's a profit that one could encounter
from having a job. A part-time job might teach you lots of valuable
things, yet it might give you some harm too.

After getting well into her essay, Vanessa changed her mind, and went back and
crossed out everything from "Nevertheless" to the end of her introduction and
replaced that part with these words:

After reading the three articles, I do not encourage high school students to look for a part-time job unless it's really necessary. The reason
is that although a job might be valuable to a student's life, it might
also be harmful to a student's life as well.

The end of this introduction could well be a lot more specific about good and
bad points, particularly the bad ones since that's what Vanessa wanted to stress
in her essay, but the main point is that she didn't let what she first wrote (and
thought) force her to write something she ended up not believing. Moral: Start
with your introduction if you want to, but don't let it lock you into a position
you won't be happy with.

PARAGRAPHS: PROVING YOUR POINTS

Everybody knows what a paragraph looks like: It looks like any other group
of sentences except that the first one is indented several spaces. But most people,
even experienced writers, would be hard put to say what a paragraph is. For one
thing, paragraphs come in radically different lengths. For instance, if you look
at the first page of any newspaper, you will find that the paragraphs are
extremely short, often only one sentence long. If you then look at any page of a
college textbook, you will of course find that the paragraphs are much longer
and that one-sentence paragraphs are rare. Paragraphs in popular magazines
lean somewhat toward the newspaper kinds. Paragraphs in more intellectual
magazines are like those in textbooks. Why is that?

Newspapers and popular magazines are designed to be read by everybody,
even people who aren't such good readers and who may not be much interested
in reading at all. So the editors of these periodicals keep the paragraphs short to
create a maximum amount of white space in the columns of text. The extra
white space makes the columns of print seem easier to read, more open. But
books and magazines designed for good readers, people who read often, do not

need to provide a lot of white space. Their readers aren't intimidated by long columns of print and will read them easily without the help of extra white space.

Newspaper paragraphs are, in a sense then, artificial paragraphs, or rather chunks of paragraphs, and to see what real paragraphs are, we need to look at the other kind, the kind you will run into in your college reading and be expected to write in your college writing. When we ask what a paragraph is, we are really asking the wrong question. A paragraph isn't what it *is;* a paragraph is what it *does.* Paragraphs are units of meaning within a book or an essay, and what they do is set up a point or a question (usually expressed in the *topic sentence* of the paragraph) and either explain it or prove it or illustrate it or discuss it or some combination of those things.

But it is not important to try to remember these things. What is important is to remember what you learned in writing summaries—that paragraphs go from general to specific. If your paragraphs consist of appropriate topic (or introductory) sentences backed up with specifics, you will be on the road to good paragraphs whether you know the four or fourteen types of paragraph development or not.

In academic and business writing, you basically *prove* or *show.* If you make a statement that requires proof, you must get specific to provide that proof. Look at this example:

> The reason the North won the American Civil War was that it was much stronger than the South. The North was a far more powerful part of the country than the South. The South just wasn't as strong as the North and so it was really impossible for the South to win.

Does this paragraph prove anything? Why not? Does it go from general to specific? Compare it with this one:

> The reason the North won the American Civil War was that it was much stronger than the South. The white population of the North was 22,340,000 while that of the South was only 5,600,000. The North had 105,000,000 acres of land under cultivation, mostly devoted to food, whereas the South had 57,000,000 acres, much of it devoted to cotton. The North had 22,000 miles of railroad to the South's 9,000 and 1,300,000 industrial workers to only 110,000 in the South.

The first paragraph, of course, is simply a succession of general sentences that all say the same thing. It proves nothing. The second one, however, gets into the specific, concrete reasons why the North was stronger than the South and, because of those specific reasons, presents a very strong case for its topic sentence.

Of course, not every paragraph you write is going to be full of specific facts like the one about the Civil War. Frequently, we argue for our ideas simply by giving our opinions, but again, the more specific (rather than general) and concrete (rather than vague) those opinions are, the more effective our argument will be. Again, compare the following two paragraphs:

> Watching a movie at home on videotape seems to me to be far more enjoyable than seeing one at a movie theater. When you're at home, you can just relax and be yourself. It's much less of a hassle than going out. I hate the nuisance of having to find the movie I want when I can just rent one and enjoy it in the comfort of my own living room.

> Watching a movie at home on videotape seems to me to be far more enjoyable than seeing one at a movie theater. Movie theaters are usually crowded at the times I can go, and there is always someone right behind me who explains the whole movie to his friend. At the theater, I have to endure the sounds and smells of popcorn being chewed all around me, while at home I can eat and drink whatever I want, whenever I want, with no fear of bothering anyone else and no worry about anyone bothering me. Finally—and this is important to someone who has to watch his expenses—the price of renting a videotape is a third or less that of going to a movie.

The second paragraph doesn't *prove* that watching videotaped movies at home is better than going to a movie theater, but it makes a good case for that view because of the concrete, specific reasons offered.

EXERCISE

Write a paragraph modeled on the second example in which you argue one of the following points:

- Watching movies in movie theaters is preferable to watching them at home on videotape.
- Commuting to work or school on public transit is preferable to doing so by car.
- Commuting by car is preferable to public transit.
- Watching a sport (specify which sport) on television is preferable to being on the scene.
- Attending a sports event (specify which kind) is preferable to watching it on television.
- Living at home while going to college is preferable to living in a dormitory.

- Living in a dormitory is preferable to living at home.
- For a college student, living in one's own apartment is preferable to living at home or in a dorm.
- Living at home or in a dorm (specify which one) is preferable to living in one's own apartment.

TOPIC SENTENCES AND THE ORGANIZATION PROCESS

Where do topic sentences come from? It would be nice if the stork or the tooth fairy or Santa Claus or someone would bring them, but we've learned from hard experience that they don't. By the same token, we've found that sitting down and scratching our heads and fretting and stewing and foaming at the mouth (all normal parts of the writing process) also won't bring them. Topic sentences come from the material you are working with. As you become more accustomed to doing academic writing, you will find that they usually come without your even thinking about them. But that won't happen right away. As you have seen in the paragraph examples you've already looked at, the topic sentence tells both you, the writer, and your reader what the paragraph is going to be about. Thus, it is easy to see that topic sentences come from your organization.

When you plan an essay, whether the plan is extremely detailed or just a kind of loose list, what you are doing is setting up the points you will cover and, usually, the order you will cover them in. Remember the planning process you went through in writing the report on men's and women's talk.

Let's say, as an example, that you have been assigned an essay in an American history class and that your subject is the relative strengths of the North and the South at the beginning of the Civil War. In your research you discover the facts about population, acreage under cultivation, railroads, and other points given in the paragraph you read earlier.

But then you discover that those facts are somewhat misleading. They make the North seem stronger than it really was. The Northern population figures, for instance, are inflated and unrealistic because they include the populations of "border states" like Missouri and Maryland, many of whose men fought for the South. They also include the populations of far western states, which contributed nothing to the North. The figures for Southern population are misleadingly low because they don't include the number of slaves in the South, and yet the slaves did valuable work that helped support the South's war effort. And so on.

Because of these complexities, you decide to organize your essay according to three main categories of strength and weakness:

Population
    white population
    black population
Economic strength
    industrial and agricultural strength
    railroad networks
Military strength
    weapons available
    leaders

This organization suggests that the completed essay might have an introduction and three body paragraphs, each with its topic sentence announcing the subject of the paragraph. But the great thing about organizations is that you never know whether they're going to work until you start writing. For example, further thought and perhaps writing might reveal that the paragraph on population should actually be two paragraphs because the population issue for both black and white populations is fairly complex, so that trying to cover both subjects in one paragraph would result in a paragraph that ran to more than a page. While there's nothing wrong with such a long paragraph, even experienced readers prefer to have them somewhat shorter.

Let's assume that you decide to give two paragraphs to population. Since the issue of white population is complicated for the North by the question of how you count the border states and whether you count the far western states at all, two questions the paragraph will have to discuss, a possible topic sentence for this paragraph might read something like this:

> The relative strength of the white populations of the North and South is complicated by which people one counts as belonging to the North.

The paragraph on black population would have to discuss not just the number of slaves in the South and the effect they had on the South's strength, but also the number of freed slaves who fought for the North. So its topic sentence might go like this:

> As complicated as counting the white population for the North is, trying to estimate the importance of the black population for the two sides is equally complex.

This topic sentence begins, as topic sentences often do, with a transition from the previous paragraph. But the important point is to see how the topic sentence develops from what you want to say in the paragraph. For instance, let's say that you wanted to make essentially the same points in this paragraph but wanted to stress that traditional history books make the mistake of over-estimating the *effective* population of the North and underestimating that of the South. The topic sentence for such a paragraph would reflect that point:

> Because traditional history books usually count whites who did not help the North and ignore blacks who did help the South, they overestimate the effective population of the North and underestimate that of the South.

It all depends on what you want to say.

Let's now assume that the material on economic strength is not so lengthy or complicated that it won't go easily into one paragraph. Since you know that the North had a huge advantage over the South in this area, your topic sentence might as well say it:

> In economic strength, the North had a huge advantage over the South.

Finally, you had thought that one paragraph might take care of the military strengths and weaknesses of the two sides, but further study revealed, again, a number of complications. Although the North began with an army and a navy, while the South had neither, the Southern states quickly seized Union war material within their borders, and many more Southern men owned firearms than did their Northern brothers. This issue would take a whole paragraph, as would the issue of the leaders on both sides. Topic sentences would be required for each of these paragraphs.

The result of all this thinking might be an outline similar to this one:

> white populations (North and South)
>
> black populations (North and South)
>
> economic strengths (North and South)
>
> military strengths (North and South)
>
> leaders available (North and South)

We see now that what had looked like a simple essay with an introduction, three paragraphs, and a conclusion turned out to be a somewhat more extensive one with an introduction, five central paragraphs, and a conclusion. And even this outline might turn out to be misleading, since some of these points, especially those about populations and military strengths, might require more than one paragraph.

We can see also how *the topic sentences of each paragraph are the result of our knowing what we wanted to write in those paragraphs.* They are the general statements expressing what the specifics of the paragraphs will tell the reader. Although the topic sentence comes first in the written paragraph, the paragraph idea has to come first before you can write the topic sentence.

Remember the steps of the thinking-writing-revising process and how topic sentences fit into it:

1. *Analyze* and *evaluate* your information.
2. *Organize* your material and *find your point.* (Here you begin grouping your material in ways that might lead to paragraphs.)
3. Write the *idea draft.* (As you write, you will find out whether your first ideas about grouping your materials will work. If they do, you are ready to write your topic sentences for each paragraph. If they don't, you can regroup your materials and then write.)
4. Write the *later drafts.* (Here you can review your paragraphs and your topic sentences, making any changes that seem necessary.)

STUDENTS AT WORK: PARAGRAPHS

When we are actually writing, it is often difficult to remember how paragraphs are shaped—that they normally start with a general sentence, the topic sentence, which introduces the ideas to be covered. Similarly, it is often hard to be sure what kind of evidence, and how much of it, one should include in a paragraph in order to make one's point adequately. Moreover, hard as these two essentials are, they are even more difficult to get right the first time—that is, as one writes one's idea draft.

In the first few papers in college English classes, teachers are used to seeing paragraphs that are faulty in either having no topic sentences or containing inadequate proof or evidence of the point being made. Here are two paragraphs from the middle of a paper about the content of Saturday morning children's television. Can you tell what points the writer is trying to make?

Dating back to God knows when, the blonde Barbie doll was intro-   1
duced to a generation of young girls. The Barbie doll is a huge success, even in today's market, being sold to girls living out their fantasies through a doll who had it all. I can imagine that many of the girls, of

all races, wished that they had blonde hair, lived in a Malibu beach home, drove a Porsche, and had a man like Ken. Barbie may have broken many dreams. Adding to the negative impact, an article last week had math teachers upset at the Barbie doll because Barbie has spoken. Now, 20 years later, Teen Talk Barbie, introduced in July by Mattel, Inc., is chattering away in the playrooms across the country, and this is what she has waited so long to say: "Math class is tough." This is the sort of thing that perpetuates the myth that girls find math harder than boys do.

One of the commercials about a new hockey game featured four white boys playing with one another. Even though professional hockey is dominated by white men, the typical minority may feel that this game may not be for him. On the other hand, many producers feature blacks playing basketball in their new hi-top basketball shoes trying to target young blacks, meanwhile it is very stereotypical to visualize that blacks always play basketball and care mostly of the shoes they wear. But we can't question the success of their methods.

Jerrold Gor, Student

Without topic sentences for these paragraphs, it is really impossible to tell what general point or points the writer was trying to make. His material is interesting, and much of his writing is very good, but what's his point? This is wonderful material for an idea draft, but it needs to be shaped to move from general to specific before it's ready for the finished paper. In a later paper, the same student did an excellent job of providing topic sentences and well-developed paragraphs. Notice here how the first sentence tells us exactly what point he wants to make:

The involvement of Asian parents may be the key in why the development of their children has escalated to such high plateaus. In the article "Japan's School System," by James Kilpatrick, Japanese parents play a major role in their children's learning process. The parents are expected to attend PTA meetings and to reinforce the school's training in "punctuality, neatness and respect for authority." I feel that the bond created between parents and their children motivates them because knowing that they have the love and support of their family gives the children incentive to do well and therefore succeed. Since American parents don't have such a close bond with their children, many students are unsure of their future and lack some incentive to learn because their parents care only about the final grades received and not how they got it. The first step in improving the American system is to have parental involvement in their children's education.

Jerrold Gor, Student

In working on the development of your paragraphs—what goes into them—the best procedure will usually be to follow these steps:

First, using your class notes, a review of the readings, and your notes on them if you have any, decide on the main points you want to make *in your essay* and list them in the order that looks best to you. This rough outline of the whole paper will make everything else much easier to do.

Second, under the main points on your list or outline, jot down any sub-points you want to make (so you don't forget them later).

Third, using these materials write your idea draft; don't worry about spelling, punctuation, grammar, and the like—just get your ideas into writing.

Fourth, make sure your paragraphs have topic sentences that tell what each paragraph will be about. Then, go back over the readings and look to see whether you've forgotten any important points; look also for any good quotations you can use to support your ideas.

After this, you'll be pretty much ready to start on the final form of your rough draft; in some cases, you may find that what you've just done is your final rough draft.

Following are some pages from students who went through this process. You'll notice that in some cases, they didn't have much to add during their fourth step, while in other cases, they felt they had a lot to add.

In the first case, Peggie Van developed one paragraph into two. Here is the paragraph in her idea draft:

There are many advantages for a student to work while going to school. For the most part, students want to earn money. If they have money, they will have independence. They can spend the money they earned any way they want to. Besides having money to spend, students are able to save money either to buy a car, for leisure spending, or to save for college use. Students can also gain work experience while they work. Depending on the job they have, they are able to learn a variety of skills such as operating a cash register or food preparation machine, learn inventory controls, bookkeeping and accounting skills, teamwork, and deal with customers. They also learn responsibility, for example, being on time and going to work regularly, taking directions and finishing assigned tasks, and also be reliable and presentable all the time.

Here is Peggie's revision of this part of her idea draft. After going back over the readings involved in this assignment, she realized that she hadn't covered the subject adequately. She also realized that when she included the important material she'd left out, she would have an unusually long paragraph, so one of her notes on her idea draft said, "Split into two paragraphs."

There are advantages for a student to work while going to school. One of the advantages is that you can ~~gain~~ earn money. For the most part, students work to earn money for their own use. Earning their own money allows them the independence to spend as they please. They would not have to ask their parents for money or for permission to do something with the money. The money they earned are ~~either~~ used for leisure ~~luxury~~ spending such as going out with friends or buying a car, or ~~for~~ saving up for college or future use. Some students may also contribute some of their money to help out the family. ~~Although most students work to earn money for use of buying things and not to save up for future use.~~ But as I said in the beginning, students usually work for money to buy personal things. It is very seldom that they chip in to help out the family.

~~Another~~ ~~Gaining experience from working is another advantage of working during highschool.~~

Besides earning money, a student can also gain work experience from working. Once a student works, he/she will learn to be responsible. By ~~saying~~ being responsible, the student must go to work regularly and be on time, taking directions and finishing assigned tasks, and also be reliable and presentable all the time. Depending on the job they have, the students are able to learn a variety of skills such as operating a cash register or food preparation machine, learning inventory controls, bookkeeping and accounting skills, teamwork, ~~and~~ dealing with customers, *and* ~~They also learn~~ supervising skills. ~~These are~~ Although these are general skills, they will help the students to find other jobs in the future in one way or another. An example of this is a highschool graduate who worked at McDonald's after graduation and worked her way up to being a professor at Hamburger University, "the

One student said that the money she earned goes "to support myself, my car and clothes and just stuff I do like going out."

McDonald's manager-training center, famous for issuing each
graduate of its one- and two-week intensive courses a degree in
Hamburgerology with a minor in fries."

Another student, Janet La, used the margins of her idea draft to write notes to
herself about examples from her own experience of the advantages of students
working. Among her notes she wrote the following, to be inserted into her final
version:

"Students who work gain benefits from work. They get discounts and free
things from the store and also special occasions off."
"My friend who works in a public library gets days off on holidays and two
months of free holidays."
"And my other friend who works in a retail store gets a discount on everything she purchases at her job."

CONCLUSIONS

We have seen in hundreds of composition textbooks many heroic efforts
to break down essay conclusions into different types for students to imitate.
And we know that students do get anxious about the conclusions of their
essays, worried that they might not end them "right," whatever "right" is. With
this in mind, we were mildly tempted to entitle this section "The Bitter End."
Since there's no getting over the fact that essays do have conclusions, the
best thing to do, we feel, is to look at some of them. Let's review three essays
from the first chapter of this book to see how their authors handled conclusions.
In the essay by Jane Brody, "Fatigue," the author tells us in her thesis sentences that "there are three main categories of fatigue"—physical, pathological,
and psychological—and then describes each in turn. Here is her conclusion:

Understanding the underlying emotional problem is the crucial first
step toward curing psychological fatigue and by itself often results in
considerable lessening of the tiredness. Professional psychological help
or career or marriage counseling may be needed.

Brody has simply finished her description of the third kind of fatigue, psychological fatigue, and stopped. She hasn't written a conclusion to the whole essay
because there would be nothing to do except repeat what she said in her introduction, that there are three main kinds of fatigue. One might say that this

kind of nonconclusion conclusion comes from the "When You're Finished, Stop" school, one we rather admire.

Here are the introductory and concluding paragraphs from Roger D. McGrath's essay, "The Myth of Violence in the Old West":

It is commonly assumed that violence is part of our frontier heritage. But the historical record shows that frontier violence was very different from violence today. Robbery and burglary, two of our most common crimes, were of no great significance in the frontier towns of the Old West, and rape was seemingly nonexistent.

McGrath's thesis sentence is: "But the historical record shows that frontier violence was very different from violence today." That is what he is going to prove in his essay.

Thus the violence and lawlessness of the trans-Sierra frontier bear little relation to the violence and lawlessness that pervade American society today. If Bodie is at all representative of frontier towns, there is little justification for blaming contemporary American violence on our frontier heritage.

Notice that McGrath has essentially just repeated the idea in his thesis sentence as the first sentence of his conclusion, adding to that a sentence relating to the underlying reason behind his study. Again, McGrath keeps his ending short and to the point.

Robert L. Heilbroner begins his essay, "Don't Let Stereotypes Warp Your Judgment," with a series of examples of common ways in which we tend to stereotype people and then comes to the point of his essay, his thesis sentences: "Stereotypes are a kind of gossip about the world, a gossip that makes us prejudge people before we ever lay eyes on them. Hence it is not surprising that stereotypes have something to do with the dark world of prejudice." Here is his conclusion:

Most of the time, when we type-cast the world, we are not in fact generalizing about people at all. We are only revealing the embarrassing facts about the pictures that hang in the gallery of stereotypes in our own heads.

Because Heilbroner is concerned about the way stereotypes lead to prejudices, he emphasizes that point in his conclusion, again, as does McGrath, tying it back in closely with his thesis sentences.

The writers of these three essays reveal several interesting similarities in their conclusions:

- They keep them as short as possible; after all, the essay has made their points and so there is no need to repeat them.
- Two of the three writers essentially repeat their main point, their thesis statements, and then stop.
- They don't use the phrase "in conclusion," and they don't repeat their thesis statements word for word.

You can conduct your own research on conclusions by looking back in Chapter 1 to see how Maynard in her essay and Sherman and Haas in theirs handle conclusions. Essentially, most writers prefer to wrap up their essays with a minimum of fuss. We have generally found that most students manage to end their essays with no great difficulty, and our chief advice to you is not to worry about it. Most of the time, your material will tell you how to conclude.

PART II

Discovering and Writing

A writer is someone for whom writing is harder than it is for other people.

Thomas Mann

3

Learning by Sorting It Out

AN IMPORTANT THINKING TOOL: MAKING INFERENCES

Certainties and Probabilities

In most of our daily actions, we govern ourselves as though our lives were surrounded by certainties—that is, truths we can count on absolutely. To illustrate, let us take a morning in the life of Mary X. She sets her electric clock for 6:00 A.M., certain that its alarm will go off at that time. She is certain that she will be able to take a shower when she gets up and that the food she has bought will still be there for her to eat at breakfast time. She is certain that her car will start, and she is certain that when she arrives at work, her job will be waiting for her. Her only concern is that sometimes the traffic is so bad, because of accidents or stalls, that the time it normally takes her to get to work may not be sufficient. Usually, however, it is.

Mary is guiding her behavior according to what, without thinking about it, she considers five certainties and one probability (that the traffic will be normal instead of slow). But of course none of these "certainties" is really certain. Power failures do occur from time to time, so that her clock may not go off at 6:00 A.M. Even if she has a battery backup for her clock, the battery may fail. Water systems fail also, especially water heaters. Perhaps Mary left her food out on the counter and her dog or roommate ate it. This could be the morning that her car battery dies, and it could also be the morning her boss decides the firm doesn't need her anymore. In other words, Mary is really dealing with six probabilities and no certainties. It is *probably* true that the morning will go as she assumes it will, but there are no certainties about it.

Still, not all probabilities are equally probable. We have degrees of probability, including, at one end of the scale, what are called *high probabilities* and, at the other end, *low probabilities*.

As a probability gets really high or really low, it gets nearer and nearer to being a certainty. For instance, if a teacher gives you a schedule of six quizzes for a course, and the first five quizzes appear exactly as scheduled, the probability that quiz number six will appear as scheduled is very high. Or, looked at another way, the probability that the quiz will be canceled or rescheduled is very low. Either way, it is almost a certainty that the quiz will appear as advertised. If, on the other hand, the teacher gave quiz number two a week after it was scheduled and skipped quiz number three altogether, the probability that number six will appear on schedule has dropped, and the class would have the right to feel very uncertain about whether it would be given and, if so, whether it would be given on its scheduled date.

In most aspects of our lives, we decide, mostly unconsciously, on the probability of an event on the basis of past experience. For instance, we know that light bulbs burn out, but we also know that they don't do so very often. We know that when we flip the light switch, there is a high probability that the light will go on, but we also know that it isn't a certainty. So we are not surprised when the light goes on, but we are mildly surprised, though not astonished, when it doesn't.

EXERCISE

On the basis of what you know about the world, evaluate the relative probability of the following events in Mary's morning. Rate them on a four-point scale:

4   certainty
3   high probability
2   low probability
1   uncertainty

Her alarm will go off at 6:00 A.M.
The water system will be functioning.
The water heater will be working.

Her food will still be there.

Her car will start.

There will not be a traffic tie-up.

She will still have her job.

In doing this exercise, you probably had difficulty rating two of the items— *her car will start* and *she will still have her job.* From your experience, you probably know that whether or not cars start as expected usually depends on various factors—the age and upkeep of the car, the temperature—and since you weren't given any of that information about Mary's car, you didn't have enough to go on to make a good judgment. Similarly, whether a person's job will be there on a given morning depends on a lot of things, including the kind of job it is, how well one does it, the economic health of the company, the economy in general, and so on.

Because people like to feel secure in their lives, they unconsciously treat as certainties matters that are only probabilities, and they often ignore evidence that makes their probabilities less and less certain. For instance, drivers who know that speeding under most circumstances increases their chances of having an accident will still speed, treating it as a certainty that they won't have an accident. Sometimes one member of a married couple will ignore numerous signs that the other member is unhappy and continue to act as always, treating it as a certainty that the other member won't end the marriage. People in these and similar circumstances are often shocked when their "certainties" turn out not to be certain at all.

EXERCISE

Using the four-point scale again, rate the probability of the following events:

You will attend your next class.

You will get an A on the next exam you have.

You will have or be able to get enough money to go out this weekend.

You will one day get married.

If you get married within the next two years, you will never be involved in a divorce.

You will not be involved in an automobile accident this week.

You will never be involved in an automobile accident.

If you do not wear a seatbelt the next time you are in a car, you will still not be injured.

If you never wear a seatbelt when riding in a car, you still will not be injured.

Try to think of at least one occasion when one of your "certainties" turned out to be wrong.

Inferences and Guesses

There is a famous short story entitled "The Lady or the Tiger," at the end of which the main character winds up alone in a room with only two doors, one of which he must go through to get out. Behind one is a beautiful lady with an agreeable disposition; behind the other is a ferocious and hungry tiger. There are no clues of any kind as to which door leads to the lady, which to the tiger. The man in the story has to guess which door to open. A *guess* is a decision based on inadequate evidence. It's a shot in the dark.

Let's play around with the lady and the tiger for a minute. Suppose our man puts his ear next to door A and hears, faintly, a low, rumbling growl of the type most of us hear only at the zoo; suppose he then listens at door B and hears nothing. Everything else being equal, he is now in a position to make a decision based on some evidence—his knowledge that tigers growl whereas people don't, or at least not like that. He can now infer that door B is the one to open. An *inference* is a conclusion drawn from evidence.

Good Inferences and Bad Inferences

Inferences are often labeled as *legitimate* or *reasonable,* on the one hand, or *illegitimate* or *unreasonable,* on the other. A reasonable inference is one based on adequate evidence or at least a well-considered judgment of the evidence available. Suppose you are in a position to hire a person to fill a particular job. The person, Michael Z, appears at his interview looking well groomed and neatly dressed. He is pleasant and answers your questions well. His work experience includes the kind of work you are hiring for, and he demonstrates an excellent command of that work. You infer from these matters that he would make a good employee, and that is a reasonable inference. If he turns out to be a poor employee, frequently late, often absent, always unproductive, you had no way of knowing that that would turn out to be the case. Your inference was still reasonable, a legitimate one, because it was logical given the evidence available.

Suppose, in another case, Henry R applies for a job. He is well groomed, well dressed, and pleasant, and he answers the questions intelligently, but he has never done this kind of work before. He is also a member of an ethnic group different from that of the interviewer. At the end, the interviewer decides not to offer Henry R the job, and this is the reasoning: "The last time we hired a member of this ethnic group without job experience we had a problem with her; she just couldn't learn the work fast enough and never did really get the hang of it.

We finally had to let her go. These people just seem to be dumb." This is an example of an illegitimate and unreasonable inference, as prejudice often is. From one instance, the interviewer has categorized all members of an ethnic group as lacking in intelligence.

In this case, two big mistakes are present. The first is to overgeneralize from too little evidence. The inference about Henry R was based on only a single example, and there is no reason to believe that one example, in a situation like this, is representative of the group. The second is to assume that all members of a group containing millions of people share a particular characteristic. It is a certainty of the same kind as our knowing that the sun will rise in the east tomorrow morning that any extremely large group of people, regardless of ethnicity, will be very diverse in all human characteristics. In this case, Henry R may or may not be bright enough to learn the job, but the inference that denied it to him was an unreasonable and illegitimate one.

EXERCISE

In the following four short cases, a certain amount of evidence is presented along with a possible conclusion. Evaluate each situation to decide whether the conclusion represents a reasonable and legitimate inference or an unreasonable and illegitimate one.

1. X rides the bus to school every Monday, Wednesday, and Friday morning at about 7:30, and almost every morning he notices another student who is always studying, reading one textbook or another. Most of the rest of the "regulars" study their work only occasionally, presumably when they've got an exam coming up. X concludes, "Boy, this must be a good student. She works all the time."

2. On the first day of his math class, X's teacher, whom X knows nothing about, comes into class smiling, a young attractive man. He reads the class roll, acknowledging each student individually, introduces the subject very entertainingly, making several genuinely funny jokes along the way, and then announces that he will give out a list of the books required and an outline of the semester's work and course requirements at the next class. With twenty-five minutes left, he dismisses the class. X is impressed. "This looks like a good teacher," he says to himself.

3. Z has been saving her money to buy a car and is now ready to do so. She consults her brother, a car buff, who tells her about a model that has been named "Car of the Year" by an auto magazine. In the library, she checks the back

issues of a consumer magazine that tests cars and finds the "Car-of-the-Year" model has had only an average frequency of repair record in the past. The company that makes it has recently had a below-average record for quality control. In a section on shopping for a new car, the magazine advises that car dealers give better prices on less popular cars than on highly popular ones. The "Car-of-the-Year" model gets excellent gas mileage, has the features she wants, and is within her price range. Z likes the way it looks. She decides not to buy it.

4. While trying to decide on a car, Z considers another model being advertised by a company that promises it makes quality the very first consideration in building its cars. The motto of this company's ad campaign is: "Quality is our middle name." However, a friend of Z bought one of this company's cars and had a lot of trouble with it. The local dealer tried to fix it seven times but was unable to do so. The company refused to replace the car, and Z's friend finally got her money back only when she went to a lawyer specializing in such cases. Z decides, "This company's ads are just designed to cover up poor quality control."

Making inferences is one of the tools we use to group or classify things. For example, Professor Drywit places John Woo and Nancy Williams in the same freshman English class because she infers that, as the result of attending the same honors English class in high school, the students have acquired equivalent skills in English. By so doing, the professor has "classified" the two students on the basis of inference. Does the professor's classification seem to you to be based on a strong inference or a weak one? Why?

CLASSIFYING TO DISCOVER

The writing assignments in this section are based on *classification*. Classification is a system for organizing things or ideas into groups according to their similarities, to make them more manageable or understandable. You encounter classification systems every day. When you go into a store, you know that the goods are going to be classified in particular ways so that you can find what you want without having to search throughout the store. In a record store, the albums will be grouped according to kind of music—all the rock in one place, all the country and western in another, all the classical in a third; in a supermarket, the foods and other goods are grouped according to type, the pickles in one place, the paper goods in another. At school, courses are grouped into departments set up according to subject matter. City zoning laws govern where businesses can be located and what kinds of housing can be built in what areas.

These laws organize or classify the city for us. This useful tool is, naturally, extremely common in academic and business work for helping us to understand large bodies of data.

Scholars and businesspeople use the tool of classification to discover underlying patterns and meanings that might not be apparent otherwise. For instance, imagine that you work for an advertising agency with an account for "Hard Rock Hairspray for Hunks," and your job is to determine in which magazines your client ought to advertise. To do so, you would want to examine carefully the kinds of items advertised in several magazines in order to draw conclusions about the audiences of those magazines. A few magazines might jump to mind as fairly obvious candidates—*GQ* and *Playboy,* for example. But what about, say, *Modern Drummer?* If you think about the bands you've seen, you would probably agree that most of them have male drummers, and so you might infer that *Modern Drummer* magazine might be a good place to advertise Hard Rock Hairspray. If you examined the magazine, you would find that while it doesn't carry as many male grooming ads as *Playboy* or *GQ,* its audience is composed for the most part of young men. From that determination, it would be reasonable to infer that *Modern Drummer*'s audience might well be interested in your client's product. Of course, your next question might be, "Yes, but does the absence of male grooming ads mean that rock musicians don't use hairspray?" That would be another possible inference.

In the early 1970s, a sociologist, William C. Martin, decided to look at the colorful world of professional wrestling in Houston, Texas. Attending some matches and studying the literature of the sport, he noticed that it was possible to classify the wrestlers—at first sight an incredible collection of colorful and outlandish characters—into several different types. First, he noticed that most of them fell into two large categories: heroes and villains. Looking more closely, he saw that even among the heroes and villains there were other smaller categories. In outline form, here is how he classified them:

Villains
    Foreign Menaces
        Nazis
        Japanese
        Russians
    Titled Snobs and Intellectuals
    Big Mean Sonofabitches
Heroes
    Clean-Cut Young Men
    Blacks and Browns
    Native Americans
Masked Men

Notice that Martin arranged both his heroes and his villains in three main classes, though he could have had four classes by making separate classes for Titled Snobs and Intellectuals, among the villains, and Blacks and Browns, among the heroes. Notice also that he found three subclasses under his Foreign Menace class. Sometimes, in classifying, one finds items that are hard to fit into one's system. This was a problem Martin ran into with his third group of wrestlers, Masked Men. The trouble with the Masked Men was that they crossed both main categories, appearing sometimes as villains, sometimes as heroes.

When one looks at Martin's classification of wrestlers, one can see that classification sometimes produces surprising results. Martin found that black and brown wrestlers were almost always cast as heroes, that Native Americans were never villains, and that Japanese usually were. An interesting and important limitation of classification is that while it reveals patterns, it doesn't necessarily reveal the *reasons* for the patterns. Further analysis and inference are almost always necessary if we are to understand what lies behind the patterns revealed by classification.

In this case, Martin found out that Japanese appeared among the villains because the audiences remembered Japan as being our enemy during World War II and because few Japanese-Americans attended wrestling matches in Houston. On the other hand, many blacks and Hispanics as well as whites attended, and so promoters, unwilling to risk racial strife in the audiences, generally cast black and brown wrestlers as heroes. American folklore pictures Native Americans as upright, dignified, and honorable, and we admire traditional Native American clothing and arts. Those facts, along with, perhaps, some guilt about the way our government has treated Native Americans, combine to make the Native American an ideal hero.

Frequently we can classify a set of data—that is, a set of individual pieces of information—in various different ways, depending on what we want to learn or how we want to look at the data. In classifying, we look for similarities between items in our data set. For instance, suppose we were going to classify the following sports: swimming, baseball, football, boxing, and water polo. We might decide to divide them into sports in which a ball is involved and those that do not use a ball, in which case we would get these categories:

Sports that use balls
    baseball
    football
    water polo

Sports that do not use balls
    swimming
    boxing

Or we could divide them into sports played in the water and those played on land:

Sports played in water
    water polo
    swimming
Sports played on land
    baseball
    football
    boxing

Or we could categorize them according to ones involving teams and ones played individually:

Team sports
    baseball
    football
    water polo
Individual sports
    swimming
    boxing

By looking at these sports lists, what immediate and general inference can you make about a way that team and individual sports differ? Does your inference *always* hold true? With what sports not listed above does it lose its legitimacy? Here is a larger list of sports. See how many different ways they can be categorized:

baseball	hockey
football	table tennis
water polo	tennis
swimming	soccer
boxing	wrestling
track	gymnastics
golf	volleyball
racquetball	diving
fishing	basketball

In the following assignments, you will be asked to classify information to discover what it means and to make reasonable inferences from your classifications.

*A*ssignments and Readings

ANALYZING TELEVISION FOR CHILDREN

In every city and town in the United States, every Saturday morning, young children settle down in front of their parents' television sets to begin watching programs—and advertisements—developed just for them.

The enormous audience of children held spellbound by stories and sales pitches beamed into their homes has left parents, educators, child psychologists, and others worried about the effects of this programming. Studies have been done from time to time looking at the amount and kinds of advertising directed at children on Saturday mornings, at the nature of the programs designed for them and the values those programs seem to teach, and at whether all segments of our society are represented on children's TV—girls as well as boys, black, Hispanic, and Asian children as well as white.

In the first of the following essays, a writer in the *New York Times* argues that children's television is doing poorly in all of these important areas; the second article reports the results of a study of gender and ethnic bias in commercials aimed at children.

Reading Assignment

Pre-reading

Before reading the following essays, think about your own experience as a child with Saturday morning television. On a piece of paper, jot down what you remember in these three categories:

- Commercials: What were they for? As you recall, were they designed to exploit children or not? Why?
- Gender representation: Do you remember the characters of children's programs as being primarily male or female?
- Ethnic representation: Do you remember the characters of children's programs as being primarily white, or not?

WHAT ARE TV ADS SELLING TO CHILDREN?
John J. O'Connor

About 20 years ago, the new Action for Children's Television, started   1
by mothers in the Boston area, prompted a national crusade when it
attacked commercials in children's programming as being **exploitative** and a disservice to society. For the past couple of weeks, I have
been dipping into the children's schedule and watching endlessly
repeated sales pitches for sugary cereals, sweet drinks, fruit-flavored
candies and blond, blue-eyed dolls with "fabulous hair" and "the
hottest clothes."

Things haven't changed much in the television business of chil-   2
dren's merchandising, and some aspects of the scene are even more
appalling.

Considering the feminist gains of the past couple of decades, for   3
instance, it is little less than astonishing to discover the **rampant** sexist stereotypes in the bulk of commercials. Boys still get to play sports
and be charmingly rowdy; girls play with dolls that look like "Charlie's Angels" rejects and that can be bought with such added-cost
extras as nail polish, makeup, perfume and, of course, cool blond
hair.

The message: little girls must be prepared for a life of buying   4
clothes and cosmetics and all those other wonderful things that will
make them irresistibly **alluring** objects. Life, it seems, is a look.

The role of television in the development of youngsters is, of   5
course, crucial and inevitably subject to public hand-wringing every
decade or so. The time has probably arrived for another national
debate. Headlines once again are telling unsettling stories about
troubled and seemingly **disaffected** teen-agers, the more notable of
recent instances involving black and Hispanic youths in gritty urban
New York, and whites in manicured suburban New Jersey.

Not surprisingly, a good many people waste no time in pounc-   6
ing on television as the culprit. Being trotted out once again are
the familiar statistics about the tens of thousands of hours of programming and the millions of commercials the average student
has consumed by the end of high school.

---

exploitative: using selfishly or unethically;   **rampant:** widespread;
alluring: attractive; **disaffected:** antisocial

Certainly, the commercials specifically aimed at young audi-   7
ences are, at the very least, suspect. They don't only sell products—
sugar-saturated and grease-clogged junk food—that arrogantly
ignore today's nutritional campaigns. They sell language. ("Ain't
life delicious," says the candy spot.) More to the point, they sell
attitudes and values. Equally as disturbing as the sexism on so many
commercials is the racism, even if unintentional, although Madison
Avenue puts so much research into its products that nothing is
likely to be unintentional.

Consider the parade of blue-eyed dolls—Beach Blast Barbie,   8
Hula-Hoop Maxie, Cool Times Barbie and the rest of the somewhat
tarty gang. Just about every commercial makes a point of mentioning the doll's hair, which is invariably blond and silky. "She's got the
best hair," brags one commercial. Is there a message here for the
black and Hispanic children with dark curled hair? It could hardly be
plainer; they do not have the best hair. They are clearly inferior. They
live in a society in which they can never be considered the best. And
then public leaders scratch their heads over the very pronounced
phenomenon of **alienation** among certain groups.

Considerably more subtle, there is the role given to "minority"   9
children in well over 90% of the commercials. In fact, in the New
York City area, black and Hispanic children are in the majority, but
they nevertheless will have a hard time finding their reflections in
the commercials surrounding the Saturday morning cartoons.

Black children are just about always placed in supporting roles. If a   10
basketball game is used to promote the virtues of a soft drink or cereal,
the single black youth will barely get into the picture frame. The leader
of the pack is invariably a white boy, preferably blond. The name of the
game remains **tokenism**. One of the few commercials to give a star-
ring role to a black youth is for a cereal and, in that case, all the players
are black. Segregation lives, and in the oddest places.

It is distressing enough that Madison Avenue's constant message   11
of "buy, buy, buy" is being delivered to homes that in many
instances may not be able to afford the products in question. But it
is downright infuriating when large sections of the audience being

---

alienation: being an outsider;   **tokenism:** representing a minority group by
using only one or two individuals

tantalized are left with the message that they are not important enough to merit equal visibility. The disservice to society noted back in 1968 is still very much with us.

FEMALES AND MINORITIES IN TV ADS IN 1987 SATURDAY CHILDREN'S PROGRAMS

Daniel Riffe, Helene Goldson, Kelly Saxton, and Yang-Chou Yu

This study updates research—some a decade old—on females   1
and minorities in children's television advertisements, examining how often minorities and females are present, and in what proportions, settings and kinds of white-minority interaction they are presented. . . .

Method

Our goal was to generalize about how minorities and females are   2
represented in the overall "world" of children's Saturday morning television commercials, regardless of which network's program a child might select. . . .

Two non-consecutive (Feb. 7 and Feb. 28, 1987) Saturdays were   3
selected for this study, in order to increase representation of *different* spots *and* total numbers of spots. . . .

All national commercials on both Saturday mornings (7–11 A.M.,   4
CST) on ABC, CBS and NBC were recorded. We coded each commercial, including repeats, that appeared, assuming greater impact for repeated messages. . . .

Product and setting were recorded for each ad, while *individual*   5
character **variables** included: race, age, gender, speaking role and interaction with minority characters. Three coders collected the data after revision of coding instructions, group training sessions and three reliability checks. . . .

Findings and Discussion

ABC presented 147 commercials, CBS 139, and NBC 133. "Snack   6
food" was the most frequently advertised (29%) product category,

---

tantalized: teased or tormented;   **variables:** things likely to change

followed by "cereal" (25%), "toys" (tied at 15%), "miscellaneous other products" (tied at 15%), "fast food" (8%), "public service announcements" (5%) and "soft drinks" (3%). . . .

As predicted, the 419 commercials were populated primarily by   7
males. Three times as many (29%) used only human male characters as used only females (9%). Nearly a fourth used only animated
characters.

When animated-only spots are excluded, nearly 38% of the 323   8
human-only commercials used only males while just over 11% had
only females. Overall, females were represented in 62% of ads. Previous comparable estimates of total female representation were 51%
in 1971 and 60% in 1973, suggesting that female representation
may have increased over the last 15 years. . . .

Our [next] prediction (no commercials with only minority char-   9
acters present) was also confirmed. Two-thirds of humans-only ads
were white-only. None were minority-only; white characters were
present in 100% of commercials. However, nearly a third had at least
one non-white character present. This may indicate increased non-
white representation. In 1974, minorities were in a fifth of Saturday
morning commercials.

But non-white "presence" is diminished even further when the   10
focus changes from percentage of commercials with "at least one"
minority, to proportion of characters who are minority. Whites . . .
totaled nearly 60% of all animated and non-animated characters, non-
whites totaled 8.2% (5.9% were black) and animated non-human
characters made up 32% of all characters.

When analysis is limited to "real" human characters, 86.5% were   11
white and 13.5% were non-white. Census data in 1985 placed the
non-white percentage of the U.S. population at 15%. . . .

Gender and race were significantly related, . . . with a higher   12
percentage of males among minority characters. Overall, white
males were the most prevalent race/gender "combination,"
accounting for a majority (52%) of all 1,429 real human characters, with white females 34.5% of characters, minority males 9.2%
of characters, and minority females 4.3% of characters. Census
projections, however, show 1985's white *females* a plurality
(43.5%) with white males 41.5%, non-white males 7.2%, and
non-white females 7.9%.

Conclusions

In 1968 the Kerner Commission warned that, "If what the white   13
American reads in newspapers or sees on television conditions his
expectations of what is ordinary and normal in the larger society, he
will neither understand nor accept the black American." With slight
emendation, that warning could still apply, and it could apply to the
television depiction of females and minorities other than blacks.

In the 1970s, scholars spurred by minority and feminist concern   14
demonstrated that racial minorities and females were underrepre-
sented on television and, if present, were used as background in
large groups, as token representatives, or to fill roles secondary
to those of white males. Similar criticism was directed at television
advertising aimed at children.

Minorities and females, in short, were shown less often than their   15
numbers in society would lead one to anticipate, *and* less often in
roles of authority or competence than logic would demand.

How have females and racial minorities fared since that 1970s   16
flurry of research? Our 1987 data *suggest* that female and non-white
presence (i.e., the presence of at least one) in children's commercials
has increased.

But despite those increases, the world of children's television   17
advertising remains predominantly male and white. In its whiteness,
that television world mirrors the real world, according to census estimates (86.5% white characters on television and 85% white in the
U.S. population). But by presenting a world with only 39% females,
children's television commercials seriously distort the real world population, where a majority—51%—is female.

Further, a form of tokenism may remain: non-white presence   18
(33% of commercials have *at least one* minority character) exceeds
non-white proportion (15%) of characters in the population of television characters. And, for the most part, non-whites have non-
speaking roles, and tend to be shown interacting among themselves
and not with whites.

Minority characters were less likely than whites to be shown   19
in home settings and adult minority males were seldom shown.
Absence of adult male role models in many black children's lives has

---

emendation: correction

long concerned those who study urban families. Absence of such models in children's "prime time"—Saturday morning—commercials is chilling. . . .

Post-reading

John J. O'Connor has written his *impressions* of some of the effects of children's television, impressions obtained, as he says, by "dipping into the children's schedule." In other words, he did not carefully or systematically study the advertising on Saturday mornings or the presence of women and minorities in children's programming. Impressions may be interesting and worthwhile, but they are still impressions.

The article by Riffe, Goldson, Saxton, and Yu represents a very careful study, rather than impressions, but it is a study only of advertising, not of the programs aimed at children on Saturday mornings. Nevertheless, it does seem to confirm many of O'Connor's impressions.

Compare the main points of O'Connor's essay and the article by Riffe et al. with your own pre-reading notes about your memories of Saturday morning TV. Were your impressions like or unlike those of O'Connor? Did they tend to confirm or not to confirm the conclusions of the study?

There are a few other matters to consider here too, before you go any further. One is whether minorities and women *should* be represented in television in proportion to their numbers in the population as a whole. Because women represent 51 percent of the total U.S. population, it is pretty clear that they should receive half of the roles in television, but what about minorities? Should they get only about 15 percent of the roles just because they represent only about 15 percent of the population? What does a black, Hispanic, or Asian child learn by watching programs in which virtually all of the main characters are white?

The Kerner Commission's question is also an interesting one. What is the effect on white children's attitudes toward minority groups if they hardly ever see them on television?

O'Connor raises two related questions. He asks whether seeing one's own ethnic group or gender poorly represented on television would produce a sense of being inferior and of not really belonging to the larger society. And he also questions the values taught to young girls about what womanhood should be—whether they should come to feel that the most important thing about being a woman is to be an attractive sex object, desirable to men.

All of these issues are worth serious exploration.

Essay Assignment

Write an essay in which you examine today's TV ads directed at children for evidence, or lack of it, of racial or gender stereotyping or bias. You may or may not wish to compare what you discover about today's ads with the evidence presented from 1987.

Pre-writing

There are many different ways to apply classification techniques to children's television. For instance, if you wanted to examine the shows, rather than commercials, for treatment of minorities, you might decide, on the basis of watching a few programs, that characters tend to fall into four groups: leading characters, important characters, minor characters, and background figures. You could then count ethnic representation in each category.

Together with your teacher and your fellow students, you will need to decide what you are going to study and how you are going to proceed. Working together, your class will have to answer the following questions:

- What do we want to learn about television's treatment of gender and/or ethnicity on Saturday mornings? (Consider the questions raised by O'Connor's article and the study by Riffe et al.; look again at the questions in the Post-reading section, page 98.)

- What system of classification will we use? (This will be determined largely by what you decide you want to find out.)

- Will each of us do our own individual study, or will we work together in pairs or small groups? Will the entire class cooperate in the same project, or will we do both, producing a series of individual papers that, when put together, offer a larger view of the issues we work on?

- Will all or some of us study the offerings of one or more of the three major networks, or will we study a local channel to see how it treats the issue we decide to study?

- Will all or some of us try to replicate—that is, redo in order to verify—the study of advertising, or will we examine the programs themselves?

- How many hours of broadcasting will we try to cover?

- Will we be able to videotape the programs or commercials we want to study? (If one person can make a videotape, two people or a small group can more easily work together on the analysis.)

When you have completed your study, you will be prepared to decide what your discoveries mean. Once again, the two articles and the questions listed in the Post-reading section above may help you with this, but you will also want to examine your own reaction to what you have learned. How *you* feel about your findings is an important consideration and should be part of your essay.

Writing

In your introduction, describe briefly what you have chosen to investigate.

In the body of your essay, you should first describe the method you used—that is, the aspects of children's television you chose to look at and how you proceeded. This is the part of your paper also where you report your findings. You may find that the article by Riffe et al. is a helpful model.

Conclude by discussing what your discoveries mean. You may also, although this is not necessary, make recommendations for changes in Saturday morning television.

Be sure to review the Writer's Checklist on pages 150–152.

ANALYZING THE JOB MARKET

Many, if not most, college students either hold jobs while they go to college, or have had jobs while in high school, or both. They are aware of the positive and negative benefits of work and usually plan—or at least hope—to find careers that will be a lot more rewarding, both personally and financially, than their part-time jobs. It comes as a surprise to most people to learn that the great majority of job holders got into their careers more or less by accident, that most people are doing work they didn't anticipate doing or prepare for when they were in college. This condition is likely to accelerate in the future, since the kinds of jobs available to Americans are changing at a very rapid rate, and most people are not even aware of the kinds of jobs that will be most in demand in the future.

To help you think about your own career in the world of work and give you some perspective on the rapidly changing nature of the job market, here are two readings: an article by a noted economist and former Secretary of Labor outlining the new categories of jobs a global market is producing in the United States, and a report from the U.S. Department of Labor on job prospects through the year 2008.

Reading Assignment

Pre-reading

Before you begin your reading, take out two pieces of paper and label them *Worksheet A* and *Worksheet B*. Write on them the answers to the questions below; it is important to do this carefully, because these worksheets will be important in your writing assignment.

Worksheet A

List all of the work characteristics in the columns below that you enjoy or think you would enjoy:

working with my hands	working independently
working with machines	working in groups
working at a desk	serving others
working with numbers	helping others
reading	working at home
writing	working in an office
drafting	working with animals
fixing things	helping animals
making things	owning own business
solving problems	working with food
meeting deadlines	working with computers
working under pressure	working outdoors
working with children	working indoors
working with senior citizens	traveling
meeting new people	working in a store

List any other job characteristics you like or might like that aren't listed above:

Write a summary of the kinds of work activities you like:

Worksheet B

Work experience you've had

Jobs:

Training required or received:

Skills acquired (list any of the following that are appropriate and add any others not on the list):

being on time	following directions
teamwork	dealing with people
training others	taking responsibility
supervising others	using your own initiative

Write a summary of your work experience. Indicate how you think it has prepared you for school and how it has helped you prepare for your future career. What have you learned from this experience that tells you what you might or might not want to do in the future?

Reading

Reminder: Highlight or underline the thesis statement and the topic sentences of each paragraph, and note the more important points in the margins. In short, *read actively.*

U.S. INCOME INEQUALITY KEEPS ON RISING
Robert B. Reich

Between 1978 and 1987, the poorest fifth of American families   1
became eight percent poorer, and the richest fifth became 13 percent richer. That leaves the poorest fifth with less than five percent of the nation's income, and the richest fifth with more than 40 percent. This widening gap can't be blamed on the growth in single-parent lower-income families, which in fact slowed markedly after the late 1970s. Nor is it due mainly to the stingy social policy of the Reagan years. Granted, Food Stamp benefits have dropped in real terms by about 13 percent since 1981, and many states have failed to raise benefits for the poor and unemployed to keep up with inflation. But this doesn't come close to accounting for the growing inequality. Rather, the trend is connected to a profound change in the American economy as it merges with the global economy. And because the merging is far from complete, this trend will not stop of its own accord anytime soon.

It is significant that the growth of inequality shows up most   2
strikingly among Americans who have jobs. Through most of the

postwar era, the wages of Americans at different income levels rose at about the same pace. Although different workers occupied different steps on the escalator, everyone moved up together. In those days poverty was the condition of *jobless* Americans, and the major economic challenge was to create enough jobs for everyone. Once people were safely on the work force escalator, their problems were assumed to be over. Thus "full employment" became a liberal rallying cry, while conservatives fretted over the inflationary tendencies of a full-employment economy. . . .

New technologies of worldwide communication and transportation have redrawn the playing field. American industries no longer compete against Japanese or European industries. Rather, a company with headquarters in the United States, production facilities in Taiwan, and a marketing force spread across many nations competes with another, similarly **ecumenical** company. So when General Motors, say, is doing well, that probably is good news for a lot of executives in Detroit, and for GM shareholders across the globe, but it isn't necessarily good news for a lot of assembly-line workers in Detroit, because there may, in fact, be very few GM assembly-line workers in Detroit, or anywhere else in America. The welfare of assembly-line workers in Detroit may depend, instead, on the health of corporations based in Japan or Canada.

More to the point: even if those Canadian and Japanese corporations are doing well, these workers may be in trouble. For they are increasingly part of an international labor market, encompassing Asia, Africa, Western Europe—and perhaps, before long, Eastern Europe. Corporations can with relative ease relocate their production centers, and alter their international lines of communication and transportation accordingly, to take advantage of low wages. So American workers find themselves settling for low wages in order to hold on to their jobs. More and more, your "competitiveness" as a worker depends not on the fortunes of any American corporation, or of any American industry, but on what function you serve within the global economy. GM executives are becoming more "competitive" even as GM production workers become less so, because the functions that GM executives perform are more highly valued in the world market than the functions that GM production workers perform.

---

postwar era: period since World War II;   **ecumenical:** worldwide

In order to see in greater detail what is happening to American ₅
jobs, it helps to view the work Americans do in terms of **functional
categories** that reflect the real competitive positions of workers
in the global economy. Essentially, three broad categories are emerg-
ing. Call them symbolic-analytic services, routine production
services, and routine personal services.

1. *Symbolic-analytic services* are based on the manipulation of ₆
information: data, words, and oral and visual symbols. Symbolic
analysis comprises some (but by no means all) of the work undertaken by people who call themselves lawyers, investment bankers,
commercial bankers, management consultants, research scientists,
academics, public-relations executives, real estate developers, and
even a few creative accountants. Also: advertising and marketing
specialists, art directors, design engineers, architects, writers and
editors, musicians, and television and film producers. Some of the
manipulations performed by symbolic analysts reveal ways of more
efficiently **deploying** resources or shifting financial assets, or of
otherwise saving time and energy. Other manipulations grab
money from people who are too slow or naive to protect themselves by manipulation in response. Still others serve to entertain
the recipients.

Most symbolic analysts work alone or in small teams. If they work ₇
with others, they often have partners rather than bosses or
supervisors, and their yearly income is variable, depending on how
much value they add to the business. Their work environments tend
to be quiet and tastefully decorated, often within tall steel-and-glass
buildings. They rarely come in direct contact with the ultimate beneficiaries of their work. When they are not analyzing, designing, or
strategizing, they are in meetings or on the telephone—giving advice
or making deals. Many of them spend **inordinate** time in jet planes
and hotels. They are articulate and well groomed. The vast majority
are white males.

Symbolic analysis now accounts for more than 40 percent of ₈
America's gross national product, and almost 20 percent of our jobs.
Within what we still term our "manufacturing sector," symbolic-
analytic jobs have been increasing at a rate almost three times that

---

functional categories: categories indicating the nature of work performed;
deploying: using;   **inordinate:** too much

of total manufacturing employment in the United States, as routine manufacturing jobs have drifted overseas or been mastered by machines.

The services performed by America's symbolic analysts are in high demand around the world, regardless of whether the symbolic analysts provide them in person or transmit them via satellite and fiber-optic cable. The Japanese are buying up the insights and inventions of America's scientists and engineers (who are only too happy to sell them at a fat profit). The Europeans, meanwhile, are hiring our management consultants, business strategists, and investment bankers. Developing nations are hiring our civil and design engineers; and almost everyone is buying the output of our pop musicians, television stars, and film producers.   9

It is the same with the global corporation. The central offices of these sprawling entities, headquartered in America, are filled with symbolic analysts who manipulate information and then export their insights via the corporation's far-flung enterprise. IBM doesn't export machines from the United States; it makes machines all over the globe, and services them on the spot. IBM world headquarters, in Armonk, New York, just exports strategic planning and related management services.   10

Thus has the standard of living of America's symbolic analysts risen. They increasingly find themselves part of a global labor market, not a national one. And because the United States has a highly developed economy, and an excellent university system, they find that the services they have to offer are quite scarce in the context of the whole world. So elementary laws of supply and demand ensure that their salaries are quite high.   11

These salaries are likely to go even higher in the years ahead, as the world market for symbolic analysis continues to grow. Foreigners are trying to learn these skills and techniques, to be sure, but they still have a long way to go. No other country does a better job of preparing its most fortunate citizens for symbolic analysis than does the United States. None has surpassed America in providing experience and training, often with entire regions specializing in one or another kind of symbolic analysis (New York and Chicago for finance, Los Angeles for music and film, the San Francisco Bay area and greater Boston for science and engineering). In this we can take pride. But for the second major category of American workers—the providers of   12

routine production services—the laws of supply and demand don't
bode well.

2. *Routine production services* involve tasks that are repeated over   13
and over, as one step in a sequence of steps for producing a finished
product. Although we tend to associate these jobs with manufacturing, they are becoming common in storage and retrieval of information. Banking, insurance, wholesaling, retailing, health care—all
employ hordes of people who spend their days processing data,
often putting information into computers or taking it out.

Most providers of routine production services work with many   14
other people who do similar work within large, centralized facilities.
They are overseen by supervisors, who in turn are monitored by
more senior supervisors. They are usually paid an hourly wage. Their
jobs are monotonous. Most of these people do not have a college
education; they need only be able to take directions and, occasionally, undertake simple computations. Those who deal with metal are
mostly white males; those who deal with fabrics or information tend
to be female and/or minorities.

Decades ago, jobs like these were relatively well paid. Henry Ford   15
gave his early production workers five dollars a day, a remarkable sum
for the time, in the (correct) belief that they and their neighbors would
be among the major buyers of Fords. But in recent years America's
providers of routine-production services have found themselves in
direct competition with millions of foreign workers, most of whom are
eager to work for a fraction of the pay of American workers. Through
the miracle of satellite transmission, even routine data-processing can
now be undertaken in relatively poor nations, thousands of miles away
from the skyscrapers where the data are finally used. This fact has
given management-level symbolic analysts ever greater bargaining
leverage. If routine producers living in America don't agree to reduce
their wages, then the work will go abroad.

And it has. In 1950 routine production services constituted   16
about 30 percent of our national product and well over half
of American jobs. Today such services represent about 20 percent
of national product and one-fourth of jobs. And the scattering of
foreign-owned factories placed here to circumvent American

---

bode: be an omen of

protectionism isn't going to reverse the trend. So the standard of living of America's routine production workers will likely keep declining. The dynamics behind the wage concessions, plant closings, and union-busting that have become commonplace are not likely to change.

3. *Routine personal services* also entail simple, repetitive work,   17 but, unlike routine production services, they are provided in person. Their immediate objects are specific customers rather than streams of metal, fabric, or data. Included in this employment category are restaurant and hotel workers, barbers and beauticians, retail sales personnel, cabdrivers, household cleaners, day-care workers, hospital attendants and orderlies, truck drivers, and—among the fastest-growing of all—custodians and security guards.

Like production workers, providers of personal services are usu-   18 ally paid by the hour, are carefully supervised, and rarely have more than a high school education. But unlike people in the other two categories of work, these people are in direct contact with the ultimate beneficiaries of what they do. And the companies they work for are often small. In fact, some routine personal-service workers turn **entrepreneurial.** (Most new businesses and new jobs in America come from this sector—now constituting about 20 percent of GNP and 30 percent of jobs.) Women and minorities make up the bulk of routine personal-service workers.

Apart from the small number who strike out on their own,   19 these workers are paid poorly. They are sheltered from the direct effects of global competition, but not the indirect effects. They often compete with illegal aliens willing to work for low wages, or with former or would-be production workers who can't find well-paying production jobs, or with labor-saving machinery (automated tellers, self-service gas pumps, computerized cashiers) dreamed up by symbolic analysts in America and manufactured in Asia. And because they tend to be unskilled and dispersed among small businesses, personal-service workers rarely have a union or a powerful lobby group to stand up for their interests. When the economy turns sour, they are among the first to feel the effects. These workers will continue to have jobs in the years ahead and may experience some small increase in real wages. They will have

---

entrepreneurial: like a person who creates a business

demographics on their side as the American work force shrinks. But for all the foregoing reasons, the gap between their earnings and those of the symbolic analysts will continue to grow.

These three functional categories—symbolic analysis, routine   20
production, and routine personal service—cover at least three out of four American jobs. The rest of the nation's work force consists mainly of government employees (including public school teachers), employees in regulated industries (like utility workers), and govern-ment-financed workers (engineers working on defense weapons sys-tems), many of whom are sheltered from global competition. One further clarification: some traditional job categories overlap with sev-eral functional categories. People called "secretaries," for example, include those who actually spend their time doing symbolic-analytic work closely allied to what their bosses do; those who do routine data entry or retrieval of a sort that will eventually be automated or done overseas; and those who provide routine personal services.

The important point is that workers in these three functional cat-   21
egories are coming to have a different competitive position in the world economy. Symbolic analysts hold a commanding position in an increasingly global labor market. Routine production workers hold a relatively weak position in an increasingly global labor market. Personal-service workers still find themselves in a national labor market, but for various reasons they suffer the indirect effects of com-petition from workers abroad. . . .

Unlike America's old . . . economy, . . . the global economy   22
imposes no particular limit upon the number of Americans who can sell symbolic-analytic services. In principle, all of America's routine production workers could become symbolic analysts and let their old jobs drift overseas. . . .

The number of such technologically empowered jobs, of course,   23
is limited by the ability of workers to learn on the job. That means a far greater number of Americans will need good health care (includ-ing prenatal and postnatal) and also a good grounding in mathe-matics, basic science, and reading and communicating. So once again, comfortably integrating the American work force into the new world economy turns out to rest heavily on education. . . .

----

demographics: characteristics of the population

TOMORROW'S JOBS
Bureau of Labor Statistics, U.S. Department of Labor

Making informed career decisions requires reliable information about   1
opportunities in the future. Opportunities result from the relationships between the population, labor force, and the demand for
goods and services.

Population ultimately limits the size of the labor force—individuals   2
working or looking for work—which **constrains** how much can be
produced. Demand for various goods and services determines
employment in the industries providing them. Occupational employment opportunities, in turn, result from demand for skills needed
within specific industries. Opportunities for medical assistants and
other healthcare occupations, for example, have surged in response
to rapid growth in demand for health services.

Examining the past and projecting changes in these relation-   3
ships is the foundation of the Occupational Outlook Program. This
report presents highlights of Bureau of Labor Statistics projections of
the labor force and occupational and industry employment that can
help guide your career plans.

Population

Population trends affect employment opportunities in a number of   4
ways. Changes in population influence the demand for goods and
services. For example, a growing and aging population has increased
the demand for health services. Equally important, population
changes produce corresponding changes in the size and demographic composition of the labor force.

The U.S. population is expected to increase by 24 million over   5
the 2002–12 period, at a slower rate of growth than during both the
1992–2002 and 1982–92 periods. Continued growth will mean more
consumers of goods and services, spurring demand for workers in a
wide range of occupations and industries. The effects of population
growth on various occupations will differ. The differences are partially
accounted for by the age distribution of the future population.

The youth population, aged 16 to 24, will grow 7 percent over   6
the 2002–12 period. As the baby boomers continue to age, the

---

constrains: restricts

group aged 55 to 64 will increase by 43.6 percent or 11.5 million persons, more than any other group. Those aged 35 to 44 will decrease in size, reflecting the **birth dearth** following the baby boom generation.

Minorities and immigrants will constitute a larger share of the   7 U.S. population in 2012. The number of Hispanics is projected to continue to grow much faster than those of all other racial and ethnic groups. . . .

Industry

Service-providing industries. The long-term shift from goods-   8 producing to service-providing employment is expected to continue. Service-providing industries are expected to account for approximately 18.7 million of the 18.9 million new wage and salary jobs generated over the 2004–14 period (chart 4).

Education and health services. This industry supersector is pro-   9 jected to grow faster, 30.6 percent, and add more jobs than any other industry supersector. About 3 out of every 10 new jobs created in the U.S. economy will be in either the healthcare and social assistance or private educational services sectors.

Healthcare and social assistance—including private hospitals, nurs-   10 ing and residential care facilities, and individual and family services— will grow by 30.3 percent and add 4.3 million new jobs. Employment growth will be driven by increasing demand for healthcare and social assistance because of an aging population and longer life expectancies. Also, as more women enter the labor force, demand for childcare services is expected to grow.

Private educational services will grow by 32.5 percent and add   11 898,000 new jobs through 2014. Rising student enrollments at all levels of education will create demand for educational services.

Professional and business services. This industry supersector,   12 which includes some of the fastest growing industries in the U.S. economy, will grow by 27.8 percent and add more than 4.5 million new jobs.

Employment in administrative and support and waste manage-   13 ment and **remediation** services will grow by 31 percent and add 2.5 million new jobs to the economy by 2014. The fastest growing

---

birth dearth: reduction in number of births;   **remediation:** corrective

industry in this sector will be employment services, which will grow by 45.5 percent and will contribute almost two-thirds of all new jobs in administrative and support and waste management and remediation services. Employment services ranks among the fastest growing industries in the Nation and is expected to be among those that provide the most new jobs.

Employment in professional, scientific, and technical services will 14 grow by 28.4 percent and add 1.9 million new jobs by 2014. Employment in computer systems design and related services will grow by 39.5 percent and add almost one-fourth of all new jobs in professional, scientific, and technical services. Employment growth will be driven by the increasing reliance of businesses on information technology and the continuing importance of maintaining system and network security. Management, scientific, and technical consulting services also will grow very rapidly, by 60.5 percent, spurred by the increased use of new technology and computer software and the growing complexity of business.

Management of companies and enterprises will grow by 10.6 per- 15 cent and add 182,000 new jobs.

Information. Employment in the information supersector is 16 expected to increase by 11.6 percent, adding 364,000 jobs by 2014. Information contains some of the fast-growing computer-related industries such as software publishers; Internet publishing and broadcasting; and Internet service providers, Web search **portals** and data processing services. Employment in these industries is expected to grow by 67.6 percent, 43.5 percent, and 27.8 percent, respectively. The information supersector also includes telecommunications, broadcasting, and newspaper, periodical, book, and directory publishers. Increased demand for residential and business land-line and wireless services, cable service, high-speed Internet connections, and software will fuel job growth among these industries.

Leisure and hospitality. Overall employment will grow by 17.7 per- 17 cent. Arts, entertainment, and recreation will grow by 25 percent and add 460,000 new jobs by 2014. Most of these new job openings will come from the amusement, gambling, and recreation sector. Job growth will stem from public participation in arts, entertainment, and

---

portals: entrances

recreation activities—reflecting increasing incomes, leisure time, and awareness of the health benefits of physical fitness.

Accommodation and food services is expected to grow by 16.5   18 percent and add 1.8 million new jobs through 2014. Job growth will be concentrated in food services and drinking places, reflecting increases in population, dual-income families, and dining sophistication.

Trade, transportation, and utilities. Overall employment in this   19 industry supersector will grow by 10.3 percent between 2004 and 2014. Transportation and warehousing is expected to increase by 506,000 jobs, or by 11.9 percent through 2014. Truck transportation will grow by 9.6 percent, adding 129,000 new jobs, while rail transportation is projected to decline. The warehousing and storage sector is projected to grow rapidly at 24.8 percent, adding 138,000 jobs. Demand for truck transportation and warehousing services will expand as many manufacturers concentrate on their **core competencies** and contract out their product transportation and storage functions.

Employment in retail trade is expected to increase by 11 percent,   20 from 15 million to 16.7 million. Increases in population, personal income, and leisure time will contribute to employment growth in this industry, as consumers demand more goods. Wholesale trade is expected to increase by 8.4 percent, growing from 5.7 million to 6.1 million jobs.

Employment in utilities is projected to decrease by 1.3 percent   21 through 2014. Despite increased output, employment in electric power generation, transmission, and distribution and natural gas distribution is expected to decline through 2014 due to improved technology that increases worker productivity. However, employment in water, sewage, and other systems is expected to increase 21 percent by 2014. Jobs are not easily eliminated by technological gains in this industry because water treatment and waste disposal are very **labor-intensive** activities.

Financial activities. Employment is projected to grow 10.5 percent over the 2004–14 period. Real estate and rental and leasing is   22 expected to grow by 16.9 percent and add 353,000 jobs by 2014. Growth will be due, in part, to increased demand for housing as the

---

core competencies: basic skills;   **labor-intensive:** requiring much human labor

population grows. The fastest growing industry in the financial activities supersector will be activities related to real estate, which will grow by 32.1 percent, reflecting the housing boom that persists throughout most of the Nation.

Finance and insurance is expected to increase by 496,000   23 jobs, or 8.3 percent, by 2014. Employment in securities, commodity contracts, and other financial investments and related activities is expected to grow 15.8 percent by 2014, reflecting the increased number of baby boomers in their peak savings years, the growth of tax-favorable retirement plans, and the globalization of the securities markets. Employment in credit intermediation and related services, including banks, will grow by 5.4 percent and add about one-third of all new jobs within finance and insurance. Insurance carriers and related activities is expected to grow by 9.5 percent and add 215,000 new jobs by 2014. The number of jobs within agencies, brokerages, and other insurance related activities is expected to grow about 19.4 percent, as many insurance carriers downsize their sales staffs and as agents set up their own businesses.

Government. Between 2004 and 2014, government employ-   24 ment, including that in public education and hospitals, is expected to increase by 10 percent, from 21.6 million to 23.8 million jobs. Growth in government employment will be fueled by growth in State and local educational services and the shift of responsibilities from the Federal Government to the State and local governments. Local government educational services is projected to increase 10 percent, adding 783,000 jobs. State government educational services is projected to grow by 19.6 percent, adding 442,000 jobs. Federal Government employment, including the Postal Service, is expected to increase by only 1.6 percent as the Federal Government continues to contract out many government jobs to private companies.

Other services (except government). Employment will grow by 14   25 percent. More than 1 out of every 4 new jobs in this supersector will be in religious organizations, which is expected to grow by 11.9 percent. Other automotive repair and maintenance will be the fastest growing industry at 30.7 percent. Also included among other services is personal care services, which is expected to increase by 19.5 percent.

Goods-producing industries. Employment in the goods- 26
producing industries has been relatively stagnant since the early
1980s. Overall, this sector is expected to decline 0.4 percent over
the 2004–14 period. Although employment is expected to decline
or increase more slowly than in the service-providing industries,
projected growth among goods-producing industries varies
considerably.

Occupation

Expansion of service-providing industries is expected to continue, 27
creating demand for many occupations. However, projected job
growth varies among major occupational groups (chart 6).

Professional and related occupations. Professional and related occu- 28
pations will grow the fastest and add more new jobs than any other
major occupational group. Over the 2004–14 period, a 21.2 percent
increase in the number of professional and related jobs is projected,
which translates into 6 million new jobs. Professional and related workers perform a wide variety of duties, and are employed throughout
private industry and government. About three-quarters of the job
growth will come from three groups of professional occupations—
computer and mathematical occupations, healthcare **practitioners**
and technical occupations, and education, training, and library occupations—which will add 4.5 million jobs combined.

Service occupations. Service workers perform services for the 29
public. Employment in service occupations is projected to increase by
5.3 million, or 19 percent, the second largest numerical gain and second highest rate of growth among the major occupational groups.
Food preparation and serving related occupations are expected to
add the most jobs among the service occupations, 1.7 million by
2014. However, healthcare support occupations are expected to
grow the fastest, 33.3 percent, adding 1.2 million new jobs.

Management, business, and financial occupations. Workers in man- 30
agement, business, and financial occupations plan and direct the
activities of business, government, and other organizations. Their
employment is expected to increase by 2.2 million, or 14.4 percent,
by 2014. Among managers, the numbers of preschool and childcare

————

practitioners: those who provide services

center/program educational administrators and of computer and information systems managers will grow the fastest, by 27.9 percent and 25.9 percent, respectively. General and operations managers will add the most new jobs, 308,000, by 2014. Farmers and ranchers are the only workers in this major occupational group whose numbers are expected to decline, losing 155,000 jobs. Among business and financial occupations, accountants and auditors and management analysts will add the most jobs, 386,000 combined. Employment, recruitment, and placement specialists and personal financial advisors will be the fastest growing occupations in this group, with job increases of 30.5 percent and 25.9 percent, respectively.

Construction and extraction occupations. Construction and extrac- 31 tion workers construct new residential and commercial buildings, and also work in mines, quarries, and oil and gas fields. Employment of these workers is expected to grow 12 percent, adding 931,000 new jobs. Construction trades and related workers will account for more than three-fourths of these new jobs, 699,000, by 2014. Many extraction occupations will decline, reflecting overall employment losses in the mining and oil and gas extraction industries.

Installation, maintenance, and repair occupations. Workers in instal- 32 lation, maintenance, and repair occupations install new equipment and maintain and repair older equipment. These occupations will add 657,000 jobs by 2014, growing by 11.4 percent. Automotive service technicians and mechanics and general maintenance and repair workers will account for half of all new installation, maintenance, and repair jobs. The fastest growth rate will be among security and fire alarm systems installers, an occupation that is expected to grow 21.7 percent over the 2004–14 period.

Transportation and material moving occupations. Transportation 33 and material moving workers transport people and materials by land, sea, or air. The number of these workers should grow 11.1 percent, accounting for 1.1 million additional jobs by 2014. Among transportation occupations, motor vehicle operators will add the most jobs, 629,000. Material moving occupations will grow 8.3 percent and will add 405,000 jobs. Rail transportation occupations are the only group in which employment is projected to decline, by 1.1 percent, through 2014.

Sales and related occupations. Sales and related workers trans- 34 fer goods and services among businesses and consumers. Sales and related occupations are expected to add 1.5 million new jobs by 2014, growing by 9.6 percent. The majority of these jobs will be among retail salespersons and cashiers, occupations that will add 849,000 jobs combined.

Office and administrative support occupations. Office and adminis-   35
trative support workers perform the day-to-day activities of the office, such as preparing and filing documents, dealing with the public, and distributing information. Employment in these occupations is expected to grow by 5.8 percent, adding 1.4 million new jobs by 2014. Customer service representatives will add the most new jobs, 471,000. Desktop publishers will be among the fastest growing occupations in this group, increasing by 23.2 percent over the decade. However, due to rising productivity and increased automation, office and administrative support occupations also account for 11 of the 20 occupations with the largest employment declines.

Farming, fishing, and forestry occupations. Farming, fishing, and   36
forestry workers cultivate plants, breed and raise livestock, and catch animals. These occupations will decline 1.3 percent and lose 13,000 jobs by 2014. Agricultural workers, including farmworkers and laborers, accounted for the overwhelming majority of new jobs in this group. The number of fishing and hunting workers is expected to decline, by 16.6 percent, while the number of logging workers is expected to increase by less than 1 percent.

Production occupations. Production workers are employed mainly   37
in manufacturing, where they assemble goods and operate plants. Production occupations are expected to decline less than 1 percent, losing 79,000 jobs by 2014. Jobs will be created for many production occupations, including food processing workers, machinists, and welders, cutters, solderers, and **braziers**. Textile, apparel, and furnishings occupations, as well as assemblers and **fabricators**, will account   •
for much of the job losses among production occupations.

Among all occupations in the economy, computer and health-   38
care occupations are expected to grow the fastest over the projection period (chart 7). In fact, healthcare occupations make up 12 of the 20 fastest growing occupations, while computer occupations account for 5 out of the 20 fastest growing occupations in the

---

braziers: people who work with brass;   **fabricators:** people who make things

economy. In addition to high growth rates, these 17 computer and healthcare occupations combined will add more than 1.8 million new jobs. High growth rates among computer and healthcare occupations reflect projected rapid growth in the computer and data processing and health services industries.

Education and Training

Among the 20 fastest growing occupations, a bachelor's or associate degree is the most significant source of **postsecondary** education or training for 12 of them—network systems and data communications analysts; physician assistants; computer software engineers, applications; physical therapist assistants; dental hygienists; computer software engineers, systems software; network and computer systems administrators; database administrators; forensic science technicians; veterinary technologists and technicians; diagnostic medical sonographers; and occupational therapists assistants. On-the-job training is the most significant source of postsecondary education or training for another 5 of the 20 fastest growing occupations—physical therapist aides, medical assistants, home health aides, dental assistants, and personal and home care aides. In contrast, on-the-job training is the most significant source of postsecondary education or training for 13 of the 20 occupations with the largest numerical increases; 6 of these 20 occupations have an associate or higher degree as the most significant source of postsecondary education or training. On-the-job training also is the most significant source of postsecondary education or training for all 20 of the occupations with the largest numerical decreases. Table 1 lists the fastest growing occupations and occupations projected to have the largest numerical increases in employment between 2004 and 2014, by level of postsecondary education or training.

Median Earnings in the Past 12 Months by Educational
Attainment US Census Bureau (2005)

Less than high school graduate	$18,435
High school graduate	$25,829
Some college or associate's degree	$31,566
Bachelor's degree	$43,954
Graduate or professional degree	$57.585

---

postsecondary: college

Post-reading

At the top of a sheet of paper, write the words Worksheet C.

Worksheet C

In the first article, Reich argues that jobs fall into three categories. Identify these categories, make sure you understand what each of them means, and, working with a classmate, match the jobs in "Tomorrow's Jobs" with Reich's categories and write this information on Worksheet C. This will give you a good start on understanding precisely what kinds of jobs hold most promise.

Essay Assignment

Write a report that will inform one of your classmates about his or her present and future employment prospects. To do so, use the information you found in the two articles. Illustrate the job trends you found with examples from the readings. Finally, use your findings to show your classmate how his or her job preferences match with job prospects for the future and make recommendations about how he or she might prepare for a career.

Pre-writing

In order to learn how job trends for the future match the experiences and hopes of one of your classmates, you will need to interview him or her. Use the following worksheet as a guide and ask any additional questions that seem important to you.

Worksheet D

What kind of jobs has your classmate had? How did he or she like each of them?

What were the hours?   What about vacation time?
Were these desirable?   Was this satisfactory?

How long were each of these jobs held?

What were the prospects for promotion and/or pay raises?

Description of the work done (get specifics; for example, have the person describe in detail the first four hours of a typical day)

What aspects of the work did he or she like best?

What aspects did he or she like least?

Does your classmate have any specific or general career aspirations now?

If so, what led to them?

Writing

The introduction should explain what the report will be about, in this case to inform your classmate about his or her prospects for the future.

The essay's body paragraphs should develop your main points—what you learned about work prospects in the future and the kinds of jobs available now, including the relationship between education and good work prospects. Be sure not to write just in general terms but to give specifics and examples. Additionally, don't feel that each of your points necessarily deserves its own paragraph. More important points may require you to write two or more paragraphs in order to develop them fully.

Your conclusion will probably contain your final recommendations to your classmate about how to achieve his or her goals.

Note: When you are writing, remember that a job is not the same as the person doing the job. In other words, a busboy, a cashier, a sales manager, and a teacher *are not jobs.* Jobs are busing dishes, working as a cashier or sales manager, and teaching. Be sure not to confuse the two. Review the Writer's Checklist on pages 150–152.

LEARNING WHAT OUR MAGAZINES TELL ABOUT US

In studying human societies, anthropologists have learned that we invent the worlds we live in and then believe that these made-up worlds of ours are "natural" and "real." Not only that, but we think our own made-up views of the way human beings behave represent the truth for everyone. This habit can produce two bad results. One is that when we encounter a world different from ours, one made up by a different society, we usually consider it wrong— perhaps even barbarian or primitive or evil.

For example, during World War II, the Japanese armed forces treated prisoners of war with contempt and brutality as a matter of course, outraging their Western enemies, who believed prisoners should be treated humanely. Thus, Western societies viewed the Japanese as barbaric and even subhuman. In Western societies, surrendering to an enemy when one's cause is hopeless is considered not dishonorable but only sensible. But the Japanese just as firmly believed that surrender was cowardly and that the only honorable end for a defeated soldier was death. Most Japanese soldiers simply could not imagine living on after surrendering. As a result, the Japanese saw Allied prisoners of war as cowardly, contemptible, and subhuman.

There can be another bad result of holding that one's own view of the world is the only one possible. If this view turns out to be destructive, it may be difficult or even impossible to change it. For instance, in some cultures certain food sources that we accept as normal are considered holy and untouchable, and people will literally starve to death rather than eat them. While many people in the United States think that Hindus are foolish for not wanting to eat cows, what would you think of having dog for dinner? In many lands, dog meat is a natural part of the diet. In our own culture, we value certain social behaviors so highly—thinking them only natural—that we find it virtually impossible to change them even though they are poisoning our environment.

In the first of the following articles, Mary Kay Blakely discusses the kind of world women's magazines have "made up" for their readers. In this world women are told they must always look beautiful and never gain weight or grow old. In the second article, Susan Dudash has examined the articles in these magazines and come to the conclusion that they do not represent the reality of women's lives today.

Reading Assignment

Pre-reading

Before you begin your reading, think about the women's magazines you have read or glanced at (*Cosmopolitan, Seventeen, Redbook, Vogue*). You may want to go to a nearby book or magazine store and skim the table of contents of several traditional women's magazines; students who have copies of these magazines may wish to bring them to class for discussion purposes.

What are the kinds of articles in these magazines? What kinds of topics are their readers interested in? What things do their readers *value*—that is, what is important to them? When you categorize these articles, do you notice any patterns? If you do, what do these patterns suggest about the world these magazines present to their readers, a world their readers clearly think valuable since they continue to buy the magazines?

Remember to take notes as you examine and discuss this topic. And remember to read the following articles *actively*, underlining or highlighting the thesis and topic sentences and making notes in the margins when you happen upon some interesting point or observation.

HELP OR HINDRANCE? WOMEN'S MAGAZINES OFFER READERS LITTLE BUT FEAR, FAILURE
Mary Kay Blakely

Journalist Maggie Scarf stumbled upon the following finding during her 10-year study of women and depression: "For every male diagnosed as suffering from depression, the head count was anywhere from two to six times as many females." The late Professor Marcia Guttentag, director of the Harvard Project on Women and Mental Health, confirmed the fact, calling depression "epidemic" among women. The strongest clue Guttentag's team of psychologists had unearthed about the reason so many women are depressed had come from a 1974 analysis of articles in women's and men's magazines. 1

The content of men's magazines "tended to concern adventure, the overcoming of obstacles; the preoccupations were with mastery and triumph," Scarf reports in her subsequent book, *Unfinished Business: Pressure Points in the Lives of Women* (Doubleday, 1980). In magazines written for women, however, "the clear preoccupation was with the problem of loss—loss of attractiveness, loss of effectiveness." The message women's magazines sent to 65 million readers was this: Whatever it is that makes you happy, you are about to lose it. 2

Twelve years after Guttentag's exhaustive study at Harvard, I conducted an informal, unscientific survey of my own. I spent $16.58 for 10 recent issues of the 10 largest magazines about women to study the reflection of women as it came back to me through 2,793 magazine pages. (The top 10 women's magazines are *Family Circle, Women's Day, McCall's, Ladies' Home Journal, Redbook, Cosmopolitan, Glamour, Mademoiselle, Woman's World,* and *Vogue.*) 3

Judging from the headlines on the covers, the foremost concern of women today is not to grow wiser but to grow smaller. The Average Reader, magazines assume, is on a perpetual diet. There were "Exercise and Diet Tips for Your Over-Fat Zones" and "The Four Hot Diets—What's Good, What's Not." The preoccupation with fat appeared as headlines on 60 percent of the covers, as articles in nine out of 10, and as advertisements in all of them. 4

Could this obsession with thinness contribute to women's ⁵
pervasive depression? A recent study of bulimia, a disorder in which
victims force themselves to vomit after eating, would indicate that it
does. Alarming reports of bulimia among college-age women have
been circulating for some time, and now there are symptoms of the
illness among 30-year-old executives.

The obsession with thinness was never labeled clearly as "van- ⁶
ity"; it masqueraded as "health." Celebrities such as Jane Fonda,
Cher, Raquel Welch and Stephanie Powers were offered as "health
experts" to advise readers on how to maintain a 25-year-old
physique well past 40. The clear message was that whatever growing and changing a woman must do psychologically to prevent
depression, she had better accomplish it in a body that never grew
or changed past 25. A youth/confidence equation appeared in several hundred pages of ads promising to fend off wrinkles with "anti-
aging complexes," "age-zone protectors," "cellular-replacement
therapy" and "line preventers." Again, unwrinkled skin was
described as "healthy" skin.

Articles creating anxiety about "what's wrong with you" pre- ⁷
ceded ads supplying the remedies. One feature called "Quick Lifts
for the Morning Uglies," a peculiar form of depression suffered by
young readers, mentioned seven tips for "improving your outlook."
Five of them involved the purchase of a bath gel, a blemish cover, a
blusher, a scarf, a perfume. Because a woman, if she lives to old age,
will become wrinkled, will shift in weight, there will always be the
need for more treatment. The Average Reader is not encouraged to
look forward to her old self as a woman of achievement, but as a
waste. "How you look" was synonymous with "who you are," and
for older women that means "invisible."

Not only does the Average Reader have to achieve her growing ⁸
and changing without bulges and wrinkles, but the current **purge** of
serious issues means that she must proceed without information. As
Elizabeth Sloan, the editor in chief of *McCall's,* recently told the press,
the magazine's past issues had been "too text-oriented. We're going
to have pictures of girls spinning, kicking, swirling. We're going to be
much younger." She promised an end to "essays on serious issues,

---

pervasive: complete, total;   **purge:** removal

society issues. They just didn't belong." The decision not to shock the Average Reader, however, can **inadvertently** contribute to another kind of depression women suffer: the prolonged, debilitating feeling of powerlessness.

Surveys indicated the Average Reader liked how-to features, especially how-tos that would solve a problem by next weekend. The quick-fix approach permeated the pages of the recent issues: "How to Stop the One You Love from Drinking," "Loving Ways to Talk Out Anything—So Your Marriage Wins," and "How Not to Look and Feel Tired." There is hardly a problem in America the Average Reader can't somehow solve with health or beauty techniques. The beauty tricks recommended made the sad-looking woman in the "before" photo look decidedly more cheerful, but can a cold, a quarrel, and a hangover really be cured by applying mascara? "The articles speak to us as if women are extremely simple-minded," says science writer K. C. Cole, a panel member for a recent symposium on the trivialization of women in magazines at the New School for Social Research in Manhattan. "Problems are cast in terms of before and after, do's and don't's, yes and no. There are rarely shades of gray. It's the language a mother uses with a child, not the language of women dealing with extremely complicated issues." 9

As the late physicist Frank Oppenheimer once explained to his students, "We don't live in the real world. We live in a world we made up." The world made up for women through 2,793 pages of the magazines I selected was this: 40-year-old bodies can look like 25 if women would only try hard enough; if "anti-aging" formulas fail to keep wrinkles off women's skin, surgery is available; and marriages can be saved in three easy steps. If women feel depressed about any of this, they probably need more blusher. 10

The "Unfinished Business" Scarf wrote about six years ago is still vastly undone. Instead of encouraging women to grow beyond childish myths and adapt to the changes of life, women's magazines have readers running in place, exhausted. The anxieties and depression instilled by these magazines have risen so high that executive women are submitting to surgery. This is the world we have "made up" for women, and it is a perilous place to exist. 11

---

inadvertently: accidentally

CONFESSIONS OF A FORMER WOMEN'S MAGAZINE WRITER
Marilynn Larkin

Writing about "hot" nutrition topics still has impact. During the   1
decade or so that I wrote for women's magazines, I received much
positive feedback from readers.

In 1989, at the height of oat bran's popularity as a panacea to lower   2
cholesterol, the president and chief operating officer of a leading cereal
manufacturer estimated that sales of oat-bran cereals would grow to
nearly $600 million annually. I wrote five oat-bran stories that year for
various women's magazines. A year later, when a study called oat bran's
health-promoting properties into question, sales plummeted 50%
within a week; at that point, I couldn't give away an article on oat bran.

I also covered other "hot" nutrition topics. But although they   3
appeared on the nutrition page, these articles tended to be either
"food-of-the-month" stories (the grapefruit diet, carrot power) or
quasi-entertainment pieces that positioned foods as medicine: to
fight cancer, strengthen the immune system, lower blood pressure,
cut cholesterol, stave off heart attacks, prevent osteoporosis, reduce
stress, or improve your sex life.

Earning a living this way was quick, easy, and—for a while at   4
least—fun. I readily recycled material from publication to publication, since all were prone to hopping on the same bandwagons. And
editors who saw my work in one magazine often asked me to "do a
story like this for *our* audience." It never dawned on me that I might
be misleading the public by promoting "food-as-magic-bullet"
mythology. I labored under the illusion that by carefully executing
assignments according to the editors' parameters, I was informing
the public and being a good writer.

What I was really doing was helping to sell magazines by pre-   5
senting a lopsided point of view: the world according to women's
magazine editors. Their world (and my assignments) was shaped
primarily by two considerations: providing a "nice environment"
for advertisers and making sure readers were not challenged by
anything more than simple tips for healthy living. . . .

Elizabeth Whelan, Sc.D., M.P.H., president of the American   6
Council on Science and Health, has repeatedly accused women's
magazines of shirking responsibility by focusing on trivia and ignoring the devastating effects of cigarette smoking. . . .

Conflicting views are seldom presented in women's magazines.   7
After all, the "logic" goes, readers might become confused if they
actually have to weigh more than one side of a story. Instead, editors
usually decide in advance what readers should think, infantilizing
readers in the process. This condescending philosophy was a major
reason why I decided to get out of the whole business and into writing for physicians. . . .

How Articles Evolve

One reason why trivial and/or incorrect nutrition advice appears so   8
often is the desire to please the magazines' lifeline: advertisers. Most
marketing executives view women's magazines as "products" or
"vehicles" that are part of a "marketing package" for their wares.
That's where the "nice environment" comes in. Before agreeing to
buy space, advertisers want to know what kinds of articles will appear
in the magazine—and, particularly, what copy will appear near the
ad. "Negative" stories—topics that may upset readers or otherwise
interfere with a "feel-good" atmosphere—are routinely rejected.
Unfortunately, this means that manuscripts that tell the truth (for
example, that the link between specific foods and specific health
effects is largely hype) seldom get published.

"Women's magazines are controlled by advertisers in ways that   9
other magazines aren't," *Ms.* co-founder Gloria Steinem told a gathering of writers from the American Society of Journalists and Authors in
1991. She described how women's magazines began as catalogs, with
short stories woven in between the ads. The link between advertising
and editorial has remained, she said, creating a situation wherein "85%
of women's magazine copy is really 'unmarked advertorial.'" . . .

When I wrote regular nutrition columns for women's magazines,   10
my topics were determined in most cases by advertisements already
commissioned or those the publication hoped to bring in. "[A major
cereal manufacturer] is advertising in September. Why don't you do
a fiber story for that issue?" one editor suggested. "We'd love to get
an ad from [a leading manufacturer of lowfat dairy products]. We
want you to do a story on foods that are low in fat and high in cal-
cium," said another. . . .

In a recent interview (*not* for a women's magazine), Richard   11
Rivlin, M.D., of New York Hospital told me: "The public is enormously

confused. They need a better understanding of the role nutrition plays with respect to disease. We haven't been doing a very good job of putting things in perspective." Writing in the *Journal of the American Medical Association*, Dr. Rivlin stressed that it is more realistic to think that good nutrition can help delay the onset or reduce the effects of such illnesses as heart disease, stroke, cancer, and diabetes—not that nutrition can prevent or eliminate these disorders entirely. He added that proper nutrition won't do much to protect an individual who continues to smoke cigarettes, drinks excessively, or leads a sedentary lifestyle.

But that type of moderate message seldom makes its way into   12 magazines where "food as medicine" themes are regarded as an essential editorial ingredient. During my tenure as a health and nutrition writer, I wrote everything from the "diet that can save your life" to the "fertility diet" and the "brain power diet." I also wrote about diets to calm your kids, boost their I.Q., and keep them from becoming overweight adults.

The Ingredients of a "Good" Nutrition Article

The other force that drives the editorial content of women's maga-   13 zines is the desire to grab attention to boost sales. The quickest, surest way to sell article ideas to a women's magazine is to come up with a great cover line. Once I learned this secret, getting assignments was a snap. Whereas some writers labored long and hard over query letters, I would think up titles and bullet them on a page, fleshing out the "story" with one or two sentences. Examples include: "16 Great Food Finds," "20 Hunger-Fighting Foods," "6 Myths That Keep You Fat," and "What Your Snacks Say About You." At least 75% of the topics I proposed in this way ended up as assignments.

Of course, the process also worked in reverse. Editors would call   14 me and say, "We want such-and-such story (naming a provocative headline). You figure out what to put in the article." Although all this smacks of deception, I did have scruples. Despite the jazzy-sounding titles, in most instances I merely repackaged basic nutrition advice into my articles, slipping in qualifiers ("there's no proof as yet") for spurious speculations and liberally peppering my articles with "may" and "they speculate." Does this excuse me? Not really. What astounds me in retrospect is how many "experts" were willing to go along with this charade.

Another essential ingredient in good articles is the voice of   15
authority. As a women's magazine writer, I needed "experts" to validate my editor's point of view. Many "experts" who regularly appear
in women's magazines are willing to trade scientific credibility for
the opportunity to have their name in print. Some would give me
quotes even when the premise of a story made little sense. For
example, one women's magazine editor asked me to do a feature
article called "Ten Foods to Make You Prettier." I balked, saying that
unless an "expert" would corroborate that such a story could include
some substance, I wouldn't do it. I was given the name of an
"authority" at the school of public health of a major university. *She*
convinced *me* it could be done and provided me with additional
sources. I not only wrote the article but recycled it to other women's
publications under such titles as "Eat Your Way to Perfect Skin" and
"Beauty Is More Than Skin Deep." . . .

"Hiring" of Writers

A little-publicized, unethical practice that is more common than writ-   16
ers would like to admit can directly affect what "expert" information
gets into a women's magazine and what doesn't. On several occasions, people from public relations agencies representing weight-loss
centers and other clients have called me with a proposition. They
would "hire" me to write a nutrition story that quoted their client if
I would "place" it in a women's magazine. For an unscrupulous
writer, this is an opportunity to be paid twice for the same article.
I have consistently refused such work, telling callers that if their
client's views were appropriate for something I am writing, they
would be used without charge.

In another typical women's magazine scenario, the writer is   17
required to skip attribution altogether—the rationale being that "we
want the magazine to be the authority." The result of this abuse of
power is that the magazine gives itself a free hand to say whatever it
wants, merely by having the writer pepper the article with convenient
phrases such as "experts agree," "scientists have found," and
"experts say." What experts? The writer and editor, of course. . . .

Style over Substance

In addition to a catchy headline and good sources, the article must   18
"lay out well" on the page. Typically this means using sidebars and

boxes, with cute little quizzes ("What's Your Nutrition IQ?"; "Are You An Emotional Eater?"), fascinating facts ("Did You Know . . ."), or 2-day "starter menus" for special diet stories. It's a plus if the article itself can be done up in an easy-to-swallow format, such as "Your A-Z Guide To Fighting Fat," "Seven Secrets Every Thin Person Knows," or "Nutrition Myths That Keep You Fat." Editors seem to assume that straightforward stories won't be read, that readers must be entertained, and that "text-heavy" pages will intimidate them.

The women's magazine writer must also understand an editor's   19
mandate to "work with the art director." In many cases, this means the writer must include points in the text to validate the accompanying photos. For example, if the art director thinks a story on summer fruit would "look great" accompanied by a photo of bananas, grapefruit, and kiwi fruit, then the writer must make sure these fruits are mentioned in the article. Sometimes the photography is planned or even executed before the article is written.

The power of the art director was carried *ad absurdum* in one article I wrote on eating "mini-meals." I had paid a registered dietitian to   20
plan meals that would meet all the Recommended Dietary Allowances for adult women. Imagine my shock when my editor called to demand that a meal be changed to include the foods that the art director thought would "look good on the page." "Luscious strawberries" and "juicy orange slices" would have to replace raisins and bananas!

The final ingredient in a "good" nutrition story is the writing   21
style. Three tones are permitted:

1. Bouncy two-year-old: "Don't wait! Start now on our power-packed, energy-boosting diet."

2. Concerned parent: "Eclairs are tempting, so have one—very occasionally . . . If you do have one, make it your only indulgence that day"; "If you must use white sauce, remember: the thinner the sauce, the thinner *you'll* stay."

3. Pseudosophisticated "friend": "Of course you can diet and lose weight. You've done it before . . . and before that . . . but each time the pounds you shed creep back, causing you to groan with disappointment when you step on the scale. Yet we all know women whose weight rarely fluctuates more than a pound or two and former fatties who managed to lose weight and *keep it off* for good . . . Now, we bring you the *real* secrets behind their success."

Once a writer has these chatty tones down pat, she simply   22
asks which style the editor wants, and bingo! Another successful
assignment! . . .

After a number of years playing at this kind of writing, I grew   23
incredibly bored. Women's magazines like to pigeonhole writers
(e.g., "health writer," "travel writer," "money writer"). Even though
I managed somewhat to defy definition by writing in all three of
these categories, editors who gave me "regular work" really wanted
me to write the same stories issue after issue, year after year: How
to shed five pounds in five days; Think yourself thin; De-stress yourself; Eat right over the holidays; Get in shape for summer; How to
stick to your diet while eating out; Why your food diary is your best
friend, etc, etc. These are women's magazine "staples"—the stories
readers presumably want to read over and over.

Perhaps it's true. Maybe all those women out there really do   24
want to read that stuff. But if that's the case, at least I have the satisfaction of knowing I no longer contribute to the propaganda that
feeds such a mindset. And I can't help but believe that women's
magazine readers are capable of taking in a healthy dose of hard
information, meaningful speculation, and controversy—about
food, nutrition, health, life—if their favorite magazines would only
make the effort, and take the risk, of presenting them.

This article is based on my experiences in writing for more than a   25
dozen women's magazines and talking with fellow journalists. There
is no question that some women's magazines have more editorial
"depth" than others. Those that cater to "educated" women generally offer less simplistic-sounding articles than those catering to "the
secretary in Middle America." And magazines with bigger editorial
budgets are apt to subject articles to more scrutiny than those with
small budgets and little money for editorial content. Nevertheless, all
operate under pressure from the market forces I have described.

NutriWatch Home Page
This article was posted on March 26, 2000.

WE'VE COME A LONG WAY, BUT MAGAZINES STAYED BEHIND
Susan Dudash, Student

*When she wrote the essay that follows, Susan Dudash was a French major at
Penn State University. The essay (in a slightly different form) appeared in 1989
in the* Daily Collegian, *the Penn State student newspaper.*

When well-known newscaster Christine Craft lost her job several   1
years ago, many people assumed that she simply was not performing her job effectively. Instead, according to my sociology professor,
Dr. Mari Molseed, Craft was fired because her employers found her
to be "Too old and unattractive. . . . [Also, she] didn't show enough
deference towards men." In an age where a woman sits on the
Supreme Court and women may vote, this certainly seems ridicu-
lous. However, this example shows the media's important role in
maintaining the **status quo** as well as in informing the public. The
information that we receive from our media can be especially misleading when they purport to be conveying a different image about
women.

One media form, working women's magazines, generally pre-   2
sents an image of women as incompetent; its traditional view mars
the chance for the status quo perceptions of women to change.
Magazines such as *Cosmopolitan, Working Woman, Mademoiselle,*
Glamour—even *Ms.*—claim to be up to date, yet still portray women
as incompetent in regard to appearance, work and knowledge.

The magazines portray women as appearance oriented, which   3
isn't in itself a problem, but the extent to which this image is presented may be. Articles and advertisements deal with clothes, hair,
make-up—not business success or how to play the stock market. In
three consecutive issues of *Glamour* I found a grand total of four
articles that dealt specifically with women's occupations. "Should
You Quit Your Job If You're Not Getting Respect?" turned out to be
a survey, simply stating the dissatisfaction of women with their
superiors, though the author *did* demonstrate that women should-
n't have to put up with disrespect or degradation. Another of these,
"Is That Just-Right Job Really All Wrong?" was a disappointing and
patronizing list of do's and don'ts. This particular article gives
good hints on what to watch out for in choosing a new occupation, but by the same token, these bits of advice should be common sense. The article tells the reader to beware of jobs whose
employees say the company is a bad place to work, or to watch out
for companies with high turnover, little financial security and

---

deference: respect;   **status quo:** existing situation;   **patronizing:** talking
down to, condescending

"nonexistent or vague" job descriptions. The third article, "Managing Your Money in the 90's: Which Old Rules Still Apply? Which Don't?", gave some useful information for those not up to date on expectations for the economy in the 1990's. This is to their credit. However, most women in the business field have probably had an elementary economics course, which makes some of the article's suggestions seem obvious. For example, of course it is better to buy a new car on credit when interest rates are lower **in lieu of** paying cash or even renting. In sum, even though these articles do deal with the job market, their advice tends to be either common sense or persuades the reader to change occupations.

This may be more apparent with our next example. The final article deals with "computeritis," a disease the article suggests is primarily caused by the repetitive motion of typing on a keyboard without enough little "breaks." Here, the article fails to follow up on the second cause of this disease: namely, thoracic outlet syndrome, a **hereditary** and easily treatable disorder. Here, the emphasis is on the work as a main cause of numb or tingly hands, not on the other causes. The article suggests that the "inflicted" worker take more breaks, hence work less.

In addition to these articles, I've found only one out of approximately fifty articles had anything to say about the woman and her job. In these same three issues, I also noted a total of three articles on the *work wardrobe*. This is not to say that there weren't countless articles on fashion, methods of seduction, and sex-related issues. These articles, along with those concerning make-up, or parties, constitute the remainder of the approximately fifty articles per issue.

The articles and advertisements in magazines for working women show perfect and unattainable images of women. Most of us don't realize the models themselves don't look this good; trick photography, silk screening, and expert make-up application present the image desired by these magazines.

These images lead women to believe their success lies not in their knowledge, but in their appearance. For example, a Nivea Skin Cream advertisement proclaims, "Is Your Face Paying the Price of Success?" A Forever Krystle cologne ad states, "CREATE YOUR OWN DYNASTY"; the accompanying photo shows a woman, arms

---

in lieu of: instead of;   **hereditary:** acquired by birth

wrapped around her man as he's dressing for work, a hard day at the office. A Pantene shampoo ad tells you to "Risk everything except your hair." Showing the **paramount** importance of the perfect appearance, a woman's face dominates the ad—a face devoid of any possible fault of complexion or hair. After skillfully applied make-up, and photo retouching, the woman is nearly perfect. Another ad for cologne, this time from Coty, tells us that we can "Make A Statement Without Saying A Word," and the beautiful flawless woman in the ad reinforces the fact; **diligence** or competence aren't required here.

According to these magazines, success depends on women's   8
appearance, and their accomplishments are secondary. Women may work, state these magazines; however, the importance of their occupations is overshadowed by numerous articles dealing with non-occupational topics and ads. Out of about fifty features in a typical issue of *Cosmopolitan,* I found four articles that were occupation-oriented; one of these even dealt with purchasing real estate. *Cosmo* scored better than most magazines of its type in this category. In place of sound advice for the working woman, this issue chose to emphasize such things as "Living with a Difficult Man," "Women Who Attract Men (And Women Who Don't)," "How Much Sex Is *Enough?*" "Beauty Bar: What a Great Smile You've Got!" The list goes on and on, and these are only the articles dealing with men. The food and decorating section boasts a feature on "Bad Girl Beds," while other sections emphasize health, the importance of staying soft, smooth, young and physically fit. The Beauty and Health Report in October's issue of *Glamour* tells its women readers to "Exercise your breasts." In November's issue, *Glamour* urges women to "Stop obsessing about your thighs, hair, breasts." I'm not making this up. These magazines are sending out conflicting signals, in addition to placing their emphasis on image and appearance.

You can take the analysis further by looking at the advertise-   9
ments yourself. In a particular issue of *Cosmopolitan* (November, 1989) at least 45 ads dealt with skincare, haircare, and make-up; 35 ads dealt with cologne; and 19 sold clothing. Also prevalent were cigarette and alcohol advertisements. Nothing occupationally oriented whatsoever was to be found. True, in some ads women were wearing work clothes; but it just so happens that none of the ads

---

paramount: highest, greatest;   **diligence:** constant effort

mention the workplace. The underlying message is the improvement of a woman's appearance—her skin and hair must look young, healthy; her scent must be attractive, if not seductive.

Advertisements abound demonstrating this point—women are   10
imperfect, but need to be perfect to succeed. Advertisements such as for Episage Ultra (THE CELLULITE SOLUTION), or Clairol haircolor (Whether you want to be noticed a little or a lot, the Clairol Highlighting Collection is who you really are), are prime examples. Countless ads for make-up—L'Oreal, Clinique, Estee Lauder, CoverGirl, Max Factor, Almay—all show models with flawless skin and hair, telling us that they use a particular brand of make-up and look so refined. Women just aren't good enough as they are.

The magazines imply that working women must accept double   11
duty—as employees in the workplace and in the traditional roles as mother and housewife. Nona Glazer, an authority in the field of women's studies and a writer for *Women's Studies International Quarterly,* put it this way: from " . . . cooking ahead . . . supervising children's homework and spending quality time with them . . . relaxing with one's husband, studying to improve oneself for the job," women are expected to retain their traditional homemaker roles in addition to their new jobs.

Advice and articles in women's magazines therefore range from   12
advice for quick one-pot meals to the proper dress-for-success attire. After work, women have to deal with decisions about whether 15-second make-up applications are better than the 12-hour process. A Coors ad states, "Our Women's Work Is Never Done." The tone of some magazines suggests that success comes with sexuality.

Even when these magazines deal specifically with the idea that   13
women work a "double" shift, they usually only address the situation and expect the reader to accept it. Not surprisingly, studies conducted within the last decade show that women are becoming more discontented with their situations in general. Women are expected to perform a double-duty job, yet the magazines often consider them so incompetent. How are they to perform these duties at all? These magazines consistently show an attitude of patronization. Typical articles give advice such as: "How to Enjoy the Superbowl—Whether You Like It or Not" or "Meeting His Mother: A Survival Guide," or "Create a New You—the Plastic Surgery Primer."

The available working women's magazines fail to give women   14
enough suggestions for future success, other than that related to a
man. The available magazines take the general attitude that women
are incompetent in respect to their appearance and work. Looking at
women in this way negates their importance in society. And the
effects of the ideals behind these magazines are all the more powerful because of their subtlety.

If these modern working women's magazines are sending out   15
conflicting messages, you can only wonder what the rest of the
media are doing. Are women's stereotypes really changing? If so,
then why are women in occupations traditionally held by men
switching out of these jobs only a few years after entrance? Why are
women's *firsts* emphasized (first woman to run for vice president,
first woman astronaut)? Even in an issue of *Ms.* only 15% of the articles dealt specifically with women and work; about half of these
addressed the problems or obstacles that women are facing on the
job. Are things really changing?

It is not merely enough to be aware of this misleading percep-   16
tion of women held by the magazines; we must demonstrate the
need for more concrete changes to give women the place in society
that, according to these magazines, is already theirs.

Post-reading

Blakely has classified certain articles in women's magazines; go back over her
article and write down her classifications. Under each one write what it suggests
about the world we have made up for women. Then write out *your* summary of
what that world's main characteristics are, what its values are. Make a few notes
for yourself about whether you think these characteristics and values are good or
bad and why. Refer to the notes you've already taken.

Essay Assignment

Write an essay in which you examine three of the top magazines listed
in Blakely's article, classify the leading articles only according to their
content, and explain what these classifications suggest about the world
these magazines project to their readers. You may use Blakely's classification if you wish, or you can make and use your own.

Pre-writing

After you have chosen the three magazines and classified the leading articles, choose two or three of the categories that best represent the world *you* think these magazines suggest. Using your pre-reading, reading, and post-reading notes, write out a brief description of that world. What are its characteristics? What are the values it projects? Then choose several *specific* articles that best exemplify that world.

At this point jot down a brief outline, ordering the categories that represent the world.

Writing

In your introduction, describe briefly the situation you are investigating. Review the section on introductions in Chapter 2 (pages 61–65) for help with this task.

In the body of your essay, describe the categories you have found, giving specific examples to illuminate the categories—to make them clear to the reader.

Conclude by discussing the values these magazines project and whether they are ones with which you agree or disagree. Review the section on conclusions for help with this task. Be sure to review the Writer's Checklist on pages 150–152.

Here are three alternate assignments:

1. Write an essay following the steps outlined above, but instead of looking at three different magazines, choose one magazine from the top ten and examine its three most recent issues.

2. Write an essay following the steps outlined above, but instead of examining one or more of the top ten magazines, study one or more of the less traditional women's magazines such as *Lear's, Working Woman,* or *Playgirl.* (Be sure you get a representative sample, at least three issues of one magazine or one copy of three magazines.)

3. Guttentag's study indicated that men's magazines "tended to concern adventure, the overcoming of obstacles; the preoccupations were with mastery and triumph." Examine three issues of a popular, general-interest magazine for men (that is, don't choose one aimed at a specific group like hunters and fishermen). Following the steps outlined above, write an essay in which you classify the leading articles according to their content and come to your own conclusion about the messages

men receive from these articles. What world do these magazines "make up"? (Compared with women's magazines, most magazines for men have very small circulations, and no other magazine for men is close to the top three—*Playboy, Penthouse,* and *Esquire*—in numbers sold.)

*A*ssignments

HOW DO ADVERTISERS TRY TO MANIPULATE US?

Americans may be the most advertisement-bombarded people on earth. Daily we are exposed to advertisements from television and radio, in newspapers and magazines, on signs we see as we go about our business, and even in our mailboxes. Often we think we see how advertisers are trying to sell us something, but what's really going on? Jib Fowles, a professor at the University of Houston, has studied and written about advertisements, and here he outlines fifteen basic emotions that advertisers try to appeal to.

Reading Assignment

Pre-reading

Before you read this article, think about a couple of advertisements you remember having seen recently, ones that struck you for one reason or another. You may not be interested in the product advertised, and you may not even remember what it was. But you remembered the ad, so it must have appealed to something in you. Jot down a list of any such ads you can recall, and when you finish the article, see whether you can figure out which of the fifteen emotional appeals Professor Fowles describes were the ones in your ads.

ADVERTISING'S FIFTEEN BASIC APPEALS
Jib Fowles

Emotional Appeals

The nature of effective advertisements was recognized full well by   1
the **late** media philosopher Marshall McLuhan. In his *Understanding*

---

late: now dead

Media, the first sentence of the section on advertising reads, "The continuous pressure is to create ads more and more in the image of audience motives and desires."

By giving form to people's deep-lying desires, and picturing   2 states of being that individuals privately yearn for, advertisers have the best chance of **arresting** attention and affecting communication. And that is the immediate goal of advertising: to tug at our psychological shirt sleeves and slow us down long enough for a word or two about whatever is being sold. . . .

An advertisement communicates by making use of a specially   3 selected image (of a **supine** female, say, or a curly-headed child, or a celebrity) which is designed to stimulate "**subrational** impulses and desires" even when they are at ebb, even if they are unacknowledged by their possessor. Some few ads have their emotional appeal in the text, but for the greater number by far the appeal is contained in the artwork. This makes sense, since visual communication better suits more primal levels of the brain. If the viewer of an advertisement actually has the **importuned** motive, and if the appeal is sufficiently well-fashioned to call it up, then the person can be hooked. The product in the ad may then appear to take on the **semblance** of gratification for the summoned motive. Many ads seem to be saying, "If you have this need, then this product will help satisfy it." It is a primitive equation, but not an ineffective one for selling.

Thus, most advertisements appearing in national media can be understood as having two orders of content. The first is the appeal to   4 deep-running drives in the minds of consumers. The second is information regarding the good or service being sold: its name, its manufacturer, its picture, its packaging, its objective attributes, its functions. For example, the reader of a brassiere advertisement sees a partially undraped but blandly **unperturbed** woman standing in an otherwise commonplace public setting, and may experience certain sensations; the reader also sees the name "Maidenform," a particular brassiere style, and, in tiny print, words about the material, colors, price. . . .

People involved in the advertising industry do not necessarily talk in the terms being used here. They are stationed at the sending   5

---

arresting: getting;   **supine:** lying on one's back;   **subrational:** not consciously aware;   **importuned:** being addressed;   **semblance:** appearance; **unperturbed:** undisturbed

end of this communications channel, and may think they are up to any number of things—Unique Selling Propositions, explosive copywriting, the optimal use of demographics or psychographics, ideal media buys, high recall ratings, or whatever. But when attention shifts to the receiving end of the channel, and focuses on the instant of reception, then commentary becomes much more elemental: an advertising message contains something primary and primitive, an emotional appeal, that in effect is the thin end of the wedge, trying to find its way into a mind. Should this occur, the product information comes along behind.

When enough advertisements are examined in this light, it   6
becomes clear that the emotional appeals fall into several distinguishable categories, and that every ad is a variation on one of a limited number of basic appeals. While there may be several ways of classifying these appeals, one particular list of fifteen has proven to be especially valuable.

Advertisements can appeal to: 7

1. The need for sex
2. The need for affiliation
3. The need to nurture
4. The need for guidance
5. The need to aggress
6. The need to achieve
7. The need to dominate
8. The need for prominence
9. The need for attention
10. The need for autonomy
11. The need to escape
12. The need to feel safe
13. The need for **aesthetic** sensations
14. The need to satisfy curiosity
15. Physiological needs: food, drink, sleep, etc. . . . .

Fifteen Appeals

1. *Need for sex.* Let's start with sex, because this is the appeal which   8
seems to pop up first whenever the topic of advertising is raised.

---

aesthetic: artistic

Whole books have been written about this one alone, to find a large audience of mildly **titillated** readers. Lately, . . . concern with sex in ads has redoubled.

The fascinating thing is not how much sex there is in advertising,   9 but how little. Contrary to impressions, **unambiguous** sex is rare in these messages. Some of this surprising observation may be a matter of definition: the Jordache ads with the lithe, blouse-less female astride a similarly clad male is clearly an appeal to the audience's sexual drives, but the same cannot be said about Brooke Shields in the Calvin Klein commercials. Directed at young women and their credit-card-carrying mothers, the image of Miss Shields instead invokes the need to be looked at. Buy Calvins and you'll be the center of much attention, just as Brooke is, the ads imply; they do not primarily **inveigle** their target audience's need for sexual intercourse.

In the content analysis reported in *Mass Advertising as Social Fore-*   10 *cast,* only two percent of ads were found to **pander** to this motive. Even *Playboy* ads shy away from sexual appeals: a recent issue contained eighty-three full-page ads, and just four of them (or less than five percent) could be said to have sex on their minds.

The reason this appeal is so little used is that it is too blaring and   11 tends to obliterate the product information. Nudity in advertising has the effect of reducing brand recall. The people who do remember the product may do so because they have been made indignant by the ad; this is not the response most advertisers seek.

To the extent that sexual imagery is used, it conventionally works   12 better on men than women; typically a female figure is offered up to the male reader. A Black Velvet liquor advertisement displays an attractive woman wearing a tight black outfit, **recumbent** under the legend, "Feel the Velvet." The figure does not have to be horizontal, however, for the appeal to be present, as National Airlines revealed in its "Fly me" campaign. Indeed, there does not even have to be a female in the ad: "Flick my Bic" was sufficient to convey the idea to many.

As a rule, though, advertisers have found sex to be a tricky   13 appeal, to be used sparingly. Less controversial and equally fetching are the appeals to our need for affectionate human contact.

---

titillated: excited;   **unambiguous:** clear, plain;   **inveigle:** use;
pander: appeal to;   **recumbent:** reclining

2. Need for affiliation. . . . The need to associate with others is   14
widely invoked in advertising and is probably the most prevalent
appeal. All sorts of goods and services are sold by linking them to
our unfulfilled desires to be in good company.

According to Henry Murray, the need for affiliation consists of   15
desires "to draw near and enjoyably cooperate or reciprocate with
another; to please and win affection of another; to adhere and
remain loyal to a friend." The manifestations of this motive can be
segmented into several different types of affiliation, beginning with
romance.

Courtship may be swifter nowadays, but the desire for pair bond-   16
ing is far from satiated. Ads reaching for this need commonly depict a
youngish male and female **engrossed** in each other. The head of the
male is usually higher than the female's, even at this late date; she may
be sitting or leaning while he is standing. They are not touching in the
Smirnoff vodka ads, but obviously there is an intimacy, sometimes
frolicsome, between them. The couple does touch for Martell Cognac
when "The moment was Martell." For Wind Song perfume they have
touched, and "Your Wind Song stays on his mind."

Depending on the audience, the pair does not absolutely have   17
to be young—just together. He gives her a DeBeers diamond, and
there is a tear in her laugh lines. She takes Geritol and preserves herself for him. And numbers of consumers, wanting affection too, follow suit.

Warm family feelings are fanned in ads when another genera-   18
tion is added to the pair. Hallmark Cards brings grandparents into
the picture, and Johnson and Johnson Baby Powder has Dad, Mom,
and baby, all fresh from the bath, encircled in arms and emblazoned
with "Share the Feeling." A talc has been fused to familial love.

Friendship is yet another form of affiliation pursued by advertis-   19
ers. Two women confide and drink Maxwell House coffee together;
two men walk through the woods smoking Salem cigarettes. Miller
Beer promises that afternoon "Miller Time" will be staffed with three
or four good buddies. Drink Dr Pepper, as Mickey Rooney is coaxed
to do, and join in with all the other Peppers. Coca-Cola does not
even need to portray the friendliness; it has reduced this appeal to
"a Coke and a smile." . . .

---

engrossed: involved;   **frolicsome:** playful

As well as presenting positive images, advertisers can play to   20
the need for affiliation in negative ways, by invoking the fear of
rejection. If we don't use Scope, we'll have the "Ugh! Morning
Breath" that causes the male and female models to avert their faces.
Unless we apply Ultra-Brite or Close-Up to our teeth, it's goodbye
romance. Our family will be cursed with "House-a-tosis" if we don't
take care. Without Dr. Scholl's anti-perspirant foot spray, the bowling team will keel over. There go all the guests when the supply of
Dorito's nacho cheese chips is exhausted. Still more rejection if our
shirts have ring-around-the-collar, if our car needs to be Midasized.
But make a few purchases, and we are back in the bosom of human
contact.

As self-directed as Americans pretend to be, in the last analysis   21
we remain social animals, hungering for the positive, endorsing feelings that only those around us can supply. Advertisers respond, urg-
ing us to "Reach out and touch someone," in the hopes our monthly
bills will rise.

3. *Need to nurture.* Akin to affiliative needs is the need to take   22
care of small, defenseless creatures—children and pets, largely.
Reciprocity is of less consequence here, though; it is the giving
that counts. Murray uses synonyms like "to feed, help, support,
console, protect, comfort, nurse, heal." A strong need it is, woven
deep in our genetic fabric, for if it did not exist we could not successfully raise up our replacements. When advertisers put forth the
image of something **diminutive** and furry, something that elicits
the word "cute" or "precious," then they are trying to trigger this
motive. We listen to the childish voice singing the Oscar Mayer
wiener song, and our next hot-dog purchase is prescribed. Aren't
those darling kittens something, and how did this Meow Mix get
into our shopping cart?

This pitch is often directed at women, as Mother Nature's chief   23
nurturers. "Make me some Kraft macaroni and cheese, please," says
the **elfin** preschooler just in from the snowstorm, and mothers'
hearts go out, and Kraft's sales go up. "We're cold, wet, and hungry," whine the husband and kids, and the little woman gets the

---

Reciprocity: mutual exchange;   **diminutive:** very small;   **elfin:** small, cute,
like an elf

Manwiches ready. A facsimile of this need can be hit without children or pets; the husband is ill and sleepless in the television commercial, and the wife grudgingly fetches the NyQuil.

But it is not women alone who can be touched by this appeal.   24
The father nurses his son Eddie through adolescence while the John
Deere lawn tractor survives the years. Another father counts pennies
with his young son as the subject of New York Life Insurance comes
up. And all over America are businessmen who don't know why they
dial Qantas Airlines when they have to take a trans-Pacific trip; the
koala bear knows.

4. *Need for guidance.* The opposite of the need to nurture is the   25
need to be nurtured: to be protected, shielded, guided. We may be
loath to admit it, but the child lingers on inside every adult—and a
good thing it does, or we would not be instructable in our advanc-
ing years. Who wants a nation of nothing but flinty personalities?

Parent-like figures can successfully call up this need. . . .   26

A celebrity is not a necessity in making a pitch to the need for guid-   27
ance, since a fantasy figure can serve just as well. People accede to the
Green Giant, or Betty Crocker, or Mr. Goodwrench. Some advertisers
can get by with no figure at all: "When E. F. Hutton talks, people listen."

Often it is tradition or custom that advertisers point to and con-   28
sumers take guidance from. Bits and pieces of American history are
used to sell whiskeys like Old Crow, Southern Comfort, Jack Daniels.
We conform to traditional male/female roles and age-old social
norms when we purchase Barclay cigarettes, which informs us "The
pleasure is back."

The product itself, if it has been around for a long time, can   29
constitute a tradition. All those old labels in the ad for Morton salt
convince us that we should continue to buy it. Kool-Aid says, "You
loved it as a kid. You trust it as a mother," hoping to get yet more
consumers to go along. . . .

So far the needs and the ways they can be invoked which have   30
been looked at are largely warm and affiliative; they stand in contrast
to the next set of needs, which are much more **egoistic** and assertive.

5. *Need to aggress.* The pressures of the real world create strong   31
retaliatory feelings in every functioning human being. Since these

---

loath: reluctant;   **egoistic:** self-centered

impulses can come forth as bursts of anger and violence, their display is normally tabooed. Existing as harbored energy, aggressive drives present a large, tempting target for advertisers. It is not a target to be aimed at thoughtlessly, though, for few manufacturers want their products associated with destructive motives. There is always the danger that, as in the case of sex, if the appeal is too blatant, public opinion will turn against what is being sold. . . .

. . . When Exxon said, "There's a Tiger in your tank," the implausibility of it concealed the **invocation** of aggressive feelings.   32

Depicted arguments are a common way for advertisers to tap the audience's needs to aggress. Don Rickles and Linda Carter trade gibes, and consumers take sides as the name of Seven-Up is stitched on minds. The Parkay tub has a difference of opinion with the user; who can forget it, or who (or what) got the last word in?   33

6. *Need to achieve.* This is the drive that energizes people, causing them to strive in their lives and careers. According to Murray, the need for achievement is signalled by the desires "to accomplish something difficult. To overcome obstacles and attain a high standard. To excel one's self. To rival and surpass others." A prominent American trait, it is one that advertisers like to hook on to because it identifies their product with winning and success. . . .   34

Sports heroes are the most convenient means to snare consumers' needs to achieve, but they are not the only one. Role models can be established, ones which invite **emulation,** as with the profiles put forth by Dewar's scotch. Successful, **tweedy** individuals relate they have "graduated to the flavor of Myer's rum." Or the advertiser can establish a prize: two neighbors play one-on-one basketball for a Michelob beer in a television commercial, while in a print ad a bottle of Johnnie Walker Black Label has been gilded like a trophy.   35

Any product that advertises itself in superlatives—the best, the first, the finest—is trying to make contact with our needs to succeed. For many consumers, sales and bargains belong in this category of appeals, too; the person who manages to buy something at fifty percent off is seizing an opportunity and coming out ahead of others.   36

---

invocation: calling forth;   **emulation:** imitation;   **tweedy:** dressed in tweed jacket or suit

7. *Need to dominate.* This fundamental need is the craving to be   37
powerful—perhaps **omnipotent.** . . . We drink Budweiser because it
is the King of Beers, and here come the powerful Clydesdales to
prove it. A taste of Wolfschmidt vodka and "The spirit of the **Czar**
lives on."

The need to dominate and control one's environment is often   38
thought of as being masculine, but as close students of human
nature, advertisers know it is not so **circumscribed.** Women's aspirations for control are suggested in the campaign theme, "I like my
men in English Leather, or nothing at all." The females in the Chanel
No. 19 ads are "outspoken" and wrestle their men around.

Male and female, what we long for is clout; what we get in its   39
place is Mastercard.

8. *Need for prominence.* Here comes the need to be admired and   40
respected, to enjoy prestige and high social status. These times, it
appears, are not so **egalitarian** after all. Many ads picture the **trappings** of high position; the Oldsmobile stands before a **manorial**
doorway, the Volvo is parked beside a **steeplechase.** A book-lined
study is the setting for Dewar's 12, and Lenox China is displayed in a
dining room chock full of antiques.

Beefeater gin represents itself as "The Crown Jewel of England"   41
and uses no illustrations of jewels or things British, for the words are
sufficient indicators of distinction. Buy that gin and you will rise up
the prestige hierarchy, or achieve the same effect on yourself with
Seagram's 7 Crown, which **unambiguously** describes itself as
"classy."

Being respected does not have to **entail** the usual **accoutrements**   42
of wealth: "Do you know who I am?" the commercials ask, and we learn
that the prominent person is not so prominent without his American
Express card.

9. *Need for attention.* The previous need involved being *looked*   43
up to, while this is the need to be *looked at.* The desire to exhibit
ourselves in such a way as to make others look at us is a primitive,
insuppressible instinct. The clothing and cosmetic industries exist

---

omnipotent: all-powerful; **Czar:** former king of Russia; **circumscribed:**
limited; **egalitarian:** politically or socially equal; **trappings:** physical objects;
manorial: like a manor or estate; **steeplechase:** kind of horse race favored by
the wealthy; **unambiguously:** clearly; **entail:** require; **accoutrements:**
physical objects

just to serve this need, and this is the way they pitch their wares. Some of this effort is aimed at males, as the ads for Hathaway shirts and Jockey underclothes. But the greater bulk of such appeals is targeted singlemindedly at women.

To come back to Brooke Shields: this is where she fits into American   44 marketing. If I buy Calvin Klein jeans, consumers infer, I'll be the object of fascination. The desire for exhibition has been most strikingly played to in a print campaign of many years' duration, that of Maidenform lingerie. The woman exposes herself, and sales surge. "Gentlemen prefer Hanes" the ads **dissemble**, and women who want eyes upon them know what they should do. Peggy Fleming flutters her legs for L'eggs, encouraging females who want to be the star in their own lives to purchase this product.

The same appeal works for cosmetics and lotions. For years, the   45 little girl with the exposed backside sold gobs of Coppertone, but now the company has picked up the pace a little: as a female, you are supposed to "Flash 'em a Coppertone tan." Food can be sold the same way, especially to the diet-conscious; Angie Dickinson poses for California avocadoes and says, "Would this body lie to you?" Our eyes are too fixed on her for us to think to ask if she got that way by eating mounds of guacamole.

10. *Need for **autonomy**.* There are several ways to sell credit card   46 services, as has been noted: Mastercard appeals to the need to dominate, and American Express to the need for prominence. When Visa claims, "You can have it the way you want it," yet another primary motive is being beckoned forward—the need to endorse the self. The focus here is upon the independence and integrity of the individual; this need is the antithesis of the need for guidance and is unlike any of the social needs. "If running with the herd isn't your style, try ours," says Rotan-Mosle, and many Americans feel they have finally found the right brokerage firm.

The photo is of a red-coated Mountie on his horse, posed on a   47 snow-covered ledge; the copy reads, "Windsor—one Canadian stands alone." This epitome of the solitary and proud individual may work best with male customers, as may Winston's man in the red cap. But one-figure advertisements also strike the strong need for **autonomy**

---

dissemble: pretend;   **autonomy:** independence

among American women. As Shelly Hack strides for Charlie perfume, females respond to her obvious pride and flair; she is her own person. The Virginia Slims' tale is of people who have come a long way from **subservience** to independence. . . .

11. *Need to escape.* An appeal to the need for autonomy often   48
co-occurs with one for the need to escape, since the desire to duck out of our social obligations, to seek rest or adventure, frequently takes the form of one-person flight. The dashing image of a pilot, in fact, is a standard way of quickening this need to get away from it all.

Freedom is the pitch here, the freedom that every individual yearns   49
for whenever life becomes too oppressive. Many advertisers like appealing to the need for escape because the sensation of pleasure often accompanies escape, and what nicer **emotional nimbus** could there be for a product? "You deserve a break today," says McDonalds, and Stouffer's frozen foods chime in, "Set yourself free." . . .

12. *Need to feel safe.* Nobody in their right mind wants to be   50
intimidated, menaced, battered, poisoned. We naturally want to do whatever it takes to stave off threats to our well-being, and to our families'. It is the instinct for self-preservation that makes us responsive to the ad of the St. Bernard with the keg of Chivas Regal. We pay attention to the stern talk of Karl Malden and the plight of the vacationing couples who have lost all their funds in the American Express travelers cheques commercials. We want the **omnipresent** stag from Hartford Insurance to watch over us too. In the interest of keeping failure and calamity from our lives, we like to see the durability of products demonstrated. Can we ever forget that Timex takes a licking and keeps on ticking? When the American Tourister suitcase bounces all over the highway and the egg inside doesn't break, the need to feel safe has been adroitly plucked.

We take precautions to diminish future threats. We buy Volkswa-   51
gen Rabbits for the extraordinary mileage, and MONY insurance policies to avoid the tragedies depicted in their black-and-white ads of widows and orphans.

We are careful about our health. We consume Mazola margarine   52
because it has "corn goodness" backed by the natural food traditions

---

subservience: being subordinate;   **emotional nimbus:** feeling;
omnipresent: being everywhere

of the American Indians. In the medicine cabinet is Alka-Seltzer, the "home remedy"; having it, we are snug in our little cottage.

We want to be safe and secure; buy these products, advertisers are saying, and you'll be safer than you are without them.   53

13. *Need for aesthetic sensations.* There is an undeniable aesthetic   54 component to virtually every ad run in the national media: the photography or filming or drawing is near-perfect, the type style is well chosen, the layout could scarcely be improved upon. Advertisers know there is little chance of good communication occurring if an ad is not visually pleasing. Consumers may not be aware of the extent of their own sensitivity to artwork, but it is undeniably large.

Sometimes the aesthetic element is expanded and made into an   55 ad's primary appeal. Charles Jordan shoes may or may not appear in the accompanying avant-garde photographs; Kohler plumbing fixtures catch attention through the high style of their desert settings. Beneath the slightly out of focus photograph, languid and sensuous in tone, General Electric feels called upon to explain, "This is an ad for the hair dryer."

This appeal is not limited to female consumers: J and B scotch   56 says "It whispers" and shows a **bucolic** scene of lake and castle.

14. *Need to satisfy curiosity.* It may seem odd to list a need for   57 information among basic motives, but this need can be as primal and compelling as any of the others. Human beings are curious by nature, interested in the world around them, and intrigued by tidbits of knowledge and new developments. Trivia, percentages, observations counter to conventional wisdom—these items all help sell products. Any advertisement in a question-and-answer format is strumming this need. . . .

15. *Physiological needs.* To the extent that sex is solely a biolog-   58 ical need, we are now coming around full circle, back towards the start of the list. In this final category are clustered appeals to sleeping, eating, drinking. The art of photographing food and drink is so advanced, sometimes these temptations are wonderously caught in the camera's lens: the crab meat in the Red Lobster restaurant ads can start us salivating, the Quarterpounder can almost be smelled, the liquor in the glass glows invitingly. **Imbibe,** these ads scream. . . .

---

bucolic: in the country;   **imbibe:** drink

Analyzing Advertisements

When analyzing ads yourself for their emotional appeals, it takes a   59
bit of practice to learn to ignore the product information (as well as
one's own experience and feelings about the product). But that skill
comes soon enough, as does the ability to quickly sort out from all
the non-product aspects of an ad the chief element which is the most
striking, the most likely to snag attention first and penetrate brains
furthest. The key to the appeal, this element usually presents itself
centrally and forwardly to the reader or viewer.

Another clue: the viewing angle which the audience has on the   60
ad's subjects is informative. If the subjects are photographed or
filmed from below and thus are looking down at you much as the
Green Giant does, then the need to be guided is a good candidate
for the ad's emotional appeal. If, on the other hand, the subjects are
shot from above and appear **deferential**, as is often the case with
children or female models, then other needs are being appealed to.

To figure out an ad's emotional appeal, it is wise to know (or   61
have a good hunch about) who the targeted consumers are; this can
often be inferred from the magazine or television show it appears in.
This piece of information is a great help in determining the appeal
and in deciding between two different interpretations. For example,
if an ad features a partially undressed female, this would typically
signal one appeal for readers of *Penthouse* (need for sex) and another
for readers of *Cosmopolitan* (need for attention).

It would be convenient if every ad made just one appeal, were   62
aimed at just one need. Unfortunately, things are often not that simple. A cigarette ad with a couple at the edge of a polo field is trying
to hit both the need for affiliation and the need for prominence;
depending on the attitude of the male, dominance could also be an
ingredient in this. An ad for Chimere perfume incorporates two
photos: in the top one the lady is being commanding at a business
luncheon (need to dominate), but in the lower one she is being
bussed (need for affiliation). Better ads, however, seem to avoid
being too diffused; in a study of post–World War II advertising . . .,
appeals grew more focused as the decades passed. As a rule of
thumb, about sixty percent of ads make one paramount appeal;

---

deferential: respectful;   **bussed:** kissed

roughly twenty percent have two conspicuous appeals; the last twenty percent have three or more. Rather than looking for the greatest number of appeals, decoding ads is most productive when the loudest one or two appeals are discerned, since those are the appeals with the best chance of grabbing people's attention.

Finally, analyzing ads does not have to be a solo activity and 63 probably should not be. The greater number of people there are involved, the better chance there is of transcending individual biases and discovering the essential emotional lure built into an advertisement. . . .

Essay Assignment

Write an essay in which you examine a selection of advertisements from a magazine you read, whether one you read frequently or infrequently. Examine ten full-page advertisements, preferably ones in color. Working with a classmate, try to figure out which of Fowles's fifteen appeals is working in each ad. Come to a conclusion about how advertisers see the readers of the magazine.

Pre-writing

Working with a classmate, choose a magazine both of you enjoy reading. Decide together which ads you will examine. It doesn't matter which ones you choose, but it will be best if they seem on the surface to be more or less representative of the ones in the magazine. Then reviewing the descriptions of the fifteen appeals, see which ones seem best to describe each of your ads. You can do this together with your partner, or you can each do it separately and then get together to see how well you agree. In case of disagreements, go back over the descriptions of the appeals to check more carefully which seem best to apply. Remember that some ads do contain more than one appeal.

As you analyze the ads, make notes for each one about not only which appeal or appeals it seems to contain but *why* you think so. Your reasons will be extremely important for your paper.

When you have found the pattern of appeals in the magazine you've studied, you are ready to make an inference about how the advertisers see the readers— who they think they are, what emotions they think are dominant in them. And then you are ready to make a further inference about how the advertisers have stereotyped the readers. You should then ask yourself what you think this means. After all, you are the one being stereotyped in a particular way.

Writing

In your introduction, briefly describe your study and why you are making it. Review the section on introductions in Chapter 2 for help with this task.

In the body of your essay, describe the categories of appeals that you found, giving specific examples to make clear to the reader why those are the correct appeals. Note how Fowles has done this in his essay.

Conclude by explaining the inferences you have made about how the advertisers see the readers of the magazine you studied and what that seems to mean to you. Review the section on conclusions for help with this task. Be sure to review the Writer's Checklist below.

THE WRITER'S CHECKLIST

The Idea Draft

1. Does your idea draft *respond fully* to the assignment?
2. Are your ideas *organized* in the way you want?
3. Does your *introduction* explain what the essay will be about and what its purpose is?
4. Do you have a *thesis* that states your point or indicates the issue the essay will address?
5. Do the *body paragraphs* each have a *topic sentence?* Do they develop the main points by giving *specifics and examples* to support those points?
6. Does your *conclusion* either summarize the main points or make a recommendation?
7. Have you *collaborated* with at least one trusted friend or fellow student who has read your draft *critically,* looking for lapses in logic or other weaknesses in content?

Sentence Combining

As part of your revision process, think consciously of using coordinators and subordinators if you have done sentence-combining work with them at this point. Be especially alert for places where *but, because* (or *for*), and *while* might clarify your meaning for your readers.

In his article on children's television programs, John J. O'Connor finds numerous occasions to use coordinators and subordinators. Here are three of them:

> Equally as disturbing as the sexism on so many commercials is the racism, *even if* unintentional, *although* Madison Avenue puts so much research into its products that nothing is likely to be unintentional.

> In fact, in the New York City area, black and Hispanic children are in the majority, but they nevertheless will have a hard time finding their reflections in the commercials surrounding the Saturday morning cartoons.

Remember that you can use the FANBOYS to introduce sentences, as in the following passage from the first paragraph of Robert Reich's essay, "U.S. Income Inequality Keeps on Rising":

> This widening gap can't be blamed on the growth in single-parent lower-income families, which in fact slowed markedly after the late 1970s. *Nor* is it due mainly to the stingy social policy of the Reagan years. Granted, Food Stamp benefits have dropped in real terms by about 13 percent since 1981, and many states have failed to raise benefits for the poor and unemployed to keep up with inflation. *But* this doesn't come close to accounting for the growing inequality. Rather, the trend is connected to a profound change in the American economy as it merges with the global economy. *And* because the merging is far from complete, this trend will not stop of its own accord anytime soon.

Why do you think Reich began three of his sentences with coordinators rather than joining them with the preceding sentences? Do you agree with his decisions?

Later Drafts

1. Taking into account the constructive criticism you have received, have you *revised* accordingly—that is, reorganized, if that was a problem, or given additional support, if that was?

2. Have you read your essay *aloud,* listening closely to what it *actually says* (not just what you think it says)?

3. Have you *revised your sentences* if they seemed unclear or awkward as you read them aloud?

4. Have you checked for those *mechanical difficulties* that you know you sometimes have? Have you used the dictionary to check words that you think may be *misspelled?*

Final Draft

If you have followed this assignment step by step, you have worked exceedingly hard on this essay. Therefore, make sure your final draft reflects your care and effort by being as professional looking as possible.

1. Type it neatly, using the format your instructor has assigned.
2. Proofread slowly and carefully, word by word, line by line. (One last time, ask a trusted friend to proofread it *after* you have, or exchange your essay with another student and proof each other's.)

Sentence Combining

JOINING IDEAS TO SHOW BASIC LOGICAL RELATIONSHIPS

Coordinating Conjunctions

The most common way we have of joining sentences is to use words called *coordinators,* or coordinating conjunctions, and the ones we use most frequently are *and, but,* and *so.*

John took typing lessons, and he never regretted it.
Mary took flying lessons, but she couldn't afford to fly often.
I needed to relax, so I put away my work.

The coordinators not only join the two sentences but also show the logical relationship between the ideas in them. *And* indicates the addition of two similar ideas; *but* tells us that there is some kind of logical opposition between them; *so* indicates that the first one is the reason for the second one. In addition to these three words, we use four others in the same way—to join sentences while showing the logical relationship between the ideas in them: *or, for, yet, nor.*

It is easy to remember these seven words if you remember the word FANBOYS. FANBOYS is an acronym, a word formed from the first letters of other words. The word *FANBOYS* is made up of the first letter of the seven coordinators:

For   And   Nor   But   Or   Yet   So

There are two reasons for remembering the FANBOYS words, the coordinators. The first is that, as in the sentence examples just given, when we use one of these words to join two complete sentences, we normally put a comma *between* the two sentences and *in front* of the coordinator. We do not do this with other connective words.

A second reason for remembering FANBOYS is that unlike other joining words, which you will learn about in the next lesson, the coordinators can introduce sentences, serving as transition words. In other words, every one of the example sentences above could have been written as two complete, separate sentences with the coordinator capitalized, as in these examples:

John took typing lessons. And he never regretted it.
I needed to relax. So I put away my work.
There was nothing for us to fear. For we were safe from any possible harm.
She did not want to marry him. Nor was he interested in marrying her.

The reason for punctuating coordinators this way is to give greater emphasis than otherwise to the idea in the second sentence. If the idea does not deserve such emphasis, the sentences should be joined rather than separated. Finally, two of the coordinators can function a little differently than the others. These two, *so* and *yet,* can be used together with the coordinator *and* to make a two-word coordinator—*and so* and *and yet:*

I needed to relax, and so I put away my work.
There was no reason for a war to take place, and yet they went to war with each other.

As you can see, the meaning does not change depending on whether one uses *so* and *yet* by themselves or with *and.* The tone becomes a little more conversational with the *and,* but that is the only difference.

Here is a summary of the logical relationships expressed by the coordinators:

- *For*—expresses a result-cause relationship:
  She flew as much as she could [result], for she loved flying [cause].
- *And*—expresses the idea of adding something like what one has just written:
  His job brought in several thousand dollars a month [one source of his money], and he got another large sum from an inheritance [a second source].

- *Nor*—Expresses a relationship like *and,* one of addition, except that *nor* relates negative statements to each other. Notice that when a sentence begins with *nor,* we must reverse the normal subject-verb positions:
  John did not like horror movies, nor did Mary like violent adventures.
- *But*—expresses opposition between two ideas:
  She got the job she wanted, but she discovered that she hated it.
- *Or*—indicates alternatives:
  She will have to find a new job, or she will continue to be unhappy.
- *Yet*—functions as does *but,* expressing opposition between ideas:
  She got the job she wanted, yet she discovered that she hated it.
- *So*—while *for* shows us *result-cause* relationships, *so* shows *cause-result* relationships:
  She loved flying [cause], so she flew as much as she could [result].

EXERCISE

Combine the following pairs of sentences using one of the coordinators. The first ten pairs are followed by an indication of the logical relationship you should express, as in these examples:

John ate too many plums. He got pretty sick. [cause-result]
Solution: John ate too many plums, and so he got pretty sick.

John ate too many plums. He got pretty sick. [result-cause]
Solution: John got pretty sick, for he ate too many plums.

The Swimming Lessons

1. John decided to take swimming lessons. He had always had a morbid fear of drowning. [result-cause]
2. He enrolled in a swimming camp on Lake Gotcha. Mary decided to enroll in it too. [addition]
3. John was in training to become a cactus inspector in the Mojave Desert. He had no real need to learn to swim. [cause-result]
4. He realized that he was doing something pointless. He felt compelled to do it anyway. [opposition]
5. Mary already knew how to swim. She thought it would be fun watching John try not to drown. [opposition]

6. The camp owners promised to teach John to swim. They would give him his money back. [alternatives]

7. Secretly, John did not believe he could learn how to swim. Mary did not think it was possible either. [addition of negatives]

8. For one week, John sank like a stone whenever he entered the water. Mary nearly drowned laughing at his antics. [addition]

9. His beautiful young instructor was about to dump him. He suddenly started swimming like an alligator. [cause-result]

10. Now that he can swim, he has decided to become a sailor. He will always have a fond spot in his heart for cactus. [opposition]

EXERCISE

What are the relationships between the ideas in the following pairs of sentences, result-cause [for] or opposition [but, yet]?

   Our basketball team had an undefeated season.
   Our football team lost most of its games.

   Our football team lost most of its games.
   The coach was really an English teacher.

   The basketball team had a terrific record.
   They did not get a national ranking.

What are the relationships between the ideas in the following pairs of sentences, cause-result [so] or opposition [but, yet]?

   Our football coach was really an English teacher.
   He knew very little about football.

   He was a pretty bad coach.
   The players liked him personally.

   The basketball players were exciting and talented.
   The students enjoyed watching them play.

What are the relationships between the ideas in the following pairs of sentences, alternatives [or] or cause-result [so]?

   Our school realized it had to hire a real football coach.
   We would never win any games.

   We could have a team that played good football.
   We could have a team that wrote great essays.

   The school decided it wanted a good football team.
   It started looking for a real coach.

What are the relationships between the ideas in the following pairs of sentences, cause-result [so] or result-cause [for]?

The school asked the coaches of its neighboring schools to recommend a new coach.
It thought they might know of some good prospects.
They all recommended that the English teacher be kept as coach.
They liked beating our team.
Finally the school hired a football coach.
Our old coach went back to just teaching English.

EXERCISE

The following exercise is like The Swimming Lessons *except that you are not given the relationship between the sentences. Choose the coordinator you think most appropriate to join the sentences and be prepared to defend your choice by telling what the relationship between the sentences is.*

Mervyn's Major

1. Mervyn Rutabaga had his heart set on being a physics major. He was hopeless at math.
2. He took extra classes. He got a tutor.
3. He could not pass the classes. The tutor couldn't seem to help him.
4. He worked incredibly hard. Everyone in the math department was willing to help him.
5. He realized he was going to have to improve. He was going to have to give up his ambition to become a great physicist.
6. In addition to his math problems, he was the despair of his physics teacher. His experiments never worked.
7. The other students could produce vacuums when they had to. Nature abhorred Mervyn's vacuums.
8. Mervyn's experiments were always unique. They inevitably proved that some basic law of nature no longer existed.
9. Mervyn finally realized that he did not have it in him to become a great physicist. He changed his major to English.
10. He believes that he can write the Great American Novel. At least he thinks he might learn to spell better.

Subordinating Conjunctions

Although coordinators enable us to express a fairly wide range of logical relationships, another group of words provides us with an even greater resource of this kind. These words are called subordinators. There are a great many subordinators, and there is no point in trying to remember all of them. Some of the most common are *because, if, since, although, while,* and *unless.*

Subordinators function in a somewhat different way from coordinators, the FANBOYS words. While coordinators go between sentences to join them, subordinators do not. Instead, subordinators *attach* to sentences, and when a subordinator attaches to a sentence, it turns a sentence into a *dependent clause—* that is, a group of words that is no longer a sentence. You will remember that coordinators can introduce complete sentences. Subordinators cannot do that; they can introduce only *former sentences,* sentences that have become dependent clauses. Go over the following examples carefully:

Coordinators

She entered law school.	[sentence]
And she entered law school.	[sentence]
For she entered law school.	[sentence]
Or she entered law school.	[sentence]
But she entered law school.	[sentence]

Subordinators

She entered law school.	[sentence]
Because she entered law school.	[not a sentence]
If she entered law school.	[not a sentence]
Although she entered law school.	[not a sentence]
While she entered law school.	[not a sentence]

The dependent clauses created by subordinators may come either at the beginning or at the end of the sentence they are attached to. Look at these examples, and notice how the dependent clauses are punctuated:

Because he was hungry, he ate the apple.
He ate the apple because he was hungry.
Although he ate the apple, he was hungry.
He was hungry although he ate the apple.
If he got hungry, he could eat the apple.
He could eat the apple if he got hungry.

Here is an easy question: When do we set dependent clauses off with commas and when do we not?

Subordinators show some logical relationships that coordinators also show, but they show some that coordinators do not show. Like the coordinators *but* and *yet,* some subordinators can show opposition:

We lost the game, but we were happy.
Although we lost the game, we were happy.
While we lost the game, we were happy.

Others can show effect-cause as *for* does:

She dumped John, for he wore cheap aftershave.
She dumped John because he wore cheap aftershave.
She dumped John since he wore cheap aftershave.

Subordinators cannot show addition, like *and,* or alternatives, like *or,* but they can show time and condition, which no coordinator can do:

Time
When you get there, I'll be gone.
After you've gone, I'll be sorry.
Don't leave the house until she tells you to.
You may go as soon as you are ready.

Condition
Unless we hurry, we are going to be late.
You can succeed at learning French if you really want to.

Here is a summary of the logical relationships expressed by the most commonly used subordinating conjunctions:

Opposition/concession: although, though, even though, whereas, while
Effect-cause: because, since, as
Condition: if, unless
Time: after, before, until, when, as soon as, while, since

You may have noticed that two words, *while* and *since,* appear under more than one heading. Because these two words can express more than one logical relationship, it is important to use them carefully so that your readers will not be confused about your meaning.

EXERCISE

Combine the following pairs of sentences by using subordinators. The sentence to be made into a dependent clause is underlined, and the logical relationship you should express is indicated, as in these examples (be sure to pay attention to the punctuation of dependent clauses in this exercise):

She had a baby. She took time off from work. [cause]
Solution: Because she had a baby, she took time off from work.

He was laid off from his job. He was a hard worker. [opposition]
Solution: He was laid off from his job although he was a hard worker.

Melanie's Masterpiece

1. No one can understand it. Melanie Birdseed considers herself a talented artist. [opposition]
2. Anyone is unfortunate enough to visit her apartment. She immediately shows them her last twelve paintings. [time]
3. It is absolutely impossible to avoid this fate. You can convince her that your ancient and beloved grandmother is dying and needs your immediate attendance at her side. [condition]
4. Melanie's paintings are so awful. They have never been exhibited outside of her living room. [cause]
5. She showed me her latest masterpiece. I couldn't figure out what it was. [time]
6. I stared at it. My eyes started to cross. [time]
7. I was trying my best to see something there. What it really looked like to me was a pile of tangled coat hangers. [opposition]
8. I finally guessed a wheat field. I knew she would never paint a pile of coat hangers. [cause]
9. I had actually put a foot through her canvas. Her reaction couldn't have been worse. [condition]
10. It was obvious I knew nothing about art, she said. At least she thought I would recognize coat hangers when I saw them. [opposition]

EXERCISE

*What are the relationships between the ideas in the following pairs of sentences, re-
sult-cause [because] or opposition [although, etc.]?*

> Carmen decided she would go to law school.
> Her parents felt that the legal profession would guarantee her a good
>   income.

> She majored in political science.
> Several people told her that would be good preparation for studying law.

> She spent three years studying governments and politics.
> She would have preferred studying biology.

*What are the relationships between the ideas in the following pairs of sentences, op-
position [although, etc.] or condition [if, unless]?*

> Carmen did a minor in biology.
> She would have liked to do a major in it.

> She had reluctantly agreed to be a lawyer.
> She tried to convince her parents that biologists could make a good living too.

> She would become a prosecuting attorney.
> She felt she had to pursue a legal career.

*What are the relationships between the ideas in the following pairs of sentences,
time [when, after] or effect-cause [because]?*

> She became a prosecuting attorney.
> She could put a lot of people in jail.

> She could punish the wicked.
> They deserved to be punished.

> She learned the law.
> She could jail parents who made their children follow careers they didn't
>   want to follow.

EXERCISE

> *The following exercise is like* Melanie's Masterpiece, *except that you are given
> no information about how to join the sentences. Choose the subordinator you think*

most appropriate to join the sentences, and be prepared to defend your choice by stating what the relationship between the sentences is.

The Chocolate Addicts

1. Almost everyone loves chocolate. John and Mary were virtually addicted to it.
2. They could not have at least one piece of chocolate every day. They started to twitch.
3. They were able to eat an entire candy bar. Their eyes gleamed with new life.
4. Their dispositions became sunny, and their coats got glossy. They were able to acquire a chocolate truffle.
5. John preferred chocolate with nuts. Mary was a purist who preferred chocolate with chocolate.
6. Mary liked a cup of chocolate in the morning and a piece of chocolate at noon. John preferred a cup of chocolate at noon and a piece of chocolate in the evening.
7. They did not get their chocolate fix when they wanted it. They got sulky and hard to be around.
8. One day John was ordered to stop eating so much chocolate. It was rotting his teeth.
9. At about the same time, Mary was told to lay off the chocolate. It was affecting her complexion.
10. They attempted to commit suicide by leaping into a vat of chocolate at the candy factory. They were saved by an alert guard and are now in a Hershey's Half-Way House.

REVIEW: COORDINATORS AND SUBORDINATORS

In the following exercises, you are asked to combine sentences using only coordinators and subordinators. You will have to do the following things in order to do these exercises:

- Decide what the logical relationship between the sentences is. (Be prepared to defend your choice; do not just leap at the first meaning that springs to mind.)

- Decide what words express that relationship. If the relationship can be expressed with either a coordinator or a subordinator, decide which you will use.

At first, you will be working only with pairs of sentences, but as you go along, you will find some triplets. As a general stylistic principle, remember that it is *usually* (not always) better *not* to join more than two sentences with coordinators. Joining three or more sentences with coordinators usually produces a sentence that sounds stringy and clumsy to most readers. For example:

John bought a cat.
Mary bought a dog.
They both really wanted a kangaroo.

The relationship between the first two sentences is one of addition, so putting an *and* there makes sense:

John bought a cat, and Mary bought a dog.

The relationship between those two sentences and the third one is opposition (what they bought is not what they wanted), and so one could use the coordinators *but* or *yet* or the subordinators *although, though, whereas,* or *while.* In speech, we would probably automatically use *but:*

John bought a cat, and Mary bought a dog, but they both really wanted a kangaroo.

That would sound all right in talk, but in writing it has a stringy effect. Using a subordinator instead of *but* would help a great deal:

Although John bought a cat, and Mary bought a dog, they both really wanted a kangaroo.

Or:

John bought a cat, and Mary bought a dog though they both really wanted a kangaroo.

Combine the following sentence pairs or triplets using coordinators and subordinators. If you think that some of the completed combinations could or should be joined with each other (for instance, sentence one with sentence two), make that connection also. As an aid to doing this exercise, here is a table of the meanings of the coordinators and the most common subordinators:

Meaning	Coordinators	Subordinators
addition	and, nor	——
alternatives	or	——
cause-effect	so, and so	——
effect-cause	for	because, since, as
opposition	but, yet, and yet	although, though, even though, while, whereas
condition	——	if, unless
time	——	after, before, until, when, as soon as, while, since

Jim the Consumer

1. Jim, who had been unemployed, got a job.
   He could barely afford to buy lunch.
2. He finally got a very well-paying job.
   He thought he was Diamond Jim.
3. His friend Robert advised him not to spend his money as fast as he earned it.
   He paid no attention.
4. He did not seek Robert's advice.
   He did not welcome it.
5. He did not know anything about either music or electronics.
   He bought a set of expensive stereo equipment.
6. He played it at full volume one evening.
   The mice all left the building.
   His downstairs neighbor thought terrorists had attacked.
7. His landlord ordered the stereo out of the building.
   It had damaged the foundation and cracked the plaster.
8. Jim had to get rid of it in thirty days.
   The landlord would move him into the street.
9. The landlord could not be reasoned with.
   Jim moved to a new place rather than get rid of his sounds.
   The mice moved back in.

10. Next Jim bought a lot of new clothes.
    His mother had chosen most of his old clothes.
    He didn't have the same taste in shirts as his mother.

11. Robert saw Jim in one of his new outfits.
    He closed his eyes.
    The glare off the sportcoat nearly blinded him.

12. Jim had to bury that sportcoat, Robert said.
    He would not be seen on the street with him.
    He would not even visit him at home.

13. Jim finally realized that his purchases were ruining his life.
    He began to rethink how he was living.

14. He did not do something about his spending.
    He was going to lose his best friend.

15. He hated to stop spending money extravagantly.
    He decided to save his money.
    He could become a college student and live happily ever after.

TRANSITION WORDS

English has another group of words, besides coordinators and subordinators, that are used to show relationships between ideas. These *transition words* do *not* join sentences; they merely show the logical relationship between them. The most common of these words are:

however	moreover
therefore	then
thus	also

Understandably, some students believe that these words actually join sentences and punctuate them as though they were coordinators or subordinators:

John leapt to his feet in alarm, however Mary remained calm.

This sentence is incorrectly punctuated. Since these transition words do not function like coordinators and subordinators—do not actually join sentences—the comma above is wrong; instead, there should be a period or a semicolon, as in the sentence you are now reading.

John leapt to his feet in alarm; however, Mary remained calm.
John leapt to his feet in alarm. However, Mary remained calm.

Unlike coordinators and subordinators, transition words are movable; you can put them at the beginning of the sentence or after the subject or at the end. They are words you can plug into a sentence, not words you join sentences with. You can see the difference between transition words and the real joining words in these two sentences:

John leapt to his feet in alarm; Mary, however, remained calm.
John leapt to his feet in alarm; Mary remained calm, however.

A final note about transition words. Despite what many textbooks and some teachers say, writers rarely use specific transition words or phrases to make transitions from one idea to another. If you've been taught to use "transitions" or transition words, you can easily check to see whether what you've been taught is true or not. Go to the bookstore to where the freshman English books are sold and pick up a collection of essays, any collection. Then open it and start looking for the transition words and phrases you've been taught about. Look in particular for the so-called transition words— *therefore, however, thus, moreover,* and so on. See if you can find even one per page. See if you can find one every five pages or every ten pages. You will probably find occasional sentences and even paragraphs beginning with the words *and* or *but,* but you will not find the transition words used much.

Transitions in real writing are more a result of good organization than anything else. If your planning has been good and your essay is well organized, transitions will, for the most part, take care of themselves. That is, your paper will read well. If it doesn't, if a reader (or your teacher) finds new points coming unexpectedly, you have an organization problem, not a transition problem.

Don't sprinkle your papers with *thus* and *therefore* and *however.* It's a sign of amateurishness. Use the coordinators and subordinators instead—and work on your organization.

REVIEW

In the following exercises, you will practice using materials from all your sentence-combining lessons so far. To assist you with coordinators or subordinators, places where they should be used to connect complete sentences are marked, as in this example:

[subord] The defense attorney argued for his client's innocence.
The defense attorney was tall.
He was wearing expensive clothes.

The assistant district attorney presented a case.

She was wearing an ordinary brown skirt and jacket.

The case was more effective.

[coord] The defendant was convicted.

Solution: *Although* the tall defense attorney wearing expensive clothes argued for his client's innocence, the assistant district attorney wearing an ordinary brown skirt and jacket presented a more effective case, *and so* the defendant was convicted.

Look Up and Say "Cheese"

1. Flying and photography are technologies.

   The technologies are two.

   The technologies are relatively new.

   The technologies are in the history of human experience.

   [coord] They are still developing.

2. The photographs were taken in 1858 by a Frenchman.

   The photographs were first.

   The photographs were primitive.

   The photographs were from the sky.

   The Frenchman was named Felix Tournachon.

   [subord] He photographed Paris from a gas balloon.

3. During the American Civil War, the Union army occasionally used balloons.

   [subord] It wished to spot Confederate troop dispositions.

   [coord] Photography did not yet have applications.

   The applications were military.

4. [subord] Aerial photography was developed in World War I.

   Aerial photography was for military purposes.

   It found its uses.

   Its uses were most numerous.

   Its uses were sophisticated.

   Its uses were in World War II.

5. [subord] Aerial photography was absolutely essential.

   It was used for spotting enemy troop movements.

   It was used for locating targets for bombers.

   Both the armies used it extensively.

The armies were Allied.
The armies were Axis.

6. Bombing raids were devastating.
The raids were on military targets.
[coord] Every nation made efforts to fool the aerial photographers.
Every nation was warring.
The efforts were strenuous.

7. Both sides used camouflage and other forms of deception.
The forms of deception included building fake airfields.
They included building fake camps.
They included fake supply dumps.

8. Today, cameras are equally useful.
The cameras are ultrasensitive.
The cameras are in airplanes.
The airplanes are flying at more than 80,000 feet.
The cameras are in satellites.
The satellites are orbiting the earth at 100 to 22,300 miles up.
[coord] They enable each side to monitor the other's military activities.

9. Pictures from weather satellites enable us to see storms.
The storms are developing far out at sea.
[coord] Aerial photographs can help in flood control.
They can help by locating snow packs.
The snow packs are unusually dense.
The snow packs are in mountains.

10. [subord] We have made aerial photography a tool.
The tool is for space exploration.
Now we can see photographs.
They are of other worlds.
They amaze us even more than those.
Those have been produced so far.

Nowhere to Hide

1. Today almost every item we buy.
We buy it in any store.
The item has a small rectangle.

The rectangle consists of black lines.

The black lines are vertical.

[coord] Underneath the lines is a string of numbers.

2. We call this rectangle with its bars and numbers a bar code.

[coord] Its official name is Universal Product Code (UPC).

3. [subord] The UPC now appears on almost every product.

It was developed to cut costs in supermarkets.

4. [subord] Supermarkets had to hire numbers of clerks.

The numbers were huge.

The clerks were to run their checkstands.

The clerks were to bag groceries.

The clerks were to take inventories.

The clerks were to stock shelves.

The clerks were to put price stickers on all the products.

The supermarkets were making only tiny profits.

5. Several companies invented coded check-out systems.

The companies were such as RCA and IBM.

[coord] They presented their designs.

The presentations were to the grocery industry.

The presentations were in January 1974.

The presentations were in San Francisco.

6. [subord] Later in the field than the RCA design.

The IBM design was selected.

7. The bar codes and checkout scanners were a great success for stores.

They were a success by enabling stores to lay off workers and cut costs.

[coord] Customers at first hated them.

8. There were protests.

The protests were by customers.

The protests were by consumer groups.

[subord] People wanted to see prices.

The prices were on the things they bought.

9. A few states even passed laws.

The laws required stores to put prices on their products.

[coord] Hardly anyone does it.

[coord] The laws have rarely been enforced.

10. Now bar codes can be used to create files.

    The bar codes are along with supermarket club cards.

    The files are personal.

    The files are on each shopper.

    [coord] This information can be sold to organizations.

    The organizations want to target individual consumers.

    They want to target them to increase their profits.

11. [subord] Your tastes were once a private matter.

    Your tastes are in food.

    Your tastes are in drink.

    Your tastes are in books and recordings.

    Now they are another product.

    The product is to be sold to whoever wants to know them.

CHAPTER 4

Learning by Comparing

COMPARING AND CONTRASTING TO DISCOVER

In this section, the writing assignments require you to notice the similarities and differences between things. Compare and contrast assignments simply reflect on paper an organizational strategy our minds use all the time. To make sense out of the disorderly and, frequently, confusing world around us, we compare (note similarities) and contrast (note differences), draw conclusions, and make decisions or recommendations accordingly.

> "I think I'll spend my day off on the beach; I've had enough sky diving for a while."
> "Take Professor James's astronomy class; Professor Stone's is impossible."
> "I hate horror movies. I'd rather see a good adventure."

Whether they realized it or not, these speakers made decisions or recommendations after examining two similar options (two outings, two classes, two kinds of movies) and after taking into account how these options differ.

Scholars and businesspeople compare and contrast constantly, and not only as a means of making a decision. Close examination of the similarities and differences between two or more items often leads to discovery. Take, for example, the student who is trying to decide between going to a state university and going to a private university.

Here is Olivia, a young woman with her AA degree from Centropolis City College, who has been working as a teller for River Valley Bank for six years. She has decided that she likes the world of finance, the work itself, and the people she works with, but she is getting a bit bored with her job as a teller. To move up the banking industry's corporate ladder, however, she needs to have her Bachelor of Arts degree, preferably with a major in finance and banking or business. So it's back to school.

The city of Centropolis has two universities—Universal University and Addams State—each of which offers a BA degree with a major in finance and banking. Located four blocks from River Valley Bank, Universal is a private university whose faculty consists of people who work within the disciplines they teach. A bank officer, for example, may teach a course in estate planning. Because this university is geared toward students who already have full-time jobs, it offers classes in the evening and does so all year round. A student enrolls in one course a month, two evenings a week; at the end of the month, he or she begins another course.

Olivia is quick to understand the benefits of this plan. She can keep her job at River Valley Bank and not take any time off from work to attend class. Additionally, she can concentrate on one course at a time and take courses during the summer. If she goes to Universal full time, Olivia can complete her BA degree in fifteen months. It will, however, cost her $7,500—not including textbooks.

Five miles away is Addams State, a public university whose faculty consists mainly of scholars and researchers who teach full time. Its student body consists primarily of full-time students, so it offers most of its undergraduate courses during the day. Unlike Universal's students, State's students enroll in five courses a semester, two semesters a year. The BA degree in banking and finance takes four semesters to complete and will cost Olivia $400 a semester—excluding textbooks, but including parking fees (Universal has free parking). Although Olivia can plan her schedule so that she takes courses only on Mondays and Wednesdays, or Tuesdays and Thursdays, she would still have to juggle her hours at work and make up the hours lost by doing fairly dull bookkeeping tasks two evenings a week at River Valley Bank.

In making an important decision like this one, Olivia would be wise to make a chart like the following one to help sort out her options and examine the similarities and differences (and the pros and cons) of each.

Issue	Universal U.	Addams State U.
Location	Centropolis (downtown)	Centropolis (edge of town)
Degree	BA	BA
Major	Banking and Finance	Banking and Finance
Minor	None	Business
Cost	$500 per month	$100 per month
Length of program	15 months	16 months
Student body	People employed full time	Full-time students
Faculty	Full-time professionals who teach part time	Full-time teachers and scholars
Number of courses	One a month	Five a semester

ORGANIZING ESSAYS BASED ON COMPARISON AND CONTRAST

How do writers organize compare/contrast essays? That depends a lot on their material and what their point is. In "The Myth of Violence in the Old West," in Chapter 1, you may remember that McGrath compares the kinds of violence characteristic of frontier towns in the nineteenth century with the kinds characteristic of our cities today. Because most readers know what kinds of violence and crime we have today but not what was most common on the frontier, he concentrates on the latter, referring to the former only occasionally to make his point—that the two are totally different.

In most compare/contrast pieces, you will probably have to concentrate equally on both things to be compared or contrasted. In cases like this, one organization usually springs immediately to mind. In this scheme, you will probably be tempted to examine all the characteristics of thing A, in one huge paragraph, and then look at all the characteristics of thing B in another, and then write your conclusion. This is not a good idea. It's likely impossible to find a professionally written article or essay organized in this way, and there is a simple reason for it. The writer who does this is, in effect, asking readers to memorize all the points in paragraph A and then to make the comparison themselves as they read paragraph B. Readers do not expect or want to do this, feeling that if the writer wants to compare two things, he or she should do the actual comparing.

Let's look at an outline of McGrath's essay on violence in Bodie, California, in the nineteenth century and that in major American cities in the twentieth. In this essay, McGrath uses the first three paragraphs as his introduction and then covers his points like this (numbers in parentheses are the numbers of the paragraphs):

Introduction (1–3)

Robbery in Bodie (4–5)

Robbery in Bodie compared with robbery in three modern cities (6)

Burglary in Bodie (7)

Burglary in Bodie compared with burglary in three modern cities (8)

Deterrence of robbery and burglary in Bodie and today (9–10)

Crimes against women in Bodie and today (11)

Juvenile crime in Bodie and today (12)

Homicide in Bodie and today (13–16)

Conclusion (17)

As you can see, McGrath makes his comparisons as he goes along—first robbery, then burglary, and so on. He does *not* cite figures for all of Bodie's crimes in one big paragraph and do the same thing for modern cities in another.

A variation of this organization might lay out first the similar characteristics and then the different ones (or the other way around). Such an organization might look like this if there were more important differences than there were similarities:

Introduction

Similar characteristics of A and B

    Characteristic 1

    Characteristic 2

Different characteristics of A and B

    Characteristic 3

    Characteristic 4

    Characteristic 5

Conclusion

The most important points in working out an organization are to make sure that it fits your material and that your reader will be able to follow it. Sometimes an organization that looks terrific on paper turns out to be terrible in practice, and then you just have to toss it and come up with a new plan. When you work on the following assignments, be sure to discuss possible organizations, along with their strengths and weaknesses, in class.

Assignments and Readings

THE OTHER BATTLE OF THE LITTLE BIG HORN
William S. Robinson

In June, 1876, a unit of the United States Army under Colonel George   1
Armstrong Custer[1] fought a battle with the combined Sioux and
Cheyenne Indians that became the most famous conflict of the Plains
Indians wars, the Battle of the Little Big Horn. The Indians, who usually
lost to the army, utterly wiped out Custer's group. There were no sur-
vivors. "Custer's Last Stand" has become the subject of books and
movies, and the Custer battlefield has been preserved. But there wasn't
just one battle at the Little Big Horn River. There were three. What happened in the other two was the subject of great controversy at the time
and is still the subject of arguments among historians today.

At this time, an ongoing dispute between the Sioux and   2
Cheyenne had reached the boiling point. The American government
wanted to open for settlement most of the land in what are now the
states of Wyoming, Montana, and North and South Dakota, and it
wanted the Indians to give up their nomadic lifestyle and go onto
reservations. The Indians did not want to do this and had no intention of cooperating. Now the Army was ordered to round them up
and force them onto the reservations. That's where Custer came in.
He was part of a force that hoped to surround the Indians and make
them do as the government wished.

Custer was in command of the Seventh U.S. Cavalry Regiment,   3
a unit that still exists today. Trying to find the Sioux and Cheyenne,
he and his regiment were riding along a string of hills about 300
feet above the valley of the Little Big Horn. Moving generally
northward, the Indians had camped in an enormous village in the
valley. Before Custer could see them, his Crow Indian scouts
informed him of their location. Custer wanted to attack them
before they could continue moving north and formulated the
following plan.

---

[1] **Colonel George Armstrong Custer:** Custer held the temporary rank of
Major General at the end of the Civil War but the permanent rank of Colonel
in the Regular Army. He insisted on being called "general" and usually was.

He divided his regiment into four groups. He took Companies   4
C, E, F, I, and L, about 225 soldiers, and went north along the hills to
get in front of the Indians. He assigned Companies A, G, and M,
about 140 men, to Major Marcus Reno[2] and ordered them to ride
down into the valley, cross the Little Big Horn River, and attack the
Indian village from the south. He formed a third force, Companies
D, H, and K, about 125 men, under Captain Frederick Benteen to
scout to the south to make sure there were no Indians there. Finally,
he assigned Company B under Captain Thomas McDougall to guard
his pack train, with his reserves of food and ammunition. Custer had
no idea he was facing some 2,000 Indians, but he probably would-
n't have cared if he did. The Army's experience with the Plains Indians was that they would usually scatter when attacked, and he was
concerned above all that they not get away. Custer, Reno, and Benteen were all experienced Indian fighters and had had distinguished
military careers during the American Civil War (1861–65). Before
sending Reno and his men into the valley, Custer told Reno that he
would follow him. For some reason, he changed his mind and went
off on his own.

As far as we can tell, Reno's detachment was the first to   5
encounter the Indians, at a sharp bend in the river where there was
a grove of trees. The Army rarely fought from horseback, and they
did not do so this time. Reno had his men dismount and form a
line across the northern bank of the river, with most of the soldiers
in the trees. The Indians immediately spotted them and attacked,
some on horseback, some on foot. They were armed with bows and
arrows and a motley collection of rifles. The soldiers outside the
trees retreated into the grove, and the Indians began to work
around them, quickly surrounding them. At this moment, Reno had
to make an instant decision—whether to stay where he was or to
retreat back across the river and up the hills and try to rejoin Benteen to make a stand there. He decided on retreat. His soldiers
mounted their horses and tried to escape through large groups of
Indians. They lost 32 killed and 7 wounded. The soldiers who made
it all said that the retreat was disorganized and chaotic, with many

---

[2] **Major Marcus Reno:** The city of Reno, Nevada, was not named after
Major Reno. His original family name was the French Renault, which is
pronounced "RenOH." It is not certain where Reno, NV got its name.

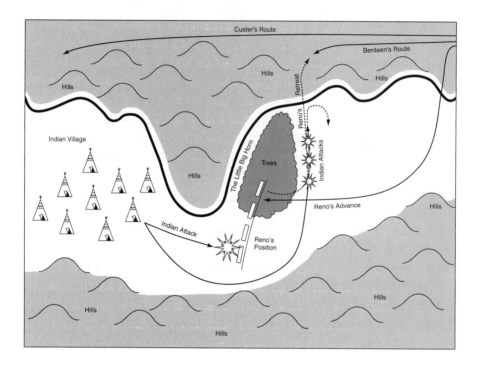

of the men inexperienced riders who could not control their horses and with the Indians shooting at them all the way, but most of them made it to the top, where they joined Benteen's group and McDougall with the pack train on what is now known as Reno Hill. There they held off the Indians for the rest of that day and all of the next until reinforcements finally arrived.

In the months after these battles, a controversy raged both within and outside the Army. Custer had become a popular hero, and his death and those of his soldiers were seen as the result of a heroic fight. But who was to blame? Neither the Army nor the populace wanted to blame Custer, so gradually blame began to fall on Major Reno, his second in command. Some believed he should have stayed in the valley, where he would have occupied many of the Indians, who could not then have attacked Custer. Captain Benteen too was under suspicion since he had gotten a written message from Custer to come quickly with the supply train and hadn't done so. He walked and then trotted his troops in Custer's direction rather than galloping to his aid. (Of course, no one could have gotten the mules of the pack train to gallop.) It became known that Custer and Benteen detested each other, and given Custer's personality, it is likely that Reno wasn't very fond of him either.

The Army finally opened an inquiry into the affair that wound up holding neither Reno nor Benteen to blame for Custer's disaster. It was impossible to say that if Reno had remained in the valley it would have made any difference in Custer's battle, and it was impossible to say that either he or Benteen could have gotten to Custer in time to save him. But both officers lived out the rest of their careers under a cloud and were never promoted. 7

The question we are going to consider here is whether Major Marcus Reno did the right thing in abandoning his position in the valley of the Little Big Horn River or whether he should have stayed. Did he save his men by retreating up the hills, or would his command have survived and benefited Custer by staying in the valley? You will be given the evidence for each of these choices, and you will be asked to compare the evidence on each side and come to your own conclusion about what Reno should have done. When you are examining this evidence and considering Reno's choices, you might want to remember that he had to make his decision very quickly, in only a matter of a few minutes, with Indians rapidly surrounding his command and bullets and arrows whizzing about his head. 8

The Situation

Reno rode into the Little Big Horn valley without knowing how many Indians were in the village there. Custer told him that he would follow him as a reinforcement. He did not know that Custer decided to ride off across the hills to try to head off the Indians from the north. The Indians, however, knew where both Custer and Reno were and prepared to attack both of them at the same time. 9

The Combatants

A standard U.S. Cavalry regiment of the period was a mixture of experienced and rookie soldiers. In the white regiments (as opposed to the two black regiments in the U.S. Army), desertion rates were very high and so a lot of the soldiers were inexperienced and untrained. Many of them could barely ride their horses and had no experience of combat. The Plains Indians were the best fighting horsemen in 10 the world, skilled riders and fierce warriors. But the white soldiers fought as units under the command of good officers who, mostly, knew what they were doing. The Indians were extreme individualists. They obeyed orders only if they felt like it. Even great chiefs like Crazy Horse and Sitting Bull could only suggest what to do. Every Indian warrior acted entirely on his own, and it was extremely rare for Indians to attack Army units. They were not sufficiently organized to do so.

Numbers

There were about 600 soldiers and Indian scouts in the Seventh Cavalry. Nobody knows how many Indians were in the village at the Little Big Horn. Estimates range from 1,000 to 3,000.   11

Fighting Methods (Tactics)

The American Cavalry had discovered during the Civil War that the best way to fight was by riding to the battlefield, dismounting, and fighting on foot. One soldier in four would hold four horses while his three comrades did the shooting. Cavalry soldiers were issued sabers, long curved swords, traditional arms of the cavalry, but the Indian-fighting army rarely if ever used them. They were armed instead with carbines (light, short rifles) and pistols. The Plains Indians hated to fight on foot and usually went into battle on their horses, though in the battles at the Little Big Horn they fought both mounted and on foot. They were equipped with whatever arms they could buy or find, a combination of rifles and bows and arrows. They did not fight as organized groups but as individuals.   12

Because of their superior organization, soldiers usually fought as groups, as companies or battalions, and if ordered to do so, would charge the enemy. Because of their highly individualistic culture, the Indians did not usually fight this way and would not normally attack an army unit. If they managed to surround a numerically inferior group of soldiers, they usually preferred to ride around it, shooting at it from their saddles. In this campaign, however, they did a few weeks earlier attack and defeat a unit of soldiers on the Rosebud River, and, of course, attacked and annihilated one of Custer's units.   13

Ammunition and Supplies

According to Lieutenant George D. Wallace, who was there, Reno's   14
men were each armed with two revolvers and a carbine. They had a
total of 24 revolver cartridges and 50 carbine cartridges in their belts,
and another 50 carbine cartridges in their saddlebags. Revolvers are
wildly inaccurate except at very close range, perhaps 10 feet or so.
The far more accurate carbines used by the cavalry could be fired at
the rate of ten to fifteen shots a minute. Lieutenant Wallace said that
a great many of the soldiers were inexperienced recruits who fired
too rapidly and too wildly and used up their 50 rounds in a few
minutes.

The soldiers carried water in their canteens but did not have food   15
with them.

We do not know how much ammunition or other supplies the   16
Indians had. It would have been up to each individual Indian to supply himself. Because they lived off the land, it would have been
impossible for one to two thousand Indians to stay in one place more
than a few days.

Testimony

During the Army's investigation of the Little Big Horn disaster, it took   17
testimony from officers, men, and scouts who accompanied Reno
into the valley. They estimated the numbers of Indians facing them
and said what they thought Reno should have done. Here are some
brief excerpts from that testimony.

Lieutenant George D. Wallace

While some of the men had been in the service for two to four years,   18
a great many were recruits who used up most of their 50 rounds . . .
Most of the recruits had never been on a horse until that campaign,
and they lost control of their horses when galloping [to escape].

F.F. Girard (a civilian scout)

I think that if Reno had been determined and resolute, he could have   19
held out against all the Indians as long as his ammunition and provisions held out. . . . Before this action, Reno had dismissed me from
my position as interpreter and Custer reinstated me, but I have no
unkind feelings toward Reno.

Lieutenant Charles A. Varnum

The position in the timber is as good as any place on the left bank of   20
the river, but I don't think we had enough men to hold it and keep
the Indians out. Of course, the position threatened the [Indian]
village to some extent and kept a containing force of Indians there,
but it was not a very safe place.

Captain Myles Moylan

The Indian fire was scattered, and the companies commenced firing   21
as soon as they were deployed. Some of the men were new, and it
was impossible to regulate their fire, but the fire of the majority was
well regulated. . . . If we had stayed 30 minutes longer in the timber,
unsupported, I doubt whether we would have gotten out with as
many as we did.

George Herendeen (civilian scout)

In my judgment, 100 men with 6,000 or 7,000 rounds of ammuni-   22
tion could have held that timber against the Indians. If they had water
and provisions, the Indians couldn't have gotten them out of there
at all.

Lieutenant L.R. Hare

The hill position was much better than the timber. If the Indians   23
had charged us in the timber, we could not have stood it more than
a few minutes. But Indians don't do that. We could have stood
them off for perhaps 30 minutes by using our ammunition judi-
ciously.

Lieutenant Charles De Rudio

Reno could have held his position in the timber three or four hours   24
by careful use of ammunition. The men out in the open fired rapidly.
Those in the woods fired slowly and deliberately.

Sergeant F.A. Culbertson

I don't think Reno could have held the timber but a very few   25
minutes. Most of the men were new and had never been under fire
before. They tended to fire at random. I fired 21 shots, but one of
the new men told me he had fired 60.

Essay Assignment

Write an essay in which you evaluate the evidence for, on the one hand, Reno having his command stay in the grove of trees along the Little Big Horn river so as to provide some distant help for Custer, or, on the other hand, doing as he did, ordering his troops through the surrounding Indians, back across the river, and up the hill to join Benteen. Come to your own conclusion as to which course of action you think would have been best *and why*.

A note

You can visit the Custer battlefield, including Reno Hill. There is a visitors center run by Native American descendants of the Indians who fought there. It is located just off Interstate 90 about 50 or 60 miles east of Billings, Montana.

COMPARING AMERICAN FAMILIES IN THE PAST AND PRESENT

The concept of hierarchy is an important one in human experience. A hierarchy among things is a graded order. For instance, if you classified all your possessions according to their value to you, with those most valuable at one end of your classification scheme and those least valuable at the other end, and all the others ranked between them, you would have created a hierarchy of your possessions. Human societies often involve hierarchies too, because we consider some people to be more important than others.

Of course, in a society in which the concept of equality is particularly important, we don't like to think of hierarchies among people, although every bureaucratic organization, whether military, governmental, academic, or business, is organized hierarchically. But equality is in many ways a modern concept, and before the eighteenth century, hierarchies were considered to be the natural state of things in all aspects of human life. In those times, most people believed that the entire universe was organized as a hierarchy, with God at the very top, the angels next, mankind in the middle, evil spirits below mankind, and the devil at the bottom. On earth, mankind was at the top followed by the animals (with the lion as most important), then birds (led by the eagle), then fish (led by the whale). Even minerals were organized hierarchically, with gold, naturally, at the top.

It followed, then, that among human beings there would also be a hierarchy, and there was. The king came first, followed by the various orders of nobles, then merchants, and so on. People who deeply believe that all things must be ordered in hierarchies will naturally organize their own affairs in the same way—even when it comes to family structure.

In colonial New England, for example, the man was at the top of the familial hierarchy, his wife and children ordered below him. Over the past three hundred years, the concept of hierarchies within families, along with the roles, responsibilities, and expectations of family members in this country, appears to have changed dramatically. Or has it?

Reading Assignment

Pre-reading

Psychologists and sociologists who study families find that most families are structured rigidly with certain family members habitually assuming certain roles, doing certain kinds of tasks, interacting in predictable ways, and having clear expectations of each other. All of these characteristics suggest an individual family's values in the same way that the hierarchical organization of colonial New England families illustrates their values.

Before you read about families in seventeenth-century New England, think about your own family. What roles do certain members of your family assume—your parents, your siblings (brothers and sisters)? Who usually does the cooking? Who gets served (or serves himself or herself) first? Who is expected to repair the roof, do the housework, discipline the children, bring home the paycheck, pay the bills, and so on? What do the individual roles and expectations suggest about your family's values?

It might be helpful to make a chart to classify the kinds of tasks and responsibilities the various members of your family have. You would want to list those of the individual adults, teenagers, and children. This will help you see how your family is organized and, perhaps, what values underlie that organization.

Reading

The following passages written by and about seventeenth-century New Englanders and contemporary Americans discuss the roles, expectations, and values of family members in these two different times.

The Social Order in Colonial New England

The essence of the [Puritan] social order lay in the superiority of   1
husband over wife, parents over children, and master over servants
in the family, ministers and elders over congregation in the church,
rulers over subjects in the state. A child might possess superior talents
and ability to his father, but within the family his father remained
superior. A church member might be the richest man in the community, but his pastor held authority over him in the church. In each
relationship God had ordained that one party be superior, the other
inferior. . . . As man ruled over the creatures and as God ruled over
man, so parents ruled over children and kings over subjects. . . .
Servants were exhorted to regard their masters as gods and to serve
them as though they were serving God. Wives were instructed that
woman was made ultimately for God but immediately for man. . . .
All social relations must be maintained with a respect to the order of
things, in full recognition of the fact that man ought to make God
his immediate end.

> Edmund S. Morgan, *The Puritan Family: Religion
> and Domestic Relations in Seventeenth-Century
> New England*

The Role of Men and Women in Colonial New England

Since marriage was an **ordinance** of God and its duties commands   1
of God, the Puritan courts enforced these duties not simply at the
request of the injured party but on their own . . . initiative. . . . Husbands and wives were forbidden to strike each other, and the courts
enforced the provision on numerous occasions. But they did not stop
there. Henry Flood was required to give bond for good behavior
because he had abused his wife by "ill words calling her whore and
cursing of her." The wife of Christopher Collins was presented for
railing at her husband and calling him "**Gurley** gutted divill. . . ."

The duty of a husband to support his wife was . . . [also] enforced   2
by judicial action. English common law provided that when a woman
married, her property passed to her husband and that he must fur-
nish her support. These provisions suited Puritan **conceptions**, and
New England courts enforced them. . . . James Harris was fined ten

---

ordinance: law;   **gurley:** surly, ill-humored;   **conceptions:** ideas shillings and required to give bond for good behavior . . . because of "disorderly carriage in his family neglecting and refusing to provide for them and for quarrelling with his wife. . . . "

In order to prevent adultery, the most grievous cause of divorce,   3 the New England governments did not rely solely upon the dread of capital punishment. To comply with the laws of God, Massachusetts, Connecticut, and New Haven made adultery a capital offense, but they seem to have carried out that punishment only three times. For the most part they sentenced offenders to fines, whippings, brand-ings, the wearing of a letter "A," and symbolical executions in the form of standing on the gallows with a rope about the neck. . . .

In seventeenth-century New England no respectable person   4 questioned that woman's place was in the home. By the laws of Massachusetts . . . a married woman could hold no property of her own. When she became wife, she gave up everything to her hus-band and devoted herself exclusively to managing his household. Henceforth her duty was to "keep at home, educating of her chil-dren, keeping and improving what is got by the industry of the man." She was "to see that nothing is wasted, or **prodigally** spent; that all have what is suitable in due season." What the husband provided she distributed and transformed to supply the everyday necessities of the family. She turned flour into bread and wool into cloth and stretched the pennies to purchase what she could not make. Sometimes she even took care of the family finances. . . .

Whatever financial or managerial ability she might possess, the   5 colonial dame remained subject to her husband's authority. Her place was "to guid[e] the house and not guid[e] the Husband." . . . She was expected to depend entirely upon his judgment. Though she clearly possessed the mental powers required for balancing family budgets, she supposedly lacked strength for more serious intellec-tual exercise. She never attended college, whatever intellectual prowess she might display in any secondary school. The accepted estimate of her capacities is revealed in the minister's exhortation to the Puritan husband not only to instruct his wife in religion but "to make it easy to her." She was the weaker vessel in both body and mind, and her husband ought not to expect too much from her. . . .

---

prodigally: wastefully

The proper conduct of a wife was submission to her husband's   6
instructions and commands. He was her superior, the head of the
family, and she owed him an obedience founded on **reverence.** He
stood before her in the place of God: he exercised the authority of
God over her, and he furnished her with the fruits of the earth that
God had provided. . . . She should therefore look upon him with
reverence, a mixture of love and fear, not however "a slavish Fear,
which is nourished with hatred or aversion; but a noble and generous
Fear, which proceeds from Love." She was not his slave or servant.
When Daniel Ela told his wife Elizabeth that "shee was none of
his wife, shee was but his Servantt," neighbors reported the incident
to the authorities, and . . . the Essex County Court fined him forty
shillings. . . .

Her husband's authority was strictly limited. He could not   7
lawfully strike her, nor could he command her anything contrary to
the laws of God. . . . In one respect she was almost his equal, for she
had "A joint Interest in governing the rest of their Family." . . .

In describing the husband's authority and the wife's submission   8
it has been necessary again and again to use the word "love." Love
was indeed, as one minister put it, "the Sugar to sweeten every
addition to married life . . ." but it was more than sugar. The minister
did not mean to imply that love was a luxury, a happy more than a
fortunate accident to the Puritans. It was a duty imposed by God on
all married couples. It was a solemn obligation that resulted directly
from the marriage contract. If husband and wife failed to love each
other above all the world, they not only wronged each other, they
disobeyed God.

Edmund S. Morgan, *The Puritan Family*

[The Puritan woman] was responsible for the care, clothing, and   9
feeding of her family, whatever her social status. If she had servants,
she had to direct them, see that they did their work properly, show
them how to do certain things, look after them when they were ill,
and maintain a watchful eye at all times. If she did not have servants,
as was the case with most of the women in the early settlements, she
had even less leisure, for she not only had to bear and care for

---

reverence: respect

children, but she had to cook and wash for the whole family without benefit of any labor-saving device; she not only had to make garments for all the family, including the menfolk, but she had to spin the thread and weave the yarn into the cloth for these garments. She also had to knit socks and stockings.

Louis B. Wright,
Everyday Life in Colonial America

The Role of Children in Colonial New England

It was the obligation of Puritan parents to make sure that their chil-   1
dren learned how to make a living and play their own part in adult life when they grew up. Since girls in colonial times were expected to become wives and mothers, they normally began learning how to do household chores when they were very young, as early as five years old. In most families, the oldest son would be expected to take up his father's business while the others became **apprentices** in some other trade or profession. Usually they began their training at about ten to fourteen years old.

Every Puritan child was taught to reverence his parents. . . .   2
Thomas Cobbett advised children to "Present your Parents so to your minds, as bearing the Image of Gods Fatherhood, and that also will help on your **filial** awe and Reverence to them." According to Cobbett, filial reverence consisted of a holy respect and fear both of a parent's person and of his words; a reverent child . . . feared to lose [his parents'] favor, feared to cross their just interests, feared to grieve them or fall short of their expectations. Moreover, he displayed these fears in his outward actions. When he spoke to his parents, he stood up. . . . If he saw his parents approaching him, he went to meet them and bowed to them; he spoke reverently to them and of them, and to express his sense of shame for his faults, he blushed and confessed his unworthiness when they corrected him. . . .

Since the training for almost every trade was gained through an   3
apprenticeship of seven years to some master of the trade, if a child wished to be free and able to earn his living by the time he became

---

apprentices: those who, in return for food and lodging, work for others to learn a trade;   **filial:** pertaining to son or daughter

twenty-one, he had to begin his apprenticeship not later than his fourteenth year. . . . Of course if he was so fortunate as to go to college, he might put off the choice of a calling until later; for the mere fact of possessing a college degree narrowed the choice: anyone with a "liberal" education would adopt a "liberal" calling, that is, a calling which required no manual labor and no long period of apprenticeship. About half the graduates of Harvard College in the seventeenth century entered the ministry. . . .

When a child became an apprentice, he went to live with his master and could not "absent himself day nor night from his Master's service without his leave." . . . The removal of a child from his parents when he was only fourteen years old or less seems a little strange, in view of the importance which the Puritans attached to family relations. The mere force of custom must have been partly responsible: apprenticeship was the only known way of learning a trade, and since the Middle Ages it had been customary for an apprentice to live with his master, even if his own home stood next door. . . . Not only were boys put out to learn a trade, but girls were put out to learn housekeeping. . . .

I suggest that Puritan parents did not trust themselves with their own children, that they were afraid of spoiling them by too great affection. The custom of placing children in other families already existed in England in the sixteenth century. Foreigners visiting the country attributed it to lack of parental affection, but Englishmen justified it on the grounds that a child learned better manners when he was brought up in another home than his own. The Puritans in continuing the practice probably had the same end in view. Certainly some parents were not fit to bring up their own children . . . [and their] children became over-familiar, "as if hail-fellow well met (as they say) and no difference twixt parent and child"; there were too many children, the ministers said, "who carry it proudly, disdainfully and scornfully towards parents."

Such conduct was inexcusable, for by the laws of God an **incorrigibly** disobedient child deserved death. New England laws provided that punishment for a rebellious son and for any child who should **smite** or curse his parents; but rather than apply this extreme

———
incorrigibly: incapable of being corrected or reformed;   **smite:** hit

penalty, the courts directed another law against parents whose affections blinded them to their children's faults. When children were allowed to become "rude, stubborn and unruly," the state might take them from their parents "and place them with some masters for years (boyes till they come to twenty one, and girls eighteen years of age compleat) which will more strictly look unto, and force them to submit unto government. . . ."

Psychologically this separation of parents and children may have had a sound foundation. The child left home just at the time when parental discipline causes increasing friction, just at the time when a child begins to assert his independence. By allowing a strange master to take over the disciplinary function, the parent could meet the child upon a plane of affection and friendliness. At the same time the child would be taught good behavior by someone who would not forgive him any mischief out of affection for his person.

Edmund S. Morgan, *The Puritan Family*

WOMEN WORKING MORE-AND PARENTING MORE
By Robert Pear
New York Times

WASHINGTON—Despite the surge of women into the workforce, mothers are spending at least as much time with their children as they did 40 years ago, and the amount of child care and housework performed by fathers has sharply increased, researchers say in a new study.

"We might have expected mothers to curtail the time spent caring for their children, but they do not seem to have done so," said one of the researchers, Suzanne Bianchi, chairwoman of the department of sociology at the University of Maryland. "They certainly did curtail the time they spent on housework."

The researchers found that "women still do twice as much housework and child care as men" in two-parent families. But they said total hours of work by mothers and fathers were roughly equal, when they counted paid and unpaid work. Using this measure, the researchers found "remarkable gender equality in total workloads," averaging nearly 65 hours a week.

The findings are set forth in a new book, "Changing Rhythms of   4
American Family Life," published by the Russell Sage Foundation and
the American Sociological Association.

At first, the authors say, "it seems reasonable to expect that   5
parental investment in child-rearing would have declined" since
1965, when 60 percent of all children lived in families with a bread-
winner father and a stay-at-home mother. Only about 30 percent of
children now live in such families.

With more mothers in paid jobs, many policymakers have   6
assumed that parents must have less time to interact with their
children. But the researchers say the conventional wisdom is not
borne out by the data they collected from families asked to account
for their time. *The researchers found, to their surprise, that married and*
single parents spent more time teaching, playing with and caring for
their children than parents did 40 years ago.

Family workload

According to a new book by sociologists at the University of Mary-   7
land, mothers are spending less time on housework, but more time
on child care.

ALL MOTHERS   (Hours per week)

Child care	Housework	Paid work	
10	32	8	1965
9	24	15	1975
8	20	19	1985
10	19	23	1995
13	19	23	2000

ALL FATHERS   (Hours per week)

3	4	42	1965
3	6	41	1975
3	10	36	1985
4	10	35	1995
7	10	37	2000

New York Times

For married mothers, the time spent on child care activities   8
increased to an average of 12.9 hours a week in 2000, from 10.6 hours
in 1965. For married fathers, the time spent on child care more than

doubled, to 6.5 hours a week, from 2.6 hours. Single mothers reported spending 11.8 hours a week on child care, up from 7.5 hours in 1965.

"As the hours of paid work went up for mothers, their hours of   9
housework declined," said Bianchi. "It was almost a one-for-one trade."

Fathers have picked up some of the slack. Married fathers are   10
spending more time on housework: an average of 9.7 hours a week in 2000, up from 4.4 hours in 1965. That increase was more than off-set by the decline in time devoted to housework by married mothers: 19.4 hours a week in 2000, down from 34.5 hours in 1965.

Rather than relying on anecdotes and images in the mass media,   11
the researchers used "time diaries" to measure how families spent their time. Using a standard set of questions, interviewers asked thousands of parents to chronicle all their activities.

FOR FIRST TIME, NUCLEAR FAMILIES DROP
BELOW 25% OF HOUSEHOLDS
Eric Schmitt

For the first time, less than a quarter of the households in the United   1
States are made up of married couples with their children, new cen-sus data show.

That results from a number of factors, like many men and   2
women delaying both marriage and having children, more couples living longer after their adult children leave home and the number of single-parent families growing much faster than the number of married couples. Indeed, the number of families headed by women who have children, which are typically poorer than two-parent fami-lies, grew nearly five times faster in the 1990s than the number of married couples with children, a trend that some family experts and **demographers** described today as disturbing.

The new data offer the 2,000 census' first glimpse into the shift-   3
ing and complicated makeup of American families and carry wide-ranging **implications** that policy makers and politicians are already struggling to address. With more communities having fewer house-holds with children, public schools often face an increasingly difficult time gathering support for renovating aging buildings and investing

---

nuclear families: traditional two-parent families;   **demographers:** people who study the characteristics of human populations;   **implications:** indirect suggestions

in education over all. Voters in Cleveland approved $380 million in levies to fix city schools, but only after two months of exhaustive lobbying by civic leaders. "This may have something to do with why our education system is not **up to snuff**," said Isabel Sawhill, a senior fellow at the Brookings Institution. "Oftentimes, those parents who still are invested in the schools don't have the money or influence to change things." Demographers expressed surprise that the number of unmarried couples in the United States nearly doubled in the 1990s, to 5.5 million couples from 3.2 million in 1990. Some of those couples have children.

Many conservative groups point to the increase as well as the statistics on single-parent households as troubling indicators of deeper societal problems. "This data shows we need to regain the importance of marriage as a social institution," said Bridget Maher, a marriage and family policy analyst at the conservative Family Research Council. "People are disregarding the importance of marriage and the importance of having a mother and father who are married." Ms. Maher and other conservatives point to the findings as justification for the enactment of policies that they say would strengthen the family, like eliminating the so-called marriage penalty in the tax code.   4

The decades-long decline in the overall number of American households with children slowed during the 1990s as two of the most troubling trends—divorce and out-of-wedlock births—moderated, demographers said. But even with that slowdown, the percentage of married-couple households with children under 18 has declined to 23.5 percent of all households in 2,000 from 25.6 percent in 1990, and from 45 percent in 1960, said Martin O'Connell, chief of the Census Bureau's fertility and family statistics branch. The number of Americans living alone, 26 percent of all households, surpassed, for the first time, the number of married-couple households with children. William H. Frey, a demographer at the University of Michigan, said, "Being married is great, but being married with kids is tougher in today's society with spouses in different jobs and expensive day care and schools." The number of married-couple families with children grew by just under 6 percent in the 1990s. In contrast, households with children headed by single mothers, which account for nearly 7 percent of all households, increased by 25 percent in the 1990s.   5

---

up to snuff: as good as they should be

The new census data paint a more detailed picture of the Ameri-   6
can family in other ways. Unmarried couples represent 9 percent of all
unions, up from 6 percent a decade ago. "It's certainly consistent with
what we've all been noting, the growth in **cohabitation** in this country, but it also tells us how complex American families are becoming,"
said Freya L. Sonenstein, director of population studies at the Urban
Institute in Washington and a visiting fellow at the Public Policy Institute of California. The number of nonfamily households, which consist
of people living alone or with people who are not related, make up
about one-third of all households. They grew at twice the rate of family
households in the 1990s. Demographers pointed to several factors to
explain the figures. People are marrying later, if they marry at all. The
median age of the first marriage for men has increased to 27 years old
from 22 in 1960; for women, it has increased to 25 years old from 20
in 1960, said Campbell Gibson, a Census Bureau demographic adviser.
The booming economy has allowed more younger people to leave
home and live on their own. Divorce, while leveling off, has left many
middle-age people living alone—at least temporarily. Advances in medicine and bulging stock portfolios have permitted many elderly people
to live independently longer. "It's easier for a young person to start out
on his own or live in a group home," said Mr. O'Connell. "And the
elderly population is healthier and economically better off." . . .

Essay Assignment

Drawing your support from your class discussion notes, the information in the preceding excerpts, and your own knowledge of the
past and the present, write an essay in which you compare and/or
contrast family life in Colonial New England with family life in
present-day America and show the importance of these similarities
and/or differences. This assignment is broad enough to result in a
book, so you'll have to limit your discussion to one or at most two
aspects of the topic. Perhaps you'll want to focus on the role of
mothers only, or fathers, or children. You could also look at female
roles in general or male roles. Concentrate on some aspect of the
subject that particularly interests you.

---

cohabitation: living together

Pre-writing

In class, discuss the roles assumed by typical family members in seventeenth-century New England. Who did what? What was expected of the father, the mother, the children? *What do their roles and expectations show us about their values?* Be sure to keep track of the main points that come out of this discussion by taking notes; otherwise when it comes time to write, you will have forgotten much of what was said.

The next step will be to exchange information about your family organization with your classmates, perhaps in small groups. There probably will be a lot of variety in how present-day families organize themselves; and it will be important for you and your classmates to exchange information in order to get a clear picture of what some of the key differences (and similarities) are.

Based on the reading assignment and class discussions, come up with a description of what seems to be a typical late contemporary American family. It probably won't look exactly like any of your individual families, but it should reflect present-day trends. For example, you might discover that most students' mothers work outside the home, that many parents are divorced, or that some fathers do the majority of the cooking.

With all this information in hand, you will be ready to examine the ways modern American families' organizations and values differ from and are similar to those of New England during the seventeenth century. Again, you may find it useful to make a chart to help in your comparisons, listing characteristics under headings like "Colonial New England" and "Present-Day United States." *What values do our present-day family organizations seem to represent?*

Writing

Your introductory paragraph should give a brief overview of the similarities and/or differences you perceive, mention what aspect of the subject you are discussing, and point to the direction your comparison/contrast essay will take. Will you emphasize the differences, the similarities, or both?

The body of the essay should give examples from the seventeenth century and the present to support your discussion. Review the opening section of this chapter for suggestions about organizing the essay. The conclusion of your essay should mention the importance of what you have learned about the changing or unchanging values of American families. Be sure to review the Writer's Checklist on page 239.

EXAMINING AMERICAN AND ASIAN EDUCATIONAL METHODS

There is much concern today that American education is not meeting the challenge of today's world, that we are not educating our children to be competitive in the future with those of other nations and cultures. A study of American education found the system so poor that the study was entitled "A Nation at Risk."

While there has been criticism of American education at all levels below graduate school, the focus of most of the concern has been on what we do, or don't do, in our elementary and secondary schools. At the same time, studies have shown a much higher achievement rate in many aspects of education, particularly mathematics, among children in other countries and especially in Asia. The Associated Press reported in February 1992 that "13-year-olds from the United States scored lower in science than top-ranked South Korea, Taiwan, Switzerland, the former Soviet Union, Hungary, France, Italy, Israel, Canada, Scotland, Slovenia, and Spain" and that math results were similar. In January 1993, Reuters news agency released a study showing that U.S. students in the first, fifth, and eleventh grades ranked behind Japanese and Taiwanese students in math, though they led in "general knowledge" questions. The math gap, however, got worse as the students got older. A *New York Times* report in April 1993 indicated improvement in American students' math scores in some states, but 75 percent of the students studied were still "below standard."

The 2005 National Assessment of Educational Progress found only 23 percent of graduating seniors tested scored at or above proficiency on the math test. In 2006, the National Assessment found that, while more U.S. fourth graders scored at basic or above on a nationwide science test than fourth graders did in 1996, the number of eighth graders scoring at basic or above remained flat. More troubling, twelfth graders performed worse on the science test in 2006 than in 1996, with 54 percent scoring at basic proficiency or above in 2006 compared to 57 percent scoring at basic proficiency or above in 1996.

Even in the most basic skill of all, reading, students seem to do worse as time goes by. The National Assessment found that graduating seniors in 2005 had the lowest reading scores since 1992.

Reading Assignment

Pre-reading

Although you may not know a great deal about Asian methods of education at this moment, you know a huge amount about American methods of education in elementary and secondary schools. As a way of beginning to think about this topic, ask yourself questions like the following: How long is the usual school year? How many students are in an average first- or third-grade class? How large is a typical high school class? Roughly, how many hours of homework are assigned weekly in elementary or high school? What subjects are taught? How do teachers teach—by lecture or discussion? What do American teaching methods suggest about the values of this society? Which values appear to be more important? Which ones less important? Remember to take notes as you come up with answers to these questions.

Reading

In the following series of articles, writers examine various aspects of the differences between Asian and American educational methods and accomplishments. Be sure to read actively, taking notes in the margins or on a sheet of paper.

NEW MATH-SCIENCE STUDY RATES U.S. STUDENTS MEDIOCRE AT BEST
William S. Robinson

In the Trends In International Math and Science Study (TIMSS), involving the students of thirty-eight nations tested in 1999, American eighth-graders did better than 17 nations in math and 18 nations in science, but they showed no improvement over their scores on the 1995 TIMSS. Singapore, Korea, Hong Kong, Japan, and the Czech Republic were the top performing countries in math and science.

On the positive side, black students improved in math, though not in science; white and Hispanic students stayed the same. On the other hand, while white students did about as well as Korean students in science, black and Hispanic students performed only as well as those in Iran and Indonesia.

The TIMSS researchers addressed the question of why American students as a whole continue to do poorly in these subjects, and they offer several answers. They found that the classroom methods of American teachers had not improved since 1995. As before, they believe that while Asian classes focus on a few subjects and study them in depth, American classes try to cover far too much and, as a result, do so superficially. Another problem is that there are no national standards in the U.S., and state and local standards are driven by number of subjects taught, not quality of teaching and learning. As a result state and district tests in the U.S. are low-level, so that too many students will not fail.

A related problem is the quality of teaching in American schools.   4
Public schools, especially city schools, have trouble finding well-trained math and science teachers. The international average for math teachers with a degree in math is 71 percent, but in the U.S. it's only 41 percent. American teachers do not have the time to prepare as thoroughly as teachers of other nations, and they do not observe each other or work together. They do not have the opportunity to learn how the best teachers work, and they are so busy getting through the curriculum that they can't give the students opportunities to work together in small groups, as is done in Japan. The presence of computers in schools had no effect or a negative one on student success. While 76 percent of American students had Internet access at school, the international average was only 25 percent.

The authors of the study believe that the home environment is   5
also a major factor contributing to success or failure. The best students lived in homes with plenty of books, a dictionary, and various study aids, and most of the highest scoring American students had college-educated parents.

One of the most disturbing aspects of the 1995 and 1999 TIMSS   6
studies is that they show American students doing worse as they move from the 4th to the 8th grades. According to Robert Schwartz, Executive Director of Achieve, a group that tries to promote higher academic standards, the 1995 study showed that "our fourth graders, relatively speaking, do very well, our eighth graders are mediocre, and our 12th-grade performance is **abysmal.** All this [1999] report tells us is that, four years later, we haven't made a sufficient number of changes to affect that dynamic."

WHY ARE U.S. KIDS POOR IN MATH?
Barbara Vobejda

A study to determine why American children lag behind those in   1
many other countries in mathematics has found that the attitudes of U.S. mothers toward their children's performance in school differ dramatically from those of Japanese and Chinese mothers.

While American mothers are likely to believe their children's   2
achievement is determined more by ability than effort, Japanese and

---

abysmal: absolutely terrible

Chinese mothers stress effort as an explanation for achievement. The Asian mothers demand more of their children and spend more time helping them with homework, according to a study released today by a National Research Council panel.

"In other countries, [the belief is] if you work hard, you're going   3
to do well," University of Michigan Professor Harold W. Stevenson said. "The mother thinks that by helping, she can improve performance. In America they say, 'The kid just isn't good in math.'"

In addition to the study of attitudes toward math among moth-   4
ers and children in Japan, Taiwan and the United States, researchers compared mathematics teaching techniques in those countries. They found that the Asian children spend more time in school, more time in math classes and, in those classes, more time working on math activities.

American children, for example, were out of their seats an average   5
of 21 percent of the period set aside for math, compared with 4 percent for the Chinese students and 2 percent for Japanese students.

Together, the studies provide more clues to what researchers say   6
is the complex question of why American children fare poorly in international comparisons. "The classrooms are radically different," said University of Chicago Professor James Stigler. Stigler pointed to a number of important differences, including a relative lack of coherence in American math classes.

In a typical American first grade, a teacher will run through a   7
series of math activities, moving, for example, from measurements to addition to telling time. "There's nothing that ties it together for the child," Stigler said.

By comparison, a Japanese teacher begins the class by stating   8
the day's goal, then rarely varies from that topic, often spending an entire class on one problem, but tackling it with different activities.

American teachers also spend more time working with individu-   9
als. In Japan and Taiwan, where the size of an average class is much larger than in this country, teachers usually work with the whole class.

FAILING SCHOOLS TRY LONGER DAYS
Cynthia G. Hicks

Spurred by the No Child Left Behind act, some schools whose stu-   1
dents didn't make the grade on the mandated standardized tests are experimenting with longer school days in an effort to raise test

scores and eliminate the threats posed by the law to schools deemed failing.

There is no one approach to adding hours to the school day or days to the school year. Some schools experimenting with the idea add an hour to school days and five extra days a year for all students. Others add a half hour to an hour several days a week just for students most at risk of performing poorly on the standardized tests, which emphasize math and reading. Still others allow teachers to choose days they will stay late. Schools also use the extra time in various ways. Some have students focus on core academic subjects, while others allow students to spend time in activities, such as tutoring or swimming, in addition to studying academics.

Lengthening the school day is expensive, raising per pupil costs by 30 percent. Lengthening the school year by just one day for all students could run about $4 million, according to some estimates. And, requiring the extra time on task certainly has critics among both teachers and parents, who worry that the extra hours will result in tiring out students, especially very young ones, and cut into family time. Critics are also concerned that the extra time will be required only of certain students, those from low-income families and poor school districts.

Even so, others support the trend, saying that middle- and upper-middle class parents provide after-school activities for their students that low income parents can't provide their children. Also, parents who work like the idea that their children will be coming home from school about the same time they come home from work. Everyone agrees that how the extra time is used is key, and Senator Edward M. Kennedy (D, MA) has proposed increased funding through No Child Left Behind to train 40,000 teachers to develop curriculum for the extra hours.

WE SHOULD CHERISH OUR CHILDREN'S FREEDOM TO THINK
Kie Ho

Americans who remember "the good old days" are not alone in complaining about the educational system in this country. Immigrants, too, complain, and with more up-to-date comparisons. Lately I have heard a Polish refugee express dismay that his daughter's high school has not taught her the difference between Belgrade and Prague.

A German friend was furious when he learned that the mathematics test given to his son on his first day as a freshman included multiplication and division. A Lebanese boasts that the average high-school graduate in his homeland can speak fluently in Arabic, French, and English. Japanese businessmen in Los Angeles send their children to private schools staffed by teachers imported from Japan to learn mathematics at Japanese levels, generally considered at least a year more advanced than the level here.

But I wonder: If American education is so tragically inferior, why   2
is it that this is still the country of innovation?

I think I found the answer on an excursion to the Laguna Beach   3
Museum of Art, where the work of schoolchildren was on exhibit. Equipped only with colorful yarns, foil paper, felt pens and crayons, they had transformed simple paper lunch bags into, among other things, a waterfall with flying fish, Broom Hilda the Witch, and a house with a woman in a skimpy bikini hiding behind a swinging door. Their public school had provided these children with opportunities and direction to fulfill their creativity, something that people tend to dismiss or take for granted.

When I was 12 in Indonesia, where education followed the   4
Dutch system, I had to memorize the names of all the world's major cities, from Kabul to Karachi. At the same age, my son, who was brought up a Californian, thought that Buenos Aires was Spanish for good food—a plate of tacos and burritos, perhaps. However, unlike his counterparts in Asia and Europe, my son had studied *creative* geography. When he was only 6, he drew a map of the route that he traveled to get to school, including the streets and their names, the buildings and traffic signs and the houses that he passed.

Disgruntled American parents forget that in this country their   5
children are able to experiment freely with ideas; without this they will not really be able to think or to believe in themselves.

In my high school years, we were models of dedication and obe-   6
dience; we sat to listen, to answer only when asked, and to give the only correct answer. Even when studying word forms, there were no alternatives. In **similes**, pretty lips were *always* as red as sliced pomegranates, and beautiful eyebrows were *always* like a parade of black

---

disgruntled: discontented;   **similes:** comparisons of two unlike things

clouds. Like children in many other countries in the world, I simply did not have a chance to choose, to make decisions. My son, on the contrary, told me that he got a good laugh—and an A—from his teacher for concocting "the man was as nervous as **Richard Pryor** at a **Ku Klux Klan** convention."

There's no doubt that American education does not meet high   7
standards in such basic skills as mathematics and language. And we realize that our youngsters are ignorant of Latin, put **Mussolini** in the same category as **Dostoievski,** cannot recite the Periodic Table by heart. Would we, however, prefer to stuff the developing little heads of our children with hundreds of geometry problems, the names of rivers in Brazil, and 50 lines from *The Canterbury Tales?* Do we really want to retard their impulses, frustrate their opportunities for self-expression?

When I was 18, I had to memorize Hamlet's "To be or not to be"   8
soliloquy flawlessly. In his English class, my son was assigned to write a love letter to Juliet, either in Shakespearean jargon or in modern lingo. (He picked the latter; his Romeo would take Juliet to an arcade for a game of Donkey Kong.)

Where else but in America can a history student take the role of   9
Lyndon Johnson in an open debate against another student playing Ho Chi Minh? It is unthinkable that a youngster in Japan would dare to do the same regarding the role of Hirohito in World War II.

Critics of American education cannot grasp one thing, something   10
that they don't truly understand because they are never deprived of it: freedom. This most important measurement has been omitted in the studies of the quality of education in this century, the only one, I think, that extends even to children the license to freely speak, write and be creative. Our public education certainly is not perfect, but it is a great deal better than any other.

STRENGTHS, WEAKNESSES, AND LESSONS OF JAPANESE EDUCATION
James Fallows

As Asian societies excel in coping with modern technology and   1
schooling people to deal successfully in the world—we need to ask ourselves how they do it. Japan's achievements are comparable to

---

Richard Pryor: famous Black comedian;   **Ku Klux Klan:** white supremist organization;   **Mussolini:** Italian dictator, 1922–1943;   **Dostoievski:** nineteenth century Russian novelist;   **soliloquy:** speech, monologue

ours, but its culture is so different that it makes a useful, revealing mirror. In Japanese education, there are aspects we should choose to emulate, and others that we would not want to adopt. There are real problems in the Japanese system, and these should point us in the opposite direction. The problems fall into four main categories.

1. **Excessive pressure**—There is unrelenting pressure on Japan- 2 ese children, due to the *all or nothing* impact that school success has on their futures. School success means university admission test scores. Test scores are virtually the only factor that determines which students get into which universities. University admission, as opposed to grades earned in university, determines what kind of career you can have in Japan.

Getting into the right university is so lastingly important that 3 many students (especially boys) who fall short on one year's test become *ronin,* wandering warriors, taking off one to four years for full-time cramming for the test. It is obviously more desirable to start preparation earlier, so students at age 8 or 10 begin the famous afternoon and evening cram schools. It is no wonder Japanese students have so little room in their lives for anything but studying, or why the motto for so many is "Pass with four, fail with five"— referring to the hours of sleep they permit themselves. Japanese parents and teachers, to say nothing of students, complain bitterly about this system but feel powerless to change it.

2. **Sexual discrimination**—Japan's school system rests on a 4 division of labor between the sexes that would be completely unacceptable to us. With minor exceptions, men carry out eco- nomic and political work. Women are completely responsible for the families, including their children's education. Women are ex- pected to have professional commitment to their children's welfare and are honored for their success. Although, from the Japanese per- spective, this approach has worked, the country loses the benefit of female talent in the business and professional worlds and male talent in child rearing.

3. **Conformity**—Much of the strict conformist mold into which 5 so many children are forced has to do with the almost total central- ization of schools. On any given day, you can walk through schools

anywhere from Hokkaido in the Siberian north to Kyushu in the trop-
ical south and find students reading the same chapters in the same
classes from the same books. Written Japanese is taught in a way that
requires students to use their right hands.

The emphasis on standardization leads to a high, consistent level   6
of competence throughout the nation, but it also constricts the
breathing space for children who do not fit or are not comfortable in
this rigid mold. Japanese educators and parents urge us not to forget the benefits our diversity and individualism bring to American
education, as they lament this weakness in their own system.

4. **Separateness and isolation**—Japan's teachers, policemen,   7
politicians, and business managers willingly point out that their society
is relatively easy to run because "We are all Japanese." Today's Japanese
population includes people whose ancestors came from Mongolia and
Polynesia; there are also several distinct minority groups. But for more
than a century, political leaders and intellectuals have promoted the
idea that to be a Japanese citizen is to be part of one pure race, separate from any other, and automatically bound together.

The cost of this engineered unity is that the differences between   8
"we Japanese" and everyone else may be viewed as negatives. For
instance, it certainly does not engender friendly feelings throughout
the rest of Asia. I often felt while living there that every white American should spend a few years in Japan, not only to experience the
culture, but to learn how it feels to be judged according to a stereotype a hundred times a day. If my children were late for school, I knew
what was going through everyone's mind, because Americans are
thought to be **indolent.**

Americans must embrace the opposite virtue. A multiracial soci-   9
ety is harder to run than a more racially unified one, but it allows us
to use talents no matter what their origin. The American multiracial
ideal (which is, of course, not fully achieved) seems far more precious
after you see how much of the world runs on racial or tribal lines.

The Japanese system has truly remarkable strengths that we   10
should try to imitate or approximate in our own cultural setting.
Some of them are the following.

---

indolent: lazy

1. **Emphasis on effort**—We should learn from Japanese and other East Asian schools the cardinal importance of stressing effort. American educators complain that schools are burdened with moral and social missions that get in the way of real teaching. But the moral burden on Japanese schools is much heavier and more explicit, especially in the elementary years. The primary element of most courses is how to be a proper Japanese, with the most important and consistent lesson being, "Try your best." 11

Japanese emphasis on effort and persistence in overcoming hardship, however, may go too far by our standards. Efforts toward these goals include "Nude Kindergartens," in which students attend school shirtless all year to build endurance, and the practice of sending boys to school in short pants throughout the winter. 12

Do not be misled into enthusiasm for the Japanese six-day school week out of belief that its purpose is principally academic. If Japanese society regarded a shorter school week desirable, the course content could easily fit into five days. *Length* is the point; it is part of an endless process of reinforcing effort. Nonetheless, we should learn from the radical idea that lies beneath this system. The more you talk about effort and the less you talk about raw ability, the more you build up the idea that all are capable of succeeding if they really try. 13

Much of America's school system focuses on early detection of differences in **innate ability.** We give tests, classify, and track students in the belief that this will help them obtain instruction that is best for them. The Japanese system spends no time at all this way. During elementary school, there is no tracking. Classes are typically 40 or 45 students per teacher, and they all move through the same books together. No one skips a grade; no one is held back. There is ruthless separation later by exams, but selection is made as late as possible, *after everyone has had a chance to try.* 14

The need for this approach is a concept so radical that we can barely grasp it here. The Japanese school system acts as though intellectual ability does not matter, assuming that just about everyone has enough ability to succeed. Japanese educators know that there are differences in ability, but they regard them as trivial. 15

---

innate ability: ability one is born with

The Japanese system contends that in normal life, determination   16
and grit will always matter more than theoretical, upper-bound
potential. Differences in raw ability will keep most of us from being
Albert Einstein or winning Nobel prizes, but they do not necessarily
bar us from achieving most possibilities in life.

The full consequence of this view is that *the key factor in success*   17
is within everyone's grasp. Emphasis on effort encourages everyone to
try and gives society a stake in developing everyone's potential. If we
took this lesson seriously, we would ask why we measure differences
in theoretical potential, when societies that care so little about these
differences do so well.

2. **High value placed on education**—Japan views the moral and   18
academic formation of children as the fundamental act of social survival, economic investment, and even national defense. Mothers and
teachers are viewed as soldiers in their homeland during war. This
devotion to education exists even though the Japanese teachers'
union is one of the few **strident** left-wing groups in the country.
Teachers are somewhat better paid than in America, but the real difference is in prestige. To call someone **sensei,** or teacher, is the ultimate honorific.

Students reflect this emphasis in a different way. A recent poll   19
compared high school students' attitudes in the U.S. and Japan.
When asked what they worried about most, Japanese students said
exams and study; American students said sex.

Of course, it is easier to say that Japan has done all this right than   20
to say how the U.S. could do the same. Japan values education partly
because of the **Confucian** tradition of rule by scholars, but also
because of the shocks administered by **Commodore Perry** and **General MacArthur,** which taught the Japanese that they had to school
themselves to survive. We could use a similar shock to our system,
some modern counterpart to *Sputnik.*

---

strident: loud, noisy, shrill;   **Confucian:** coming from Confucius, an ancient
Chinese philosopher;   **Commodore Perry:** U.S. naval officer who forced
Japan to open its doors to international trade;   **General MacArthur:** U.S.
general in charge of Japan after its defeat in World War II;   *Sputnik:* name
of the first satellite to orbit the earth, launched by Russia at a time when
American rockets failed to fly—the success of Sputnik prompted a major
funding of education programs in the United States

3. **Collective responsibility**—Japanese education deliberately   21
builds a sense of collective responsibility and group well-being in classrooms, communities, corporations, and the nation. The spirit is easier
for Japan to evoke than for America; Japan can fall back on racial unity,
along with broader emphasis on traveling, working, playing, and living
in groups. However, the Japanese system takes deliberate steps that
could be used in any society. Each class is graded as a class; teachers
talk to students every day about their group welfare. It would not be
easy for American schools to develop this attitude, but the Japanese
system goes out of its way to try, and the American system could too.

4. **Fairness**—By some measures of social equity and social   22
democracy, Japanese education and society may strike us as snob-
bish and unfair. **Hierarchy** runs through every aspect of Japanese life.
Moreover, money has begun to distort the Japanese school system
as it has ours. Because the cram schools are so important and so
expensive, an increasing number of students who enter Tokyo University are children of the rich.

However, the fairness of the Japanese system has a different   23
philosophical base than that of Western societies. The most important fact about Japan's educational success is that average performance is so good not because the *best* scores are so high, but
because the *worst* ones are. Principals and teachers are rotated from
school to school every few years in an attempt to keep achievement
levels uniform throughout Japan. This central control keeps one
school, region, or class of people from falling too far behind.

Americans can learn about this kind of fairness from Japanese   24
education. We may have the most fortunate upper and middle
classes in the world, but Japan has the most fortunate lower class. As
our two systems have competed, the best bottom has proven more
important than the best top.

Although I am not an educational specialist, I would like to offer   25
some personal suggestions gleaned from Japan's success.

- First, the effects of school and family are difficult to separate. In
  the short term, there is little to do about the high incidence of
  broken families in America, but something *can* be done about the

---

hierarchy: ranking of people according to wealth or power

economic harm that divorce often inflicts on children. Currently, the federal government **garnishees** our wages to cover the obligations we owe our parents through Social Security. Similarly, we could use the IRS to garnishee divorced parents' wages to make sure they carry out their obligations to their children.

- Second, we could **temper** the power and autonomy of local school boards. Every other major society has decided that all its students need to know certain things and meet national standards. I think America has to do the same.

- Third, we need to even out the funding extremes that make our best and worst schools so different from each other. We need to find fairer ways to pay for schools.

- Fourth, we need to focus on the real school problem—not lack of perfection at the top, but real failure at the bottom. Every time we talk about saving the schools, we should define the task as making the worst 30 to 40 percent much better, rather than adding Advanced Placement courses and further enriching schools that already perform very well. One way to do this is to expand Head Start; another is to generate a national spirit of service and crusade with a Peace Corps or National Service Corps that would bring talented young Americans or even foreign volunteers to work in our worst schools.

Although many U.S. analysts hold up Japanese education as an   26
ideal, a closer look reveals that the solution to America's education problem is not so simple. Because American schools are part of American society, they will always differ from Japanese schools—and so they should. In closing, I would like to offer American educators the challenge I addressed to American cultural, political, and economic leaders in *More Like Us: Making America Great Again*:

"Many of the practices that make Japan so efficient would simply   27
stifle us. If, for some reason, America really tried to make itself like Japan . . . it could never be more than a second-rate version of the real thing. If it tried that, America would also give up the values that not only are crucial to its success but constitute its example to the world. American society is the world's purest expression of the individualist belief—the

---

garnishee: seizing by government of all or part of one's wages to pay a debt; here the social security tax is meant; **temper:** reduce

idea that a society can flourish if each person is freed to pursue happiness as he or she sees fit. If we think these values are worth defending, we need to show that a society based on them can continue to succeed. Fundamentally, we owe it to ourselves, not to the Japanese . . ., to make our society as flexible, decent, and democratic as it can be. But **chastening** examples from outside can help us concentrate on our task."

SCHOOL HERE IN THE UNITED STATES
AND THERE IN VIETNAM
Student Essay

In the West, the educational system teaches students to think and to experiment with ideas that are important. In the East, it teaches students facts and self-discipline.   1

In Western countries, people have more freedom, which means that some students are not concerned about their education. Yet, to look on the bright side, the instructors teach students the thinking process and to experiment with ideas. The problem in Eastern countries is that teachers always force students to do what they tell them to do; but the students respect themselves and learn more.   2

In Vietnam if the teacher assigns the student homework to do but the student forgets to do it, that student will get in big trouble. Not only will his grade be lowered but he will be suspended or his parents will be called. Sometimes grade-school children will be spanked in front of the class. In the United States, the teachers don't care. If the students do the work, it's fine with them; if they don't, it's okay. When I was just in the United States for a few weeks, my junior high school teacher gave us homework that was very hard for me, and I got stuck. On the following day, I was almost crying because I was thinking that the teacher was going to punish me. When I entered the class, the teacher noticed that I hadn't done my homework, but she said it was okay, not to worry about it. When she said that, I felt as though I was in heaven. Since then, if I don't understand my homework, I just put it aside. As a result, I'm getting lazier every day. It's like I don't care about my education.   3

In the United States, the important point is that the instructor teaches students to think and to experiment with ideas. This is very   4

---

chastening: correcting or making better

different from Vietnam, where we never do experiments by ourselves. In high school, I took an Introduction to Physical Science class, and the teacher gave us a partner to work with on experiments. Whenever it was time to do an experiment, I just depended on my partner. While she mixed all the substances together, I just stood there, and if she needed anything, I got it for her. Toward the end of the semester, the teacher announced that the final would include an experiment, and we had to do it ourselves without a partner. So during the last week, I kept asking my partner questions about how to finish our experiment, and she took lots of her time to show me. But during the final I was "dead meat." I flunked it.

Inventing the New World

One indicator of future wealth is the value of the patents a nation holds. It has long been assumed that the United States had nearly an insurmountable lead in basic scientific research, and therefore an ultimate advantage in the world's industrial competition. Recent studies have shown, however, that while the United States is strong in a variety of academic fields like environmental studies, agricultural sciences, and clinical medicine and life sciences, it is behind in areas necessary for supporting industrial advances: engineering, computer science, electronics, communications, robotics and instrumentation. Several studies have attempted to measure not just the overall number of patents, but also the number of important and influential ones—those that will most likely generate wealth and growth for a nation. These studies show a new world in which Japan is rapidly overtaking the United States. U.S. spending on research and development has only nominally increased over the past 10 years, holding between 1.5 and 2 percent of the gross national product. In Japan, R&D spending has reached 3 percent of GNP.

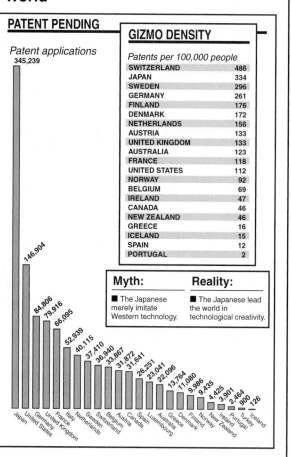

PATENT PENDING

Patent applications

345,239 — Japan
146,904 — United States
84,806 — Germany
79,916 — France
66,095 — United Kingdom
52,939 — Italy
40,115 — Netherlands
37,410 — Sweden
36,940 — Switzerland
33,867 — Belgium
31,872 — Austria
31,641 — Canada
26,251 — Spain
23,041 — Luxembourg
22,096 — Australia
13,764 — Greece
11,080 — Denmark
9,986 — Finland
9,435 — Norway
4,425 — New Zealand
3,901 — Ireland
2,464 — Portugal
900 — Turkey
126 — Iceland

GIZMO DENSITY

Patents per 100,000 people

SWITZERLAND	486
JAPAN	334
SWEDEN	296
GERMANY	261
FINLAND	176
DENMARK	172
NETHERLANDS	156
AUSTRIA	133
UNITED KINGDOM	133
AUSTRALIA	123
FRANCE	118
UNITED STATES	112
NORWAY	92
BELGIUM	69
IRELAND	47
CANADA	46
NEW ZEALAND	46
GREECE	16
ICELAND	15
SPAIN	12
PORTUGAL	2

Myth:	**Reality:**
■ The Japanese merely imitate Western technology.	■ The Japanese lead the world in technological creativity.

Source: World Rank Research Team

SOME PUBLIC SCHOOLS DON'T MAKE THE GRADE
Richard Morin

What grade do America's public schools deserve? Depends on who's   1
doing the grading. Public school teachers and parents give high
marks to the schools—but college professors and employers say the
schools fail to give their graduates the skills they need to succeed in
college or the workplace.

More than nine out of 10 public school teachers and two out of   2
three parents say the schools in their areas are doing an "excellent"
or "good" job educating children, according to a series of surveys
released [in January 1999] by the Public Agenda Foundation and
Education Week magazine.

But the people who deal directly and most immediately with the   3
products of the public school systems disagree—strongly. Only a
third of all employers and slightly more college professors say that
today's public high school students have the skills necessary to succeed in the working world or in college, the polls found.

Employers are particularly critical. Levels of dissatisfaction on   4
some key measures of performance declined dramatically from
results of a similar poll conducted just one year ago.

Three out of four employers—77 percent—say recent job   5
applicants rate only fair or poor in terms of "their work habits, such
as being organized and on time," up from 58 percent in early
1998. A majority of those employers interviewed—54 percent—
grade recent applicants low in terms of "being respectful and
polite"; just 32 percent offered a similarly negative assessment one
year ago.

Perhaps it's unfair to hold schools accountable for students with   6
dismal social skills or bad manners. But it's quite fair to ask about the
3 R's—and again, public school students were graded low by employers. Big majorities say young applicants are inadequate in terms of
basic math skills (64 percent) and their grammar and spelling
(80 percent), both up, but only significantly, from last year's poll. . . .

Post-reading

After having read the passages above and using your pre-reading notes,
list the characteristics of Asian and American educational systems. You might

---

3 R's: reading, writing, and arithmetic

use two sheets of paper—one each for Asian and American methods—and make two columns:

American   Asian

Another way would be to put all the advantages for both systems on one sheet and all the disadvantages on another:

Advantages   Disadvantages

As you do this, be sure to think further about educational methods, and don't hesitate to include your own ideas. For instance, an advantage of one system might seem to you to involve a corresponding disadvantage. When you read, for example, that Asian children get less individual attention than American children and so their classes can move faster and cover more material, you might recognize a disadvantage: slower children are more likely to be left behind and feel defeated. Also, as you make your lists, be sure to identify which writer talks about which advantages and which disadvantages so that when you are ready to write, you will be able to find your references easily and to use quotations.

Essay Assignment

Because of years of declining test scores and behavioral problems, the American educational system has come under attack for failing to provide students with the basic skills needed for college and the work force. As a result, some people have suggested that we use the Asian model of education in our schools, while others argue that we need to retain our own system but merely implement it better. Write an essay in which you examine American and Asian educational methods, noting the advantages and disadvantages of each. Come to a conclusion about *either* which system you think is best for the United States and why *or* what combination of the two systems you think should be instituted.

Pre-writing

Since the assignment asks you to examine the advantages and disadvantages of the two systems, your first step should be to study and evaluate your lists. Remember that you can go in two directions with this assignment. Either you can decide which system seems superior or you can pick out elements of each and recommend a combination of the best of both systems.

In the first case, remember that a system can be superior without being perfect. As a result, you may find yourself writing sentences acknowledging both strengths and weaknesses, for example, "*Although* the Asian system has X weaknesses, it still seems better in Y and Z ways." Because issues like this are rarely black and white, there is almost always much to be said on both sides. When you have decided which way you want to deal with the assignment, go back over your lists, grouping your points as you think you will want to use them in your paper, and make a brief outline. Also jot down a working thesis to help direct and focus your essay.

Writing

Although the basic organization of the comparison section of the essay might be pretty much the same regardless of your final goal, keep in mind a point about the actual writing of this section. If, for instance, you plan to argue that the American way is better, you will want your comparison paragraphs to focus as much as possible on the strengths of the American system. Don't ignore or leave out the weaknesses, but focus on the strengths.

The concluding section of an essay in which you try to say that one system is better will require some argument. For example, suppose you read a review comparing two restaurants. Let's say the writer had much to say about the relative good and bad points of each in terms of service, atmosphere, salads, meat and poultry dishes, desserts, and prices. Suppose the review claimed that one place had wonderful salads and low prices, but that the other one was really just about as good or even better in every other respect. Then the writer concludes, "And so I recommend the Bug-Eyed Lobster on Main Street over the Great Dirt on 24th because of its superior salads." You'd think, "Whoa! How did salads suddenly get so important? What about the other place's better meat dishes, great chicken, and only slightly higher prices?" And so on. A conclusion in a comparison/contrast essay really has got to take everything into consideration—not just one or two of the writer's favorite points. The real conclusion of the essay, then, might not be a single paragraph; it might be several paragraphs.

If, on the other hand, you plan to write about the best of both systems, you should focus about equally on their strengths and weaknesses: the strengths and weaknesses of the American system are such-and-such and why; those of the Asian system are such-and-such and why. Or the strengths of both are such-and-such and why; their weaknesses are such-and-such and why.

No matter what organization you use, the concluding section of an essay on the best system or the best of both systems should simply summarize what you think *is* the best. For suggestions about organizing your essay, review the opening section of this chapter. Be sure to review the Writer's Checklist on page 239 for reminders to help you complete this assignment.

THE HEALTH-CARE CRISIS: EXAMINING TWO APPROACHES TO NATIONAL HEALTH

The United States does not have a national health insurance system because, it is argued, it would be inefficient and expensive and would put our health care in the hands of "government bureaucrats." Yet we spend about $4,500 a year for every American, whether they're insured or not—and a lot aren't—while the next most costly system is Switzerland's at about $2,500 per citizen, and all are insured. Among the major industrialized nations—Canada, the European countries, and Japan—American citizens have the highest uninsured rate and the least access to medical attention. Our life expectancy is shorter, our infant mortality rate is higher, our childhood immunization rate is lower, and it is harder and more expensive to see a doctor for anything. In a study conducted by the World Health Organization in the year 2000, the United States ranked thirty-seventh in overall health-care quality worldwide.

In the last two and a half years, the following subjects made the news:

May 14, 2004: A 22 year-old Utah woman injured in an auto accident had nearly half her skull removed by doctors and could not get it back for nearly four months because of a dispute between Medicaid and the hospital over who would pay for the surgery. (Associated Press)

July 18, 2004: A 64-year-old California man, uninsured and a few months short of being eligible for Medicare, was injured in an auto accident, spent about 38 hours in a hospital being treated for his injuries, and was billed $72,000. (*San Francisco Chronicle*)

September 10, 2004: Premiums for job-based health insurance rose 11.2 percent over those for the previous year, the fourth straight year for double-digit increases in these premiums. The average annual premium for job-based health insurance in 2004 was now $9,950.00. (*San Francisco Chronicle*)

In addition, the U.S. Census Bureau reported in 2003 that 45 million Americans lack health insurance, a record high number. By 2007, that number had risen to 46 million. In 2004, the U.S. Health and Human Services Department announced that Medicare premiums would rise by 17.4 percent in 2005, the largest increase in the program's history.

In recent years 2001 to 2006, private health insurance premiums in the U.S. rose 73 percent. Republican commentators like Allan B. Hubbard, director of the National Economic Council, argued that health insurance has gotten so expensive because people use it too much.

In 2005, Tenet Healthcare Corp., which owned one of two hospitals in Redding, CA, paid $300 million to settle lawsuits brought against two of its doctors. The doctors performed unnecessary cardiac surgery on many patients, and the hospital overcharged for its services, because Tenet Corp. demanded that its hospitals increase profits every year.

On March 26, 2007, the *New York Times* reported that aged persons who have paid for long-term-care insurance policies frequently find that when they file a claim for admission to an assisted living home, the insurance companies deny the claim. The *Times* says that "some long-term-care insurers have developed procedures that make it difficult—if not impossible—for policyholders to get paid."

In 2007, many pediatricians stopped giving children vaccinations of new medicines to immunize them from diseases because the medicines are too expensive and insurers do not fully reimburse them for their costs.

In 2007, CBS News reported that the major brand-name drug companies have begun paying companies that make cheaper generic drugs not to market their products. They call it "pay to delay."

On May 9, 2007, the *New York Times* reported that two major drug companies, Amgen and Johnson & Johnson, have paid millions of dollars to doctors to prescribe anemia medicines to their patients, even though studies have shown that the drugs have not improved the lives of patients and may even have shortened them. The medicines had a combined sales of $10 billion in 2006 and are given to about a million patients each year. This is only one example of numerous reported cases in which drug companies have paid doctors to prescribe unnecessary or harmful drugs.

At the same time, there is violent opposition to changing the system. Presidents as diverse as Harry Truman, Richard Nixon, and Bill Clinton have tried and failed to get national health insurance approved, and the arguments against it are as vigorous as ever.

Opponents of government-sponsored single-payer health insurance often point to Europe, where, they say, health care is rationed. This is not, however, the case. Health care is not rationed in any of the leading government-sponsored systems. One problem encountered by two countries, Canada and Great Britain, is a shortage of doctors, which can make timely treatment difficult to obtain. France, as you will see, has solved this problem by making medical and nursing education free for all qualified students. If you want to look further into this issue, you have two resources available to you on the Internet. For articles opposed to national health insurance, search for "socialized medicine." For those advocating national health insurance, search for "single-payer health plan."

For this writing assignment, we are going to include only a few of these arguments. The main documents you will find here are ones that allow you to make a comparison yourself between two national health plans, the American and the French. We've chosen the French rather than, say, the Canadian or the Japanese because in the WHO study referred to above, where the United States came in thirty-seventh, France came in first.

Reading Assignment

Pre-reading

Perhaps you haven't had much experience with the American medical system, haven't been hospitalized, and haven't had to pay for whatever treatments you might have needed. For you, the chances are this is a non-issue. But it won't be for long—for any of us. As we age, however gradually and gracefully, things that once worked so well we took them for granted start to work not so well, and we have to call upon our medical system to get them fixed. The older we get, the more medical insurance starts to loom as an expense we are going to have to deal with.

To get some perspective on this problem, we suggest you ask your parents and, if possible, your grandparents or someone their age, whether they worry about medical insurance and possible medical expenses and try to find out what, if anything, they are doing about these actual or potential problems. Ask them what they like and dislike about our system, and jot down notes on what they tell you. Try to get them to be specific. Is it too expensive? Is it hard to see a doctor? Ask them specifically if there's anything that really worries them. Ask what they would change if they were in charge and could do anything they wanted.

There's another little matter we'd like you to consider as you approach this question. You're going to find references to European approaches to medical insurance, which some call "socialized medicine." You may have grown up thinking that socialism in all its forms is bad and that our capitalistic system is good. You may also believe that, in the standard cliché, the United States is number one in everything. We're the best and the smartest, and that's that.

Well, all those countries with "socialized medicine" are just as capitalistic in their economic systems as we are. They all know, just as well as we do, that state-run economies, such as that in the former Soviet Union, don't work. (On the other hand, in 1941, Nazi Germany and Imperial Japan were purely capitalistic countries; there is nothing inherently virtuous about capitalism.) The Canadians, Europeans, and Japanese think there are places where the national government is more efficient than private enterprise. For example, neither Japan nor any European country thinks private enterprise can run its transportation systems better than the government can, and they have the transportation systems to prove it. Their trains all run well over 100 miles per hour (the French TGV passenger trains run at 190 mph), run everywhere, and run on time, and their highways make many of our interstates look like cowpaths. European municipal public transit is the most modern and efficient in the world. We're really great at a lot of things, but we aren't the best at everything.

The point here is not to run down the United States but to caution you not to bring a bunch of stereotyped prejudices to this discussion.

Reading

You are going to get a very small sampling of arguments for and against a national health service to replace the one we have, and you will find information enabling you to make at least a superficial comparison between our system and a completely different one. We've already suggested where you can get more information on the Internet.

THE AMERICAN HEALTH-CARE SYSTEM

General

In 2000 the United States spent 12.9 percent of its gross domestic product on health care. This percentage continues to grow. It has an infant mortality rate of 6.82 deaths/1,000 births. American life expectancy is 74.24 years for men and 79.9 years for women. American health care is primarily in the hands of private insurers, whose principle aim is to make a profit. The government provides Medicare (insurance for those over 65 and for those with certain disabilities) and Medicaid (insurance for the poor and disabled). Since there is no government-subsidized insurance plan for the overwhelming majority of the population, over 60 percent of U.S. health expenditures come from the pockets of individuals. It is difficult to provide a short summary of the American system because it is extremely complex; so the following is only a general outline of what it does and how it works.

Details

The Medicare plan comes in two parts, Part A and Part B. Most do not pay for services covered under Part A, but do have to pay if they choose Part B coverage. As of 2007, Part B covered some medical expenses but not others, with deductables depending on the medical services used. A monthly premium of between $93.50 and $161.40, depending upon income, is changed.

Part A "helps cover" hospital stays, home health care, stays in skilled nursing facilities and home hospice visits. Part B "helps cover" doctors, outpatient hospital care, physical therapy, and some home health care. Most physical aids such as wheel chairs, crutches, walkers, and the like are covered.

In addition, there is a "Medicare + Choice" plan. In this case, the individual signs up with a Health Maintenance Organization (HMO)—essentially a medical insurance company—which offers a range of services and for that gets direct Medicare payments. The company receives the payments whether it has to provide patient services or not. Most companies stay in this business as long as they are making a profit, but if the profit disappears, because too many patients are showing up with too many expensive problems, the company may drop out of the business regionally or nationally. It is in the company's interest, therefore, to limit the services it will offer patients. It often does this by refusing the service of specialists in many cases. Patients in an HMO must use the doctors in the plan, usually must get a doctor's referral to see a specialist, and must stay within the HMO's service area or areas. A patient who signs up with an HMO may change to another company anytime between January and June, but after June must stay with the company for the rest of the year. An HMO can discontinue its services at the beginning of any year.

In Northern California in 2001, HMOs differed slightly in services offered and patient co-pays (the amount the patient must pay out of pocket for a particular service). The co-pay to see a physician ranged from $7 to $15. Prescription drug co-pays ranged from $7 to $10. Of 25 companies, 13 had no limit on number of drugs per year, 6 had an annual limit, and 6 offered no drug coverage at all (Medicare does not offer drug coverage). The monthly premiums for these HMOs ranged from $40 to $90.

Medicaid is even more difficult to describe than Medicare because, as the Health Care Financing Administration says, it is a joint federal-state program and thus "varies considerably from State to State, as well as within each State over time." Each state "establishes its own eligibility standards; determines the type, amount, and scope of services; sets the rate of payment for services; and administers its own program." There are some federal guidelines for who must receive payments. These are, roughly, anyone receiving welfare, some low-income families with children, some aged, blind, and disabled people; infants born to Medicaid-eligible women, children under 6 and pregnant women whose income is at or below 133 percent of the Federal poverty level, some recipients of adoption insurance and foster care, some Medicare recipients, and "special protected groups."

More complete descriptions of the Medicare and Medicaid programs may be found by searching under those words on the Internet.

THE FRENCH HEALTH-CARE SYSTEM

General

France spends 7.4 percent of its gross domestic product on health care. It has an infant mortality rate of 4.51 deaths/1,000 births. French life expectancy is 74.85 years for men and 82.89 years for women. The country has national health insurance funded by compulsory payroll contributions (13% of wages); employers contribute 70 percent and employees 30 percent. Though funded nationally, the system is administered regionally. All spouses and dependents of wage earners are covered. Coverage is for 99 percent of the population and 75 percent of total national health expenditures. Private insurance plans are available to cover what the government does not.

Details

Patients are free to choose their doctors and there are no limits on number of visits or services. Patients pay their doctors ($18 for general practitioners and $25 for specialists) but are reimbursed by the government. All medical and nursing education is free for qualified students.

The patient chooses his or her physician and may consult with specialists without having to be referred by his or her doctor. The fees of dentists, podiatrists, and midwives are 70 percent reimbursable by the state. Services such as x-rays, lab work, nurses, and so on are 60 percent reimbursable. The fees of state-run hospitals and hospices are fully reimbursable and those of clinics offering more specialized services are partially reimbursable. Prescription drugs are reimbursable as are over-the-counter drugs if prescribed by a doctor. Fees caused by catastrophic illnesses or accidents are fully reimbursable. The system provides salary subsidies for those completely disabled.

U.S. SPENDS MOST ON HEALTH, BUT FRANCE NO. 1 IN TREATMENT
Lauran Neergaard

The United States spends more per person on health care than any   1
other country, yet in overall quality its care ranks 37th in the world,
says a World Health Organization analysis. It concluded that France
provides the globe's best health care. Italy ranked No. 2, says the
World Health Report, being published Wednesday, a highly contentious first attempt to compare the world's health systems. Tiny
countries with few patients to care for—San Marino, Andorra, Malta—
crowd onto the World Health Organization's surprising best list.
Singapore, Spain, Oman, Austria and Japan round out the top-10.

    That doesn't mean the French and Italians are the world's health-   2
iest people. Japan actually won that distinction. Instead, the WHO
report basically measures bang for the buck: comparing a population's health with how effectively governments spend their money on
health, how well the public health system prevents illness instead of
just treating it and how fairly the poor, minorities and other special
populations are treated. When each country's measurements were
added together, even study co-author Dr. Christopher Murray, a Harvard health economist and the health organization's chief of health
policy evidence, was surprised. He had expected Scandinavian countries or Canada to be the world's best, because they're always presented as models. Instead, Norway hit No. 11, Canada 30. Britain,
with its much-debated free national health service, came in 18th. . . .

    It's long been clear "the U.S. is woefully lacking," E. Richard   3
Brown, director of the UCLA Center for Health Policy Research said.
Proof, he said, is in the 40 million uninsured Americans amid a patchwork of different quality private insurance and government programs.
While good at expensive, heroic care, Americans are very poor at the
low-cost preventive care that keeps Europeans healthy, said Princeton

University health economist Uwe Reinhardt. Take prenatal care, vital to a healthy start in life. Reinhardt called France the world's role model, while many poor Americans never get prenatal care. . . .

The United States spends a stunning $3724 per person on health   4
each year. But measuring how long people live in good health not just how long they live, the Japanese beat Americans by $4^1/_2$ years, and the French lived three more healthy years. Yet Japan spends just $1759 per person on health and France $2125. "That's a pretty big gap," noted Murray. "For the money we're spending, we should be able to do a lot better." . . .

HEALTH CARE IN FRANCE AND THE UNITED STATES: LEARNING FROM EACH OTHER
Paul V. Dutton

The health care systems of both France and the U.S. face crisis of   1
unprecedented scope. Both countries possess large and growing elderly populations that threaten to push the pace of health care price increases even higher than their already faster-then-inflation rates. Observers in both countries fear that outlays for increasingly expensive medical treatments and technologies will **wreak havoc** on public spending priorities. In the U.S., unchecked health care inflation will imperil Medicare and Medicaid, spur ever-larger federal budget deficits, and push up the embarrassingly large number of Americans without any medical insurance at all. In France, already insufficient resources have spurred strikes and demonstrations by doctors, while health care price hikes endanger that country's commitment to its European partners to maintain low budget deficits. A **delinquent** performance by France could place the entire project of European Monetary Union in peril.

Beyond these impending crises, American and French health care   2
systems share several fundamental principles. Nonetheless, a World Health Organization report published in 2001 found that France has the best overall health care system among the 191 countries surveyed while the U.S. ranked 37th behind virtually all European countries as well as Morocco, Oman, and Costa Rica. Several factors explain the

---

wreak havoc: destroy;   **delinquent:** failure to do what the law requires or what is necessary

differences in the rankings of France and the United States. The most important factor was the large number of Americans whose access to care is limited because of their lack of health insurance—estimates range between 39 and 43 million. Despite this lack of coverage, America still spends far and away the most on its health care system at 13.7% of GDP while France spends 9.8%, placing it in the fourth position.

	France	U.S.
Disability-Adjusted Life Expectancy	3	24
Distribution of Health in the Population	12	32
Fairness in Health Care Financing	6	54
Responsiveness	16	1
Health Care Spending per capita	4	1
Overall Rank	1	37

The WHO rankings, however, do not mean that the French sys-   3
tem is **unequivocally** superior to the American. In fact, both systems could profit from an understanding of the other's strengths. Toward that end, this analysis paper compares the health care systems of both countries and assesses how they can learn from each other in order to deal with their impending health care crises.

The Health Care Market

The health care market suffers from several **inherent** imperfections,   4
which have motivated government intervention in both the United States and France. Many of the very young, chronically ill, and aged could not obtain medical care if it were not for government sponsored assistance or insurance. In order to remedy market imperfections and improve access to quality medical care, governments have generally taken one of two approaches: a *national health service* or the promotion of *health insurance*. Great Britain possesses the **archetypal** national health service (NHS); everyone has access to medical care from providers whose **remuneration** flows largely from the government budget. Health insurance also socializes the demand for health

---

unequivocally: in all respects;   **inherent:** built-in;   **archetypal:** original standard;   **remuneration:** repayment

care by grouping consumers in order to spread risk and cost. Although the U.S. system relies much more heavily on private insurers, health insurance in both France and America is closely tied to one's employer or socio-professional category. This basic similarity is joined by other fundamental principles, especially in regard to the freedom of medical practice and patient choice.

Similarities: The Ideal of Private Medicine

As in the U.S., **autonomous** physicians dominate **ambulatory health**   5
care in France. Patient choice of physician, direct access to specialists, patient payment of fees (with subsequent reimbursement), physicians' freedom of diagnosis and prescription, fee for service, and ultra-high levels of medical confidentiality remain well-entrenched features of French medicine. Also like in the U.S., French workers and their employers pay for the bulk of their medical care through premiums assessed on gross wages. French employers and their employees pay wage levies of approximately 20%; employers contribute 13% and workers 7%.

Simple comparisons with U.S. expenditures are difficult because   6
of the wide array of [American] medical insurance plans whose premiums vary considerably according to firm size. Also, U.S. health insurance is priced not as percentage of wages, as in the French case, but in flat dollar premiums. A large employer, such as the state of Arizona, that provides coverage that approximates French medical insurance—pays $9,348 per year for each enrollee with dependents and leaves $1,704 per year to the employee. Hence, for a moderate-income earner ($40,000 annually), medical insurance costs are significantly higher than the French case—approximately 27% of **gross wages**.

In France, insurance premiums flow into one of several quasi-   7
public insurance funds that are jointly administered by employer and employee representatives. These insurance funds negotiate national medical fee schedules with the leading French physician associations. These *conventions*, as they are called, form the basis of physicians' remuneration. Although over 25% of French physicians charge fees

---

autonomous: independent;   **ambulatory health care:** nonhospitalized;
gross wages: total wages before taxes or other deductions; net wages are
what you actually take home

above the *convention* rates, their patients' reimbursement—usually
70% of expenses in ambulatory care—is tied to it. Thus, as in the
U.S., where private insurers and Medicare employ "normal and customary" fee schedules to determine payments to physicians, French
doctors' fees are ultimately constrained by insurers' willingness to
pay. . . .

France also possesses a significant private not-for-profit and for-   8
profit medical insurance sector (over three hundred companies)
that, while competing against each other, work in complementary
fashion with the quasi-public insurance funds. Indeed, fully 84% of
the population benefits from supplementary insurance coverage
that pays all or part of the medical fees that are uncovered by their
health insurance fund. In 1996, these supplementary providers
financed 12% of all health care expenditures while 13% of what
Americans would term deductibles or co-payments was left to
households.

U.S. private insurers account for nearly three times the share of   9
total expenditures than their French counterparts do (35% versus
12%) and Americans pay more out of their own pockets than the
French (17% versus 13%) for personal health care spending. [Of
course, these figures do not take into account the high percentage
of Americans who have insurance but cannot use it because they
cannot afford the personal payments they would have to make.] The
federal and state governments in the U.S. play a substantial role in
health care, mostly through Medicare and Medicaid (43%). But even
this large fraction is dwarfed by France's quasi-public insurance
funds, which account for almost three-quarters of total health care
spending.

Differences: Doctor Pay, Managed Care and Access

Medical practice and health care in France and the United States   10
are also marked by deep differences in hospital practices, efficiency,
and access to preventative and curative care. French hospitals lie
mostly in the public sector and their physicians, about one third of
the country's total, are salaried. As in the U.S., regional medical
centers are closely associated with medical education and research,
and therefore benefit from the relatively low-paid services of interns
and residents.

The French health care system is one of the most expensive in   11
the world and cost containment is an imperative for the government and insurers alike. Yet French costs remain far outpaced by
the U.S. France spends $2,047 **per capita** on health care compared
to America's $4,095. One of the major factors behind the relative
expense of the U.S. system is the higher earnings of health professionals. The average American physician earns over five times the
average U.S. wage while the average French physician makes only
about two times the average earnings of his or her compatriots. That
said, French physicians have remained more firmly attached to fee-
for-service medicine, albeit at lower rates, than their American colleagues and continue to enjoy a very high level of prescriptive
freedom. Their services are prospectively approved for payment
through the national *conventions* and are rarely questioned by insurers. This is in great contrast to the increasingly strict post-service
payment reviews that American doctors face from American insurers and Medicare.

The relatively low income of French physicians is allayed by two   12
factors. Practice liability is greatly diminished by a system that discourages a **tort-adverse** legal system, and medical schools, although
extremely competitive to enter, are essentially free. Thus, French
physicians enter the market with little if any debt and pay much
lower malpractice insurance premiums. . . .

At the same time, the French system exhibits enviably low   13
administrative costs: 5% of total expenditures versus 14% in the
U.S. U.S. physician fee increases are increasingly driven by doctors'
efforts to recover office-personnel and non-physician payroll
expenses, which have risen at a compounded annual growth rate of
7.1% since 1986. These increases far exceed hikes in liability insurance premiums (3.5%) and medical supplies (1%) during the same
period. Although numerous, French insurance funds adhere to a
nationally standardized billing and reimbursement procedure.
This practice, along with the fact that physicians' services are
pre-approved for payment through the national *convention*, permits
French medical offices to operate with relatively few administrative
personnel.

———

per capita: per person;   **tort-adverse:** a system that discourages law suits

Access constitutes the most striking difference between the   14
American and French health care systems. 16% of the U.S. population
lacks health insurance altogether and many possess insurance with
such high deductibles that they forego medical needs for financial reasons. A large number of uninsured puts additional strains on a health
care system. In order to recuperate the costs of uncompensated care,
providers raise the price of services for the insured, thereby creating a
vicious cycle, since higher insurance premiums ultimately lead to more
uninsured patients. One needs to return to France of the 1960s to find
America's current rate of un-insurance. Ninety nine percent of the
French population obtained health insurance by 1980, either through
the above-mentioned work-related insurance funds, as a dependent
of an insured person, or through special insurance funds for the unemployed. A 2000 law extended coverage to the remaining 1% who
somehow fell through the cracks of these health insurance funds.

Learning from Each Other

Breakthroughs in medical science and pharmacology have made   15
possible dramatic improvements in health in France and the United
States. But those improvements remain in peril without an effective
containment of rising medical costs, especially as populations age
and require more and increasingly expensive medical care. Under
these stresses, a health care system will depend on the achievement
of cost containment, efficiency of delivery, and equity of access. The
simultaneous mastery of these three inter-related objectives will be
critical to the health and prosperity of all.

THE AMERICAN HEALTH CARE CRISIS

Invited Testimony by Sara Collins to the Subcommittee on Oversight and
Investigations of the Committee on Energy and Commerce U.S. House of
Representatives

June 24, 2004

A Commonwealth Fund Report

The recent reports of uninsured patients struggling to pay **exorbitant**   1
hospital bills have lent a human face to a health care system under
enormous strain. . . . The number of people without health insurance

---

exorbitant: for too expensive

climbed to 43.6 million in 2002, nearly 4 million more than two years before. At the same time, national health care spending grew at a rate of 9.3 percent in 2002, the highest annual increase in a decade. Health insurance premiums rose even more rapidly, increasing by 13.9 percent in 2003, the third consecutive year of double-digit inflation.

Employers are responding to rising premiums by sharing more of   2 their costs with employees and offering new insurance products that shift more financial risk to workers. A severe fiscal crisis has led many state governments to restrict eligibility for public programs such as Medicaid and the Children's Health Insurance Program (CHIP)—a development that is likely to increase the number of people without coverage.

The Commonwealth Fund Biennial Health Insurance Survey, a   3 nationally representative survey of more than 4,000 adults, interviewed people about the extent and quality of their health insurance coverage in late 2003. The survey revealed growing instability in insurance coverage, particularly among people with low incomes and minorities. It also found evidence of an erosion in the quality of benefits received by people who have health insurance. Gaps in insurance coverage and rising health care costs are preventing large shares of both uninsured and insured Americans from getting the health care they need. In addition, the survey found high rates of medical bill problems, among the insured and uninsured alike. Many families with medical debt face stark trade-offs between life necessities like food and rent and paying down their debt.

Key findings from the survey include: 4

- The share of working-age adults (ages 19 to 64) who experienced a time without insurance coverage increased to 25 percent in 2003, up from 24 percent in 2001, the last year the Commonwealth Fund survey was conducted. In 2003, 17 percent of adults said that they were uninsured at the time of the survey, while an additional 9 percent had coverage at the time of the survey but had been uninsured for part of the previous 12 months.

- Insurance coverage was most unstable among those with the lowest incomes and among minorities. More than half (52%) of adults ages 19 to 64 in households earning less than $20,000 per year were uninsured for some time during 2003. The erosion of health insurance was most marked for families with incomes between $20,000 and $35,000—35 percent were without coverage during the year, up from 28 percent in 2001. Nearly half (47%) of all Hispanics experienced a time uninsured, and coverage for African Americans worsened considerably—the share of those with a time uninsured rose from 27 percent in 2001 to 38 percent in 2003.

- In addition to eroding insurance coverage, the survey found evidence of a decline in the quality of coverage among those who are insured. Nearly half (49%) of those who were insured all year through private coverage said that they had experienced either an increase in the amount they pay for their premiums, an increase in their share of medical bills, or cutbacks or new limits in their health benefits.

- Nearly everyone with private coverage pays something out-of-pocket when they obtain health care services. The survey asked adults how much they paid out-of-pocket over the last 12 months, excluding premiums, for their own personal pre-scription medicines, dental and vision care, and all other med-ical services, including doctors, hospitals, and tests. Two of five adults (41%) with employer-sponsored coverage paid less than $500 annually in out-of-pocket costs; a third (36%) paid between $500 and $2,000 per year; 13 percent paid $2,000 or more per year; and 10 percent did not respond or did not know. People with coverage in the individual market paid more than those with employer sponsored coverage—23 percent had annual out-of-pocket costs of $2,000 or more.

- Adults with low or moderate incomes spend the greatest share of their earnings on out-of-pocket health care costs. Of those with private coverage who had annual incomes of less than $20,000, 29 percent spent 5 percent or more of their income on out-of-pocket costs and 17 percent spent 10 percent or more. More than one-fifth (23%) of those in the next income bracket ($20,000 to $34,999) spent 5 percent or more of their income on out-of-pocket costs. Among those with annual incomes of $60,000 or more, just 2 percent spent that much on out-of-pocket costs.

- Erosion in insurance coverage appears to be impeding Ameri-cans' ability to get health care. The share of people who reported problems getting the health care they needed because of cost increased from 29 percent in 2001 to 37 percent in 2003. Those problems included: not filling a prescription; having a medical problem but not going to a physician or clinic; skipping a medical test, treatment, or follow-up visit recommended by a doctor; or not seeing a specialist when a doctor or the respondent thought it was needed.

- Access problems were most severe among those who experienced a period without health insurance in the previous 12 months. Around three of five of those who had a time uninsured said they had problems getting the care they needed because of cost. But even those with coverage all year reported problems. Three of 10 (29%) of those who were continuously insured reported that they did not get the care they needed because of cost, up from 21 percent in 2001.

- Many Americans are having problems paying their medical bills. In the survey, two of five adults (41%) ages 19 to 64—more than 70 million people—said they had problems with their medical bills in the last 12 months or were paying off medical debt accrued over the last three years. . . .

- Medical bills are creating financial hardship among many families. Among those who said they had a medical bill problem in the last 12 months or were paying off **accrued** medical debt, more than a quarter (27%) reported that they had been unable to pay for basic necessities like food, heat, or rent because of medical bills. More than two of five (44%) said they had used all or most of their savings to pay their medical bills; one-fifth (20%) said that they had run up large credit card debts or had to take out loans against their homes in order to pay these bills. . . .

NAME-BRAND DRUG COSTS SOAR, SENIOR GROUPS SAY
Washington Post

WASHINGTON—The price of name-brand prescription drugs most used   1
by seniors has increased by rates substantially above inflation for the past four years, undercutting the potential value of the new Medicare drug discount card, two senior advocacy groups reported Tuesday.

---

accrued: acquired

In a study tracking the prices of 197 of the most widely used   2
brand-named drugs from 2000 to 2003, the group AARP found a
cumulative increase of 27.6 percent, compared with a general inflation increase of 10.4 percent.

Analyzing the prices of the top 30 name-brand drugs prescribed   3
for seniors, Families USA found an increase on average 4.3 times
greater than inflation between January 2003 and January 2004.

The AARP report also found that the price escalation had picked   4
up during the past four years. Approximately one-quarter of the
most-used name-brand drugs more than doubled the general inflation rate in 2000, while 87 percent of those same drugs doubled the
inflation rate in 2003. . . .

As the nation's overall drug budget has increased by double-   5
digit rates in recent years, the Pharmaceutical Research and Manufacturers of America has said most of the increase is the result of
greater use of prescription drugs rather than inflation in drug
prices.

Jeff Trewhitt, a spokesman for the trade group, told the Associ-   6
ated Press that the studies overstated the rate of inflation for prescription drugs and did not account for the industry's substantial
research and development costs.

Prices of prescription medicines have risen 4.4 percent on aver-   7
age in each of the past three years, slightly slower than medical
inflation, Trewhitt said. "That's a more accurate basis for comparison," he said.

According to Families USA, the price of the five most prescribed   8
drugs for seniors increased at an especially fast rate last year. Lipitor,
used to lower cholesterol, rose 5.5 times more than inflation; blood-
clot preventer Plavix increased 5.3 times inflation, osteoporosis drug
Fosamax increased 4.6 times inflation, blood-pressure medication
Norvasc increased 6.6 times inflation, and arthritis drug Celebrex
rose by 5.4 times inflation.

THE INCREDIBLE SHRINKING HEALTH CARE DEBATE
Micah L. Sifry and Nancy Watzman

Dr. Arthur Kellerman is the chair of the department of emergency med-   1
icine at Emory University. A few years ago, he treated a middle-aged,
working mother who had a massive stroke and then was brought to

his emergency room in a coma. She died, "despite an all-out effort to save her," Dr. Kellerman later recalled. "In treating her, I learned she had stopped taking her blood pressure medicine two weeks before. Her blood pressure shot up, causing an artery in her brain to burst. Why had she stopped taking her medicine? Because she was poor and uninsured, and she had to choose between buying food for her kids or medicine for herself. Like most moms, she chose food, and paid for the decision with her life."

In the fall of 2003, Pete and Mary MacDowell of Chapel Hill,   2
North Carolina, went shopping for individual health insurance. Pete had recently retired and his group insurance had expired. The couple applied for coverage from the Blue Cross Advantage Plan. Though both are in their early 60s, neither has a serious health condition. Nor do they smoke, another red flag for insurance actuaries. Pete does have diabetes, but it's under control without medication, and his high blood pressure is also under control. "Nothing more than getting older," Pete told us in an e-mail. But when he heard back from Blue Cross, he could have had a heart attack. "The good news about this plan is that they would not reject you, just adjust the price according to the underwriting," he e-mailed some of his friends. "The quote: For a standard $500 deductible plan, no dental or glasses, for both of us: $4,189/mo. or $50,268/yr. For a tripped-down $5,000 deductible plan, $2,934/mo. or $35,208/yr."

With no irony or sarcasm he added, "Time to riot."   3

Over 43 million Americans currently lack health insurance. Like Dr. Kellerman's patient, some 18,000 of them will die unnecessarily this year for that basic reason, according to a recent series of studies by the Institute of Medicine, an arm of the National Academy of Sciences.

In addition, one out of three Americans will probably experience   4
a gap in coverage over the next four years, as they or other family members change jobs or lose coverage for other reasons. Contrary to conventional wisdom, lack of insurance is not solely tied to unemployment—in fact, 80 percent of the uninsured live in a home where at least one person works. Another trend that is driving up the number of uninsured—more companies are stripping health insurance out of their retirees' benefit packages.

While many of the uninsured do go to hospital emergency 5
rooms to get essential treatment, they are not getting the same quality of medical care as people with insurance. Lack of insurance also
leads to shorter lives, one major reason why the United States ranks
25th in male life expectancy and 19th in female life expectancy
among 29 developed countries.

People who are uninsured get fewer preventive services—like 6
regular checkups, mammograms, and prostate screenings. If they
have a chronic condition like high blood pressure, asthma, or diabetes, they are less likely to obtain vital medications on a regular
basis. In general, people without insurance are less likely to see a
doctor, or even to have a regular doctor. And the lack of regular
care can lead to more expensive care for preventable or treatable
conditions. Ultimately, taxpayers, who pay almost $30 billion a year
to cover unreimbursed medical expenses, absorb much of these
costs.

Why is America doing so little about the crisis of the uninsured, 7
especially when surveys show that more Americans worry about
health care costs than about losing their job, paying their rent or
mortgage, losing money in the stock market, or being a victim of a
terrorist attack?

An even harder question: why are people with power in Wash- 8
ington proposing to do so much less about the uninsured than they
did just a few years ago? This is true of both Republicans and
Democrats, by the way.

In 1992 the first President Bush proposed to cover 85 percent of 9
uninsured people by offering to spend $50 billion a year on tax cred-
its that could amount to $5,100 per year per family. Nine years later,
his son, George W. Bush, proposed a similar plan, only it was much
stingier—covering just 14 percent of the uninsured at a cost of
$9 billion a year.

Democrats have also scaled back their ambitions, which once— 10
when Harry Truman ran for president—even included universal
national health insurance. In 1993 President Bill Clinton and Hillary
Rodham Clinton put forward a complicated plan that would have
eventually provided public insurance to 95 percent of all Americans.
Fast-forward to 1998–2000 and Democrats were focused on something they called the Patients' Bill of Rights, which would guarantee
those with HMO coverage greater access to vital medical services

and allow people to sue their insurer if it denied them needed care, but did nothing to expand coverage for the uninsured.

Why the incredible shrinking health care debate?   11

One big reason for this gap in legislative coverage can be summed up rather easily: uninsured Americans don't have a powerful lobby and they don't make campaign contributions. Making sure that everyone has health insurance means going after powerful moneyed interests that now dominate the health care business, and by extension, the political debate. As Representative Pete Stark (D-CA) said back in 1992, "The doctors don't like [national health insurance]. The hospitals don't like it. The drug companies don't like it, and the insurance companies don't like it."

The last time Washington tried to do anything serious about   12
the health care crisis, in 1993–1994, groups representing these industries spent somewhere between $100 million and $300 million to lobby Congress and the public in defense of their interests, according to Haynes Johnson and David Broder, two veteran *Washington Post* reporters who wrote *The System*, a definitive reconstruction of the health care battles of the Clinton years. The insurance industry lobby was so strong that the Clintons rejected outright any discussion of a Canadian-style "single-payer" plan in favor of "managed competition," even though single-payer could cover everyone while saving hundreds of billions of dollars. The efforts by the insurance companies, doctors and hospitals, and the pharmaceutical industry—along with broader business lobbies like the National Federation of Independent Business and the Chamber of Commerce—to kill the Clinton bill "were almost indistinguishable from presidential campaign organizations in the scope of their fundraising, the scale of their field organizing, the sophistication of their advertising and public relations skills, and the speed of their electronic communications," Johnson and Broder write. Supporters of health care reform, by contrast, were divided and far less well funded.

Since then, health care reform has become a new "third rail of   13
American politics"—an issue that politicians don't want to touch.

As Representative Patrick Kennedy (D-RI), who chaired the House Democrats' fund-raising arm in 1999–2000, admitted not long ago, the failure of Clinton-style health care reform taught Democrats that "to change the status quo here, we would have to overturn too many vested relationships."

One out of every seven dollars in the American economy is gen-   14
erated in the health care industry. So perhaps it's not surprising that the health sector has also been a generous contributor to political campaigns, furnishing over $478 million to federal candidates and parties since 1989. That includes money from health professionals, hospitals, nursing homes, medical suppliers, nutritional and dietary supplement makers, and pharmaceutical manufacturers. On top of that, the giant insurance sector provided $213.7 million.

When politicians do approach health care, it's with far more   15
incremental proposals, like a bill passed in 1996 that requires insurers to offer coverage to people when they lose or change jobs (without placing any limits on what they can charge), or efforts to get more children enrolled under Medicaid. Even the broadly popular notions that patients should be able to go to an emergency room without prior approval from their HMO or that patients should have the right to appeal restrictive care decisions made by their insurance company have **foundered.** These issues have been entangled in the fierce fight between trial lawyers and business groups over so-called tort reform.

The Association of Trial Lawyers of America is one of the richest   16
Political Action Committees in the country—delivering over $22.9 million to candidates and parties since 1989, 85 percent to Democrats. Its leading adversary, the American Medical Association, isn't far behind, having given a tad over $20 million during that same period, 59 percent to Republicans. So far, these two sides have fought each other to a draw over the issue of arbitrarily capping medical malpractice awards.

All this money, and the lobbying that goes along with it, has had   17
the effect of completely clogging the legislative arteries, blocking any consideration of fundamental solutions to the health care crisis. Each special interest group has subsidies it wants supported and privileges protected. But seen from the perspective of someone who is uninsured, Congress appears to be a private hospital that only treats paying patients, instead of a public institution accessible to all.

---

incremental: partial;   **foundered:** failed

DRUG COMPANIES INCREASE SPENDING ON EFFORTS TO LOBBY CONGRESS AND GOVERNMENTS
Robert Pear

WASHINGTON—Lobbyists for the drug industry are stepping up spending to influence Congress, the states and even foreign governments as the debate intensifies over how to provide prescription drug benefits to the elderly, industry executives say. 1

Confidential budget documents from the leading pharmaceutical trade group show that it will spend millions of dollars lobbying Congress and state legislatures, fighting price controls around the world, subsidizing "like-minded organizations" and paying economists to produce op-ed articles and **monographs** in response to critics. 2

The industry is worried that price controls and other regulations will tie the drug makers' hands as state, federal and foreign governments try to expand access to affordable drugs. 3

The documents show that the trade association, the Pharmaceutical Research and Manufacturers of America, known as PhRMA, will spend at least $150 million in the coming year. 4

That represents an increase of 23 percent over this year's budget of $121.7 million. 5

Directors of the trade association approved the new budget, together with an increase in membership dues to pay for an expanded lobbying campaign, at a meeting last week. 6

"Unless we achieve enactment this year of market-based Medicare drug coverage for seniors, the industry's vulnerability will increase in the remainder of 2003 and in the 2004 election year," says one document, which laments the "demonization of the industry." . . . 7

The trade association and its tactics have become an issue. In debate on the Senate floor last summer, Senator Richard J. Durbin, Democrat of Illinois, said, "PhRMA, this lobby, has a death grip on Congress." 8

Senator Charles E. Schumer, Democrat of New York, said the drug industry made wonderful products, but was becoming "despised and hated" because of its aggressive efforts to keep prices and profits high. 9

---

monograph: a scholarly book or article

But Senator Orrin G. Hatch, Republican of Utah, defended the   10
trade group, saying it had been vilified as a "satanic" force, "a bunch
of greedy, money-grubbing companies." In fact, he said, drug makers
do more than any other industry to help people. . . .

In its budget for the fiscal year that begins on July 1, the phar-   11
maceutical lobby earmarks $72.7 million for advocacy at the federal
level, directed mainly at Congress; $4.9 million to lobby the Food
and Drug Administration; and $48.7 million for advocacy at the state
level.

In addition, the budget sets aside $17.5 million to fight price   12
controls and protect patent rights in foreign countries and in trade
negotiations.

The PhRMA budget allocates $1 million "to change the Cana-   13
dian health care system" and $450,000 to stem the flow of low-price
prescription drugs from online pharmacies in Canada to customers
in the United States.

WHY THE U.S. NEEDS A SINGLE PAYER HEALTH SYSTEM
David U. Himmelstein, M.D. and Steffie Woolhander, M.D.

1. Our pluralistic health care system is giving way to a system   1
run by corporate **oligopolies**. A single payer reform provides the
only realistic alternative.

A few giant firms own or control a growing share of medical   2
practice. The winners in the new medical marketplace are determined by financial clout, not medical quality. The result: three or
four hospital chains and managed care plans will soon corner the
market, leaving physicians and patients with few options. Doctors
who don't fit in with corporate needs will be shut out, regardless of
patient needs.

A single firm—Columbia/HCA—now owns one quarter of all   3
Florida hospitals, and has announced plans to move into Massachusetts. In the past year alone the firm has purchased more than a
dozen hospitals in Denver and Chicago, closing unprofitable ones
and shutting out unprofitable physicians and patients. In Minnesota,
the most mature managed care market, only three or four plans and
three or four hospital chains are left. In many rural areas a single plan

---

oligopoly: power held by a few

dominates the market, presenting patients and physicians with a take-it or leave-it choice. Managed care plans in California, Texas and Washington, DC have "delisted" thousands of physicians—both primary care doctors and specialists—based solely on economic criteria. One Texas physician was featured in Aetna's newsletter as "Primary Care Physician of the Month," and thrown out of the plan shortly thereafter when he accumulated high cost patients in his practice. In Massachusetts, BayState HMO "delisted" hundreds of psychiatrists, instructing their patients to call an 800 number to be assigned a new mental health provider. The for-profit firm running Medicaid's managed mental health care plan has just informed psychiatrists that many of them will be barred from the plan as a cost cutting measure. . . .

2. A single payer system would save on bureaucracy and investor profits, making more funds available for care.   4

Private insurers take, on average, 13% of premium dollars for overhead and profit. Overhead/profits are even higher, about 30%, in big managed care plans like U.S. Healthcare. In contrast, overhead consumes less than . . . 1% in Canada's program. Blue Cross in Massachusetts employs more people to administer coverage for about 2.5 million New Englanders than are employed in all of Canada to administer single payer coverage for 27 million Canadians. In Massachusetts, hospitals spend 25.5% of their revenues on billing and administration. The average Canadian hospital spends less than half as much, because the single payer system **obviates** the need to determine patient eligibility for services, obtain prior approval, attribute costs and charges to individual patients, and battle with insurers over care and payment.   5

Physicians in the U.S. face massive bureaucratic costs. The average office-based American doctor employs 1.5 clerical and managerial staff, spends 44% of gross income on **overhead,** and devotes 134 hours of his/her own time annually to billing. Canadian physicians employ 0.7 clerical/administrative staff, spend 34% of their gross income for overhead, and trivial amounts of time on billing (there's a single half page form for all patients, or a simple electronic system).   6

---

obviate: eliminate;   **overhead:** operating expenses

According to U.S. Congress' General Accounting Office, administrative savings from a single payer reform would total about 10% of overall health spending. These administrative savings, about $100 billion annually, are enough to cover all of the uninsured, and virtually eliminate co-payments, deductibles and exclusions for those who now have inadequate plans—without any increase in total health spending.

   3. The current market-driven system is increasingly compromising quality and access to care.   7

   The number of uninsured has risen rapidly, to . . . over 42 million.   8
The proportion of people with coverage paid by an employer is dropping, and those with employer-paid coverage face rising out-of-pocket costs. Only massive Medicaid expansions—10.5 million nationally since 1989—have averted a much larger increase in the uninsured. Proposals for welfare reform and Medicaid managed care programs would shrink Medicaid enrollment (increasing the number of uninsured) and threaten the quality of care for those left on Medicaid. . . .

   HMOs have sought to profit from Medicare and Medicaid contracts by providing substandard care, and even **perpetrating** massive fraud. The largest Medicare HMO, IMC in Florida, induced thousands of the elderly to sign over their Medicare eligibility and then **absconded** with $200 million in federal funds. Nationwide, Medicare HMOs provide strikingly substandard homecare and rehabilitation to the disabled elderly. Tennessee Medicaid HMOs have failed to pay doctors and hospitals for care. After 360,000 women and children were enrolled (and $650 million was spent annually), Florida suspended enrollment in its Medicaid HMO program because of flagrant abuses. Administrative costs consumed more than 50% of Medicaid spending in at least 4 Florida HMOs. In one plan that enrolled 48,000 Medicaid recipients, 19% of total Medicaid dollars went for the three owners' salaries. Thousands of patients were denied vital care; sales **reps** often illegally pressured healthy people into joining HMOs, while discouraging those who were ill; patient complaints and inspectors' findings of substandard care were repeatedly ignored. Overall, a **cursory** state audit found serious problems

---

perpetrating: doing;   **absconded:** ran away with;   **reps:** representatives;
cursory: superficial

at 21 of the 29 HMOs participating in the program. A more extensive evaluation is just beginning. These Florida scandals are a virtual
replay of California's earlier Medicaid HMO experience.

HMO payment **incentives** increasingly pressure primary care   10
physicians to avoid specialty consultations and diagnostic tests. In
this **coercive** climate, errors of judgment will inevitably occur, denying patients needed specialty care, while specialists are idle. In some
areas of the nation (e.g. New York City and California) market **imperatives** have led to growing unemployment of physicians, while huge
numbers of patients don't get adequate care. . . .

4. A single payer system is better for patients and better for doc-   11
tors. Canada spends $1,000 less per capita on health care than the
U.S., but delivers more care and greater choice for patients. Combining the single payer efficiency of Canada's system with the much
higher funding of ours would yield better care than Canada's or ours
at present.

Canadian patients have an unrestricted choice of doctors and   12
hospitals, and Canadian doctors have a wider choice of practice
options than U.S. physicians. Canadians get more doctor visits and
procedures, more hospital days, and even more bone marrow, liver
and lung transplants than Americans. While there are waits for a
handful of expensive procedures, there is little or no wait for most
kinds of care in Canada . . . The average waiting time for knee
replacement in Ontario is 8 weeks, as compared to 3 weeks in the
U.S. But patient satisfaction levels with the procedure and care are
identical. The time from first suspicion to definitive therapy for
breast cancer is actually shorter in British Columbia than in
Washington State. There are virtually no waits for emergency
coronary artery surgery in Canada, though elective cases face
delays, particularly with the surgeons held in highest regard. . . .
Finally, under a single payer system we would face much less
restraint on care than Canada because we spend (and would
certainly continue to spend) much more, and have many more specialists and high tech facilities. Hence even the modest limitations
on care seen in Canada are unlikely here. . . .

---

incentives: motivations to an action;   **coercive:** use of force;
imperatives: forces

Many of us have negative feelings toward government, and exam- 13 ples of government inefficiency and incompetence bound. Yet the record of private insurers is far worse. Their overhead is, on average, 600% above that of public programs, and no private insurer's overhead is as low as Medicare's. Dozens of financial scandals have wracked insurers and HMOs in the past year alone. . . . Moreover, Medicare treats doctors and patients more respectfully than most private insurers, funds virtually all residency training, and pays Massachusetts hospitals higher rates than do most HMOs. Finally, when a public program misbehaves we have channels to seek redress; we know where Congress meets, and can vote them out. For-profit firms must answer only to their stockholders.

Essay Assignment

Using your class discussion notes, notes you have made from talking with your parents and others, and the information and arguments you've been given here, write an essay in which you compare and/or contrast the American and French health-care systems to show which you think is the better or what combination of qualities of the two you think might produce the best system.

Pre-writing

In class, it would probably be a good idea to share what everyone has learned about their parents' and grandparents' feelings about our health-care system, what they like and don't like, what they would change if they could. With a list of these things on the board, you can then match up the two health-care systems with those criteria and see which one comes closest to satisfying them.

Writing

Your introductory paragraph should outline briefly what the problem seems to be or at least what the controversy is over. In the body of the essay, the first thing to do is compare the most important characteristic of the two systems. You want to establish what you're talking about before getting to the arguments about it. You should be able to do this in one or two paragraphs.

You could then outline and compare the most important arguments for and against the systems. In your conclusion, you will use your previous discussion and comparison to support your view of which system you think is best or what combination of qualities of the two you think might produce the best system.

THE WRITER'S CHECKLIST

The Idea Draft

1. Does your idea draft *respond fully* to the assignment?
2. Are your ideas *organized* in the way you want?
3. Does your *introduction* explain what the essay will be about and what its purpose is?
4. Do you have a *thesis* that states your point or indicates the issue the essay will address.
5. Do the *body paragraphs* each have a *topic sentence?* Do they develop the main points by giving *specifics and examples* to support those points?
6. Does your *conclusion* make one or more recommendations?
7. Have you *collaborated* with at least one trusted friend or fellow student who has read your draft *critically,* looking for lapses in logic or other weaknesses in content?

Sentence Combining

When you revise your idea draft, remember to use coordinators and subordinators when possible. Be especially alert for sentences *or pairs of sentences* in which you are comparing or contrasting two things or ideas. In such cases, words like *while, whereas,* and *but* will help you show the relationship you have in mind.

In the essay about why American kids are poor at math, Barbara Vobejda wants to contrast the attitudes toward their children's achievement of American and Asian mothers, and at the same time she wants to put her emphasis on what Asian mothers think. So she writes her sentence this way:

> *While* American mothers are likely to believe their children's achievement is determined more by ability than effort, Japanese and Chinese mothers stress effort as an explanation for achievement.

When contrasting two ideas, James Fallows uses the most obvious method:

> Japan's achievements are comparable to ours, but its culture is so different
> that it makes a useful, revealing mirror.

Sometimes a writer will use *but* to introduce a sentence or even a paragraph in order to give what follows particular emphasis. Kie Ho does this to introduce a transitional paragraph:

> *But* I wonder: if American education is so tragically inferior, why is it that
> this is still the country of innovation?

Finally, don't forget that concession—admitting that there is another side to an issue or that you could be challenged on your point—is used a great deal in professional writing. In the two examples below, Fallows grants that there is another perspective from the one he believes is best.

> Although, from the Japanese perspective, this approach has worked, the
> country loses the benefit of female talent in the business and professional
> worlds and male talent in child rearing.

> Although I am not an educational specialist, I would like to offer some per-
> sonal suggestions gleaned from Japan's success.

Other phrases that you might find handy in writing about contrasting things or ideas are *on the other hand, in contrast,* or *by comparison.*

Later Drafts

1. Taking into account the constructive criticism you have received, have you *revised* accordingly—that is, reorganized, if that was a problem, or given additional support, if that was?
2. Have you read your essay *aloud,* listening closely to what it *actually* says, not just what you think it says? (This is another good place to work with a trusted fellow student or friend. Have him or her read your essay aloud and both of you listen closely to what it says.)
3. Have you *revised your sentences* if they seemed unclear or awkward as you read them aloud?
4. Have you checked for those *mechanical difficulties* that you know you sometimes have? Have you used the dictionary to check words that you think may be *misspelled?*

Final Draft

If you have followed this assignment step by step, you have worked exceedingly hard on this essay. Therefore, make sure your final draft reflects your care and effort by being as professional looking as possible.

1. Type it neatly, using the format your instructor has assigned.
2. Proofread slowly and carefully, word by word, line by line. (One last time, ask a trusted friend to proofread it *after* you have, or exchange your essay with another student and proof each other's.)

Sentence Combining

JOINING IDEAS TO SHOW CONTRAST AND CONCESSION

One of the most common writing tasks you are likely to encounter in college, in almost any classes you take, is that of making comparisons between two ideas or things, to show their similarities, or making contrasts between them to show their differences. An allied task—one that is even more common than comparisons and contrasts—is to show relationships of concession.

Here is a short comparison passage:

I have here two objects. Both are round and about three inches in diameter. Both grow on trees, and both are edible. The one in my left hand is considered a fruit, and the one in my right hand is also. So both are normally found in the same section of the supermarket.

Here is a short contrast passage:

I have here two objects. The one in my left hand has a smooth red skin and a stalk on one end, but the one in my right hand has a slightly pebbled orange skin and no stalk. The one in my left hand has a firm texture and sweet flavor, while the one in my right hand is pulpy and juicy and has a slightly acidic taste. The red one is grown in northern climates in the summer, whereas the orange one grows in southern, warmer climates all year round.

Notice the connecting words in the two passages:

In the first: *and, and, and, so*
In the second: *and, but, and, and, while, and, and, whereas*

While both passages make liberal use of the most common joining word in the language, *and,* the contrast passage employs three other words in central places: *but, while,* and *whereas.*

Here is another short passage; what joining words does it use?

> Mary is faced with a dilemma, which of two cars to buy. The red one is sleek and attractive, and it has been newly painted, but it leaks oil and smokes slightly, and its brakes and tires are in poor condition. The green one is rather dingy, but it is in excellent mechanical condition. Although Mary finds the red one much more attractive, she decides that the green one is a better purchase.

Up until the last sentence, we have the familiar words of comparison and contrast: *and* and *but.* Then we find a new word, *although.* This word enters because the last sentence does something none of the other sentences does; it shows a relationship of concession between the two parts of the sentence. You will remember from studying subordinators that these words indicate opposition between ideas: *although, though, even though, while,* and *whereas.* It is now time to qualify that statement. It is true that all of those words do show opposition, but three of them—*although, though,* and *even though*—also show concession, and in fact that is their main function.

WHAT IS CONCESSION?

To concede a point is to admit that it is true. In argument or discussion, we often must admit that some of the things our opponent says are true. For instance, John argues that oranges are better than apples, while Mary argues the opposite. Mary points out that the skin of apples is more pleasant to the touch than the skin of oranges. John has to admit that this is true, so he says:

> Although apples have more pleasant skins, oranges are superior in many other ways.

John has used *although* to concede a point. He could also have used *though* (more informal) or *even though* (more emphatic). He might even have used *while* or *whereas,* although these words are better at showing contrasts than at showing concession. You will remember the mention of *transition words* at the end of Chapter 3. Two common transition words that you may want to use occasionally in writing comparison/contrast essays are *however* and *on the other hand.*

SUMMARY OF COMPARISON/CONTRAST WORDS

We have now looked at a number of joining words that you will need to use in writing essays, paragraphs, or sentences involving comparison, contrast, and concession. These words fall into three categories:

Coordinators	**Subordinators**	**Transition Words**
and	although	however
but	though	on the other hand
	even though	
	while	
	whereas	

Remember the differences among types of words. *Coordinators* may join independent sentences; when they do, put a comma in front of the coordinator. Coordinators may also introduce sentences:

Mary likes handball, but John prefers jogging.
Mary likes handball. But John prefers jogging.

Subordinators join dependent clauses to sentences; when the dependent clause comes first, put a comma after it; when it follows the sentence, do not use a comma.

While Mary likes elephants, John prefers penguins.
John prefers penguins while Mary likes elephants.

Transition words do not join sentences and may be placed within or at the end of a sentence instead of at the beginning of it.

Mary likes a good time; however, John mopes.
Mary likes a good time; John, however, mopes.

USING JOINING WORDS TO SHOW EMPHASIS

There is one final difference between coordinators and subordinators that you need to know. When the coordinator *but* joins two sentences, the ideas in the two sentences get equal emphasis. But when the subordinators such as *although, whereas,* and *while* join sentences, the idea following the subordinator gets played down somewhat.

Here you are trying to sell your battered old car, which you have taken beautiful care of. It doesn't look very good, but it runs like a whiz. You have two customers, A and B, who have looked it over and taken it for a test drive. They now speak:

A: "Well, although it doesn't look very good, it certainly runs well."
B: "Well, although it runs well, it certainly doesn't look very good."

Who do you think is most likely to buy it?

As it turns out, neither A nor B buys it. (A would have, but at the last moment, she got a phone call telling her that her rich uncle Fred had just given her a Mercedes-Benz.) So here you are again, facing two prospective customers along with the friend of one of them, who is not in the market for a car. The three people make the following comments. Who is leaning toward buying the car, who is leaning toward not buying it, and who is the neutral observer?

C: "Although it's rather ugly, it's in excellent condition."
D: "It's rather ugly, but it's in excellent condition."
E: "Although it's in excellent condition, it's rather ugly."

In all of the examples above, the subordinate clause (the *although* clause) has come at the beginning of its sentence, but, as you know, such clauses can just as easily come at the end of sentences:

It's in excellent condition although it's rather ugly.

EXERCISE: JOINING TO SHOW EMPHASIS—1

The following exercises will give you practice in using although, while, and whereas to join ideas and to give emphasis. Remember that all of these words can show contrast or opposition, but only although (or its friends even though and though) can show concession. Examples:

Showing contrast/opposition:

While Jamaal was a stellar math student, his English was just barely passing.

Kevin was terrible at sports *whereas* his sister Athena got a scholarship to play basketball.

Showing concession:

Although I love meeting new people, I hate blind dates.

Maria would not sell her old car *even though* it was costing her too much money to run.

Remember that the contrast/concession words play down the part of the sentence they are attached to and emphasize the part of the sentence they are *not* attached to. Example:

Show contrast/opposition; emphasize second sentence:

Whereas my pet tarantula does helpful things around the house such as eating bugs, my cat just spreads fleas everywhere.

Show concession; emphasize first sentence:

Marlissa knows that she studies best in the mornings *although* she'd rather go jogging then.

1. Most women like to shop.
    Men generally go to the store just to buy something they want.
    a. Show opposition; emphasize first sentence.
    b. Show concession; emphasize second sentence.
    c. Which version do you prefer? Why?

2. For women, it's the process that counts.
    For men, it's the results.
    a. Show opposition; emphasize second sentence.
    b. Show opposition; emphasize first sentence. (Don't use the same joining word you used in *a*.)
    c. Which version do you prefer? Why?

3. This idea may be generally true.
    There are many complications and exceptions to it.
    a. Show concession; emphasize second sentence.
    b. Show concession; emphasize first sentence.
    c. Which version do you prefer? Why?

4. Women do seem to shop more than men.
    They don't shop just for anything.
    a. Show opposition; emphasize second sentence.
    b. Show concession; emphasize second sentence.

5. A woman may spend several hours shopping with a friend.
    They will probably not, for example, shop in a hardware store.
    a. Show opposition; emphasize second sentence.
    b. Show concession; emphasize first sentence.
    c. Join the two sentences in another way of your choice.
    d. Which version do you prefer? Why?

6. Men rarely go out just to shop.
    It is possible to find men wandering around aimlessly in hardware or automotive stores.
    a. Show opposition; emphasize first sentence.
    b. Show opposition; emphasize second sentence.
    c. Show concession; emphasize the sentence of your choice.
    d. Which version do you prefer? Why?

EXERCISE: JOINING TO SHOW EMPHASIS—2

You have practiced using the subordinators that indicate opposition and concession. In these exercises, you will continue to use these words, but you will now also practice using the word but *to show contrast. Remember that while the subordinators give differing emphasis to the two parts of a sentence, the word* but, *a coordinator, gives the same emphasis to the two parts. Examples:*

Mary's python, Filbert, died.
Mary was not particularly sad.
   Show concession; emphasize sentence two.

Solution: *Although* Mary's python, Filbert, died, Mary was not particularly sad.

Mary preferred fairly independent pets, like cats.
She found Filbert to be rather clinging.
   Show opposition; emphasize sentence one.

Solution: Mary preferred fairly independent pets, like cats, *while* she found Filbert to be rather clinging.

Filbert was a well-behaved python.
He didn't seem to have much personality.
   Show opposition; give equal emphasis.

Solution: Filbert was a well-behaved python, *but* he didn't seem to have much personality.

Musical Tastes

1. John liked rock and roll.
   Mary preferred classical music.
   a. Show opposition; give equal emphasis.

2. Rock and roll is the music of today.
   Classical music has retained its popularity over generations.
   a. Show concession; emphasize sentence one.
   b. Show concession; emphasize sentence two.

3. Lovers of rock and roll often like classical music too.
   Those who prefer classical music usually hate rock and roll.
   a. Show opposition; emphasize sentence one.
   b. Show opposition; emphasize sentence two.

4. Jazz came from popular black sources in the South.
   Some of it has since developed in the direction of classical music.
   a. Show opposition; give equal emphasis.
   b. Show opposition; emphasize sentence one.
   c. Show opposition; emphasize sentence two.

5. Jazz in its original forms was an African-American art.
   It influenced many white musicians, even including the French composer Maurice Ravel.
   a. Show opposition; give equal emphasis.
   b. Show concession; emphasize sentence two.
   c. Show concession; emphasize sentence one.

6. Tastes in popular music change every generation or so.
   Those who like the new music always heap scorn on the music that preceded them.
   a. Show concession; emphasize sentence one.
   b. Show concession; emphasize sentence two.

EXERCISE: JOINING TO SHAPE SENTENCES

In the following exercises, you are asked to "shape" the sentences, joining them to show a particular point of view or emphasis. As an example, look at the following two sentences:

Strikes are an essential part of the labor-management bargaining process.
They are very costly and disruptive to both management and workers.

If the president of General Motors were going to write these two sentences as one sentence, he would surely want to "shape" it in such a way as to emphasize the bad aspects of strikes, and so he might write this:

Although strikes are an essential part of the labor-management bargaining process, they are very costly and disruptive to both management and workers.

The head of a labor union, on the other hand, would probably "shape" the sentence this way:

Strikes are an essential part of the labor-management bargaining process although they are very costly and disruptive to both management and workers.

To do the following exercises, you need to know, if you don't already, that two baseball teams in the American League, the New York Yankees and the Boston Red Sox, are unusually fierce rivals. As a result, Red Sox fans usually hate the Yankees, and Yankee fans usually hate the Red Sox.

The Yankees and the Red Sox

1. In 1978, the Boston Red Sox led the Eastern Division of the American League almost all year.
   The New York Yankees won the championship on the last day.
   a. Show opposition; join the sentences as you would if you were a neutral sportswriter.
   b. Show opposition; join them as you would if you were a New York Yankees fan.
   c. Show opposition; join them as you would if you were a Boston Red Sox fan.

2. Recently, the Yankees have spent great amounts of money trying to buy the best players available.
   They had little success in winning championships until recently.
   a. Show concession; join the sentences as you would if you were a solid supporter of the Yankees.
   b. Show concession; join the sentences as you would if you disliked the Yankees.

3. In 1986, the Red Sox won the American League championship.
   The New York Mets beat them in the World Series.
   a. Show opposition; join the sentences as you would if you were merely reporting the facts.

    b. Show opposition; join the sentences as you would if you were
       a Red Sox fan.

    c. Show opposition; join the sentences as you would if you were from
       New York.

4. The 1986 Red Sox had many great hitters, such as Wade Boggs and
    Jim Rice. They were a very slow team.

    a. Show concession; join the sentences as you would in a paragraph
       about the strengths of the Red Sox.

    b. Show concession; join the sentences as you would in a paragraph
       about their weaknesses.

5. Until the late 90s, the Yankees had excellent hitters.

    Their pitching was rather poor.

    a. Join the sentences as you would in a paragraph about the
       weaknesses of the Yankees.

    b. Join the sentences as you would in a paragraph about the strengths
       of the Yankees.

6. The Red Sox have excellent players.

    We Yankee fans can't stand them.

    a. Join these two sentences.

7. We Red Sox fans have had to admire the numerous great teams the
    Yankees have had over the years.

    They still drive us crazy.

    a. Join these two sentences.

REVIEW

In the following exercises, you will practice using modifiers and showing relation-ships of opposition and concession. The places where you should use a subordinator have been indicated (as in sentence 2 below).

What Carolyn Did on Her Summer Vacation

1. The previous summer, Carolyn had a job.

    The job was boring.

    The job was low paying.

    The job was working in the stockroom.

    It was the stockroom of a department store.

    The department store was small.

    The department store was local.

2. This summer, she hoped to find a job.
   The job would be more stimulating.
   The job would be with a better salary.
      [join: equal emphasis]
   For six weeks, she could find nothing.
   The weeks were long.
   The weeks were anxious.
   The weeks were in March and April.

3. She was discouraged by her search.
   Her search was fruitless.
   Her search was for a summer job.
      [join: emphasize second sentence]
   She kept up her effort.
   Her effort was painstaking.

4. Her patience and her searching were rewarded when she found
   two jobs.
   Her searching was careful.
   Her searching was scrupulous.
   The jobs were interesting looking.

5. One was a job.
   The job was standard.
   The job was moderately exciting.
   The job was in sales.
   The job was in a women's store.
   The store was in town.
      [join: equal emphasis]
   The other was a position.
   The position was extremely interesting.
   The position was in an advertising agency.
   The agency was in a distant city.

6. Carolyn liked the idea of a job.
   The job was well paying.
   The job was selling women's clothes.
      [join: emphasize second sentence]
   She did not like the idea of staying in town.

7. She was not excited about a position.

   The position was an internship.

   The position was with low wages.

       [join: emphasize second sentence]

   She was excited about a job.

   The job was glamorous.

   The job was in an advertising agency.

   The job was in a large city.

8. Carolyn's mother hoped she would take the job.

   Her mother was worried.

   The job was in sales.

   The job was near home.

       [join: decide whether to emphasize the first or second sentence or to give them equal emphasis.]

   Her father thought the internship was an opportunity.

   The internship was in advertising.

   The opportunity was great.

   The opportunity was to get experience.

   The experience was practical.

   The experience was in the business world.

9. Carolyn loved her home and the town where she grew up.

       [join: decide whether to emphasize the first or second sentence or to give them equal emphasis]

   She wanted to have the experience of living in a city and working at a kind of job.

   The experience was novel.

   The experience was challenging.

   The city was big.

   The kind of job was completely new.

10. The internship required work and hours.

    The work was very hard.

    The hours were very long.

    The hours were at low pay.

        [join: decide whether to emphasize the first or second sentence or to give them equal emphasis]

    Carolyn found it very rewarding.

The Black Death

1. Modern medicine has almost eliminated the danger.
   The danger is to humans.
   The danger is from plague.
       [join: emphasize second sentence]
   It still does not understand some forms.
   The forms are of this disease.
   This disease is terrifying.
   This disease is deadly.

2. The plague wiped out millions.
   The millions were of people.
   The millions were in China.
   The millions were in India.
   The millions were in the Middle East.
       [join: equal emphasis]
   Most Europeans had never heard of it.
       [subord] It struck them in the fourteenth century.

3. It is believed that people died.
   The people were between forty and fifty million.
   The people were in Europe.
   They died of plague.
   They died by the end of the century.

4. There are three forms of plague.
       [coord] Each form has different symptoms.

5. The form produces lymph nodes, blotches, destruction, and blackening.
   The form is the most famous.
   The lymph nodes are swollen.
   The blotches are purple.
   The blotches are caused by blood hemorrhaging.
   The hemorrhaging is under the skin.
   The destruction is of the nervous system.
   The blackening is of the body.
   The blackening is just before death.

6. Many historians believe that the rhyme refers to the blotches.
   The rhyme is sung by children.
   The rhyme is "Ring Around the Rosey."
   The blotches are under the skin.
   The blotches are caused by plague.
       [coord] They think that the last line, "All fall down," refers to the death
       of the victim.

7. The fourteenth-century Europeans tried cures and methods.
   The methods were preventive.
   The cures and methods were of every kind.
       [join: emphasize second sentence]
   They were unsuccessful.
       [subord] They did not know the virus was carried by fleas.

8. The victims were cared for.
   The victims were the very first.
   The caring was by their fellow citizens.
   Their fellow citizens were goodhearted.
       [join: emphasize second sentence]
   Victims were left to die.
   The victims were later.
   The dying was on their own.
       [coord] The entire social order collapsed.
   The social order was of Europe.
   The collapse was total.

9. People killed strangers.
   People killed gypsies.
   People burned Jews to death.
   The strangers were innocent.
   The burning was in many European cities.
       [join: emphasize first sentence]
   The Jews were dying.
   The dying was of plague.
   The dying was just as rapidly as anyone else.

10. The black death should teach us lessons.
    The black death was of the fourteenth century.
    The black death was in Europe.
    The lessons are about the effects.
    The effects are of fear.
    The effects are of ignorance.
    The effects are of superstition.

CHAPTER *5*

Arguing

FACTS AND OPINIONS

We all hold opinions about almost any subject. For example, Janet might believe that *Netty's Neighborhood* (a television show about a divorced black woman with three children who lives in Beverly Hills) realistically portrays the life of the black, single mother. Her neighbor, Anna, who is black, might believe that *Netty's Neighborhood* is about as close to being representative of a black family as Bill Cosby is to being the average American father.

Okay. There's no harm in either opinion. Janet and Anna can sit on their front steps on an evening and have the following dialogue.

> JANET: Netty's family sure represents the average American black family.
> ANNA: No, they don't.
> JANET: Yes, they do.
> ANNA: No, they don't.

And this dialogue can drag boringly on—and might if Janet and Anna were small children. ("That's my toy." "No, it isn't." "Yes, it is." "No, it isn't.") But they're not. Therefore, a more predictable turn for the discussion is that one woman starts supporting her position—often by citing facts.

> ANNA: According to the 1985 Census Report, black female heads of families have a median family income of $9,574. As a divorce lawyer to some of Hollywood's most affluent stars, Netty makes at least $135,000 annually.

JANET: Oh. Then they aren't representative financially?

ANNA: No, they are not.

Both women hold opinions. The difference between their viewpoints, how-ever, is that Anna possesses facts upon which to base her opinion; Janet doesn't. This is a vital difference.

On a daily basis, most of our opinions are relatively unimportant. Who, for example, really cares whether or not Janet thinks Netty's family is an average American family? Besides Anna, no one. However, if Janet were writing a term paper on the status of American black families with a single head of household and, relying solely on her opinion, cited Netty and her children as the average family, her professor might very well fail the paper. And for good reason; she would be wrong. Her opinion, to which she is entitled, would be unsupported by facts.

Many people think that because they are entitled to hold opinions on any subject they want, those opinions are just as good as anyone else's. But they aren't. An opinion is only as good as the facts behind it. Basic to critical thinkers and writers is the ability to distinguish between facts and opinions.

Fact versus Opinion

A fact can be verified. We can find out whether it is true or not, at least theoretically. Is it a fact that the moon is 568 feet from Earth? We can check it. Is it a fact that New York City is the largest city in the United States? Again, we can find out. Is it a fact that Ohio is the best state of all fifty? How would one check that out? It is a matter of opinion.

An opinion can be the result of a number of factors: a knowledge of facts, an unexamined acceptance of others' opinions (those of our parents, our friends, or the nightly news anchorperson), a bias (often unconscious), a "gut response" (it just feels "right"), or a combination of these and other factors. One of the goals of a college education is to help students form opinions founded upon an examination of the facts.

EXERCISE

Based on your own knowledge, decide which of the following statements are facts and which are opinions:

- The Los Angeles Lakers won the 1987 National Basketball Association championship.
- Chicago is situated on the southwest shore of Lake Michigan.

- The United States Navy is the finest fighting force in the world today.
- Cats are a lot more fun than dogs.
- The Constitution of the United States was approved in Philadelphia, Pennsylvania.
- As a result of the Watergate investigations, President Nixon resigned from office.
- Sacramento, California, possesses as many Mexican restaurants as a porcupine has quills—they're everywhere.
- In July 1987, the world's population grew to 5 billion.
- The movie *Full Metal Jacket* was rated R.
- It should have been rated NC-17 because of all the violence in it.
- William Shakespeare is the world's greatest playwright.
- Ted Williams, of the Boston Red Sox, was the finest hitter in baseball during the 1940s and 1950s.

Distinguishing Fact from Opinion

As you can see, it is not always easy to distinguish fact from opinion. Let's look at the case of Ted Williams. We know that he was the last player to bat .400 for a season and that he had a higher lifetime batting average and hit more home runs than any other player of the 40s and 50s. Those statistics make it sound like he was the best hitter of the time. But Joe DiMaggio was also an extremely good hitter, and he got hits in fifty-six consecutive games, a record most baseball people think is the greatest hitting feat ever. So is Williams still the greatest hitter of the time?

Sometimes whether we consider a statement to be a fact or an opinion will depend upon its source. In Williams's case, we would probably accept it as a fact that he was the best batsman if a number of respected authorities on baseball said he was. If, however, your roommate, who is a diehard Boston Red Sox fan, said Williams was the greatest, then you might question whether it was fact or opinion; it still might be a fact, or it might be the opinion of an overly enthusiastic fan.

Another, perhaps more difficult aspect of distinguishing fact from opinion has to do with interpretation. Take, for example, the statement, "Shakespeare is the world's greatest playwright." In order to determine whether that's fact or opinion, we must determine not only the source of the statement ("Said who?") but also what the source meant by "greatest." Is a great playwright designated so by the number of plays he or she wrote? By the quality of the plays? (And how do we determine a play's quality?) Is the best play the funniest and most entertaining? The most thought provoking? The list of questions we need to answer in order to determine whether that statement is fact or opinion goes on and on and on. Finally, because we cannot answer with any certainty all the questions, we must assume that the statement, "Shakespeare is the world's greatest playwright," is an opinion, perhaps a reasoned and thoughtful opinion, but an opinion nonetheless.

Facts and "Facts"

That a fact is a fact does not mean necessarily that it is correct. It may appear to be so. However, if it is based on false or inaccurate information, it may be downright wrong. Remember that for centuries, it was a fact that the Earth was flat. Or take our friends Anna and Janet. Anna convinced Janet that *"Netty's Neighborhood"* did not represent a typical black family by using a statistic, the fact that in 1985 the median family income of a single-parent, female-headed black family was $9,574. Anna got that figure from the 1985 U.S. Census Report, a fairly reliable source for that kind of information.

However, Anna might have remembered the figure incorrectly, inverted the numbers ($9,754?), gotten the information from a supermarket rag like the *National Enquirer,* or just made it up to win her point. Janet, however, believed in Anna's honesty, respected the statistic's source, and had faith in her friend's memory. But if Janet were assigned to write a term paper on the status of single-parent, black families in America in the 1980s, she'd be well advised to check the Census Report herself to make sure her friend did have the fact right.

EXERCISE

Relying on your own knowledge and judgment, determine which of the following are statements of fact and which statements of opinion, and discuss with your classmates the reasons why:

- The sun rises in the east.
- Teenagers spend more money on renting home movies than they do on going to movie theaters.
- Agatha Christie's play *The Mousetrap* played longer in London than any play in the history of English theater.
- It is by far the best play of the modern English stage.

- More people have enjoyed this play in the past twenty years than have enjoyed everything written by Shakespeare put together.
- According to a 1986 Yale University study, a single woman of thirty has a 20 percent chance of marrying.
- By the time she is thirty-five, her chances are only 5 percent.
- Anything is fair in love and war.
- People who own pit bull terriers have the same moral values as drug runners and thieves.
- The Golden Gate Bridge was fifty years old in 1987.
- It is the most beautiful bridge in the world.
- It is one of the main tourist attractions in San Francisco.

EVALUATING EVIDENCE AND SHAPING YOUR ARGUMENT

A lot of the problems students and professional people face are issues in which it is important to sort out facts from opinions and, in the case of the opinions, decide how much they can be trusted. A group of people may think that capital punishment deters crime and ought to be the mandatory sentence for murder. In order to convince the state of this view, they would try to prove that the death penalty is a greater deterrent to crime than life imprisonment is. They might examine homicide rates in states that had capital punishment and in those that didn't, they might look at the before-and-after homicide rates in a state that abolished the death penalty, or they might study the rates of homicide in a state before and after a much publicized execution.

In fact, scholars have done just that, and this group might cite the work of Isaac Ehrlich, who published a study in 1975 which shows that a decline in executions in the United States led to a corresponding increase in murders. Unhappily for Ehrlich, a group of other social scientists found his work seriously flawed. Ehrlich's findings were based entirely on evidence he gathered from 1962 to 1974, a time when, it is true, the number of executions declined and the number of homicides rose. The trouble is that the increase in the number of homicides was part of an overall rise in crime—of all sorts—a fact that Ehrlich didn't take into consideration in his study. Therefore, his findings were debunked because there was no reason to think that the rise in murders was the result of the decline in executions.

Professional people are often asked to offer suggestions, give reports, choose between possible options, or make recommendations. A grocer might have to decide from which of two vegetable distributors to buy; a broker might have to advise a client on investment options; a city manager might have to report to the city council on whether or not to allow a twenty-story Holiday Inn to be built downtown. The quality of all such decisions depends entirely on how well the issue is examined and how carefully the various facts, opinions, and inferences are examined and used.

Preparation

There are four important things to remember in dealing with arguments:

1. *Don't make up your mind about the issue ahead of time.* You may have believed for years that X was true and Y was false, and your family or your friends may still believe it, but that doesn't mean they're right. If you're smart, you'll be aware that such beliefs are often based on weak or biased information (or no information at all, just prejudice). Wait until you've examined all the evidence. Remember that you may have just as many prejudices and groundless opinions as the next person.

2. *Don't fall for the fallacy of "common sense."* Common sense leads to all sorts of erroneous conclusions. For instance, legislatures have learned that increasing criminal punishments for particular crimes doesn't always lead to a reduction in those crimes, as common sense would suggest it would. Why not? For one thing, a jury will often hesitate to convict a person of a particular crime if the penalty for it seems disproportionately severe. When the crime then goes unpunished, where is the deterrent value of the severe penalty? And severe penalties for lesser crimes may lead to more severe crimes. For instance, if we instituted the death penalty for dealing certain dangerous drugs, then drug dealers would realize that they might as well kill in order to prevent being caught, since the penalty would be the same anyway. Common sense once told us that the world was flat, that the sun rotated around the Earth. Common sense isn't always wrong, but it often is.

3. *When examining an issue, sort out the facts from the opinions.* In the case of opinions, ask yourself whose opinions they are. Are they likely to be biased for some reason? Are they likely to be based on self-interest? Are they "expert" opinions, ones that should be given strong consideration?

4. *When "facts" contradict each other, consider who has produced the contradictory "facts" and which side has the greater weight of "facts."*

For instance, in the 1970s and 1980s, numerous studies carried out by independent researchers consistently showed that cigarette smoking and other forms of tobacco use were extremely harmful to people's health. A much smaller number of studies commissioned by the tobacco industry showed that smoking was not very harmful. These two sets of "facts" clashed with each other, but the antismoking studies were more credible because they came from independent researchers and were more numerous than the others.

Arranging Your Argument

When you write, don't ignore the other side. The writer who argues only his or her own point is much less effective than the writer who takes his or her opponent into consideration. How do you feel about someone who doesn't seem to listen to your side in a dispute and just keeps arguing his or her own views? How, on the other hand, do you feel about a person who says, "Yes, I see what you mean, and I agree with you about so and so" before going on to give his or her own opinions?

When you organize the paragraphs of an argument essay, you may be tempted to write an introduction, a paragraph covering the pro side, a paragraph covering the con side, and a conclusion. On the face of it, this seems to make a lot of sense, but it is usually not a good idea.

Pro or con paragraphs usually feature two problems. One is that they are like sacks. You can throw everything into one of them, but then there's no order inside it; within the sack everything is a hodgepodge. The other problem is that the length of such paragraphs often fools the writer into thinking the paragraph is well developed when it isn't.

Suppose, for instance, that in 1948 an executive for a major American railroad was preparing a paper in which he was going to argue that his company should immediately begin replacing its steam locomotives with diesels. This would be a pro/con issue, and he would have plenty of opposition. Suppose he wrote a paragraph like the following:

> Diesel locomotives offer numerous advantages over steam. They are easier
> to maintain. They create less wear on tracks, ties, and roadbed. They offer
> greater flexibility in use. And they are cheaper to run.

He would certainly get nowhere because he has failed to explain *why* they are easier to maintain, *why* they create less wear on tracks, *how* they are more flexible, and finally, *why* they are cheaper to run and *how much* cheaper they are. His argument would be completely vulnerable to attack. In short, rather than one paragraph of advantages, he would need at least four—and possibly more if any of these points was sufficiently complex.

Generally speaking, there are three ways to organize pro/con arguments. One is to begin with all the points on one side and then to conclude with all the points on the other side. In cases like this, most writers like to start with the position they oppose, the one they think is the weaker, and conclude with the side they favor, the stronger one in their view. Let's say you want to argue that all grading systems should be abolished in college. You might organize your essay as follows. *Remember that this outline does not indicate the paragraph divisions of an essay, only the sequence of the argument.*

Introduction
Arguments in favor of grading systems
Arguments against grading systems
Conclusion

If the argument involves more than one issue, the organization will naturally be less straightforward. Suppose you wanted to argue that a credit/no credit grading system should be instituted instead of the letter-grade system. You would have to deal with the arguments for and against each of these systems. So your organization might look like this (again, the outline does not indicate the paragraphing):

Introduction
Arguments in favor of letter grades
Arguments against letter grades
Arguments against credit/no credit grades
Arguments in favor of credit/no credit grades
Conclusion

A third way of handling these kinds of arguments is to argue each issue point by point instead of in separate paragraphs or sections of the paper.

Writing Your Argument

While you are analyzing your information, try to decide which side has the better arguments. You may, of course, decide that A is correct and X is wrong and then realize, while writing, that X is really right. There's nothing wrong with that; it happens to writers all the time. But it is certainly inconvenient. It's much better to think everything through as carefully as possible first so you don't surprise yourself.

When you're sure about what you think, try to write your essay in such a way that you emphasize the point you will finally want to make. For example, suppose you are writing on the topic "Bananas should be outlawed." You have read the relevant documents and have the following list of points:

Facts	**Opinions**
Last year 136 people were injured in banana-related accidents.	Herbert Clutch believes that the yellow color of bananas causes jaundice.
Medical studies have shown that bananas are high in potassium, a preventative of heart disease.	The Mothers Opposed to Seductive Stuff (MOSS) argue that bananas have an immoral shape. (This group also opposes flagpoles.)
A survey by the Banana Institute showed that 96.7 percent of cereal eaters believe that sliced bananas improve the taste of their cereal.	After nearly choking to death on a banana, Arcana Wedgefeather reports that she and others like her grow nauseated in the produce section of supermarkets.
Since most bananas come to the United States from foreign countries, they have a slight negative effect on our trade balance.	

You decide that the opinions are weak and the facts are on the side of bananas. Mr. Clutch and Ms. Wedgefeather have no medical credentials to support their views, while the potassium studies were undertaken by impartial researchers. In a population of well over 250 million, 136 injured people isn't very many. The Banana Institute survey is suspicious (96.7 percent of people never agree on anything), but in your experience most people do like bananas. Meanwhile, MOSS seems to be a group of cranks.

While you want to report the arguments for banning the banana, you should word your paragraphs in such a way that you try to affect how the reader will view this material. You might write your essay in this way:

> While a move to outlaw the sale of bananas has sprung up in some parts of the country, the proponents of this view have little credibility. For instance, a group calling itself Mothers Opposed to Seductive Stuff argues that the very form of the banana tends to undermine our morals, but no other group concerned with morals has ever found the shape of the banana offensive or indecent, and MOSS would even like to get rid of flagpoles. It has also been argued that

bananas can have a sickening effect in the supermarket on those who have had accidents with them, but no medical evidence supports this view.

Some statistics indicate that bananas do create some problems. In the United States last year, 136 people were injured in banana-related accidents, and since most of our bananas come from foreign countries, they have a slight negative effect on our trade balance. But 136 accidents in a population of over 250 million is very few, and the trade balance problem is too small to be important.

Writing your argument in this way, you will not have to review every single point in detail when you get to your conclusion because you have already shown that the anti-bananas arguments have little merit.

In the event that you don't feel the case is so one-sided, you should, of course, write the pro and con points in a more balanced way. Then your conclusion will have to sum up the main points on both sides. You may even decide—and write your conclusion to show—that you aren't able to make up your mind on this issue with the evidence you have. That is a perfectly reasonable and intelligent conclusion to come to in many cases.

*A*ssignments *and Readings*

DECIDING CARMEN HERRERA'S FUTURE

Difficult pro/con issues can come up in our personal lives just as they emerge at the local or national level. Often these personal issues involve values that are just as important as those behind the big public issues, and they usually involve passions and prejudices as well. It is essential for our happiness and well-being that we try to resolve our own problems as objectively as we can, for our prejudices and feelings—and those of our friends and relatives—can often lead us into trouble, or at least lead our lives in undesirable directions. The following case is such an issue.

Carmen Herrera's family emigrated from El Salvador to the United States ten years ago when Carmen was in the second grade. Carmen got excellent grades in elementary school and did so well in high school (she has maintained a 3.8 GPA) that Ms. Aguilar, her guidance counselor, is encouraging her to continue her education by attending the University of Mountainfield, a prestigious state university, in New Berryford, a city two hundred miles away. Although Carmen has no specific career goals, she enjoys school and would like to continue.

As the oldest of five children, she also feels a responsibility to her family. Since their move to the United States, they have been living in a three-bedroom apartment, saving for a down payment on a house. Carmen has been contributing some of the money she makes working part time as a clerk-typist to the house fund, but she realizes that she will not be able to work during the academic year if she attends school full time and must meet the grade-point average required of a scholarship student.

Ms. Aguilar feels that because of her high school record, test scores, and financial need, Carmen has an excellent chance of being awarded a scholarship that would cover her tuition, books, and room and board.

A friend, Alicia Casillas, is planning to attend a small private business school in town, Radcliffe Business College, which guarantees job placement at the end of an eight-month training program in secretarial skills, including word processing. Although the program would take some initial investment from her parents, Carmen thinks that she could easily pay this back and in a few years contribute enough to the house fund so that her family could purchase their own home. Then she could still go to college if she wanted to.

Reading Assignment

Pre-reading

Before you read the following recommendations from Carmen's family and acquaintances, think about her dilemma. Although you know little about her situation, you should consider the differences between liberal arts and vocational educations. In general, what are the benefits of a liberal arts education? What are those of vocational education? As you think about this issue, remember to take notes so you won't forget your thoughts as you read other people's.

Reading

Carmen has been talking to people about her problem and has gotten the following reactions. Remember to read actively, taking notes in the margins or on another sheet of paper.

VARIOUS COMMENTS ON CARMEN'S DILEMMA

Ms. Aguilar (her high school counselor): "It doesn't matter that you   1
don't know what you might major in at college. Most majors
require only two years to complete, so you have plenty of time to

find out what you like. Meanwhile, you'll be taking courses in a number of disciplines and getting the kind of liberal education you're going to need in order to succeed in whatever field you decide to enter. You know, hardly anyone from this school ever goes to college, except perhaps to the community college, or even thinks about getting a scholarship. You would set a wonderful example to the younger students if you made it."

Mr. and Mrs. Herrera (her parents): "*When* we get a house or even   2
whether we get a house is not your worry. You are young. You have to live your life and do what is best for you. One of the reasons we moved from El Salvador was so that you children could have opportunities that we were denied, and the biggest one is education. You must get the best education you can."

Victor Oquendo (her boyfriend): "You can't afford to go away to   3
college even if you get a scholarship. Where are you going to get spending money for clothes, movies, things like that? Are you going to hit your parents up every time you want to go shopping? Every time you want a hamburger? I think you're being unrealistic. You should stay here, go to Radcliffe, and get a good job, help your parents, and save for the future."

Mr. Hansen (her employer at ABC Clerical Services): "You're a terrific   4
word processor. If you go to Radcliffe and learn something about programming, I'd be happy to hire you full time. In fact, I'll keep the position open for you. It's guaranteed. And, if you want, you can keep your part-time job here. We'll make arrangements to fit your schedule at Radcliffe."

Alicia Casillas (her friend): "I'd be scared of college, a place   5
like Mountainfield or something. It's different. The people are different. You wouldn't know anybody. Besides, if you go to Radcliffe you can keep your job at ABC and start making *big* money in eight months instead of maybe four years from now. Remember Dwana Brown, who graduated two years ago? She's working for

Bechtel now and makes $24,000 a year. She's even got her own apartment!"

Maria Herrera (her fourteen-year-old sister): "I'd give anything to go 6 to Mountainfield. Think of all the new people you'll meet. Think of the courses you could take—music, dance, drama—not like in this school where you have to sit through boring classes where the teacher reads from the textbook. At Mountainfield you'd really get good teachers. Plus, if you go and do well, then Mom and Dad might help me go to someplace like that. I don't think I'll be able to get the scholarships you can."

Thomas Herrera (her sixteen-year-old brother): "Our parents will 7 never get a house with the prices what they are around here unless we both keep helping them. And you really could help them out if you were earning a decent salary and living at home. I think we owe it to them. They gave up a lot to get us out of El Salvador and give us a chance. We should help them out now."

Post-reading

Go over the background to Carmen's problem, listing the most important facts. Then go through the opinions of her friends and relatives. In each case, ask yourself whether each one is expressing a fact or an opinion and list the facts and opinions separately. In the case of the facts, you will want to indicate how important each one is. (You could use a star system, as in rating the movies, with four-star facts, three-star facts, and so on.) With the opinions, it will be important to note not just what they are but also who holds them. Which opinions seem to be based on a genuine concern for Carmen and which seem based more on the concerns of the people holding the opinions? You could then rate the opinions in order of value also.

In examining the opinions, it is important for you to think about each one yourself. It is perfectly possible for a person with no axe of his or her own to grind to have a pretty worthless opinion of a matter, just as it's possible that an opinion based on self-interest might really express an important point. You will need to think for yourself about the financial realities and future consequences for Carmen's life that are involved in either of her two possible courses of action.

Essay Assignment

Write an essay in which you examine the evidence for and against Carmen's attending the University of Mountainfield and Radcliffe Business College. Carefully considering both options, come to your own conclusion about which school she ought to attend.

Pre-writing

Before you begin organizing your essay, review the section "Evaluating Your Evidence and Shaping Your Argument." In particular, keep in mind the following four points:

1. Be sure to include the strongest arguments of both sides.

2. Don't make "sack paragraphs," with all the arguments on one side in one paragraph and all the arguments on the other side in a second one.

3. Remember that a statement isn't an argument; statements are often like topic sentences—that is, sentences that have to be explained or backed up.

4. Make sure your conclusion is based solidly on the arguments preceding it. It should reflect the strengths and weaknesses of the arguments covered in your essay, not be merely your own unsupported opinion tacked on at the end.

Writing

Your introduction should briefly outline the issue and state your thesis, which may well be your recommendation. Your paragraphs will probably pretty much follow the essay assignment itself, and your conclusion, of course, will either make a recommendation or restate your thesis. Be sure to review the Writer's Checklist on pages 338–340 as you work on this assignment.

SHOULD HIGH SCHOOL STUDENTS WORK?

In an earlier age, it was rare for high school students to work, unless they had to do so in order to help support their families. Those who did work part time usually did so only for two or three hours after school, leaving the evenings and the weekends for study and socializing. The relatively small amounts of money teenagers made at these jobs generally went toward financing dates or into a college-saving fund.

Now, however, the proliferation of franchise businesses, particularly fast-food outlets, that seek inexperienced, easily trained young people to do repetitious work at the minimum wage has created many job opportunities for teens. At the same time, teenagers have become a prime target for advertisers, who bombard them with glossy inducements to buy the latest in clothes and electronics. The pressure is on, particularly among teens who come from working- and middle-class families, to get jobs and to work long hours in order to get as much of their own disposable income as possible.

As a result, the issue of whether—or how much—teenagers who don't have to work should work has gradually become a major concern to parents, educators, psychologists, and sociologists, who worry about the effects of part-time work on the physical, educational, psychological, and social well-being of teenagers. However, other professionals, especially those employers who benefit from the low wages awarded to teenagers, maintain that teenagers profit, more than just financially, from working because they learn responsibility and become accustomed to adult life.

Reading Assignment

Pre-reading

As a way of beginning to think about this topic, you might consider these questions on the basis of your own experience or that of others you know: What is positive about high school students holding jobs during the school year? What is negative about it? What are the issues involved besides the problem of work interfering with school? Take notes that you can refer to after you've read what others have to say on the subject.

Reading

Remember to take notes in the margins or on a separate sheet of paper as you read the following four essays.

PART-TIME WORK ETHIC: SHOULD TEENS GO FOR IT?
Dennis McLellan

John Fovos landed his first part-time job—as a box boy at Alpha Beta   1
on West Olympic—the summer after his sophomore year at Fairfax
High School in Los Angeles. "I wanted to be independent," he said,
"and I felt it was time for me to see what the world was really like."

Now an 18-year-old senior, Fovos works the late shift at the   2
supermarket stocking shelves four nights a week. He saves about $50
a week, but most of his paycheck goes to his car payment and
membership at a health spa. "The rest is for food—what I don't eat
at home—and clothes."

Shelley Staats went to work part time as a secretary for a Cen-   3
tury 21 office when she was 15. Since then, she has worked as a
cashier for a marine products company, scooped ice cream at a
Baskin-Robbins, cashiered at a Video Depot and worked as a "floater"
at May Co.

The Newport Harbor High School senior currently works about   4
25 hours a week in the lingerie department at the new Broadway in
Costa Mesa. Although she saves about $200 a month for college,
she said she works "to support myself: my car and clothes and just
stuff I do, like going out."

Working also has helped her to learn to manage both her time   5
and money, Staats said, and her work in the department store is
providing experience for a future career in fashion merchandising.

But, she acknowledged, there are times when working while   6
going to school has taken its toll.

"Last year I was sleeping in my first-period class half the time,"   7
admitted Staats, who occasionally has forgone football games and
school dances because of work. "After a while, it just wears you out."

Nathan Keethe, a Newport Harbor High School senior who   8
works more than 20 hours a week for an exterminating service,
admits to sometimes feeling like the odd man out when he sees that
fellow students "are out having a good time after school and I'm
working. But then I think there's a lot of other kids out there working,
too, and it doesn't seem so unusual."

Indeed, what clearly was the exception 40 years ago is now   9
the rule.

Fovos, Staats and Keethe are riding the crest of a wave of   10
part-time student employees that began building at the end of
World War II and has steadily increased to the present. In 1981,
according to a study by the National Center for Education Statistics,
80% of high school students had held part-time jobs by the time
they graduated.

Part-time work during the school years traditionally has been   11
viewed as an invaluable experience for adolescents, one that builds

character, teaches responsibility and prepares them for entering the adult world.

But the authors of a **provocative** new book challenge conven- 12 tional wisdom, contending that an over-commitment to work during the school years "may make teenagers economically wealthy but psychologically poor. . . ."

The book, *When Teenagers Work: The Psychological and Social* 13 *Costs of Adolescent Employment,* is by Ellen Greenberger, a developmental psychologist and professor of social ecology at the University of California, Irvine, and Laurence Steinberg, a professor of child and family studies at the University of Wisconsin.

Based on national research data and on the authors' own 14 study of more than 500 working and non-working students at four Orange County [California] high schools, the book reports that:

- Extensive part-time employment during the school year may undermine youngsters' education. Students who work long hours are more likely to cut back on courses at school, taking easier classes and avoiding tougher ones. And, say the authors, long hours of work begun early in the school years increase the likelihood of dropping out.

- Working leads less often to the accumulation of savings or financial contributions to the family than to a higher level of spending on cars, clothes, stereos, concerts and other luxury items.

- Working appears to promote, rather than deter, some forms of delinquent behavior. About 30% of the youngsters in their first part-time job have given away goods or services; 18% have taken things other than money from work; 5–1/2% have taken money from work; and 17% have worked under the influence of drugs or alcohol, according to the Orange County study.

- Working long hours under stressful conditions leads to increased alcohol and marijuana use.

---

provocative: challenging, stimulating

- Teen-age employment—typically in dull or monotonous jobs
  for which the sole motivation is the paycheck—often leads
  to increased **cynicism** about working.

Moreover, the authors contend that adolescents who work long   15
hours may develop the superficial social skills of an adult, but by
devoting too much time to a job they severely curtail the time
needed for **reflection, introspection** and identity experimentation
that is required to develop true maturity.

Such findings lead Greenberger and Steinberg to conclude "that   16
the benefits of working to the development of adolescents have been
overestimated, while the costs have been underestimated."

"We don't want to be read as saying that kids shouldn't work   17
during the school year," Greenberger said in an interview. "Our argument is with over-commitment to work: That working long hours
may interfere with other very important goals of the growing years."

The authors place the blame partly on the types of jobs available   18
to young people today. By working in unchallenging, monotonous jobs
in fast-food restaurants or retail shops, they contend, teenagers learn
few new skills, have little opportunity for meaningful contact with
adults and seldom gain work experience that will lead to future careers.

"Parents and schools," Greenberger said, "should wake up from   19
the dream that having a kid who works 30 hours a week is promoting his or her transition to adulthood."

Greenberger and Steinberg's findings, not surprisingly, do not   20
sit well with the fast-food industry.

"The fast-food industry is probably the largest employer of   21
young people in the United States," said Paul Mitchell, spokesperson
for Carl Karcher Enterprises, which employs thousands of teenagers
in its Carl's Jr. restaurants.

"For most of those young people," Mitchell said, "it's their first   22
job, the first time they are told that you make a product a certain
way, the first time they work with money, the first time they are
made aware to be there on time and do it right . . . and it's just a
tremendous working experience."

Terry Capatosto, a spokeswoman for McDonald's, calls Green-   23
berger and Steinberg's findings "absurd, to say the least."

---

cynicism: scornful, sneering attitude;   **reflection:** thoughtfulness;
introspection: self-examination

"Working at McDonald's contributes tremendously to [young   24
people's] personal development and work ethic," said Capatosto,
noting that countless McDonald's **alumni** have gone on to professional careers and that about half of the people at all levels of
McDonald's management, including the company's president and
chairman of the board, started out as crew people.

"The whole idea of getting students out in the community   25
during the time they're also a student is a very productive thing to
do," said Jackie Oakes, college and career guidance specialist at
Santa Ana High School.

Although she feels most students work "for the extras kids   26
want," Oakes said they worked for a variety of reasons, including
earning money to go on a trip with the school band and saving for
college.

As for work taking time away from studying, Oakes said, "I think   27
if a kid isn't interested in studying, having a job doesn't impact that."

Newport Harbor High School's Nathan Keethe, who usually   28
earns B's, doesn't think he'd devote more time to schoolwork if he
weren't working. "Not really, because even when I wasn't working
I wasn't too devoted to school," he said, adding that "for somebody
who is, I wouldn't recommend working too much. I do think it would
interfere."

Fairfax High's John Fovos, who works about 27 hours a week,   29
however, said his grade-point average actually has risen since he
began working part time. The motivation? "My parents told me if
my job hindered my grades, they'd ask me to quit," he said.

Although she acknowledges that some teen-age workers may   30
experience growth in such areas as self-reliance and improved work
habits, Greenberger said, "It's not evident that those things couldn't
be **realized** in other settings as well. There's no evidence that you
have to be a teen-age drone in order to grow in those areas."

As for the notion that "it would be great to get kids out into the   31
workplace because they'll learn," Greenberger said that "the news is
not so good. On the one hand we find that relatively little time on the
job is spent using anything resembling higher-order **cognitive** skills,"
she said. "Computation nowadays is often done automatically by the

---

alumni: graduates;   **realized:** made real or actual;   **cognitive:** process
of acquiring knowledge

cash register; so much for practicing arithmetic. Kids do extremely little writing and reading [on the job]. There's also very little job training. In fact, most of the youngsters in our survey reported their job could be done by somebody with a grade-school education or less."

MCJOBS
Ben Wildavsky

According to the standard lament, the 18 million jobs created in   1
America since the 1982 recession are an **illusory** measure of economic expansion; a nation of hamburger-flippers, goes the argument, is a nation in decline.

As the **archetypal** fast food establishment, serving close to 7 per-   2
cent of the U.S. population every day and employing a remarkable 1 out of 15 first-time job seekers, McDonald's has been a frequent target for those **expounding** the "dead-end jobs" thesis. . . .

While the typical complaints critics voice about McDonald's   3
certainly have some basis in reality—annual turnover often surpasses 100 percent, and it is not difficult to find crew members who complain of high pressure and low wages—the overall picture is more positive. A closer look at the people who work at McDonald's shows that a surprising number of burger-flippers advance through the ranks and enjoy the benefits that go with managerial responsibility in a demanding business. More important, most employees who pass through McDonald's gain the kinds of skills that help them get better jobs. . . .

Marion Foran started working at McDonald's in July 1973, a   4
month after graduating from high school in Helena, Montana. She planned to attend the University of Northern Arizona at Flagstaff, and her mother told her to go out and get a job. "In my family," says Foran, "there were five kids, and it was assumed that if you wanted to go to college you'd have to pay your own way." She was hired at $1.60 an hour, intending only to stay until she had financed her first year of college. . . .

Soon, Foran was awarded the first in a series of promotions.   5
She became a second assistant manager, working six days a week

---

illusory: deceptive;   **archetypal:** original model or type;
expounding: arguing for

supervising employees, hiring and training crew members, taking inventory, and helping with the financial reports, all for the grand sum of $350 a month.

By the time she was 18, Foran was first assistant manager, had 6 purchased a new Volkswagen bug with her own money, and had trained two new second assistants. . . .

At age 20 . . . she moved to Las Vegas and started work as a 7 manager trainee at a McDonald's in a poor section of town, a far cry from small-town Montana. By 1978, Foran was promoted to restaurant manager and was asked to open a brand new outlet on the Las Vegas Strip. . . .

After managing another Las Vegas store for one and a half years, 8 Foran was promoted to area supervisor in 1982 at age 26; she oversaw operations at five or six stores and earned $24,000 a year, with the added benefits of a company car and weekends off. After two more years, she became a field consultant, then a training assistant, running the Basic Operations Course that all would-be McDonald's managers must take. . . .

In April, 1988, she started her current job as a professor at 9 Hamburger University, the McDonald's manager-training center at company headquarters in Illinois, famous for issuing each graduate of its one- and two-week intensive courses a degree in Hamburgerology with a minor in Fries. . . .

A less spectacular but perhaps more typical example of some- 10 one who has progressed through the ranks is David Fisher. Fisher was recently promoted to second assistant at a McDonald's in a suburb of Washington. The average salary nationally for those in his position is $19,500, with full medical benefits. . . .

Fisher disagrees with people who think McDonald's jobs lead 11 nowhere. He is exasperated by the high turnover that plagues the tight D.C.-area labor market—"some kids just hop from job to job"— and thinks that too many employees expect something for nothing: "There's an amazing amount of opportunity available, but no one's going to hand it to you." He cites three successful second assistants, all in their early 20s, who started at the bottom—one from Korea, one from Nigeria, and one from Jamaica. Apparently, recent immigrants, who may find few other jobs as easily available, can achieve considerable mobility at McDonald's. . . .

Not everyone paints as rosy a picture of McDonald's as those   12
who have made it. In addition to low wages and a hot, high-speed
work environment, some employees complain of poor treatment by
managers. Mark Kershaw, a 33-year-old manager from Ogden, Utah,
who started at McDonald's in high school and came back as a manager when a back injury caused him to lose his railroad job, agrees
that "there are some managers who treat them like slaves." He tries
to avoid this, and has gotten to know his employees well, to the
point of advising them about problems outside the workplace. . . .

Lou DeRosa, the 29-year-old manager of a Connecticut   13
McDonald's, grew up in a tough New Haven neighborhood. He
offers a blunt assessment of McDonald's jobs that seems realistic for
many of those who take them: "This is a survival job. A lot of people
can't handle it. This is something that shows you if you can work or
not. It's not like a department store where you can lay back." DeRosa
stresses the time constraints and high standards crew members must
work to: "It separates the men from the boys." . . .

While the number of success stories to be found within   14
McDonald's belies the notion that jobs there are **irredeemably**
worthless, these examples are not intended to suggest that such
career paths are typical, only that they are possible. The vast majority of those who work at McDonald's come and go with great frequency, and not everyone sees anything wrong with this. "*All* jobs
are dead-end," says Walter Williams, professor of economics at
George Mason University. "We as a nation suffer from the Horatio
Alger myth, where a guy comes in as a porter and becomes president of the company." The typical person, according to Williams,
achieves upward mobility *across* jobs, not within a job. This
process involves working at a particular job, gaining experience,
finding out about other jobs, and moving on. . . .

What exactly do fast food jobs teach? A 1984 study by Ivan   15
Charner and Bryna Fraser . . . attempted to answer that question. . . .
As might be expected, high percentages of employees reported
learning such directly job-related skills as operating a cash register
(80 percent) and operating food preparation machines (85 percent).
Seventy percent of employees believed they had learned "some" or

---

irredeemably: hopelessly

"a great deal" about training other workers, 50 percent learned supervisory skills, and 40 percent learned inventory control, while fewer than 20 percent developed bookkeeping or accounting skills.

More important than the specific skills learned are what Charner 16 and Fraser call "general employability skills," the kinds of qualities an employee—particularly a young person with limited work experience—must possess to be successful in any job. Ninety-four percent of employees said their jobs helped them learn teamwork, 89 percent learned how to deal with customers, and 69 percent developed an awareness of how a business runs. Respondents learned such crucial work skills as taking directions (73 percent), getting along with coworkers (75 percent), being on time (57 percent), finishing an assigned task (64 percent), taking responsibility for mistakes (65 percent), coming to work regularly (59 percent), and being well groomed (44 percent). . . .

The not-so-hidden secret of McDonald's success lies in the 17 **meticulous** operating procedures for food preparation and service that all its stores follow. Before being shown the ropes by a crew trainer, new employees watch an orientation video that stresses neatness and hygiene. Employees are told they must bathe daily, have clean hair and teeth, keep moustaches and sideburns trimmed, wear only neutral nail polish, and wash their hands with soap before and after using any work station.

Another video, "Counter 1: The Six Steps," teaches the funda 18 mentals of customer service. Crew members are told to be at the counter before the customer arrives, to look him or her in the eye, and to smile. A beaming teenager is shown greeting a customer with an upbeat "Good afternoon! May I take your order please?" The narrator instructs crew people, "Vary the greeting and the tone of your voice from customer to customer—you don't want to sound like a robot." . . .

Training tapes with titles like "Fries," "Opening the Store," and 19 "A Study in Breakfast" are used to teach various stations and responsibilities, with detailed station observation checklists used both as a reference point for crew people and a performance assessment tool for managers. No point is too small to be left out—making french fries

---

meticulous: extremely careful and precise

involves 15 separate steps, with seven more to be followed for bagging—though a number of tasks require more human initiative than a checklist can spell out. If counter people are not busy, for example, they should help their coworkers, clean the counter, and replenish supplies. Those working the grill are guided by a timer, but must rely on visual inspection to decide exactly when to turn the patties. And counter people have standing instructions to replace any items dropped by customers at no cost, informing the manager afterwards so the product can be accounted for in the store's inventory. . . .

By looking at the qualities that large employers of entry-level   20
personnel say they are looking for, it becomes clear that these closely **coincide** with the employability skills taught in fast food jobs. Alan Wurtzel, chairman of Circuit City, a chain of electronics stores based in Richmond, Virginia, says that when his stores hire new cashiers and stock clerks, specific skills are unimportant. "The most important thing we're looking for is attitude and energy. We want people who are reliable, presentable, clean shaven, honest, can get along with coworkers, and can follow directions." When a new store opens, Wurtzel says, 10 applicants have to be screened for every one hired; people with these basic work skills are apparently not easy to find.

Ninety percent of Mike O'Shea's new employees have fast food   21
experience, mostly at McDonald's. While the 20-year-old assistant manager of a downtown Chicago shoe store says he is unimpressed by applicants with a string of short-term hitches at fast food restaurants, he understands people who rise to a certain level and decide it's not worthwhile to continue. . . .

As senior human resources coordinator at the Washington-area   22
Capital Centre entertainment complex, Kim Whittington considers fast food experience a plus in a candidate for entry-level positions: "For me it shows the motivation, the initiative, especially if they've been there over a year. They learn people skills, cash handling, getting people in and out quickly; they could even learn some management skills if they're training other people." Whittington stresses the importance of "basic, basic work skills," adding, "we have problems with dependability, especially among young people." . . .

---

coincide: correspond exactly

Evidently, the kinds of skills learned at McDonald's are the kinds   23
of skills employers are looking for. This does not mean that the jobs
are a **panacea** whose abundance offers a magic solution to the
nation's problems. Although McDonald's jobs undeniably fulfill various people's needs for part-time and seasonal employment, they are
just as undeniably plain hard work. Like all jobs that are easily available to many different people, what they can do and are doing . . .
is to give people a chance to work hard and get ahead, even—
perhaps especially—those whose lack of skills and advantages might
seem to limit their prospects enormously.

WHY FAST-FOOD JOINTS DON'T SERVE UP
GOOD JOBS FOR KIDS
Amitai Etzioni

McDonald's is bad for your kids. I do not mean the flat patties and   1
the white-flour buns; I refer to the jobs teenagers undertake, mass-
producing these choice items.

As many as two-thirds of America's high-school juniors and   2
seniors now hold down part-time jobs, according to studies. Many
of these are in fast-food chains of which McDonald's is the pioneer,
trend-setter and symbol.

At first, such jobs may seem right out of the Founding Fathers'   3
educational manual for how to bring up self-reliant, work-ethic-driven,
productive youngsters. But in fact, these jobs undermine school attendance and involvement, impart few skills that will be useful in later
life, and simultaneously skew the values of teenagers—especially their
ideas about the worth of a dollar.

It has been a longstanding American tradition that youngsters   4
ought to get paying jobs. In folklore, few pursuits are more deeply
revered than the newspaper route and the sidewalk lemonade stand.
Here the youngsters are to learn how sweet are the fruits of labor
and self-discipline (papers are delivered early in the morning, rain or
shine), and the ways of trade (if you price your lemonade too high
or too low . . .).

Roy Rogers, Baskin-Robbins, Kentucky Fried Chicken, et al., may   5
at first seem nothing but a vast extension of the lemonade stand. They

---

panacea: cure-all

provide very large numbers of teen jobs, provide regular employment, pay quite well compared to many other teen jobs and, in the modern equivalent of toiling over a hot stove, test one's **stamina.**

Closer examination, however, finds the McDonald's kind of job   6
highly uneducational in several ways. Far from providing opportunities for **entrepreneurship** (the lemonade stand) or self-discipline, self-supervision and self-scheduling (the paper route), most teen jobs these days are highly structured—what social scientists call "highly routinized."

True, you still have to have the gumption to get yourself over to   7
the hamburger stand, but once you don the prescribed uniform, your task is spelled out in minute detail. The franchise prescribes the shape of the coffee cups; the weight, size, shape and color of the patties; and the texture of the napkins (if any). Fresh coffee is to be made every eight minutes. And so on. There is no room for initiative, creativity, or even elementary rearrangements. These are breeding grounds for robots working for yesterday's assembly lines, not tomorrow's high-tech posts.

There are very few studies of the matter. One of the few is a 1984   8
study by Ivan Charner and Bryna Shore Fraser. The study relies mainly on what teenagers write in response to questionnaires rather than actual observations of fast-food jobs. The authors argue that the employees develop many skills such as how to operate a food-preparation machine and a cash register. However, little attention is paid to how long it takes to acquire such a skill, or what its significance is.

What does it matter if you spend 20 minutes to learn to use a cash   9
register, and then—"operate" it? What "skill" have you acquired? It is a long way from learning to work with a **lathe** or carpenter tools in the olden days or to program computers in the modern age.

A 1980 study by A. V. Harrell and P. W. Wirtz found that, among   10
those students who worked at least 25 hours per week while in school, their unemployment rate four years later was half of that of seniors who did not work. This is an impressive statistic. It must be seen, though, together with the finding that many who begin as part-time employees in fast-food chains drop out of high school and are gobbled up in the world of low-skill jobs.

----

stamina: strength, endurance;   **entrepreneurship:** organizing a business;
lathe: a wood-working machine

Some say that while these jobs are rather unsuited for college-   11
bound, white, middle-class youngsters, they are "ideal" for lower-
class, "non-academic," minority youngsters. Indeed, minorities are
"over-represented" in these jobs (21 percent of fast-food employees).
While it is true that these places provide income, work, and even
some training to such youngsters, they also tend to perpetuate their
disadvantaged status. They provide no career ladders, few marketable
skills, and undermine school attendance and involvement.

The hours are often long. Among those 14 to 17, a third of   12
fast-food employees (including some school drop-outs) labor more
than 30 hours per week, according to the Charner-Fraser study. Only
20 percent work 15 hours or less. The rest: between 15 and 30 hours.

Often the stores close late, and after closing one must clean up   13
and tally up. In affluent Montgomery County, Md., where child labor
would not seem to be a widespread economic necessity, 24 percent
of the seniors at one high school in 1985 worked as much as five to
seven days a week; 27 percent, three to five. There is just no way
such amounts of work will not interfere with schoolwork, especially
homework. In an informal survey published in the most recent
yearbook of the high school, 58 percent of the seniors acknowledged
that their jobs interfere with their schoolwork.

The Charner-Fraser study sees merit in learning teamwork and   14
working under supervision. The authors have a point here. However,
it must be noted that such learning is not automatically educational
or wholesome. For example, much of the supervision in fast-food
places leans toward teaching one the wrong kinds of compliance:
blind obedience, or shared **alienation** with the "boss."

Supervision is often both tight and woefully inappropriate.   15
Today, fast-food chains and other such places of work (record shops,
bowling alleys) keep costs down by having teens supervise teens with
often no adult on the premises.

There is no father or mother figure with which to identify, to   16
emulate, to provide a role model and guidance. The work-culture
varies from one place to another. Sometimes it is a tightly run shop
(must keep the cash registers ringing); sometimes a rather loose pot
party interrupted by customers. However, only rarely is there a master
to learn from, or much worth learning. Indeed, far from being places

---

alienation: being apart from, outside of;   **emulate:** copy, imitate where solid adult work values are being transmitted, these are places where all too often delinquent teen values dominate. Typically, when my son Oren was dishing out ice cream for Baskin-Robbins in upper Manhattan, his fellow teen-workers considered him a sucker for not helping himself to the till. Most youngsters felt they were entitled to $50 severance "pay" on their last day on the job.

The pay, oddly, is the part of the teen work-world that is most   17
difficult to evaluate. The lemonade stand or paper route money was for your allowance. In the old days, apprentices learning a trade from a master contributed most, if not all, of their income to their parents' household. Today, the teen pay may be low by adult standards, but it is often, especially in the middle class, spent largely or wholly by the teens. That is, the youngsters live free at home ("after all, they are high-school kids") and are left with very substantial sums of money.

Where this money goes is not quite clear. Some use it to support   18
themselves, especially among the poor. More middle-class kids set some money aside to help pay for college, or save it for a major purchase—often a car. But large amounts seem to flow to pay for an early introduction into the most trite aspects of American con-sumerism, flimsy punk clothes, trinkets, and whatever else is the last fast-moving teen craze.

One may say that this is only fair and square; they are being   19
good American consumers and spending their money on what turns them on. At least, a cynic might add, these funds do not go into illicit drugs and booze. On the other hand, an educator might bemoan that these young, yet unformed individuals, so early in life are driven to buy objects of no intrinsic educational, cultural or social merit, learn so quickly the dubious merit of keeping up with the Joneses in ever-changing fads, promoted by mass merchandising.

Many teens find the instant reward of money, and the youth   20
status symbols it buys, much more alluring than credits in calculus courses, European history, or foreign languages. No wonder quite a few would rather skip school—and certainly homework—and instead work longer at a Burger King. Thus, most teen work these days is not providing early lessons in work ethic; it fosters escape from school and responsibilities, quick **gratification** and a short cut in the consumeristic aspects of adult life.

––––––––
gratification: satisfaction of desires

Thus, **ironically,** we must add youth employment, not merely   21
unemployment, to our list of social problems. And, like many other
social ills, the unfortunate aspects of teen work resist easy correction.

Sure, it would be much better if corporations that employ teens   22
would do so in conjunction with high schools and school districts.
Educators could help define what is the proper amount of gainful
work (not more than "X" hours per school week); how late kids may
be employed on school nights (not later than 9 p.m.); encourage
employer understanding during exam periods, and insist on proper
supervision. However, corporations are extremely unlikely to accept
such an approach as that, which in effect, would curb their ability to
draw on a major source of cheap labor. And, in these **laissez-faire**
days, Congress is quite disinclined to pass new social legislation
forcing corporations to be more attentive to the education needs of
the minors they so readily employ.

Parents who are still willing to take their role seriously may   23
encourage their youngsters to seek jobs at places that are proper
work settings and insist that fast-food chains and other franchises
shape up or not employ their kids. Also an agreement should be
reached with the youngsters that a significant share of teen earnings
should be dedicated to the family, or saved for agreed-upon items.

Above all, parents should look at teen employment not as   24
automatically educational. It is an activity—like sports—that can be
turned into an educational opportunity. But it can also easily be
abused. Youngsters must learn to balance the quest for income with
the needs to keep growing and pursue other endeavors that do not
pay off instantly—above all, education.

Go back to school.   25

WHY NOT ASK THE STUDENTS? URBAN TEENAGERS
MAKE THE CASE FOR WORKING
Katherine Cress

For many of today's urban minority high school students from   1
low-income families, the future looks bleak. In their neighborhoods,
violence is a fact of life. Some teenagers face pressure to join gangs
and get involved in drug activity, and 50% or more of all inner-city

---

ironically: in contrast to expectations;   **laissez-faire:** let (business) alone

students drop out of high school. For these and other reasons, such teenagers are considered to be "**at risk**" for various problems, including unemployment. The question is, How can minority high school students in urban areas be helped to make a successful transition from school to higher education or to the adult world of work?

The business community has long endorsed one popular answer.   2 Business believes that jobs are "good" for young people. More specifically, business claims that jobs help disadvantaged students make a successful transition from school to work. According to the Committee for Economic Development, part-time work during high school can give at-risk youth

> a sense of purpose and an important connection with the outside world. Young people from disadvantaged homes often lack knowledge about the world of work, have few positive adult role models, and have limited access to the job market. Businesses can offer valuable real-world experiences for these youths and offer the role models they lack. In addition, appropriate job experience can help teach or reinforce the basic skills in which disadvantaged youth are so often deficient.

Others, however, doubt whether working can perform this link-   3 ing function. William Behn, John Ogbu, Michelle Fine, and others suggest that the experience of working cannot by itself magically provide the access to opportunity that poor minority students in urban areas lack. Rather, they fear, if students take on employment, it may simply serve to train them earlier in life to accept a **subservient** place in a society that remains **intractably** discriminatory. In effect, jobs may reproduce inequality rather than break down barriers.

At the same time, others have begun to worry about how work-   4 ing affects students' performance in school. Brooke Workman maintains that students in the midwestern college-prep high school where he teaches work simply because it is "the thing to do" and then suffer as a result from fatigue, falling grades, and a diminished interest in schooling. Linda McNeil, who studied students from four midwestern high schools, found that working students tended to feel tired in class, to take easier electives, and to avoid upper-level

---

at risk: likely to fail;   **subservient:** inferior, subordinate;   **intractably:** stubbornly

courses. McNeil summed up her findings by commenting that "increased student employment has become one of the factors which has caused teachers and students to expect less from each other." While both Workman and McNeil studied populations in the Midwest rather than the urban minority students on which I focus here, their warning must be considered: some jobs, for some students, have been shown to diminish commitment to schooling.

What do the students themselves think? Missing from the research ₅ is any attempt to find out from urban students what working means to them. There are two good reasons to pursue this question. The first is an **ethnographic** one: if we want to conduct thorough analyses of programs that are being implemented in schools, we need to begin to listen to what students themselves think. Second, as businesses begin to play an increasing role in the **socialization** of the young, we need to find out if their youth programs accomplish what they claim. Surprisingly, little or no **evaluation** has accompanied the raft of business-led employment programs that have sprung up in recent years, and this lack of accountability must be corrected.

In 1989 I interviewed high school juniors and seniors in Boston ₆ regarding the nature of their work experiences. These students were working part-time under the auspices of the Boston Compact, a school/business/ university partnership that has been admired and **replicated** across the country. Such initiatives represent a key component in the business community's renewed commitment to public education. Focusing on an all-urban, predominantly at-risk population made it possible to understand for the first time the work experiences of the group most in need of any positive benefits employment may provide.

The interviews explored three interrelated questions. How do ₇ part-time jobs in Boston businesses affect students' understanding of the adult world of work? How do these jobs affect students' sense of their potential access to that world? And how do these jobs influence the way students view their future? In interviewing a sample of at-risk high school students, I found that work can offer such students a valuable growth experience when the conditions and the relationships in the workplace are right. Prior research suggests that

---

ethnographic: cultural, social;   **socialization:** adjustment to the values of society;   **evaluation:** testing;   **replicated:** copied

work does more harm than good; the results of my study suggest that the reverse *can* be true.

Findings on five central issues emerged from the interviews and   8
shed light on the questions of how at-risk students experience work and how they plan for the future. The issues were: (1) the role of work relationships in students' lives, (2) students' conscious acquisition of skills and work habits on the job, (3) work as an alternative to "the street," (4) the way students regard money, and (5) whether work during high school affects the way students plan for college and careers. There seems to be a great deal about the work experience that educators and businesspeople must strive to understand better—and to do so, they need information that only working students themselves can provide.

The most significant finding of my study was that relationships   9
on the job, especially relationships with adults, matter a great deal to students. Students spoke again and again about their interactions, both positive and negative, with adult supervisors. Kevin's description of his relationship with his supervisor was positive:

> I used to be cold-hearted and ruthless. If I wanted something,
> I'd take it. But I look at my boss . . . he's nice. He does things,
> you know? He travels the world, he owns his own plane, he
> flies across country and to Europe and stuff, he's a nice guy,
> you know? He doesn't fight anybody for something. That's
> what I'd like to be.

Students look up to their supervisors and admire their clothes,   10
speech, office skills, and behaviors. Students also value their accessibility, warmth, and personal ethics. When Kevin vowed to model himself after his boss, who taught him that you can succeed without "stomping on people to get to the top," he was showing that he had learned from this man a new way of *being* in the world.

On the negative side, some students described adults who were   11
inconsiderate and even cruel. Jeffrey, who led a team of environmental service workers at one of the city's large hospitals, was falsely accused by a nurse with whom he worked of shirking his duties. As it turned out, she had forgotten to tell him about the assignment in question. Before the situation was resolved, however, Jeffrey felt that she was wrong. "And then she didn't talk right [to me], the way she

was supposed to. Even if she was angry, she shouldn't have talked down to us. She said we don't want to work there, [that] all the kids who work there won't do anything on the weekends—things she felt inside about some of the other workers, this was the time she let it all come out." In the end the nurse apologized to Jeffrey, which he says made him feel "relieved. Because it was my trust that was on the line. My dependability."

Students' experiences on the job vary by race. Interviews brought   12
to light a difference in the frequency with which white and nonwhite students experienced positive and negative relationships with adults in the workplace. White students were more likely than nonwhite students to talk about positive experiences with adults on the job; non-white students spoke more often than whites about negative experiences with adults on the job. Because the ability to relate well to adults in positions of power enhances students' opportunities in the adult world of work, white students may experience a smoother entry into the working world.

The literature on student work suggests that many student   13
workplaces are segregated by age (at least in the naturally occurring student job market), and the literature characterizes this segregation as a negative phenomenon. However, the students I interviewed saw both advantages and disadvantages to age-segregated workplaces. A positive aspect of working with peers was being with college-age co-workers who served as role models. "They tell you what to expect when you get to college," Richard explained, "and we kind of want to be like them when we get there." Ivonne agreed: "Being around college students—that sort of made me want to broaden my mind."

On the negative side, students described age-segregated work-   14
places gone wild, with little or no adult supervision. Stephen called the insurance company in which he worked "the zoo," and, at Jacques' job at a hospital cafeteria, a fight broke out when another student worker slapped Jacques' girlfriend. In his words, "I just got in a fight because she got smacked and was on the floor crying."

Significant differences existed between white and nonwhite   15
students' attitudes concerning the experience of working with peers. The most striking difference was that twice as many nonwhite students as white students talked about both the advantages and the disadvantages of working with peers. Males were more likely than

females to see disadvantages to working with peers. The reasons for these differences are unclear. The findings simply raise questions about relationships between students on the job and draw attention to the particular importance of peer relationships for students of color.

None of the previous studies of students who work mentioned 16 the finding of my study that some urban students clearly recognize and consciously seek the future-oriented benefits of working. While Ellen Greenberger and Laurence Steinberg observed that improved work habits develop on the job, Milfred Dale's study of inner-city youth showed no connection between working and the development of more mature work habits. None of the prior research has revealed the belief of some working students that they are gaining valuable job skills and work habits. However, the students in my study made it clear that they wanted, valued, and sought out these skills and habits. James stated that he worked to acquire the skills that he "would need in a job in the future," explaining that, thanks to his work in a record store, "by senior year I'll be able to run the whole store, because they're showing me everything right now. These skills will really help in the future—like managing, marketing, stocking—so I will be able to do all that." James' goal is to own and operate his own business after college. Akeem stressed the prestige of having a "respectable" job during high school: "You tell people you have a job at a bank, and they say, 'Yeah, that boy's real clever.'"

Cultivating good work habits was also important to these 17 students. Matt said that working had helped him learn to control his temper: "I've learned not to snap the gun when my boss tells me something. Not that it's wrong, but he'll be picking something out so the next time I won't do it, and I tend to get a little snappy. I tend to get a little bent out of shape about it sometimes. So I don't think it would be good to have an attitude like that down the line."

Career counselors who work with students see the acquisition of 18 job skills and good work habits as the key to opportunities in the adult world of work, especially for at-risk students. One counselor explained that urban students, many of whom come from "chaotic backgrounds," operate on impulse. When their desires are thwarted, they get angry and go off. They need to learn, this counselor continued, that "there are ways to deal with your frustrations in a responsible manner."

It is encouraging to note that nonwhite students more so than   19
whites said that they valued gaining job skills and appropriate work
habits through their jobs. This may mean that jobs help at-risk
students put together the pieces that will secure them access to
success in the adult world of work.

Work can also serve as an important alternative to "the street."   20
Students reported that school demanded little of them and that the
only alternatives to working after school were going home to watch
television or getting into trouble. Male students were particularly
aware of the lure of the street, where drugs were bought and sold
and gang activity lent structure to life. Reggie talked about the
teenagers who chose the street over jobs:

> Oh yeah, there's kids out there—stealing cars, selling drugs, and
> all that. This kid in my class, he goes and pulls out his money and
> flashes $850, in 50s and 20s. And he says, "I have money—
> mucho moolah." And I say, "Well, I have money too, it may not
> be as much as yours, but it's cleaner than yours." And he looked
> at me and didn't even talk. It's like he thought about it, and there
> was nothing he could say.

However, previous research does not suggest that jobs can   21
provide an escape from delinquency and dangerous environments.
Among the students sampled by Steinberg and his colleagues, working caused an increase in cigarette and marijuana use; the
researchers also found that other work-related behaviors—such as
materialism, cynicism, and acceptance of unethical business
practices—could push students toward delinquency. The studies by
Denise Gottfredson and by Milfred Dale did not present evidence
that working increased delinquent behavior in students, but neither
did they show work as a way out of delinquency or as protection
against a dangerous and **pervasive** youth culture. They did not find
what seemed to be true for some of the students interviewed here—
that work was often the safest place to be.

It is generally assumed that high school students work "for the   22
money." However, the above revelations about how important it is
to students to establish good working relationships, to acquire

---

materialism: belief that only material goods are important;   **cynicism:** belief
that people are motivated by selfishness;   **pervasive:** spread everywhere

productive job skills and work habits, and to avoid the street clearly
show that work means more to students than simply making money.

Even when they do talk about the financial benefits of working,   23
students speak in relatively unselfish terms. For example, many
students mentioned that, before they had jobs, they were constantly
forced to ask their parents for money—but once they became
moneymakers themselves, they could use their income to take pressure off their families. As James put it, "I used to ask my mother for
money. Then I had to get a job. I'm getting too old to ask my mother
for money. I like to be my own person." Laronda actually lent her
mother money; Kevin paid for his family's groceries. Seventeen-year-
old Carmen, already married, worked to pay household expenses.
Kevin, J. T., and Matt paid their own room and board. Contributing
to their own support—and thereby contributing to the welfare of
the family as a whole—was a significant way students found to connect with their families. It made students feel useful and independent at the same time. . . .

Overall, schools and businesses should take steps to enhance   24
students' work experiences. Schools should integrate work into the
curriculum, recognize work as a powerful after-school intervention,
and help students reflect on and learn from their workplace experiences. Businesses should ensure that students' work experiences are
carefully structured and supervised. In addition, they should
establish mentoring and college-preparation programs to help
students plan realistically for the future. Finally, businesses should
begin to evaluate their efforts; up to this point, jobs programs have
seldom been carefully evaluated. If schools and businesses put their
efforts into improving young people's experience of working, then
the energy, enthusiasm, and skills that students gain from it will not
be wasted.

Post-reading

These reading selections raise numerous questions bearing on the issue of
whether high school students should work. The most obvious one is whether
part-time work tends to interfere with school, including both social and homework time, but there are several others. Before you can get very far with the
planning of this essay, you will, therefore, have to make notes in two separate
areas: (1) What are the issues involved besides the problem of work interfering

with school and (2) What facts and opinions in these articles bear on each of these issues?

It is going to be essential to list the issues, and it will certainly be a good idea to work with others in your class to make sure you have identified all of them. Then you will need to list the facts and opinions under each of the issues (unless some of the facts and opinions apply equally to several issues at the same time).

As always in the case of opinions, it is essential to look at where they come from (does the person have some reason to be biased in favor of one view?) and at how they are backed up. For instance, which of the following two opinions do you think has better support?

> "I think horror movies are bad. They show all kinds of terrible things happening to people."
>
> "I think horror movies are bad. They cheapen human life by making murder, the worst act a human being can commit against another, merely a form of entertainment."

Now is also the time to go back to your pre-reading notes or any of the other thoughts you had while reading these articles. In the same way that you test those of others, you need to test your own ideas. Write them down under the appropriate issue headings, and look as objectively as you can at how well supported *your* opinions are.

People often make the mistake of thinking that their own experiences are representative—that is, that what they have gone through proves something is true for everyone. Individual experiences rarely *prove* anything. If they did, scientists investigating this or almost any other issue could simply study one person, find out how he or she was affected, and write up a report. But, of course, they can't do that. They have to study many people who are as representative as possible of the whole population being examined. Keep in mind, then, that while your own experiences are important, they are probably not conclusive.

Essay Assignment

Write an essay in which you examine the evidence for and against high school students working part time. Carefully consider both sides of the question and, weighing the pro and con arguments, come to your own conclusion on this issue.

Pre-writing

Before you begin organizing your essay, review the section "Evaluating Evidence and Shaping Your Argument." Be sure to keep in mind these four points:

1. Include the strongest arguments of both sides.
2. Don't put all the arguments on one side in one paragraph and all the arguments on the other side in a second one.
3. Remember that a statement isn't an argument. Statements often resemble topic sentences—that is, sentences that have to be explained or supported.
4. Make sure your conclusion is based solidly on the arguments preceding it. It should reflect the strengths and weaknesses of the arguments covered in your essay, not be merely your own unproven opinion tacked on at the end.

Jot down a working outline, organizing your main points and citing your support, and a working thesis.

Writing

Your introduction should briefly outline the issue and state your thesis. Your paragraphs should support your thesis while dealing with the complexity of the problem as you see it. Your conclusion, of course, should either summarize your essay's main points or make a recommendation.

Be sure to review the Writer's Checklist on pages 338–340 to help you complete this assignment.

SHOULD PEOPLE KEEP HANDGUNS AT HOME?

It has often been said that the United States is a country built upon guns. Our Revolutionary War began when some ordinary farmers in Massachusetts went home, got out their hunting guns, and attacked a unit of the British army. And, of course, the frontiersmen who explored and gradually opened up the North American continent for settlement all carried guns of one kind or another. During the nineteenth century, our old west was famous for its gun-toting cowhands, criminals, and lawmen. This long tradition has resulted in a society that today is more heavily armed than any other in the world.

Although many people favor outlawing guns of all kinds and others would legalize weapons of every type, the argument in recent years has centered primarily on handguns and assault rifles—weapons of use primarily to kill human beings, though some kinds of handguns are used in target shooting.

Although the United States has the highest homicide rate by firearms of any country in the world, other countries have shown concern about guns. After a massacre of schoolchildren and their teacher in Scotland, Britain declared all firearms illegal and collected every gun in the nation under penalty of prison sentence. In 1997 Australia, responding to a similar massacre, declared all semiautomatic weapons and pump-action shotguns illegal and spent more than $260 million to pay citizens to turn in their weapons. Canada has tightened its already very tight gun-control laws.

The American response to numerous massacres, both of school children and adults, has been less drastic. In 1994 Congress passed the Brady Bill, which requires a five-day waiting period and background check of anyone seeking to buy a gun from a licensed dealer. In 1998 a new FBI computerized check system went into effect that blocked 11,584 gun sales during its first 41 days. But 1,030,606 gun sales went through. Laws have been passed both locally and nationally to bar the sales of assault rifles, but these laws exempted the most popular models and permitted gun manufacturers to make "copycat" models that can be sold legally. Finally, 31 states have no laws banning the private sale of guns, and in most states dealers at gun shows can sell whatever they want to whoever wants to buy it.

But more important than whether we have national or local legislation to make it more difficult to own guns, in particular handguns, is the decision by individuals to buy a gun. Many feel that with handguns in the hands of criminals, it makes no sense for law-abiding citizens not to be armed. Others argue that since handguns are useful for only one purpose, to kill human beings, it is unwise and perhaps even immoral to own them.

Reading Assignment

Pre-reading

Before you read the following articles and essays, ask yourself how you stand on this issue and why. Write down your position and the reasons for it so you can refer to them after you've finished reading what other people have to say about handguns.

Reading

Read actively, making notes in the margins or on a separate sheet of paper.

THE SECOND AMENDMENT TO THE U.S. CONSTITUTION

The argument over whether handguns should be outlawed or strictly licensed often begins with the Second Amendment to the Constitution of the United States, part of the Bill of Rights. One side points to it as their Constitutional sanction to own handguns; the other argues that owning handguns has little to do with maintaining a militia—that is, a citizen army or a reserve military force.

A well regulated militia being necessary to the security of a free state,   1
the right of the people to keep and bear arms shall not be infringed.

FIREARM-RELATED DEATHS IN THE UNITED STATES AND 35 OTHER HIGH- AND UPPER-MIDDLE-INCOME COUNTRIES

E. G. Krug, K. E. Powell, and L. L. Dahlberg Division of Violence Prevention, National Center for Injury Prevention and Control, Centers for Disease Control and Prevention

Background. The Forty-Ninth World Health Assembly recently declared   1
violence a worldwide public health problem. Improved understanding of cross-national differences is useful for identifying risk factors and may facilitate prevention efforts. Few **cross-national** studies, however, have explored firearm-related deaths. We compared the incidence of firearm-related deaths among 36 countries.

Methods. Health officials in high-income (HI) and upper-middle-income   2
(UMI) countries with populations greater than one million were asked to provide data . . . on firearm-related homicides, suicides, unintentional deaths and deaths of undetermined intent, as well as homicides, and suicides, for all methods combined. Thirty-six (78%) of the 46 countries provided complete data. We compared age-adjusted rates per 100,000 for each country and pooled rates by income group and geographical location.

---

cross-national: across national boundaries, international

Results. During the one-year study period, 88,649 firearm deaths were ₃
reported. Overall firearm mortality rates are five to six times higher in
HI and UMI countries in the Americas (12.72) than in Europe (2.17), or
Oceania (2.57) and 95 times higher than in Asia (0.13). The rate of
firearm deaths in the United States (14.24 per 100,000) exceeds that
of its economic counterparts (1.76) eightfold and that of UMI countries (9.69) by a factor of 1.5. Suicide and homicide contribute equally
to total firearm deaths in the U.S., but most firearm deaths are suicides
(71%) in HI countries and homicides (72%) in UMI countries.

Conclusions. Firearm death rates vary markedly throughout the ₄
industrialized world. Further research to identify risk factors associated with these variations may help improve prevention efforts.

Keywords. Firearms, violence, suicide, homicide, cross-cultural com- ₅
parison, developed countries, epidemiology. . . .

In 1990, self-directed and interpersonal violence caused 2.7% of the ₆
world's disability adjusted life years (DALY) lost—the numbers of
years of life lost from premature death combined with the loss of
health from disability. This percentage is projected to increase to
4.2% in 2020. In view of what it described as a dramatic increase in
the incidence of intentional injuries, the Forty-Ninth World Health
Assembly recently adopted a resolution declaring violence a leading
worldwide public health problem and urged member states to assess
and develop science-based solutions to the problem.

    Violence can be defined as the intentional use of physical force— ₇
against another person or against oneself—which results in or has a
high likelihood of resulting in injury or death. Much of the previous
research conducted on violent deaths has focused on homicide or
suicide. In some countries, firearms are the most frequently used
weapons in homicide and suicide. This is particularly true in the
United States, where 71% of homicides and 61% of suicides are
firearm-related. In 1993, a firearm was involved in the deaths of
39,595 people in the U.S. (15.6 per 100,000), making firearm
injuries the seventh leading cause of death. . . .

    International comparisons of firearm-related fatality rates are not ₈
common. . . . International comparisons, however, may provide
important insights into the magnitude of and risk factors for a health

problem. These risk factors can be further studied and may lead to new prevention strategies. In this report, we describe firearm-related deaths in 36 countries and address several questions: How do firearm-related death rates in the U.S. compare with rates in other countries of similar and lower economic status? Are firearm-related death rates similar among geographical regions? Do sex- and age-specific firearm death rates vary across income groups? We also place firearm death rates into the broader context of violent deaths by presenting overall homicide and suicide rates. . . .

RESULTS
Homicide and Suicide Rates

During the one-year study period, the 36 countries combined   9
reported 82,465 homicides (6.9 per 100,000) and 130,546 suicides (10.9 per 100,000). Homicide rates for individual countries range from 0.55 in England and Wales to 25.12 in Estonia. Suicide rates range from 1.46 in Kuwait to 34.05 in Estonia (Table 5.1). Some countries reported extremely high violent death rates. . . . The highest rates for homicide are mainly found in Estonia, Mexico, Brazil and the U.S. The highest suicide rates were reported by Estonia, Hungary and Slovenia, the only countries from Eastern Europe that are included in our study.

A firearm was involved in over half of the deaths classified as   10
homicides in Northern Ireland (86%), Italy (74%), the U.S. (71%), Brazil (56%), Mexico (56%) and Greece (51%). In the remaining countries a firearm was involved in less than half the homicides reported. A firearm was involved in almost one-quarter (24%) of the deaths classified as suicides in all of the countries. A firearm was involved in less than half the suicides reported by each of the countries individually, with the exception of the U.S. (61%).

Firearm-Related Deaths

Variations by country. During the one-year study period, 88,649   11
firearm deaths were reported by the 36 countries, for a pooled rate of 7.4 deaths per 100,000. . . . Firearm homicide rates range from a low of 0.00 in Mauritius to 10.35 in Mexico. Firearm suicide rates range from 0.02 in South Korea to 6.30 in the U.S. Unintentional firearm death rates range from 0.00 in Hong Kong, Japan, Kuwait, and Singapore to 1.32 in Mexico.

Table 5.1   Violent Death Rates per 100,000 Population for 36 Selected
High-Income and Upper-Middle-Income Countries

	Year	Population	Firearm total	Firearm homicide	Firearm suicide
High-income countries					
United States	1993	257,783,004	14.24	7.11	6.30
Northern Ireland	1994	1,641,711	6.63	5.07	1.32
Finland	1994	5,088,333	6.46	0.84	5.39
Switzerland	1994	7,021,000	5.31	0.57	4.53
France	1994	57,915,450	5.15	0.40	4.08
Canada	1992	28,120,065	4.31	0.68	3.33
Norway	1993	4,324,815	3.82	0.26	3.44
Austria	1994	8,029,717	3.70	0.37	3.25
Israel	1993	5,261,700	2.91	0.70	1.78
Belgium	1990	9,967,387	2.90	0.53	2.07
Australia	1994	17,838,401	2.65	0.41	2.10
Italy	1992	56,764,854	2.44	1.47	0.81
New Zealand	1993	3,458,850	2.38	0.15	1.88
Denmark	1993	5,189,378	2.09	0.22	1.74
Sweden	1993	8,718,571	1.92	0.18	1.65
Kuwait	1995	1,684,529	1.84	0.34	0.03
Germany	1994	81,338,093	1.24	0.20	0.88
Ireland	1991	3,525,719	0.97	0.03	0.75
Spain	1993	39,086,079	0.78	0.19	0.36
Netherlands	1994	15,382,830	0.70	0.30	0.31
Scotland	1994	5,132,400	0.54	0.18	0.30
England/Wales	1992	51,429,000	0.41	0.08	0.28
Taiwan	1994	21,086,686	0.37	0.12	0.11
Singapore	1994	2,930,200	0.21	0.05	0.15
Hong Kong	1993	5,919,000	0.14	0.09	0.05
Japan	1994	124,069,000	0.05	0.02	0.03
Upper-middle-income countries					
Brazil	1993	160,737,000	12.95	9.59	0.72
Mexico	1994	90,011,259	12.69	10.35	1.01
Estonia	1994	1,499,257	12.26	7.73	2.86
Argentina	1994	34,179,000	8.93	2.10	2.89
Portugal	1994	5,138,600	3.20	1.17	1.00
Slovenia	1994	1,989,477	2.60	0.30	2.13
Greece	1994	10,426,289	1.29	0.52	0.71
Hungary	1994	10,245,677	1.11	0.22	0.80
Mauritius	1993	1,062,810	0.19	0.00	0.12
South Korea	1994	44,453,179	0.12	0.04	0.02

Variations by geographical region. When responding countries are   12
grouped by region, firearm mortality is highest in the Americas and
lowest in Asia (Figure 5.1). In fact, the overall firearm mortality rate
is five to six times higher in the Americas (12.72 per 100,000) than
in Oceania (2.57) or Europe (2.17), and it is 95 times higher than
in Asia (0.13). In the Americas most (58%) firearm deaths are
homicides. Suicides make up most of the firearm deaths in Europe
(69%) and Oceania (80%). In Asia, 35% of the firearm deaths are
reported as homicides, 37% as suicides, 20% as unintentional deaths
and 8% as deaths of undetermined intent.

Rates by income group. The rate of firearm death in the U.S.   13
(14.24 per 100,000) is eight times the pooled rate for the other HI
countries (1.76) and is 1.5 times the pooled rate for the UMI
countries (9.69) (Figure 5.2). Firearm homicide rates are about

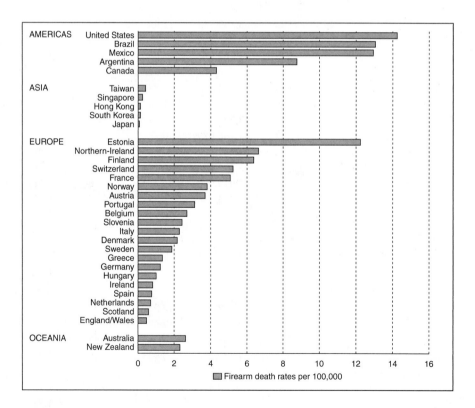

Figure 5.1   Firearm death rates, by country and region, in 36 high- and
upper-middle-income countries

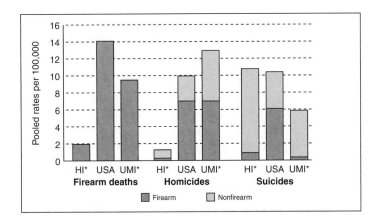

Figure 5.2   Firearm death, homicide, and suicide rates, by income, in 36 high- and upper-middle-income countries

19 times higher in the U.S. (7.11) and UMI countries (6.89) than in HI nations (0.37). In comparison, the U.S. firearm suicide rate (6.30) is five times higher than the rate for HI nations (1.21) and is nearly seven times higher than the rate for UMI nations (0.91).

Comparing the proportion of homicides and suicides that involve a [14] firearm, the U.S. emerged as having a far greater proportion than either HI or UMI countries. Seventy-one percent of homicides in the U.S. involve a firearm, compared with 33% in HI countries and 54% in UMI countries. Sixty-one per cent of suicides in the U.S. involve a firearm, compared with 11% in HI countries and 17% in UMI countries.

When we assessed the proportion of firearm deaths that are [15] homicides and suicides, we observed marked variations in the income groups. . . . In the U.S., the proportion of firearm deaths that are homicides (46%) is almost equal to the proportion that are suicides (48%). In the HI countries, however, the proportion of firearm deaths that are suicides is much greater (71%) than the proportion of such deaths that are homicides (19%). The reverse is true for UMI countries, where most firearm deaths are homicides (72%) rather than suicides (9%).

Variations by age and sex. Age and sex patterns of firearm mortality [16] in HI and UMI countries are similar, differing only in magnitude. Firearm homicide and unintentional death rates are higher in younger age groups and firearm suicide rates are higher for older adults. However, when compared with their counterparts in the HI and UMI groups, the young people (15–24 year age group) in the U.S. stand out in several ways. In the U.S., the 15–24 year age group has the highest age-specific rate of firearm homicide, whereas the rate is higher in the 25–34 year age group in HI and UMI countries. . . . The 15–24 year age group in the U.S. also has the highest age-specific rate of unintentional firearm deaths, but this is not the case in HI countries. . . . Finally, in the U.S., firearm suicide rates among people 15–24 years old are higher than for those 25–54 years old. . . . The reverse is true in the HI and UMI groups.

Although firearm mortality rates among males uniformly exceed   17
rates among females, the rates among females are relatively closer to the rates among males in the U.S. than in either the HI or UMI group. The male/female firearm mortality ratio in the U.S. (6.0) is two-thirds to almost one-half the ratio in the HI (9.7) and UMI (10.9) countries. Five countries, however, have a lower male/female firearm mortality ratio than the U.S.: Hong Kong (1.9), Kuwait (2.3), South Korea (3.2), Portugal (4.4) and Argentina (4.9).

Discussion

Our study explores the incidence of firearm-related deaths among   18
36 wealthier nations of the world. It is, to our knowledge, the first cross-national comparison of firearm death rates among males and females of all ages. During a one-year period, a firearm was involved in almost 90,000 deaths in the 36 countries included in our study. We observed marked variations in firearm deaths among these nations whether considered individually or grouped by income or geographical location. Among these 36 countries, the U.S. is unique in several aspects. It has the highest overall firearm mortality rate, a high proportion of homicides that are the result of a firearm injury, and the highest proportion of suicides that are the result of a firearm injury. The U.S. also has a relatively low male/female firearm mortality rate ratio—a finding which indicates that the difference between the rates for males and females is smaller in the U.S. than in most other countries. Finally, the age-specific patterns indicate that the impact of all causes of firearm mortality—homicide, suicide, and unintentional injuries—is more pronounced in the younger age groups (**<25 years old**) in the U.S. than in other nations.

<25 years old: 25 years old and under

Particularly high firearm mortality rates were noted among four   19
nations in the western hemisphere (the U.S., Mexico, Brazil and
Argentina). In contrast, firearm mortality among the five participating Asian countries (Japan, South Korea, Hong Kong, Singapore and
Taiwan) was very low. Higher rates of homicide in general and
firearm homicide in particular were noted among UMI countries.
HI countries reported low firearm suicide rates, but overall rates of
suicide were otherwise comparable with the U.S. rate.

The explanations for these observations [are] undoubtedly com-   20
plex and in need of further study. A few areas worthy of pursuit have
been identified, and future research is likely to expand the list. For
the purposes of discussion, factors influencing firearm injury mortality can be separated into three general areas that are not mutually
exclusive: factors that influence the use of a firearm, factors that
influence the homicide rate, and factors that influence the suicide
rate. Factors that have been suggested to influence the use of
firearms include the social norms concerning the use of firearms, the
availability of firearms in general, and the types of firearms that
people choose to use. Social norms may play a role in firearm-related
mortality, homicide and suicide, in part by influencing if a weapon is
used and what type of weapon is used. The use of firearms should
be low in places where strong social norms inhibit people from using
firearms. Social norms, for example, may be part of the reason for
the very low rates of firearm mortality in all five Asian countries
participating in our study.

Firearm availability varies greatly among nations: among the   21
14 countries in our study for which such data are available, the proportion of households possessing a firearm ranges from <1% in Japan
to 48% in the U.S. A positive association between firearm ownership
and rates of firearm homicide, firearm suicide, and overall suicide has
been reported. Research findings are mixed, however, about the
relationship between firearm ownership and overall homicide rates.
Because firearms are more lethal than other weapons, such as knives,
choosing a firearm as a weapon increases the likelihood of a fatal out-
come. The types of firearms available may also influence mortality
rates, because some models are more likely to be lethal than others.

Firearm mortality rates may also be influenced by underlying   22
causes of homicide and suicide that operate independently of the

firearm-related factors just described. Social factors that may influence homicide rates include income inequality, low funding for social programs, divorce, the proportion of households with working women, ethnic-linguistic **heterogeneity**, and social acceptance of violence. Factors that may influence suicide rates include economic instability, unemployment, breakdown of the family group structure, **intergenerational** pressures and competition, **secularization**, and substance use and misuse. . . .

We should strive to improve our understanding of the factors that   23
account for cross-national variations in violent and firearm death rates. For example, in most HI countries, suicide rates are high, but firearms play a relatively small role. In most UMI countries, firearms are involved in more than half of all homicides. In some nations, such as the U.S. and Estonia, firearm death rates of all types are high, whereas in other nations, such as the five Asian nations in our study, firearm death rates of all types are low. A better understanding of the economic, socio-cultural and other factors that underlie these differences will help in the design and implementation of national or regional interventions. The low rates in Asia show that such deaths can be prevented and provide hope that other nations may achieve similar levels.

HANDGUN REGULATIONS, CRIME, ASSAULTS, AND HOMICIDE: A TALE OF TWO CITIES
Drs. J. H. Sloan, A. L. Kellermann, D. T. Reay, J. A. Ferris, T. Koepsell, F. P. Rivara, C. Rice, L. Gray, and J. LoGerfo

The following study examines the effect of handgun ownership on homicide rates in two cities similar in every respect but one: their handgun control laws. One city, Vancouver, British Columbia, has very strict handgun ownership laws, as does Canada as a whole. The other city, Seattle, Washington, has very loose handgun ownership laws. The study appeared in the November 10, 1988, issue of The New England Journal of Medicine, *a highly respected medical journal.*

Approximately 20,000 persons are murdered in the United States   1
each year, making homicide the 11th leading cause of death and the 6th leading cause of the loss of potential years of life before age 65.

---

heterogeneity: differences;   **intergenerational:** between the generations; **secularization:** drawing away from a religious orientation

In the United States between 1960 and 1980, the death rate from homicide by means other than firearms increased by 85 percent. In contrast, the death rate from homicide by firearms during this same period increased by 160 percent.

Approximately 60 percent of homicides each year involve   2 firearms. Handguns alone account for three fourths of all gun-related homicides. Most homicides occur as a result of assaults during arguments or **altercations**; a minority occur during the commission of a robbery or other felony. S. P. Baker has noted that in cases of assault, people tend to reach for weapons that are readily available. Since attacks with guns more often end in death than attacks with knives, and since handguns are disproportionately involved in intentional shootings, some have argued that restricting access to handguns could substantially reduce our annual rate of homicide.

To support this view, advocates of handgun control frequently   3 cite data from countries like Great Britain and Japan, where the rates of both handgun ownership and homicide are substantially lower than those in the United States. . . .

Opponents of gun control counter with statistics from Israel and   4 Switzerland, where the rates of gun ownership are high but homicides are relatively uncommon. However, the value of comparing data from different countries to support or refute the effectiveness of gun control is severely **compromised** by the large number of potentially **confounding** social, behavioral, and economic factors that characterize large national groups. To date, no study has been able to separate the effects of handgun control from differences among populations in terms of socioeconomic status, aggressive behavior, violent crime, and other factors. To clarify the relation between firearm regulations and community rates of homicide, we studied two large cities in the Pacific Northwest: Seattle, Washington, and Vancouver, British Columbia. Although similar in many ways, these two cities have taken decidedly different approaches to handgun control.

---

altercations: heated, noisy quarrels;   **compromised:** made suspicious; **confounding:** confusing

Study Sites

Seattle and Vancouver are large port cities in the Pacific Northwest.   5
Although on opposite sides of an international border, they are only
140 miles apart, a three-hour drive by freeway. They share a
common geography, climate, and history. Citizens in both cities have
attained comparable levels of schooling and have almost identical
rates of unemployment. When adjusted to U.S. dollars, the median
annual income of a household in Vancouver exceeds that in Seattle
by less than $500. Similar percentages of households in both cities
have incomes of less than $10,000 (U.S.) annually. . . . The two
communities also share many cultural values and interests. Six of the
top nine network television programs in Seattle are among the nine
most watched programs in Vancouver.

Firearm Regulations

Although similar in many ways, Seattle and Vancouver differ markedly   6
in their approaches to the regulation of firearms. In Seattle, handguns
may be purchased legally for self-defense in the street or at home.
After a 30-day waiting period, a permit can be obtained to carry a
handgun as a concealed weapon. The recreational use of handguns is
minimally restricted.

In Vancouver, self-defense is not considered a valid or legal   7
reason to purchase a handgun. Concealed weapons are not permitted. Recreational uses of handguns (such as target shooting and
collecting) are regulated by the **province,** and the purchase of a
handgun requires a restricted-weapons permit. A permit to carry a
weapon must also be obtained in order to transport a handgun, and
these weapons can be discharged only at a licensed shooting club.
Handguns can be transported by car, but only if they are stored in
the trunk in a locked box.

Although they differ in their approach to firearm regulations,   8
both cities aggressively enforce existing gun laws and regulations,
and convictions for gun-related offenses carry similar penalties. . . .
Similar percentages of homicides in both communities eventually
lead to arrest and police charges. In Washington, under the Sentenc-
ing Reform Act of 1981, murder in the first degree carries a minimum

---

province: Canadian equivalent of U.S. state

sentence of 20 years of confinement. In British Columbia, first-degree murder carries a minimum sentence of 25 years, with a possible judicial parole review after 15 years. Capital punishment was abolished in Canada during the 1970s. In Washington State, the death penalty may be invoked in cases of aggravated first-degree murder, but no one has been executed since 1963.

Rates of Gun Ownership

Because direct surveys of firearm ownership in Seattle and Vancouver have never been conducted, we assessed the rates of gun ownership indirectly by two independent methods. First, we obtained from the Firearm Permit Office of the Vancouver police department a count of the restricted-weapons permits issued in Vancouver between March 1984 and March 1988 and compared this figure with the total number of concealed-weapons permits issued in Seattle during the same period. . . . Second, we used Cook's gun prevalence index, a previously **validated** measure of intercity differences in the **prevalence** of gun ownership. This index . . . **correlates** each city's rates of suicide and assaultive homicide involving firearms with survey-based estimates of gun ownership in each city. Both methods indicate that firearms are far more commonly owned in Seattle than in Vancouver. . . .

Ownership of Firearms in Seattle and Vancouver

	Seattle	**Vancouver**
Long guns (rifles, shotguns)	Not registered	Not registered
Total concealed-weapons permits issued 1984–1988	15,289	_____
Total restricted-weapons permits issued 1984–1988	_____	4,137
Cook's gun prevalence index	41%	12%

Results

Over the whole seven-year study period, 388 homicides occurred in Seattle (11.3 per 100,000 person-years). In Vancouver, 204 homicides occurred during the same period (6.9 per 100,000 person-years). . . .

---

validated: proven;   **prevalence:** existence;   **correlates:** relates to each other

When homicides were subdivided by the mechanism of death,   11
the rate of homicide by knives and other weapons (excluding
firearms) in Seattle was found to be almost identical to that in
Vancouver. . . . Virtually all of the increased risk of death from
homicide in Seattle was due to a more than **fivefold** higher rate of
homicide by firearms. Handguns, which accounted for roughly
85 percent of the homicides involving firearms in both communities, were 4.8 times more likely to be used in homicides in Seattle
than in Vancouver. . . .

Discussion

In order to exclude the possibility that Seattle's higher homicide   12
rate may be explained by higher levels of criminal activity or
aggressiveness in its population, we compared the rates of burglary,
robbery, simple assault, and aggravated assault in the two communities. Although we observed a slightly higher rate of simple and
aggravated assault in Seattle, these differences were relatively small—
the rates in Seattle were 16 to 18 percent higher than those reported
in Vancouver during a period of comparable case reporting. Virtually
all of the excess risk of aggravated assault in Seattle was explained
by a sevenfold higher rate of assaults involving firearms. Despite
similar rates of robbery and burglary and only small differences in
the rates of simple and aggravated assault, we found that Seattle had
substantially higher rates of homicide than Vancouver. Most of the
excess mortality was due to an almost fivefold higher rate of murders
with handguns in Seattle.

Critics of handgun control have long claimed that limiting access   13
to guns will have little effect on the rates of homicide, because
persons who are intent on killing others will only work harder to
acquire a gun or will kill by other means. If the rate of homicide in a
community were influenced more by the strength of intent than by
the availability of weapons, we might have expected the rate of
homicides with weapons other than guns to have been higher in
Vancouver than in Seattle, in direct proportion to any decrease in
Vancouver's rate of firearm homicides. This was not the case. During
the study interval, Vancouver's rate of homicides with weapons

---

fivefold: five times

other than guns was not significantly higher than that in Seattle, suggesting that few would-be assailants switched to homicide by other methods.

Ready access to handguns has been advocated by some as an   14 important way to provide law-abiding citizens with an effective means to defend themselves. Were this true, we might have expected that much of Seattle's excess rate of homicides, as compared with Vancouver's, would have been explained by a higher rate of **justifiable** homicides and killings in self-defense by civilians. Although such homicides did occur at a significantly higher rate in Seattle than in Vancouver, these cases accounted for less than 4 percent of the homicides in both cities during the study period. When we excluded cases of justifiable homicide or killings in self-defense by civilians from our calculation of relative risk, our results were almost the same.

It also appears unlikely that differences in law-enforcement   15 activity accounted for the lower homicide rate in Vancouver. Suspected offenders are arrested and cases are cleared at similar rates in both cities. After arrest and conviction, similar crimes carry similar penalties in the courts in Seattle and Vancouver. . . .

Our analysis of the rates of homicide in these two largely similar   16 cities suggests that the modest restriction of citizens' access to firearms (especially handguns) is associated with lower rates of homicide. This association does not appear to be explained by differences between the communities in aggressiveness, criminal behavior, or response to crime. Although our findings should be **corroborated** in other settings, our results suggest that a more restrictive approach to handgun control may decrease national homicide rates.

A Note on Vocabulary in Academic Studies

In the last paragraph of the preceding article, the authors use the word *suggest* twice. In normal use, of course, *suggest* means *imply* or *propose*. In academic research, however, it means something much stronger than that, more like *indicate*. Researchers will use the word to mean that they feel they have proven something.

You should also note the use of the phrase *associated with* and the word *association*. Why do the authors say that lower homicide rates are associated

---

justifiable: proven right, valid;   **corroborated:** supported

with restrictions on gun ownership instead of being caused by such restrictions? They do so because they are aware that they haven't shown any causation. They haven't proven that restrictions on firearms cause few homicides. A distinction like this is extremely important in academic research. Researchers are very careful not to make extravagant claims that they cannot strictly support. Notice the difference between this approach and that by Mr. LaPierre in the next article.

CRIME IS THE BASIC PROBLEM, NOT GUNS
Wayne LaPierre

Wayne LaPierre is executive director of the National Rifle Association's Institute for Legislative Action.

America has a crime problem, not a gun problem. Misguided attempts   1
to control crime by restricting the law-abiding only serve to divert
attention and resources from direct action against the criminal.

Advocates of further gun restrictions are making the U.S. a much   2
more dangerous place in which to live.

More than 20,000 laws regulate the rights of peaceful, honest   3
citizens to buy and use firearms—and yet the crime rate continues to
rise. When will we stop kidding ourselves? Do we really believe law
No. 20,001 will make any difference?

How many more people will die before we realize it's time to   4
devote our resources and public debate toward a direct confrontation with violent criminals?

The nearly 3 million members of the National Rifle Association   5
are leading the fight to deal with the insanity of our plea-bargaining
system, the tragedy of early-release programs for violent criminals
and the failure to enforce minimum mandatory sentences.

It's a tragedy that we don't enforce a law already on the books.   6
This stipulates that a criminal dealing drugs on the street who carries
a gun is subject to a five-year-to-life mandatory sentence. The streets
of Los Angeles and Washington would be safer tomorrow if this law
were enforced tonight.

When we begin swift and sure prosecution we may finally send   7
the message that people who commit violent crimes will be behind
bars for a long time.

The NRA has consistently supported programs like the McCollum-   8
Staggers amendment and legislation passed last week in Virginia

establishing an instant identification system—similar to checks done for credit card purchases—that stops felons from trying to circumvent the law to buy guns.

The technology and information are in place to make such   9
checks a reality. But most criminals do not purchase firearms over the counter. They buy them on the black market or steal them and never enter our system of regulatory law.

The NRA is advocating a plan of attack called Project Crime   10
Control. It's designed to get criminals off the streets for good, and that's the only way to curb crime. Project Crime Control calls for the following immediate steps:

- Prosecute and jail felons found in possession of firearms.

- Create new prison space. We can no longer afford the system's standard excuse, "There's no place to put these criminals."

- Establish a federal death penalty for killing a police or corrections officer.

- Deny probation and parole to violent felons who misuse deadly weapons.

- Stop the travesty of plea bargaining by enacting a tough federal law that allows only one felony in a five-year period to be bargained down to a misdemeanor. This will keep lawbreakers such as Patrick Purdy, the Stockton [Calif.] schoolyard gunman, off our streets and in jail.

- Require a 10-year sentence for using kids in a trafficking crime. Let drug kingpins know we're going to protect our kids.

From Los Angeles to Washington, drugs and violent crime are   11
making our cities increasingly unlivable. Problems that were once only associated with the "big city" are infecting other areas. With each felon committing over 187 felonies per year, the $430,000 it costs to let one roam free makes the $20,000 per year spent to keep one behind bars seem like a bargain.

We have some hard choices to make right now. Will we create   12
more political placebos, laws that add nothing to public security and only regulate the law-abiding?

Or will we finally begin fixing a criminal-justice system that   13
would set a Patrick Purdy loose on society seven times? Our limited

supply of human, monetary and time resources cannot be wasted in even beginning to follow the wrong course. We must decide right now whether to fight crime, or freedom.

DO GUN LAWS WORK? STUDY IS INCONCLUSIVE
Kristen Wyatt

ATLANTA—A sweeping federal review of the nation's gun control   1
laws—including mandatory waiting-periods and bans-on certain weapons—has found no proof such measures reduce firearm violence.

The review was conducted by a task force of scientists appointed   2
by the Centers for Disease Control and Prevention. The CDC said the report suggested more study was needed, not that gun laws don't work.

But the agency said it had no plans to spend more money on   3
firearms research.

Firearms injuries were the second-leading cause of injury deaths,   4
killing 28,663 people in 2000, the most recent year for which data were available. About 58 percent of the deaths were suicides. Gun accidents claimed about 775 lives that year.

Some conservatives have said that the CDC should limit itself to   5
studying diseases, and some have complained in the past that the agency has used firearms-tracking data to push gun control. In fact, since a 1996 fight in Congress, the CDC has been prohibited from using funds to press for gun control laws.

Since then, the task force reviewed 51 published studies about   6
the effectiveness of eight types of gun-control laws. The laws included bans on specific firearms or ammunition, measures barring felons from buying guns, and mandatory waiting periods and firearm registration.

In every case, a CDC task force found "insufficient evidence to   7
determine effectiveness."

"I would not want to speculate on how different groups may   8
interpret this report," said Dr. Sue Binder, director of CDC's Center for Injury Prevention and Control. "It's simply a review of the literature."

Most of the studies were not funded by the CDC. Gun-control   9
advocates quickly called on the government to finance better research.

"There have not been enough good surveys to know whether   10
these laws work, and that's a very sad and troubling fact," said Peter
Hamm, spokesman for the Brady Campaign to Prevent Gun Violence.

The National Rifle Association said it needed more time to review   11
the report before commenting on it.

About the only conclusion the task force could draw from the   12
surveys was that mandatory waiting periods reduced gun suicides in
people over 55. But even that reduction was not big enough to affect
significantly gun suicides for the overall population.

The task force complained that many of the studies were incon-   13
sistent, too narrow or poorly done.

"When we say we don't know the effect of a law, we don't mean   14
it has no effect. We mean we don't know," said Dr. Jonathan Field-
ing, chairman of the CDC task force. "We are calling for additional
high-quality studies."

Among the problems: 15

- Studies on firearm bans and ammunition bans were inconsistent.
  Some showed the bans decreased violence, yet others found the
  bans actually increased violence. Many firearm bans grant
  exemptions to people who already owned the weapons, making
  it hard to tell how well a ban worked. Other evidence showed
  that firearms sales go up right before bans take effect.

- Studies on background checks were also inconsistent, with
  some showing decreased firearm injuries and others showing
  increased injuries.

- Only four studies examined the effectiveness of firearm registration
  on violent outcomes, and all of the findings were inconsistent.

CONGRESS'S FIREARMS PROBLEMS
Micah Sifry and Nancy Watzman

According to the University of Chicago's nonpartisan National   1
Opinion Research Center, nearly 79 percent of the public believe that
a police permit should be required for purchasing guns. Large
majorities also favor restricting individual gun purchases to no more
than one a month and requiring safety training for gun purchasers.
Three-fourths support mandatory registration for handguns. Surely
popular opinion is due to the endless death toll: *The United States*

has the dubious honor of having the highest rate of homicide and suicide by gun among developed countries, and guns are the leading cause of death for people ages 10 to 24. In 2001 alone, nearly 30,000 people died from gun wounds.

Yet none of these overwhelmingly popular gun control propos- 2
als are law, primarily because Congress and the administration regularly capitulate to the tough lobby of the NRA and other gun rights groups. Together these groups have contributed $17.2 million since 1989 to federal political campaigns, 85 percent to Republicans. In contrast, gun control groups have contributed just $1.6 million over the same time period, 94 percent to Democrats, according to the Center for Responsive Politics.

Over the past 25 years, the gun lobby has shot down numerous 3
attempts to regulate guns. The NRA has beaten off proposals to require chemical "tags" in explosives, which would make them easier to trace in preventing terrorism; it has successfully opposed the ban of "cop-killer" bullets designed to pierce body armor. The gun group has thwarted proposals to require gun locks on guns, or to put limits on how many guns can be purchased per month. The list goes on and on.

To appreciate the firepower of the gun lobby, flash back to 4
1999. In April, twelve students and a teacher died at Columbine High School in suburban Colorado, after they were shot by stu-dents Dylan Klebold and Eric Harris. All four guns they used were purchased by an 18-year-old friend at Denver-area gun shows from private sellers who are not required to run background checks on buyers the way that gun shops must under the 1993 federal Brady Law. . . .

In the aftermath of the tragedy, Congress considered legislation 5
to require background checks for gun show purchases. Not once but twice the Senate voted against this commonsense measure. The 44 senators who said no to strong background checks over the course of a week in May 1999 were the beneficiaries, on average, of nearly 29 times more campaign cash from gun rights groups than the 40 senators who said yes to background checks on three votes— $23,340 versus $815. . . .

The Senate finally approved a bill requiring a three-day waiting 6
period for gun purchases, but only because then—vice president

Al Gore broke a tie. Their colleagues in the House disagreed. The 212 House members who voted the NRA's way on two separate roll call votes were the beneficiaries of 31 times more campaign cash from gun rights groups than the 189 members who voted in favor of background checks—$11,195 versus $355. The measure never became law, because the House and Senate couldn't agree on a final version. You can go to a gun show today and buy a gun from a private seller without going through a background check. . . .

WHY I BOUGHT A GUN
Gail Buchalter

I was raised to wear black and cultured pearls in one of Manhattan's more desirable neighborhoods. My upper-middle-class background never involved guns. If my parents felt threatened, they simply put another lock on the door. . . . 1

Today, I am typical of the women whom gun manufacturers have been aiming at as potential buyers—and one of the millions who have succumbed: Between 1983 and 1986, there was a 53 percent increase in female gun-owners in the U.S.—from 7.9 million to 12.1 million, according to a Gallup Poll paid for by Smith & Wesson, a gun manufacturer. . . . 2

I began questioning my beliefs one Halloween night in Phoenix, where I had moved when I was married. I was almost home when another car nearly hit mine head-on. With the speed of a New York cabbie, I rolled down my window and screamed curses as the driver passed me. He instantly made a U-turn, almost climbing my back bumper. By now, he and his two friends were hanging out of the car windows, yelling that they were going to rape, cut and kill me. 3

I already had turned into our driveway when I realized my husband wasn't home. I was trapped. The car had pulled in behind me. I drove up to the back porch and got into the kitchen, where our dogs stood waiting for me. The three men spilled out of their car and into our yard. 4

My adrenaline was pumping faster than Edwin Moses' legs clearing a hurdle. I grabbed the collars of Jack, our 200-pound Irish wolfhound, and his 140-pound malamute buddy, Slush. Then I 5

kicked open the back door—I was so scared that I became aggressive—and actually dared the three creeps to keep coming. With the
dogs, the odds had changed in my favor, and the men ran back to
the safety of their car, yelling that they'd be back the next day to
blow me away. Fortunately, they never returned.

A few years and one divorce later, I headed for Los Angeles with   6
my 3-year-old son, Jordan (the dogs had since departed). When I
put him in preschool a few weeks later, the headmistress noted that
I was a single parent and immediately warned me that there was
a rapist in my new neighborhood.

I called the police, who confirmed this fact. The rapist had no   7
modus operandi. Sometimes he would be waiting in his victim's
house; other times he would break in while the person was asleep.
Although it was summer, I would carefully lock my windows at night
and then lie there and sweat in fear. Thankfully, the rapist was
caught, but not before he had attacked two more women.

Over some time, at first imperceptibly, my suburban neighbor-   8
hood became less secure. A street gang took over the apartment
building across from my house, and flowers and compact cars gave
way to graffiti and low-riders.

Daytime was quiet, but these gang members crawled out like   9
cockroaches after dark. Several nights in a row they woke me up. It
was one of the most terrifying times in my life. I could hear them talking and laughing as they leaned against our fence, tossing their empty
beer cans into our front yard. I knew that they were drinking, but were
they also using violence-inducing drugs such as PCP and crack? And if
they broke in, could I get to the police before they got to me?

I found myself, to my surprise, wishing that I had a loaded pistol   10
under my pillow. In the clear light of day, I found this reaction shock-
ing and simply decided to move to a safer neighborhood, although
it cost thousands of dollars more. Luckily, I was able to afford it.

Soon the papers were telling yet another tale of senseless horror.   11
Richard Ramirez, who became known as "The Walk-In Killer," spent
months crippling and killing before he was caught. His alleged crimes
were so brutal and bizarre, his desire to inflict pain so intense, that I
began to question my beliefs about the **sanctity** of human life—his,
in particular. The thought of taking a human life is repugnant to me,

----

modus operandi: consistent method of operating;   **sanctity:** sacredness but the idea of being someone's victim is worse. And how, I began to ask myself, do you talk pacifism to a murderer or a rapist?

Finally, I decided that I would defend myself, even if it meant   12
killing another person. I realized that the one-sided pacifism I once so strongly had advocated could backfire on me and, worse, on my son. Reluctantly, I concluded that I had to insure the best option for our survival. My choices: to count on a cop or to own a pistol. . . .

I . . . called [a] friend. He was going to the National Rifle Associ-   13
ation convention that was being held in Reno and suggested I tag along. . . . The next day at the convention center, I saw a sign announcing a seminar for women on handguns and safety. I met pistol-packing grandmas, kids who were into competitive shooting and law-enforcement agents. I listened to a few of them speak and then watched a video, "A Woman's Guide to Firearms." It explained everything from how guns worked to an individual's responsibilities as a gun owner.

It was my kind of movie, since everything about guns scares   14
me—especially owning one. Statistics on children who are victims of their parents' handguns are overwhelming: About 300 children a year—almost a child a day—are killed by guns in this country, according to Handgun Control, Inc., which bases its numbers on data from the National Safety Council. Most of these killings are accidental.

As soon as I returned to Los Angeles, I called a man I had met a   15
while ago who, I remembered, owned several guns. He told me he had a Smith & Wesson .38 Special for sale and recommended it, since it was small enough for me to handle yet had the necessary stopping power.

I bought the gun. That same day, I got six rounds of special   16
ammunition with plastic tips that explode on impact. These are not for target practice; these are for protection.

For about $50 I also picked up the metal safety box that I had   17
learned about in the video. Its push-button lock opens with a touch if you know the proper combination, possibly taking only a second or two longer than it does to reach into a night-table drawer. Now I knew that my son, Jordan, couldn't get his hands on it while I still could. . . .

Today he couldn't care less about the gun. Every so often, when   18
we're watching television in my room, I practice opening the safety box, and Jordan times me. I'm down to three seconds. I'll ask him

what's the first thing you do when you handle a gun, and he looks at me like I'm a moron, saying for the umpteenth time: "Make sure it's unloaded. But I know I'm not to touch it or tell my friends about it." Jordan's already bored with it all.

I, on the other hand, look forward to Mondays—"Ladies' Night"   19
at the target range—when I get to shoot for free. I buy a box of bullets and some targets from the guy behind the counter, put on the protective eye and ear coverings and walk through the double doors to the firing lines. . . . I am keeping my promise to practice. Too many people are killed by their own guns because they don't know how to use them.

It took me years to decide to buy a gun, and then weeks before I could load it. It gave me nightmares.

One night I dreamed I woke up when someone broke into our   20
house. I grabbed my gun and sat waiting at the foot of my bed. Finally, I saw him turn the corner as he headed toward me. He was big and filled the hallway—an impossible target to miss. I aimed the gun and froze, visualizing the bullet blowing a hole through his chest and spraying his flesh all over the walls and floor. I didn't want to shoot, but I knew my survival was on the line. I wrapped my finger around the trigger and finally squeezed it, simultaneously accepting the intruder's death at my own hand and the relief of not being a victim. I woke up as soon as I decided to shoot.

I was tearfully relieved that it had only been a dream.   21

I never have weighed the consequences of an act as strongly   22
as I have that of buying a gun—but then again, I never have done anything with such deadly **repercussions.** Most of my friends refuse even to discuss it with me. They believe that violence begets violence.

They're probably right.   23

FIREARM DEATHS OF CHILDREN AND TEENS IN THE U.S.
Cynthia G. Hicks

For one reason or another, the deaths of children and teenagers by   1
gunfire in the United States has reached startling proportions and the numbers are growing.

In 2000, researchers at Harvard University studied the relationship   2
between firearm availability and the deaths of children 5–14 years old.

---

repercussions: results

They found that 6,817 U.S. children in that age group were killed by firearms between 1988 and 1997 and that the death rates were highest in states where firearms were most easily available. The Centers for Disease Control revealed that in 2003, 2,827 children and teens were killed by firearms. By comparison, the most devastating losses incurred by the American Army in World War Two came during the Normandy invasion of Europe in 1944, when about 2,000 American soldiers were killed. The number of children and teens killed in 2003 was greater than all American casualties in the Iraq war from 2003 to April 2006.

According to Matthew Miller, Deborah Azrael, and David Hemenway, authors of the Harvard study, children in other industrialized nations "are not dying from guns." Drs. Miller, Azrael, and Hemenway write, "Compared with [these] children . . . the firearm-related homicide rate in the United States is 17 times higher, the firearm related suicide rate 10 times higher, and the unintentional firearm-related death rate 9 times higher. Overall, before a child in the United States reaches 15 years of age, he or she is 5 times more likely than a child in the rest of the industrialized world to be murdered, 2 times as likely to commit suicide and 12 times more likely to die a firearm-related death." 3

In the five states with the highest rates of gun ownership— Louisiana, Alabama, Mississippi, Arkansas, and West Virginia—children were far more likely to be killed by guns than in the five states with the lowest rates of gun ownership, 16 times more likely from unintentional firearm injury, 7 times from firearm suicide, 3 times from firearm homicide, and "overall, twice as likely to die from suicide and homicide." The states with the lowest rates of gun ownership were Hawaii, Massachusetts, Rhode Island, New Jersey, and Delaware. 4

In their study, published in the February 2002 *Journal of Trauma,* Miller, Azrael, and Hemenway controlled for (that is, eliminated as factors) state-level poverty, education, and urbanization. This study is important because it suggests that children aged 5–14 are more likely to die from guns when more guns are present. 5

A TEACHER CONSIDERS GUN VIOLENCE ON CAMPUS
By William S. Robinson

I taught English for 36 years at the University of California at Berkeley and at San Francisco State University. In that time, at both schools, there was only one person killed by someone with a gun. 1

Unfortunately, he was a friend of mine in graduate school, and he was killed by accident, as it were. The killer was trying to get the professor he was working for.

Now, in April 2007, a deranged student at Virginia Tech University has killed, at this writing, 32 students and wounded at least 20 others. Some of them may die, while others will certainly be crippled for life.

What will be the American response to this massacre? Probably, nothing. It doesn't bother most of us that people are killed by guns. It happens every day. According to the *New York Times,* in 2004, an average of about 81 people a day were killed by guns in the United States. A total of 29,569 people were killed by guns that year. So what?

The Republican Party is adamantly opposed to gun control in almost any form, and the Democrats have recently regained majorities in the two houses of congress only by running against gun control in many districts, particularly in the south and west. The National Rifle Association is opposed to gun control in any form; its members vote according to its wishes, and politicians are terrified of them.

President George W. Bush and Senator John McCain, a leading candidate for the Republican nomination for president in the 2008 election, have both said that they oppose any legislation restricting gun ownership. The president's spokeswoman, Dana Perino, said, "The president believes that there is a right for people to bear arms, but that all laws must be followed." In the Virginia Tech case, all laws were followed except the one against murder.

There have been three responses to the 2007 massacre. The one that you never hear on radio or television is that guns, and in particular easily-concealed handguns, should be completely banned. After a much smaller school-yard massacre in Scotland, the United Kingdom parliament did just that. It is now illegal in the UK to own a handgun, and the gun killings have stopped.

A second response is to try to tighten the loose and porous checks on gun purchases. A few states and cities have enacted very modest controls on who can buy a handgun, while others, such as Virginia, allow virtually anyone to purchase as many guns as they want. None of these laws is likely to be changed very much if at all.

But there was been a third response, and the spokesmen (never women) for it have received all the air time they could wish. In this view, students and teachers should be armed so that they can kill potential killers. Philip Van Cleve, president of the Virginia Citizens Defense League, said that if students and teachers were armed, "they wouldn't die like sheep, at least, but more like a wolf with some fangs, able to fight back." I personally would prefer not to die like either a sheep or a wolf, and I try to imagine the chaos and death that would result if a deranged killer entered a classroom, and he and half the students opened fire on each other in that confined space.

On a large campus like Virginia Tech or U.C. Berkeley or San Francisco State, disputes, arguments, and heated quarrels among students occur every day. It's inevitable. Students get drunk and do amazingly stupid things. That's inevitable too. Suppose all these students were armed.   9

After every failed exam or poorly received paper, students take bitter exception to the low grade they've received, and they often complain loud and long to the teacher who is, as they see it, responsible. Suppose all these students were armed.   10

If I had to teach in a classroom of 25 or more students, all entitled to carry concealed handguns, I would have to bring my own gun to class and put it on the desk before starting the day's work. If I had to make an appointment for a student doing poor or failing work, I'd have to have my gun on my own desk in my office, ready for his or her appearance.   11

Is this what we want American higher education to look like, and be?   12

Is the solution to gun violence in this country to have everyone packing heat whenever they leave the house? Strangely, there are no other countries that see it that way, and even stranger, they don't have the gun deaths and massacres that we have.   13

MAN SHOOTS OWN SON

The following story appeared in the San Francisco Chronicle, *dateline Los Angeles.*

A North Hollywood man, victimized by burglars two months ago, shot and killed his 3-year-old son early yesterday when he mistook the boy's shadow for that of an intruder, police said.   1

Manuel Sesmas, 30, told police that he and his wife, Nely,   2
were awakened by the opening and closing of their bedroom door
at 3:45 A.M.

Mrs. Sesmas told her husband, "Here they come," said police   3
Detective Kevin Harley.

Sesmas said he jumped out of bed, grabbed a pistol and opened   4
the bedroom door. He said he saw a shadow and fired downward to
avoid seriously hurting anyone.

The shadow turned out to be that of his son, Victor Manuel   5
Sesmas, just days away from his fourth birthday.

Post-reading

Controversial issues always rouse people's passions strongly on one side of
the question or another; the more controversial the issue, the stronger the passions. And the question of handgun control is one of the most controversial in
American society. In cases like this, it is particularly important to sort out facts
from opinions and, when dealing with opinions, to decide which seem to be
the best-founded ones.

With these matters in mind, take the following steps in the analysis stage
of your writing process. First, go back over the reading assignments above
and make notes about what is fact and what is opinion in each. In the case of
articles that are entirely or almost entirely opinions, evaluate and make brief
notes about how well founded the opinions are. Are they the opinions of
someone who has actually studied the issue? Or are they opinions based on
personal experience? In the latter case, you should ask whether the person's
experience has been the same as yours or as that of many people or only a
few. You might want to keep separate sets of notes in some or all of the
following categories:

Very important facts
Less important facts
Well-supported opinions
Poorly supported opinions

Be sure to make notes about *why* you consider some facts or opinions more
important than others.

> ### Essay Assignment
>
> **Study the information above and write an essay in which you examine this issue and come to a conclusion as to whether handguns should be banned or licensed on a national basis.**

Pre-writing

If you have taken all the steps outlined above, you are now ready to let the facts and opinions argue with each other, to decide which side of the issue seems to have the stronger case. And you will also need to decide *how much* stronger the stronger case is. Is it very much stronger or only marginally stronger? In the former instance, you may decide that it is so strong that there is no question about the issue. In the latter instance, you may decide that one side has a *slightly* stronger case but that the issue is really still open to question.

As you think about organizing your essay, remember four important points from the section "Evaluating Evidence and Shaping Your Argument" (pages 259–261):

1. Be sure to include the strongest arguments of both sides. You may not wish to include weak ones, particularly ones based on poorly supported opinions.

2. Don't make "sack paragraphs," with all the arguments against gun control in one paragraph and all the arguments for it in another.

3. Remember that a statement isn't an argument; statements are often topic sentences—that is, sentences that have to be explained or backed up.

4. Make sure your conclusion is based solidly on the arguments preceding it. It should reflect the strengths and weaknesses of the arguments you cover in your essay, not be your own unsupported opinion tacked on at the end.

Create a working outline, with supporting examples, plus a working thesis.

Writing

Your introduction should probably acknowledge the controversial nature of this topic, as well as introducing your topic and stating your thesis. The body paragraphs should deal with the strongest opposing arguments, either by rebutting them or by acknowledging their validity. (Note how Buchalter ends her essay "Why I Bought a Gun.") However, your arguments and their support should be more compelling than those of your opposition. The conclusion should either make a recommendation or summarize your main points in order to emphasize your thesis. Be sure to review the Writer's Checklist on pages 338–340.

CENSORSHIP OF HIGH SCHOOL NEWSPAPERS

Censorship in a democracy such as the United States is an extremely controversial issue. Do people in power have the right to restrict what others say and write within a system of government that professes freedom of expression? For example, should even a democratic government have the power to forbid certain kinds of information from being reported to the public on the grounds that it might endanger the safety of the nation? Similarly, should certain books be taken off public library shelves because they may corrupt the country's youth—for instance, *Catcher in the Rye* or *Lady Chatterley's Lover*— as some have argued? When, if ever, is censorship in the best interests of a group of people?

So concerned with this issue were the men who wrote the Constitution of the United States of America that they added an amendment to it—the First Amendment, ratified December 15, 1791:

> Congress shall make no law respecting an establishment of religion or prohibiting the free Exercise thereof; or abridging the freedom of speech, or of the press; or the right of the people peaceably to assemble, and to petition the Government for a redress of grievances.

Clearly this amendment guarantees our right to freedom of speech—or does it? The next question that arises is who is guaranteed the freedom of expression and under what conditions? Do all of us have equal rights? Do high school students, for example, have the same rights as adults?

In 1983 the principal of Hazelwood East High School, in a suburb of St. Louis, ordered two pages of the *Spectrum,* the student newspaper, to be deleted because he found two articles objectionable—one on teenage pregnancy and one on the impact of divorce on students. Cathy Kuhlmeier and two other students who worked on the *Spectrum* brought suit because they thought their First Amendment right to freedom of expression had been violated.

The case, *Hazelwood School District, et al., v. Cathy Kuhlmeier, et al.,* was tried first at the District Court, which upheld the rights of the principal to censor the paper. The students then appealed to the Court of Appeals, which reversed the District Court's decision and said the First Amendment had been violated. The case ended up in the Supreme Court, which, on January 13, 1988, ruled in favor of Hazelwood School District and against the students.

However, not all of the Supreme Court justices agreed. Justices White, Rehnquist, Stevens, O'Connor, and Scalia were in the majority, but Justices Brennan, Marshall, and Blackmun dissented, and did so strongly—proving that even some of the finest legal minds in this country disagree on this issue.

Reading Assignment

Pre-reading

As a way of beginning to think about this topic, ask yourself what your position is. Do high school students have the same rights as adults? Why or why not? Discuss this issue with your classmates and others. And remember to take notes so you won't forget their positions and arguments.

Reading

PREGNANCY AT HAZELWOOD HIGH
Christine de Hass

The following excerpts are from a lengthy article on teenage pregnancy. The article discusses teenage sexuality, birth control, parents' ability to discuss sex with their teenage children, abortion, and the squeal law (which would require doctors or clinics to notify the parents of anyone under 18 years of age who requested any form of birth control). The article then presents three accounts by Hazelwood East High School students who became pregnant—the part of the article the principal found objectionable even though the names were changed to protect the students' privacy. Here are parts of those accounts.

Terri: I am five months pregnant and very excited about having my   1
baby. My husband is excited too. We both can't wait until it's born.

After the baby is born, which is in July, we are planning to move   2
out of his house, when we save enough money. I am not going to

be coming back to school right away (September) because the baby will only be two months old. I plan on coming back in January when the second semester begins.

When I found out I was pregnant, I really was kind of shocked   3
because I kept thinking about how I was going to tell my parents. I was also real happy. I just couldn't believe I was going to have a baby. When I told Paul about the situation, he was really happy. At first I didn't think he would be because I wasn't sure if he really would want to take on the responsibility of being a father, but he was very happy. We talked about the baby and what we were going to do and we both wanted to get married. We had talked about marriage before, so we were both sure of what we were doing.

I had no pressures (to have sex). It was my own decision. We   4
were going out four or five months before we had sex. I was on no kind of birth control pills. I really didn't want to get them, not just so I could get pregnant. I don't think I'd feel right taking them.

At first my parents were upset, especially my father, but now   5
they're both happy for me. I don't have any regrets because I'm happy about the baby and I hope everything works out.

Patti: I didn't think it could happen to me, but I knew I had to start   6
making plans for me and my little one. I think Steven (my boyfriend) was more scared than me. He was away at college and when he came home we cried together and then accepted it.

At first both families were disappointed, but the third or fourth   7
month, when the baby started to kick and move around, my boyfriend and I felt like expecting parents and we were very excited!

My parents really like my boyfriend. At first we all felt sort of   8
uncomfortable around each other. Now my boyfriend supports our baby totally (except for housing). . . . After I graduate next year, we're getting married. . . .

I want to say to others that it isn't easy and it takes a strong, will-   9
ing person to handle it because it does mean giving up a lot of things. Secondly, if you're not going to give your child all the love and affec-tion around, you won't be a good parent. Lastly, be careful because the pill doesn't always work. I know because it didn't work for me.

This experience has made me a more responsible person. I feel   10
that now I am a woman. If I could go back to last year, I would not get pregnant, but I have no regrets. We love our baby more than

anything in the world (my boyfriend and I) because we created him! How could we not love him??? . . . He's so cute and innocent. . . .

Julie: At first I was shocked. You always think, "It won't happen to me." I was also scared because I did not know how everyone was going to handle it. But then I started getting excited.   11

There was never really any pressure (to have sex). It was more of a mutual agreement. I think I was more curious than anything.   12

I had always planned on continuing school. There was never any doubt about that. I found that it wasn't as hard as I thought it would be. I was fairly open about it and people seemed to accept it. Greg and I did not get married. We figured that those were the best circumstances. So we decided to wait and see how things go. We are still planning on getting married when we are financially ready. I also am planning on going to college at least part time.   13

My parents have been great. They could not have been more supportive and helpful. They are doing everything they can for us and enjoy being "grandma and grandpa." They have also made it clear it was my responsibility. . . .   14

DIVORCE'S IMPACT ON KIDS MAY HAVE LIFELONG EFFECTS
Shari Gordon

This is the other article the principal of Hazelwood East High School censored from the May 13, 1983, edition of the Spectrum.

In the United States one marriage ends for every two that begin. The North County percentage of divorce is three marriages end out of four marriages that start.   1

There are more than two central characters in the painful drama of divorce. Children of divorced parents, literally millions of them, are torn by the end of their parents' marriage.   2

What causes divorce? According to Mr. Ken Kerkhoff, social studies teacher, some of the causes are: 3

- Poor dating habits that lead to marriage
- Not enough variables in common
- Lack of communication
- Lack of desire or effort to make the relationship work

Figures aren't the whole story. The fact is that divorce has a   4
psychological and sociological change on the child.

One junior commented on how the divorce occurred. "My dad   5
didn't make any money, so my mother divorced him."

"My father was an alcoholic and he always came home drunk   6
and my mom really couldn't stand it any longer," said another
junior.

Diana Herbert, freshman, said, "My dad wasn't spending   7
enough time with my mom, my sister, and I. He was always out of
town on business or out late playing cards with the guys. My parents
always argued about everything."

"In the beginning I thought I caused the problem, but now I   8
realize it wasn't me," added Diana.

"I was only five when my parents got divorced," said Susan   9
Kiefer, junior. "I didn't quite understand what the divorce between
my parents really meant until about the age of seven when I understood that divorce meant my mother and father wouldn't be
together again."

"It stinks!" exclaimed Jill, a junior. "They can, afterwards, remarry   10
and start their lives once again, but their kids will always be caught
in between."

Out of the 25 students interviewed, 17 of them have parents   11
that have remarried.

The feelings of divorce affect the kids for the rest of their lives,   12
according to Mr. Kerkhoff. The effects of divorce on the kids lead to
the following:

- Higher rate of absenteeism at school
- Higher rate of trouble with school, officials and police
- Higher rate of depression and insecurity
- Run a higher risk of divorce themselves

All of these are the latest findings in research on single parent   13
homes.

A LIMIT ON THE STUDENT PRESS
Jean Seligmann and Tessa Namuth

This article, published in Newsweek, *discusses the Supreme Court's
decision on the Hazelwood case.*

Abortion, teen suicide, AIDS, runaway kids. They're all standard fare   1
on local television news shows and the stuff about which teenagers
endlessly chatter. But when these topics begin making headlines in
high school newspapers, local school boards and high-school principals often feel compelled to ban them. Such juvenile prior restraints
are not rare: last year the Student Press Law Center in Washington
received more than 500 reports of censorship battles from student
editors around the country. Now these youthful editorialists have few
weapons left. Last week, in a 5–3 ruling, the U.S. Supreme Court
gave school administrators broad latitude to suppress controversial
stories. "A school need not tolerate student speech that is inconsistent with its 'basic educational mission'," Justice Byron White wrote
for the majority. "School officials may impose reasonable restrictions
on the speech of students, teachers and other members of the school
community."

Last week's decision arose from a suit by journalism students at   2
Hazelwood East High School in Missouri. They went to court after their
principal, Robert E. Reynolds, deleted two pages from the May 13,
1983, issue of the *Spectrum,* a student newspaper produced as part of
an elective course called Journalism II. Reynolds pulled the pages
because of two stories about teen pregnancy and divorce. In his view,
the articles did not adequately disguise the identities of girls who had
been pregnant or [protect] the **anonymity** of a parent who was getting divorced. Further, he said, references in the first story to sexual
activity and birth control were inappropriate for younger students to
read. Because of a printer's deadline, he says he had no chance to ask
students to make revisions.

In a stinging dissent, Justice William Brennan (joined by Justices   3
Thurgood Marshall and Harry Blackmun) charged that Reynolds had
"violated the First Amendment's prohibitions against censorship of
any student expression that neither disrupts classwork nor invades
the rights of others." The decision, Brennan warned, could convert
public schools into "**enclaves** of **totalitarianism** . . . that strangle
the free mind at its source."

---

anonymity: the state of remaining unknown or unrecognized;   **enclave:** an
area within the boundaries of another area;   **totalitarianism:** authoritarian
rule of many by one person or one group;

Reaction at Hazelwood East High was mixed. "I think the princi-   4
pal should have some say in what stories the paper does," says
Tammy Hawkins, current editor of the *Spectrum,* "but he should have
consulted the students." Cathy Kuhlmeier, one of those who filed
the suit, was disturbed by the decision, which she said might "turn
kids off to journalism." Principal Reynolds felt **vindicated.** "We're
glad the court gave us local control over the curriculum," he said.
Reynolds didn't wait for judicial permission: last semester he vetoed
a proposed story on AIDS, telling a faculty adviser that "the climate
wasn't right."

The ruling, which does not affect private schools because their   5
administrators are not state officials, is also not expected to have
much impact on college newspapers. At that level, where most
students are not minors, the courts have almost always extended full
First Amendment protections. But all student newspapers financed
and supervised by the public schools would seem to come under the
new ruling, not only those that are produced as part of a journalism
curriculum. The school could be considered the newspaper's publisher, explains Ivan B. Gluckman, legal counsel for the National
Association of Secondary School Principals, and thus has the authority to veto articles on subjects it doesn't approve of. "But I don't think
the court means for principals to have absolute rights to censor," he
says. The rights they do have "are meant to be exercised within
reason, for example, when something is obscene, indecent or just
bad journalism."

Unfortunately that may prove a murky standard in practice. The   6
court vigorously defended the **prerogatives** of high-school officials.
But the justices might have prevented another round of disputes if
they had also urged administrators to use their power cautiously. Can
a student paper, for instance, run a story about a local anti-abortion
center that works with high-school girls or the formation of a
teenage gay-rights group? It will now depend on the principal's
views. "The papers will be more **orthodox** and bland," predicts Alan
Levine, a New York lawyer and author of a book called *The Rights of
Students.* "The only alternative will be leaflets and an underground
press." That's an unlikely route, although, in this age of home

---

vindicated: cleared of blame or accusation, justified   **prerogatives:** exclusive rights or privileges;   **orthodox:** following accepted traditions or beliefs

computers, not impossible. The Constitution may no longer extend very far into the schoolhouse, but surely it protects desktop publishing by editors of all ages.

HIGH SCHOOL PAPERS GROW UP
Jerry Carroll

Carroll, a reporter, writes about topics being covered in some California high school newspapers. Unlike most of the country, the Hazelwood School District v. Kuhlmeier *decision will have little effect in California because an amendment to the State Education Code says that school authorities will have no say in what the newspapers print with the exception of materials that are libelous, obscene or slanderous, that "create a clear and present danger of unlawful acts . . . [or that] cause substantial disruption to the orderly operation of the school." Nonetheless, people in California feel strongly about the decision.*

San Lorenzo journalism teacher Richard Lloyd remembers when high   1
school newspapers did not deal with anything more weighty than cars, sock hops and football games. OK, maybe the lousy food at the cafeteria.

How times have changed. . . . "Right now, my students are   2
writing in-depth feature stories about alcoholism in the home, AIDS and a sociological study of our school," said Lloyd.

The gradual but startling shift in high school journalism—from   3
covering campus high jinks to reporting on such serious issues as date rape and teenage pregnancy—is such that last week the Supreme Court gave school administrators greater powers of censorship.

Justice Byron White wrote in the majority opinion that school   4
officials "must be able to take into account the emotional maturity of the intended audience in determining whether to **disseminate** student speech on potential sensitive topics, which might range from the existence of Santa Claus in an elementary school setting to the particulars of teenage sexual activities in a high school setting."

The case involved a Missouri high school where a principal   5
refused a student newspaper permission to publish an article about teenage pregnancy and the effect of divorce on students.

---

disseminate: spread around, distribute

The ruling has no effect in California, where Lloyd and a few   6
other high school journalism teachers successfully lobbied in the
early 1970s for an amendment to the State Education Code that
ensured broad press freedom for students. . . . The education code
language prompted the principal at Homestead High School in
Cupertino last week to reverse a decision to stop publication of an
article in the newspaper there about a 17-year-old student who
tested positive to HIV virus, which can lead to AIDS. . . .

Written by Kathryn Pallokoff, 17, the article is a careful and   7
responsible account of the problem, giving figures on the spread of
the disease and warning of the importance of "safe sex."

Other articles in the newspaper detailed complaints about   8
students being harassed by Army recruiters, Governor George
Deukmejian's spending plan for schools, and the risks involved in
drinking and driving. . . .

The AIDS article wouldn't raise a brow if seen in another publi-   9
cation. But reports like it will not be seen in high school newspapers
in most of the rest of the country after the Supreme Court decision.

Even though it doesn't apply in California, high school journalists   10
and their newspaper advisers view the ruling with scorn.

"My students are very much offended by the idea they are not   11
considered mature enough to handle these topics," said Steve
O'Donoughue, the newspaper adviser at Fremont High School in Oakland. "They feel in general—and I'm sure it's just not my students—
that it is hypocritical, especially when the two topics in the original
case, divorce and teen pregnancy, are common topics in the lives of
these kids.

"I don't know when it changed, but I'd say certainly in the '80s,   12
despite the image of students being wrapped up in their Esprit outfits
and MTV, that a lot of the high school press has been covering what
you might call the hard topics, the topics they feel affect them. These
include AIDS, teenage pregnancy—the topics the Supreme Court
ruled the principal had the right to censor. . . .

"I think students are more aware of topics that earlier genera-   13
tions wouldn't even talk about. They can talk a lot more clinically
about sexual topics. Just listening to student discussions about AIDS
amazes me how detached and informed they are." . . .

Donal Brown, faculty adviser to the *Redwood Bark* at Larkspur's
Redwood High School, said the switch from fluff to substance in

student newspapers coincided with "the awareness of young people that they have to do something about the problems they are facing." 14

He said the *Redwood Bark* last spring did an article about the rape of a 16-year-old girl who had become drunk at a party. 15

"It was extremely important for our community that this come out. It increased the awareness of students of how evil this was. We had an editorial talking about how students should give each other support and not allow these things to happen. There were a lot of people at the party who could have been more aware and protective of the girl who let herself get drunk," Brown said. . . . 16

He said allowing students to come to grips with the real problems that lie beyond the campus gives them the sense "they can improve things, help shape the society. They don't have to be passive robots taking their place in some sort of totalitarian enclave." 17

Said Rebecca Jeschke, 17, one of the editors in chief: "If you give kids responsibility, they rise to the occasion." 18

HIGH COURT GIVES A CIVICS LESSON
Fred M. Hechinger

Some people argue that the schools have the duty, indeed an obligation, to introduce students to only the highest values and morals with the hopes that the students will emulate them. Others argue that schools must also introduce students to the "real world" with the hopes that the students will be prepared to deal with the social and political problems that exist outside the high school walls; not doing so, they argue, amounts to repressing students' minds. In an essay published in the New York Times, *Hechinger discusses these two theories about the role of schools that underlie the* Hazelwood School District v. Kuhlmeier *decision.*

In 1969, the Supreme Court ruled that students "do not shed their constitutional rights to freedom of speech or expression at the schoolhouse gate." 1

Last week, in a 5 to 3 ruling, the court put some limits on this broad view of the Bill of Rights when it decided that a student newspaper was part of a high school's curriculum and subject to censorship of any content that conflicted with a "valid educational purpose." 2

The case, *Hazelwood School District v. Kuhlmeier,* grew out of a   3
long-standing conflict between two theories of education. The court
sided with the traditionalists, who see the school as a molder of
values for the immature. In the words of Justice Byron R. White, who
wrote the majority opinion, schools must set "standards that may be
higher than those demanded by some newspaper publishers or
theatrical producers in the 'real' world."

On the other side of the controversy is a view of schools set forth   4
by Horace Mann, the 19th-century patron saint of universal public
education, and, more recently, by John Dewey, the philosopher of
progressive education. These men, though not rejecting limits on
students' rights, held that schools are not enclaves apart from the
"real world." Dewey described them instead as "embryonic" versions
of society in which students learn to act as citizens in a democracy.

In a dissent that was solidly in the tradition of Dewey, Justice   5
William J. Brennan Jr. wrote that the mere claim by school officials
that student expression is incompatible "with the school's pedagogi-
cal message" does not justify suppression. Otherwise, he wrote,
school officials could convert public schools into "enclaves of
totalitarianism."

Justice Brennan conceded that educators have an "undeniable,   6
and undeniably vital, mandate to **inculcate** moral and political
values" but [argued] that this is "not a general warrant to act as
thought police."

"The young men and women of Hazelwood East," he wrote,   7
"expected a civics lesson, but not the one the Court teaches them
today." . . .

In the Supreme Court's reversal of the appellate court, Justice   8
White upheld the school authorities' right to censor speech that is
"ungrammatical, poorly written, inadequately researched, biased or
prejudiced, vulgar or **profane,** or unsuitable for immature audiences,"
none of which (with the possible exception of the last point) was at
issue in the Hazelwood case. . . .

The Hazelwood ruling is not likely to put an end to the controversy.   9
There is much agreement, shared by the dissenting Justices . . . that
limits exist to student rights, in particular those of the student press.

---

inculcate: teach by frequent repetition;   **profane:** contemptuous,
blasphemous;

But there is no consensus about how far school administrators can go in imposing their own views, or those of the political mainstream.

On this point the disagreement is clear-cut: Justice White 10 believes that principals may reject any student expression that could "associate the school with any position other than neutrality on matters of political controversy." Justice Brennan emphasizes the importance of "teaching children to respect the diversity of ideas that is fundamental to the American system."

For decades the student press has taken a zig-zag course 11 between **docile** publications that attract little attention and the more enterprising or provocative ones that are read and debated. During the campus upheavals of the late 1960's, students came to equate supervision with suppression, and rebelled by creating an under-ground press that eluded adult influence altogether. . . . With last week's ruling, the principals have regained lost ground, but they will be under an even greater burden to draw the difficult distinction between instilling values and repressing developing minds.

CENSORSHIP: A FACT OF LIFE STUDENTS ARE FORCED TO FACE
Jonathan Yardley

Yardley, the book critic of the Washington Post, *addresses the theory that schools have a traditional mission and the Supreme Court's decision supports just that. High school students do not have, he argues, the same rights as adults. His conclusion, however, points not to the ease with which school authorities should censor students but to the complexity of the tasks that teachers and administrators face.*

Apart from teenage newspaper editors, self-appointed guardians of 1 journalistic rights and First Amendment extremists, few Americans are likely to take serious exception to the Supreme Court's ruling last week on censorship of high-school newspapers. Its support for a prin-cipal in Missouri who had deleted stories from a student newspaper is sound both constitutionally and educationally. But the decision should not be interpreted as **carte blanche** for censorship, and it must not be taken as an excuse to sweep under the rug the serious issues with which the student journalists were attempting to deal. . . .

---

docile: ready to be taught, submissive;   **carte blanche:** full permission, ability to do what you want (French)

The Hazelwood student paper is not an independent publication,   2
but a teaching instrument of its journalism department. Had the students chosen to express themselves in an independent publication—
an underground or counter-culture newspaper, perhaps—Reynolds
would have had no authority to censor or discipline them, and presumably would have had the good sense not to try. But stories published in the student newspaper are another matter altogether. . . . As
Justice Byron White put it in his majority opinion . . .

"A school must be able to take into account the emotional   3
maturity of the intended audience in determining whether to
disseminate student speech on potentially sensitive topics, which
might range from the existence of Santa Claus in an elementary
school to the particulars of teenage sexual activity in a high school
setting. A school must also retain the authority to refuse to sponsor
student speech that might reasonably be perceived to advocate drug
or alcohol abuse, irresponsible sex or conduct otherwise inconsistent
with the shared values of a civilized social order."

In conclusion, White wrote that Reynolds "could reasonably   4
have concluded that the students who had written and edited these
articles had not sufficiently mastered those portions of the Journalism II curriculum that pertained to the treatment of controversial
issues and personal attacks [and] the need to protect the privacy of
individuals. . . ." Or, to put it another way, high school isn't the real
world, and the rules of the real world do not always apply there.

To Justice William Brennan, writing in dissent, the majority   5
decision is "brutal censorship," but even as one who usually agrees
with Brennan on questions of civil liberties and rights, I think in this
instance he goes too far. The decision does not, as he contends,
overturn a 1969 ruling denying that students "shed their constitutional rights to freedom of speech or expression at the schoolhouse
door"; the majority quite specifically reaffirmed that broad principle,
qualifying it only by the observation, also based in precedent, that
"a school need not tolerate student speech that is inconsistent with
its 'basic educational mission,' even though the government could
not censor similar speech outside the school."

This seems to me a matter of simple common sense. Even   6
though the legal rights of children have gained broader recognition
in recent years, it remains that children are not adults and that they

have no **explicit** or **implicit** right to behave with the full freedom granted to adults. Freedom entails the responsibility to exercise it with mature judgment, and this neither young children nor adolescents possess. One of the most important functions of the schools is to prepare them for that exercise; the principal of Hazelwood High School, in restricting the contents of an issue of *Spectrum,* was attempting among other things to teach his journalism students a lesson about what is and is not a responsible exercise of journalistic freedom.

But it was also an act of censorship, no question about that, and no doubt the court's endorsement of it will be interpreted in some quarters as license to clamp down on other, less offensive forms of student expression. Should that lead to heavy-handed restraints on student publications, performances and other activities—especially any restraints involving the expression of political or ideological sentiment—the result would be a bad civics lesson for the students and an **abrogation** of sound educational practice by the schools.

But this isn't likely to happen, at least on a widespread basis; the initial reaction to the decision was measured, except among the few alarmists who see it as the death **knell** for student rights, and no principals seemed to be in a great hurry to haul out the scissors and red pencils. Most school authorities probably agree with the Hazelwood school superintendent, who said the decision "reaffirms our position that the board of education has authority to establish curricula."

What nobody seemed to be saying, though, is that the ruling gives school administrators no help in dealing with the questions that the *Spectrum* articles raised. Like it or not, reality at the high schools is very different from what it was only a generation ago, and reality is what school administrators have to contend with. Sexual promiscuity, teenage pregnancy, drug and alcohol abuse: These and "conduct otherwise inconsistent with the shared values of a civilized social order" are scarcely new to the schools, but they are present now to an extent without precedent and they simply cannot be scissored away by censorship or other forms of escape.

---

explicit: directly expressed, clearly defined, explained; **implicit:** indirectly expressed, not clearly defined, implied; **abrogation:** abolishment by authority, nullification; **knell:** slow, solemn sounding of a bell

However clumsily and immaturely, the editors and writers of   10
Spectrum were trying to discuss these questions in a manner that
they hoped would help their fellow students; their journalistic
qualifications may have been limited, but their intentions were good.
The court's reaffirmation of the schools' disciplinary powers certainly
is welcome, but if the schools now use those powers to push reality
out of sight, they will be doing no one any good, least of all the
students. A society that expects its educational system at all levels to
act **in loco parentis** cannot insist that this same system willfully
ignore the facts of its students' lives. Somehow the schools have to
reconcile their traditional educational mission with the responsibility
we have **foisted** on them to teach students how to live in the real
world; it's a tough assignment.

Post-reading

As you are now aware, if you weren't already, the question of students'
rights and the problems of censorship are extremely complex. As in all really
tough arguments, intelligent and educated people disagree vehemently, and
their arguments are frequently well reasoned and thoughtful. Now, it's your
turn.

Go back to the selections above and ask yourself the following:

- Who is the author?
- Who is the audience?
- What does the author hope to accomplish?

In the margins or on a separate sheet of paper, write brief summary notes of
each article, including in them the author's position and his or her main
support. Also note any questions you think the article raises and doesn't answer
and/or any places you disagree with the author. In the latter case, make sure
you jot down *why* you disagree. (The articles by Hechinger and Yardley are
particularly important for the purposes of this assignment.)

Now, make lists of the arguments for the censorship of high school
publications and the reasoning behind them (noting the circumstances when

---

in loco parentis: in the place or position of a parent (Latin);   **foisted:**
imposed

censorship may be justified) and of the arguments against it and the reasoning behind them. After having carefully evaluated the lists, you are ready to write the paper.

Essay Assignment

Write an essay in which you discuss not just the *Hazelwood* case but also the broader issue of censorship in high school publications. You may want to take a firm position on this issue, or you may wish to explain the arguments surrounding the issue without taking a firm position.

Pre-writing

As you think about organizing your essay, remember these important points:

1. Give your readers sufficient background to understand the complexity and importance of the issue.
2. Cite the strengths, as well as the weaknesses, of the arguments you mention, including your own.
3. Support statements with facts and/or well-founded opinions to strengthen your argument.

For further ideas on structuring your essay, refer to the section "Writing Discussion Essays" (pages 363–365), then jot down a working thesis and outline.

Writing

Although you may feel strongly one way or the other on this issue, remember that there's no right or wrong answer. There are, however, stronger and weaker arguments. In order to compose the strongest one you can, keep an open mind while you write and use the most compelling support you can muster. Be sure to review the Writer's Checklist below.

THE WRITER'S CHECKLIST

The Idea Draft

1. Does your idea draft *respond fully* to the assignment?
2. Are your ideas *organized* in the way you want?
3. Does your *introduction* explain what the essay will be about and what its purpose is?
4. Do you have a *thesis* that states your point or indicates the issue the essay will address?
5. Do the *body paragraphs* each have a *topic sentence?* Do they develop the main points by giving *specifics and examples* to support those points?
6. Does your *conclusion* express your view on the issue and is it based on the argument in the body of your essay?
7. Have you *collaborated* with at least one trusted friend or fellow student who has read your draft *critically,* looking for lapses in logic or other weaknesses in content?

Sentence Combining

In revising your idea draft, keep in mind the possibility of using appositives, if you have studied them. Generally, you will probably use adjective clauses automatically because we use them in speech a great deal, but appositives are constructions that writers, not speakers, use. One of the most common uses of appositives is to identify someone or something, as in these instances from Dennis McLellan's article on part-time work for teenagers. (Note that the appositive in the first example contains an adjective clause too.)

> Nathan Keethe, a *Newport Harbor High School senior who works more than 20 hours a week for an exterminating service,* admits to sometimes feeling like the odd man out. . . .
> John Fovos landed his first part-time job—*as a box boy at Alpha Beta on West Olympic*—the summer after his sophomore year at Fairfax High School in Los Angeles.
> The book, *When Teenagers Work: The Psychological and Social Costs of Adolescent Employment,* is by Ellen Greenberger, *a developmental psychologist and professor of social ecology at the University of California, Irvine,* and Laurence Steinberg, *a professor of child and family studies at the University of Wisconsin.*

Often professional writers use appositives to develop their ideas, as in this case from Amitai Etzioni's essay:

> But in fact, these jobs undermine school attendance and involvement, impart few skills that will be useful in later life, and simultaneously skew the values of teenagers—*especially their ideas about the worth of a dollar.*

McLellan does the same thing but uses a common appositive + adjective clause construction starting with the word *one:*

> Part-time work during the school years traditionally has been viewed as an invaluable experience for adolescents, *one that builds character, teaches responsibility and prepares them for entering the adult world.*

Later Drafts

1. Taking into account the constructive criticism you have received, have you *revised* accordingly—that is, reorganized, if organization was a problem, or given additional support, if support was?
2. Have you read your essay *aloud,* listening closely to what it *actually says* (not just what you think it says)?
3. Have you *revised your sentences* if they were unclear or awkward? (This is another good place to work with a trusted fellow student or friend. Have him or her read your essay aloud, and both of you should listen closely to what it says.)
4. Have you checked for those *mechanical difficulties* that you know you sometimes have? Have you used the dictionary to check words that you think may be *misspelled?*

Final Draft

If you have followed this assignment step by step, you have worked exceedingly hard on this essay. Therefore, make sure your final draft reflects your care and effort by being as professional looking as possible.

1. Type it neatly, using the format your instructor has assigned.
2. Proofread slowly and carefully, word by word, line by line. (One last time, ask a trusted friend to proofread it *after* you have, or exchange your essay with another student and proof each other's.)

S*entence Combining*

SHAPING SENTENCES TO SHOW RELATIONSHIPS: APPOSITIVES

Among the words that can modify nouns are nouns themselves. In English, we can use nouns to add to the meaning of other nouns in ways that some other languages cannot do. For instance, in some languages, if you want to specify what kind of hunter someone is, you have to add a prepositional phrase to the noun meaning hunter. In these languages you would have a hunter of deer or a hunter of alligators. In English we simply put the qualifying noun in front of the main noun, thus: deer hunter, alligator hunter. Similarly, we speak of office buildings instead of buildings for offices or student union buildings rather than buildings for the union of students.

In addition to these common usages, in which we put nouns in front of other nouns, we also put noun modifiers behind the nouns they modify. Studies show that experienced writers use this kind of noun construction very frequently while inexperienced writers do not. Thus, learning this construction will take you a long way toward making your writing like that of writers in the academic and professional worlds.

Noun modifiers that follow the nouns they modify normally rename or identify or describe in different words the nouns they refer to. Two other points are worth mentioning here. First, these noun modifiers often have modifiers of their own, sometimes very long strings of them. Second, writers usually set these modifiers (together with their modifiers) off with commas. Here is an example:

Everyone looked up to George, the tallest <u>student</u> in the freshman class.

In this case, the noun *student* is the main modifier of George, but it has other words modifying it—*the tallest* and *in the freshman class*. All of those words together are a *noun phrase* modifying *George,* telling something about him. Here are a few more examples:

I'm going to make one of my favorite dishes tonight, <u>chicken Marengo</u>.
The street I live on, *a noisy, dirty, busy <u>thoroughfare,</u>* is not a pleasant place to be.
He had yet another idea for solving all our problems, *the third <u>one</u> that evening.*

Mary's car, *a dreadful clunker due to fall apart any day*, was purchased by a friend of hers, *a guy who was sure he could fix anything that ran on wheels*.

PUNCTUATING NOUN PHRASES IN SENTENCES

1. Single phrases are set off by commas. Remember to put a comma *after* the phrase as well as in front of it:

   Martha Goggle, a retired airline pilot, lives next door.

   I love her house, a redecorated 747.

2. Series of nouns or noun phrases are set off by dashes when they occur in the middle of sentences:

   My favorite forms of entertainment—concerts, movies, books, and records—are all fairly expensive.

3. Series of noun phrases at the ends of sentences are most often set off with a comma or a dash, less often with a colon:

   There are several dangers involved in skiing—broken legs, wind-burned skin, and death by avalanche.

EXERCISE

Combine the following sentences using noun phrases whenever you can, as in this example:

Melvin hated his cage.
Melvin was an oversized Indian elephant.
His cage was an undersized cell with poor room service.

Solution: Melvin, an oversized Indian elephant, hated his cage, an undersized cell with poor room service.

Rashaad and Gloria

1. Rashaad was dedicated to his studies.
   He was a nineteen-year-old math major.

2. Until she met him, Gloria studied hard but also enjoyed the good times.
   She was his girlfriend.
   The good times were parties.
   The good times were movies.
   The good times were concerts.

3. Rashaad could rarely be dragged to anything.
   He was the ultimate nerd.

4. He told her his idea of a great evening.
   It was dinner.
   It was calculus until 11:00.
   It was a glass of wine.
   It was her to snuggle with.

5. After she missed three of her favorite events, Gloria decided to dump Rashaad.
   One event was the Fifties Sock Hop.
   One event was the Homecoming Dance.
   One event was the Butchers' Meat Ball.

6. One night a mysterious object came crashing through Rashaad's window.
   It was a calculator with a note wrapped around it.

7. The note said, "Dear Rashaad. Here is my idea of a good time.
   It is dinner with Fred.
   Fred is an art major I have just met.
   It is dancing with Fred until 1:00.
   It is snuggling with Fred."

8. The note concluded with these words.
   These words were, "Use this to count on, from now on, because you can't count on me."

EXERCISE

Following are three sample sentence-combining exercises using noun phrases:

1. They bought some furniture.
   The furniture was a new sofa.
   The furniture was a bookcase.

   Solution: They bought some furniture, a new sofa and a bookcase.

2. He won the grand prize at the big raffle.
   The grand prize was a set of dishes purchased at a secondhand store.

   Solution: He won the grand prize at the big raffle, a set of dishes purchased at a secondhand store.

3. David and Martha pulled the roast out of the oven.
    David and Martha are my favorite cooks.
    The roast was a piece of meat big enough to feed the First Infantry
    Division.

    Solution: David and Martha, my favorite cooks, pulled the roast out of
    the oven, a piece of meat big enough to feed the First Infantry Division.

*In the first four exercises below, the noun phrases are underlined to help you
identify them.*

Albert's Pets

1. Albert Lee moved into a new place.
    Albert is an old friend of mine.

2. His apartment is attractive, but Albert had a problem.
    His apartment is a condominium not far from here.
    Albert is a man newly divorced.

3. Albert had a love-hate relationship with his condominium.
    His condominium was an attractive, sunny, two-bedroom apartment.

4. He loved the place but hated being there because nobody else was around.
    The place was the first apartment he had ever had all to himself.
    Nobody else was there, no other creature of any kind.

5. In short, Albert was lonely.
    Albert was a gregarious man from a large family.

6. That's why Albert decided to get a couple of pets.
    The pets were a dog and a cat.

7. The dog was a mutt he got from the pound, and the cat came from a
    friend of his.
    The dog was a puppy he named Animal.
    The cat was a kitten he called Kitty.

8. Animal quickly ate a major portion of his wardrobe.
    Animal was a frisky and untameable little beast.
    His wardrobe was his slippers, a shoe, several socks, and the leg of a pair of
    trousers.

9. Kitty used her claws to produce shredded furniture when she tired of
    chasing Animal.

The shredded furniture was a shredded couch, a shredded chair, and a handsome set of shredded drapes.

10. Albert's expensive new condominium was a wreck, but Albert was happy as a clam.

The wreck was nothing but a large playground for Animal and Kitty.

Creating Noun Phrase Modifiers

Because these noun phrases are so important to good writing and so useful to anyone who has to write much, some additional exercises follow to assist you in actively using them to express information you have. In each case, you are given a short sentence with an underlined noun and a blank to be filled in:

She bought the <u>car</u> she had been longing for _____.

Your task is to fill in the blank with a noun referring to the underlined noun:

She bought the car she had been longing for, a Ford _____.

Of course, because specific writing is usually better than general writing, it would be better to be more specific than that, to add a whole noun phrase:

She bought the car she had been longing for, an almost new maroon and gray Ford convertible.

Start with thinking first of a single noun, like *Ford,* and build on it because you are working here with using noun phrases. In the following exercises, questions follow the first four sentences to help you find first a noun and then a whole noun phrase that will work. Be sure to provide the normal punctuation used to set off appositives.

1. I saw a <u>movie</u> the other day _____.
   (What kind of movie? A comedy? A horror film? What was it about?)

2. I visited her <u>house</u> last week _____.
   (What kind of house? A mansion? A cottage? Or was it just a normal residence with some particular characteristics?)

3. A new <u>store</u> just opened in the mall _____.

(What kind of store? A store selling what? A store you want to visit? Why?)

4. Mary observed the <u>monster</u> through her binoculars _____

_____.

(What kind of monster? A huge beast of some sort? A creature from outer space? Your younger brother dressed in an outlandish costume? Your younger brother dressed in his normal way?)

5. I play my current favorite <u>record</u> all the time _____.

6. My <u>homework</u> _____ is going to keep me up all night.

7. My current <u>job</u> _____ is taking up too much of my study time.

8. The birthday <u>present</u> I got last year _____ was just what I wanted.

9. There are <u>four things</u> that I wish I could afford to buy myself now _____

_____

_____.

10. Of my three favorite <u>TV shows</u> _____ I think I enjoy the last one the most.

EXERCISE

The following exercises are similar to the ones you have just done. In the first five, you are given a model sentence to imitate. Use the model word for word but instead of copying the noun phrases of the model, use your own, drawing on your own thoughts and experiences.

1. **Model:** I get a lot of enjoyment out of my car, an aging 280Z that gets me where I want to go about as fast as I want to get there.

   Your sentence: I get a lot of enjoyment out of my car [or some other object], _____.

2. **Model:** I went to an interesting high school, a place where basketball was more important than American history and you were graded according to how much money your parents had.

   Your sentence: I went to an interesting high school, _____

_____

_____.

3. **Model:** I really enjoyed a book I read last week, an odd novel about a man living in New York City with three women.

    Your sentence: I really enjoyed [or hated] a book I read last week,

    _____.

4. **Model:** There is one teacher I always remember fondly, a high school speech teacher who took us to see Broadway musicals.

    Your sentence: There is one teacher I always remember fondly,

    _____

5. **Model:** I could eat one of my favorite dishes, chicken and vegetables cooked in apple brandy, just about every week.

    Your sentence: I could eat one of my favorite dishes, _____

    _____

    just about every week.

6. Write a sentence in which you use a noun phrase to describe a television show you enjoy.

7. Write a sentence in which you use a noun phrase to describe one or more members of your family.

8. Write a sentence in which you use a noun phrase to describe a job you have or once had or would like to have.

9. Write a sentence in which you use a noun phrase to describe your room or your house.

10. Write a sentence in which you use a noun phrase to describe a hobby of yours or an activity you enjoy.

REVIEW

In the following exercises, you will practice using modifiers and joining words. In the first three, noun phrases are underlined, but in the rest, you will have to find them on your own. As in previous exercises, places where you should use joining words have been indicated.

Note: When you use a noun phrase to modify a noun that already has a prepositional phrase following it, your noun phrase modifier should always follow the prepositional phrase. For example, if you wanted to use the noun phrase *my mother* to modify any of the following nouns + prepositional phrases, you would write them this way:

The woman of the house, my mother
The doctor in charge, my mother
The person with the best idea, my mother
The speaker on the platform, my mother

The Statue of Liberty

1. The most famous statue was the creation of a sculptor.
   The statue is in the United States.
   The statue is the Statue of Liberty.
   The sculptor was French.
   The sculptor had grandiose ideas.
   The sculptor was Frédéric-Auguste Bartholdi.

2. He was assisted by an engineer.
   The engineer was celebrated.
   The engineer was Alexandre-Gustave Eiffel.
   Eiffel was the designer and builder of the Eiffel Tower.
   The Eiffel Tower is famous.
   The Eiffel Tower is in Paris.

3. The world associates the Statue of Liberty with New York.
   New York is the main American center for finance and the arts.
   [join to show concession]
   Bartholdi originally created a series of models.
   The series is fascinating.
   The models are of the statue.
   The models were designed for the Suez Canal in Egypt.

4. These models of female figures were part of Bartholdi's plan.
   The female figures were holding a torch aloft.
   The plan was for a lighthouse.
   The lighthouse was in the shape of an enormous female figure.
   The figure was standing at the entrance to the canal.

5. The light would come from the figure's torch and from a crown on her head.
   The light was shining from the lighthouse.
   The torch and the crown are both features of the Statue of Liberty.

6. His Suez statue rejected, Bartholdi came to the United States and proposed a statue.

Bartholdi was a believer in freedom in an age of European despotism.
The statue was dedicated to liberty.

7. Many Americans of the time were suspicious of Europeans.
   [join to show opposition or concession]
   His idea gained support in America, and he even secured a location.
   His idea was unique.
   His idea was grandiose.
   The location was for the proposed statue.
   The location was Bedloe's Island in New York harbor.

8. The statue was made of copper.
   The copper was beaten into shape over plaster forms.
   The copper was mounted on a steel skeleton.
   The skeleton was designed by Eiffel.

9. Americans of the time were apprehensive that the statue might not be fully clothed.
   The Americans were a prudish bunch.

10. The man who swung public opinion in favor of the statue was Joseph Pulitzer, who drummed up support through his two newspapers.
    Pulitzer was an immigrant from Hungary.
    The newspapers were the *New York World* and the *St. Louis Post-Dispatch.*

In the following exercise, you will practice using modifiers, including appositives, and joining words. To assist you with the joining words, places in which coordinators and subordinators should be used are marked.

Cold Comfort

1. [subord] The first caveman had the first case of sniffles.
   We have begun to understand the cold only in years.
   The cold is common.
   The years are recent.

2. A cold results.
   [subord] A virus enters our upper respiratory tract and begins to kill the cells there.
   The virus is a microscopic organism.

Our upper respiratory tract is our nose and throat.

It kills the cells there in order to reproduce.

3. The symptoms of a cold are the results of the body.

The symptoms are most frequent.

The symptoms are congestion.

The symptoms are a drippy nose.

The symptoms are coughing and sneezing.

The body is attempting to get rid of the virus.

The virus is invading.

4. Many of our cold remedies really interfere with our bodies' attempts.

The attempts are to kill the virus.

The virus is causing the cold.

[coord] We should take as few such remedies as possible.

5. One would think we could develop drugs.

The drugs are to kill the cold viruses.

[coord] There is one complication.

The complication is little.

The complication prevents us from doing that.

6. [subord] Scientists have so far identified more than two hundred different cold viruses.

These are only a fraction of the ones.

The ones are harmful.

The ones are in existence.

[coord] It would require a different drug to kill each different virus.

7. [subord] You could get shots against every cold virus.

The virus is known.

You could still catch a cold.

The cold would be every year of your life.

The cold would be from an unknown virus.

8. Linus Pauling believed that vitamin C can prevent colds.

He was a famous scientist.

He won the Nobel Prize in chemistry.

[coord] Scientists have concluded that vitamin C has little or no effect.

The effect is deterrent.

9. The only thing that has prevented people from catching each other's colds is a facial tissue.

The tissue is impregnated with iodine.

The tissue is called "the killer Kleenex."

10. [subord] Most people believe that kissing is an easy way to transmit a cold virus.

Fortunately, it is not.

11. [subord] You wish to catch a cold.

The cold is good.

The cold is annoying.

The cold is sneezy.

The cold is drippy.

Simply shake hands with someone or touch an article.

The article belongs to that person.

SHAPING SENTENCES TO SHOW RELATIONSHIPS: ADJECTIVE CLAUSES

So far you have worked with adding individual words or phrases to nouns to amplify their meanings. In this lesson, you will add clauses to nouns. Unlike a phrase, a clause contains both a subject and a verb. Following, for example, are phrases of the kinds you have been working with. Note that although some of them contain forms of verbs, none of them contains both a subject and a verb; that is, none of them could be changed into a sentence.

a groaning monster
groaning loudly
bored by the company of frogs
at the local shopping center
with all kinds of clothes
in violent reds, luminescent blues, blazing yellows
the tallest student in the freshman class
a piece of meat big enough to feed Godzilla

Length has nothing to do with whether a group of words is a phrase or a clause; the only thing that counts is whether there is a subject and a verb in the group of words. Here are some common clauses; their subjects and verbs are underlined:

because <u>he</u> <u>had eaten</u> it
while the <u>wind</u> <u>blew</u>
how <u>nobody</u> in the house <u>knows</u> about the leak
what the <u>woman</u> with the new coat <u>will want</u>

The clauses that modify nouns are different from the four above. Noun-modifying clauses—which, you will not be surprised to hear, are called *adjective clauses*—generally begin with the word *who, that,* or *which.* They begin with *who* if the noun the clause modifies is a person word, and they begin with *that* or *which* if it is a word referring to anything that isn't a person.

The woman/who took the plane to Paris
The coat/that I wore to the concert last night

In the exercises below, you will find pairs of short sentences. You are to make the second sentence of each pair into an adjective clause modifying the underlined noun in the first sentence. In each case, find the word in the second sentence that either repeats or refers to the underlined noun and change it into *who* if the underlined noun is a person word or *that* or *which* if it is a thing word. Here are some examples:

1. The <u>woman</u> is my aunt.
    She bought me a new kangaroo.

    Solution: The woman who bought me a new kangaroo is my aunt.

    Explanation: The word in the second sentence that refers to *woman* is *she. She* is a person word, so it is replaced by *who.*

2. The <u>box</u> contained the birthday present.
    It fell off the table.

    Solution: The box that fell off the table contained the birthday present.

    Explanation: The word in the second sentence that refers to *box* is *it. It* is a thing word and so is replaced by *that* or *which.*

3. The <u>plan</u> is really interesting.
    You proposed it.

    Solution: The plan which you proposed is really interesting.

    Explanation: The word in the second sentence that refers to *plan* is *it. It* is a thing word and so is replaced by *that* or *which.* But one cannot say *The plan/ you proposed which / is really interesting,* and so one must move the word *which* to the front of the clause.

EXERCISE

In the first five pairs of sentences below, the noun in the first sentence that the adjective clause is to modify is underlined, and the noun or pronoun in the second sentence that refers to it and must be changed to who, that, or which is also underlined.

Cars and the Environment

1. George bought a used car.
   It gave him endless problems.

2. He took it to a mechanic.
   He told him it would cost $450 to fix it.

3. George bought a car.
   He thought he would like it.

4. But now he owns one.
   He hates it.

5. However, he has found a mechanic.
   He does excellent work.

6. A problem is the harmful effect of automobiles on the environment.
   We have to face this problem.

7. Cars have a particularly damaging effect.
   The cars are not maintained properly.

8. But the gases still create serious atmospheric problems.
   Even new cars emit these gases.

9. The cars are primarily responsible for the smog in most of our cities.
   People drive these cars to and from work and around town on errands.

10. However, the pollution comes from other sources as well.
    We suffer from this pollution.

SPECIAL RULES

Using adjective clauses can involve some rules that you and your instructor may or may not want to get into. Here are two special rules.

Adjective Clauses: Special Rule 1

Sometimes adjective clauses should have commas around them and some-times they should not. Although most of the time it does not matter whether a particular adjective clause is set off with commas or not, sometimes it does, at least in American (as opposed to British) usage.

Let us begin by calling these clauses *comma clauses* (for those with commas around them) and *no-comma clauses* (for those without). Most adjective clauses are no-comma clauses, and whenever you are in doubt about whether to put commas around an adjective clause, follow one simple rule: Don't.

Whether or not we put commas around adjective clauses has *nothing whatever to do with the content of the clause, with what the clause says*. It is the noun the clause modifies that determines whether the clause will be a comma clause or a no-comma clause. If the noun requires no further identification for us to know who or what it refers to, the clause following it will be a comma clause. Here are some typical kinds of nouns that usually produce comma clauses after them:

- Proper nouns:
  Mary Smith, who works night and day, is an excellent lawyer.
  The Golden Gate Bridge, which spans the entrance to San Francisco Bay, is by no means the longest bridge in the world.

- Any noun indicating all members of a class of things or group of people or other living creatures:
  Copper, which has numerous important uses, is growing scarce.
  Homeowners hate crabgrass, which spoils the appearance of their lawns.
  Japanese automobiles, which are very well built, have captured an important share of the American market.
  Let us salute the crocodile, which has survived from the Age of Reptiles.
  The English, who have produced some of the world's greatest writers, have not produced many first-rate painters.

- Nouns preceded by possessive words usually will produce comma clauses following them:
  George's houseboat, which is a wreck, is no place to bring people you like.

Sometimes we do or do not use commas around a clause depending on whether we want to indicate that the information in the clause refers to all the members of the class indicated by the noun or only to some of those members:

> American lawyers, who charge outrageous fees, are a disgrace. (indicates that all American lawyers charge outrageous fees)
>
> American lawyers who charge outrageous fees are a disgrace. (indicates that only some charge outrageous fees and that only those are a disgrace)

EXERCISE

In the following exercise, decide whether the adjective clauses, which are underlined, should have commas around them and, if so, why:

1. Mark Twain who is probably America's greatest humorist came from a small town in Missouri.

2. Wolverines which live only in the far north are generally considered to be among the most intelligent of animals.

3. Many animals which are not as intelligent as the wolverine have adapted better to living near human beings.

4. Most people enjoy the paintings of Winslow Homer which are rich in color and often quite dramatic.

5. The boulevards of Paris which are spacious and tree lined are among the most beautiful streets in the world.

6. These broad straight boulevards are surrounded by narrow little streets that twist and turn.

7. My neighborhood which has both broad and narrow streets does not quite have the same charm as most of Paris.

8. The *Journal of Unforeseeable Disasters* which I subscribe to provides my favorite bed-time reading.

9. I am a great admirer of women athletes who are as dedicated to their sports as men without, on the whole, getting the same monetary rewards.

10. I have become a fan of lightly flavored mineral water which is both thirst quenching and tasty.

Adjective Clauses: Special Rule 2

When the noun an adjective clause modifies is a personal one and when the clause is a comma clause, good writers must decide whether to use *who* or *whom* in the clause. It isn't necessary to make this decision in no-comma clauses. To tell whether you should have *who* or *whom,* you need to see your adjective clause as a sentence, like this:

> John, who ate the cake, wore a big smile.
>> who ate the cake (clause)
>> he ate the cake (sentence)
> John, whom the alligator ate, was missed by all.
>> whom the alligator ate (clause)
>> the alligator ate him (sentence)

You can see that when the subject of the clause (*who, he*) refers to the noun the clause modifies, you use *who,* but when some word that is not the subject of the clause refers to the noun (*whom, him*), you use *whom.*

The following exercises involve choosing between *who* and *whom*; in the first five, the clause has been rewritten for you so you can see which word, the subject or some other word, refers to the noun the clause modifies.

1. Mary, (who/whom) loves parties, gave one last week.
   she loves parties

2. John, (who/whom) Mary can't stand, found out about it.
   Mary can't stand him

3. John came to the party with Jane, (who/whom) he had dated once.
   he had dated her once

4. Jane, (who/whom) liked Mary, was happy to be there.
   she liked Mary

5. Mary, (who/whom) nothing could faze, tossed John out.
   nothing could faze her

6. John, (who/whom) was fazed by everything, went home alone.

7. Jane, (who/whom) Mary invited to stay, did so.

8. Jane danced a great deal with Fred, (who/whom) Mary was secretly interested in.

9. Mary scowled a great deal at Fred, (who/whom) Jane was dancing with.

10. Fred, (who/whom) was having a great time, wondered what Mary was scowling about.

11. At that point, George, (who/whom) was madly in love with Jane, entered the room.

12. Now George, (who/whom) no one wanted to dance with, started scowling at Jane.
13. Jane and Fred, (who/whom) all the dark looks were being directed at, just wanted to have a good time.
14. Jane and Fred said good night to the others, (who/whom) were disappointed, and left.
15. But Mary and George, (who/whom) Jane and Fred had run away from, got over it and lived happily ever after anyway.

REVIEW

To do the following exercises, you will need to remember the difference between adjective clauses, which you have just been studying, and noun phrases, which you studied in the previous lesson. They can be easy to confuse since both do essentially the same thing—modify nouns.

> George bought the camera of his dreams, *an expensive new Japanese model* (noun phrase modifying *camera*)
>
> George bought the camera *that he had always wanted.* (adjective clause modifying *camera*)

As you can see, these two constructions do the same general kind of thing but do it in ways that are often quite different. For instance, we could use both our noun phrase and our adjective clause in the same sentence, modifying the same word.

> George bought the camera that he had always wanted, an expensive new Japanese model.

Remember: Adjective clauses begin with *who, which,* or *that.* Noun phrases do not.

In the following exercises, you will practice using modifiers and joining words. To help you with adjective clauses, sentences that should be changed into adjective clauses are marked with the appropriate clause word—*who, which,* or *that.* When a sentence is not marked with an adjective clause word, it should not be turned into an adjective clause; try to use a noun phrase instead. As in previous exercises, places where you should use joining words have been indicated. *IMPORTANT: Before doing this exercise, review the punctuation of noun phrases on page 341,* just before the exercises.

Don't Go Near the Water

1. Until well into the nineteenth century, men wore nothing in the water and swam only with other men.
   (*who*) The men swam for pleasure and exercise.

2. Women wore gowns with weights.
   The weights were sewn into their hems.
      [join]
   They bathed only with other women.
   (*who*) Women got into the water only to get wet.

3. Sea bathing did not begin until around the 1830s.
   The sea bathing was sexually mixed.
   The sea bathing was an American invention.

4. Women wore a number of clothes.
   (*who*) Women intended to go into the sea.
   The number of clothes was incredible.
   The clothes were a long dress.
   The clothes were long, full undergarments.
   The clothes were gloves.
   The clothes were a bathing cap.
   The clothes were overshoes.
   The drawers were under the dress.
   The bathing cap was with a straw hat over it.

5. By the second half of the nineteenth century, baths encouraged mixed bathing and even swimming.
   The baths were public.
   The baths were built in most cities.
   The cities were American.
   The swimming was by women.

6. Of course, the clothes had to give way to attire.
   (*which*) The clothes had made swimming impossible.
   The clothes were the dresses, gloves, and overshoes.

The attire was more practical.

The attire was less bulky.

The attire was for bathing.

7. The 1920s was a time.

The 1920s was the "jazz age."

The time was characterized for women by skirts.

The time was characterized for women by the right to vote.

The time was characterized for women by the first great woman swimmer.

The skirts were short.

The swimmer was Gertrude Ederle.

(*who*) Gertrude Ederle swam the English Channel faster than any man had ever done.

8. Men's and women's swimsuits now looked similar.

The swimsuits were tank tops.

The swimsuits were shorts.

The tank tops and shorts were woolen.

The shorts were belted.

    [join]

Most communities made rules.

The rules were foolish.

The rules applied only to women.

(*which*) The rules said that only a few inches of skin could show above the knee.

9. In the 1940s, bathing suits covered less body, and the swimsuit came in.

The bathing suits were for both men and women.

(*who*) The men and women were now beginning to seek tans.

The swimsuit was two-piece.

The swimsuit was for women.

10. The bikini made its initial impact in France in the 1950s, and the famous string bikini seems to have been an invention.

The bikini was named after an island.

The island was in the Pacific.

(*that*) The United States destroyed the island in an atomic bomb test.

(*which*) The string bikini leaves almost nothing to the imagination.

The invention was Brazilian.

Cats That Love the Water

1. Catfish are found in large numbers in almost every part of the world.
   They come in more than two thousand species.
   The parts of the world are North and South America.
   The parts of the world are Africa.
   The parts of the world are Asia.
   The parts of the world are Europe.
   The species range from gigantic to tiny and from harmless to dangerous.

2. The biggest catfish can weigh more than five hundred pounds and will eat virtually anything.
   The biggest catfish is the wels.
   The wels is huge.
   The wels is voracious.
   The wels lives in eastern Europe and western Asia.
   Anything swims in its waters.

3. Many varieties of catfish are found in the United States.
   [join]
   The largest species are the flathead cat and the blue fulton.
   The flathead cat is ugly.
   These live in the Mississippi River and its tributaries.
   These can weigh over one hundred pounds.

4. Among the oddest catfish are the electric cat of Africa and a South American catfish.
   The electric cat is dangerous.
   It can give an 800-volt shock.
   The South American catfish is tiny.
   It swims into the gills of other fish.
   It lodges there.
   It feeds on their blood.

5. The "walking" catfish can stay out of water for hours and slither across land.
   It is a variety.
   The variety is from southeast Asia.
   It was brought to Florida.

6. American catfish will not shock you or drink your blood.
      [join]
   Many have spines.
   The spines are sharp.
   The spines are sawlike.
   The spines are behind their heads.
   The spines are covered with a substance.
   The substance is slightly poisonous.
   The substance can produce a sharp sting.
   The sting can last for several hours.

7. Catfish come in such a variety.
   The variety is astonishing.
   It is a variety of sizes.
   It is a variety of shapes.
      [join]
   All catfish have at least two characteristics in common.
   These characteristics are the "whiskers."
   The "whiskers" give them their name.
   These characteristics are the fact that none of them has scales.

8. Among the tales are those about the wels.
   The tales are astonishing.
   The tales are told about catfish.
   The wels is gigantic.
   The wels is Eurasian.
   The wels is said to eat birds.
   The birds are swimming on the water's surface.
   The wels is said to have swallowed a small child.
   The child was playing near the shore.

9. Equally amazing is the description of "noodling."
   "Noodling" is a method of catching catfish.
   The catfish are large.
   The catfish are in backwaters of the Mississippi.

10. The fisherman wades into the water, gropes under logs and in holes, feels
    around until he finds a fish, then puts his hand in its mouth and pulls it
    out into the open.

The water is muddy.
The logs are old.
The holes are deep and dark.
The holes are the places that big catfish like to hide in.
Its mouth is huge.

CHAPTER *6*

Discussing

ARGUMENT AND DISCUSSION IN SCHOOL AND ON THE JOB

One of the words you are likely to find most often on essay examinations and written assignments is *discuss*. When teachers use this word, they want you not to ramble on about a matter, writing whatever comes into your head, but to formulate a carefully organized, complete argument or discussion of the issue.

We are all used to arguing a point. We often try to convince someone else, or a great many other people, to accept our position on an issue. As parents, we may want to convince our children to get good grades at school; as children, we may want to convince our parents that a C+ in chemistry really is a good grade given the difficulty of the course.

In college and in the professional world, argumentation is often a little different. One kind of argument may be intended to produce a decision—to change a university's admissions policies, for example. Another kind may be intended to describe or explain something—what the university's admissions policies are, how they developed historically, and what results they are currently having on society, to continue our example. This kind of argumentation, which we will call "discussion" from now on, may involve considering which of all the causes of World War I are the most significant or trying to find a relationship between economic and voting patterns in a particular place at a particular time.

Academic and professional discussion sometimes leads to a clear-cut preference for one position over another, but it often seeks instead to help us gain a better understanding of an issue or a situation.

The assignments that follow do not have "right" answers or solutions. For instance, one examines the availability, cost, and quality of child care for the small children of women who work outside the home. While the problems surrounding quality child care have no simple solutions, just as obviously any question that bears on child care is extremely important and one we should try to understand as well as we can.

The best way of trying to understand such a complex issue is to examine it from as many points of view and with as much information as possible. Then when we discuss the necessity of increased funding to support day care, we can support our position with thoughtful and well-founded discussion.

Opinion, as you have already learned, can be well founded or ill founded. We all have opinions, some based on fact (well founded), some solely on gut response (ill founded). As you have also already learned, opinions based on feelings alone are out of place in an academic or professional discussion. Only the most simple-minded audience—one you are not apt to find in a university or the professions—will accept an argument whose support is based solely on its author's emotional reaction. "We should impeach President X because his position toward women annoys me." Well, it might. But that won't convince the House of Representatives to initiate the impeachment process. "We should impeach Richard Nixon because we have hundreds of feet of recorded tape that prove he encouraged his subordinates to conceal illegal activities and so committed a criminal offense." Once the House members hear the tapes (the support for this opinion) and if those tapes do indeed convince them of Nixon's involvement, then the argument to impeach him acquires some basis.

All of the following assignments are issues about which reasonable, intelligent, well-intentioned people disagree. Although they have no "right" answer, each issue has evoked thoughtful and compelling arguments. Read the articles and essays with an open mind—one which acknowledges that *your* opinions, as well as those of the writers you read, may be well or ill founded.

WRITING DISCUSSION ESSAYS

In discussion essays, the first paragraph should *introduce* the subject and *acknowledge* its complexity. It may also *present* your position, or you may save that for your conclusion. The next paragraph (or paragraphs) should give your readers as much background as you think they will need to understand the issue. Then the organization may start to look somewhat like that of a typical argument essay.

As in argument essays, you must show that you understand the arguments on the other side in order to successfully convince readers of your views. If you appear to have looked at only one side of an issue, readers might very well conclude that you are only partially informed and don't understand the entire issue. Understandably, they might then simply dismiss your essay as being one-sided.

Therefore, you have to discuss opposing positions, acknowledging their strengths and/or pointing out their weaknesses. Some writers do this first, saving their own arguments for last. Additionally, they will show that they know what their weak points are (and may even concede their weakest ones) as well as make sure they cover their strong ones. As in the case of argument outlines, remember that the outlines here do not represent paragraph divisions.

> Approach 1 (address opposition first)
>   Introduction
>   Background
>   Opposing arguments and their reasoning
>   Writer's arguments and their reasoning
>   Conclusion

Other writers take up the opposition point by point. This is easier to do if the number of points to be considered is relatively small. Here are typical outlines for these two approaches. Again, remember that these do not represent paragraph divisions.

> Approach 2 (discuss issue point by point)
>   Introduction
>   Background
>   Argument 1
>   Opposing argument and reasoning
>   Writer's argument and reasoning
>   Argument 2
>   Opposing argument and reasoning
>   Writer's argument and reasoning
>   Arguments 3, 4, 5, and so on, as above
>   Conclusion

Another way to deal with a complex and thorny issue, particularly when you aren't necessarily trying to argue for one side or the other, is to spend the body of the essay discussing the various aspects of the issue. Then, in the conclusion, either summarize the whole issue or, if it is appropriate, make a recommendation about what should be done. This is really not very different from the approaches above except that rather than taking a position on one side or another, the writer is merely trying to clarify the whole issue, to show what is involved in it and what its implications are. Such an essay might have this kind of organization:

Introduction
Background
Explanation of aspect 1 (including arguments for and against)
Explanation of aspect 2 (including arguments for and against)
Explanations of aspects 3, 4, 5, and so on, as above
Summary conclusion or recommendations

*A*ssignments and Readings

WHO SHOULD CARE FOR THE CHILDREN?

Biologically and historically, women have been the family members primarily responsible for raising the children, at least the young ones. But now two trends that have been developing for some time are beginning to catch up with our old assumptions about child care. One is that an increasing number of women are deciding to enter the workforce, either out of financial necessity or for personal gratification. The other is that a high rate of divorce and a high rate of pregnancy out of wedlock have produced single mothers in unprecedented numbers, and for the most part, these women are young and poor. In both cases, the result is children with no one to take care of them.

Yet society needs children to grow up as healthy, happy, productive human beings who will be able to run things when their turn comes. It also needs women who can use their education and training in the workforce and women who can get the training they need to get off welfare. For all of these things, it needs people who can bring up children to be physically, psychologically, and emotionally healthy adults. The question is: Who's going to do it?

Reading Assignment

Pre-reading

As a way of beginning to think about this topic, ask yourself questions like the following and jot down your answers.

Should biological mothers be the ones to care for children? Why?

Should child care be available for women who want or need to work? If so, who should pay for it?

What role should married fathers play in child care?

Should society penalize unmarried fathers who contribute nothing to child care?

What role should government play in child care?

How many families do you know in which either both parents work or only one parent is present? In these cases, how is child care managed? Is it managed well?

As far as you know, are the children adequately supervised? Do they tend to get into trouble? Do you see or have you heard of any problems with juvenile delinquency or criminality as a result of inadequate child care?

Reading

WHO'S TAKING CARE OF THE CHILDREN?
Michael Ryan

Energetic and outspoken, Angela Roffle, at 31, is halfway toward her   1
college degree and fulfilling her dream of climbing out of welfare. Nothing has come easily to her. She is a single mother with a 10-year-old and 2-year-old twins living on the economic brink in a crime-ridden area. But for Roffle, those are not the biggest obstacles to achieving her goal. Child care is.

   "This is a bad day to talk about child care," she told me the   2
afternoon we met in St. Louis. "A neighbor usually takes care of my kids while I'm in school, but she had to take today off. I have two backups, but my second babysitter is in the hospital, and I couldn't get to the third because my car broke down." Because of her difficulties, Roffle missed several classes and lost precious study time.

Still, she is not defeated. "You know," she said, "there are plenty of women who go through this, just like me, at least once a week. You just have to."

Every day in America, millions of parents struggle to find ways   3 and means to provide care for their children while they go to work or school. Today, two-thirds of mothers work outside the home. One-quarter of the kids in this country live with only one parent. An esti-mated 23 million children require child care.

Of those kids, 8.3 million go to licensed day-care settings that   4 are inspected and required to meet minimum standards for health, safety and educational content. That leaves 14.7 million children in unlicensed settings. Some will get first-rate care with highly moti-vated caretakers. But others will go to substandard settings where they may run the risk of fire or accident and, in some cases, abuse. Still others have no regular child care. Their parents must depend on a shifting network of friends and relatives, and sometimes, in desper-ation, even leave their children unsupervised.

Child-care experts report that obtaining good day care is a   5 nationwide problem. It is frequently either in short supply, not up to standards or out of reach financially. "I call it a 'trilemma,'" said Arlyce Currie of Bananas, an Oakland, Calif., resource center for parents.

For many parents, the cost is the biggest problem. "Affordability   6 is the big issue," said Nancy Travis of Atlanta's Save the Children agency. "Child-care costs here range from $46 to $160 a week." Even for many in the middle class, such costs are prohibitive.

As Kathy Doellefeld-Clancy discovered, however, even having a   7 good income does not guarantee quality care. She and her husband both have good jobs, and she took great care in choosing a day-care center for her son Jonathan. Almost immediately, though, she started to worry.

"One day, I went in and there were about 40 kids with only four   8 teachers watching them," Doellefeld-Clancy said. "I had to stop a piece of equipment from falling on one of the children. I called the director, and she said it was just a fluke. But I went back another time and found one teacher supervising 14 kids."

The last straw came when Jonathan, then 16 months, bit another   9 child. A trained child-care worker would have understood that this behavior can occur at a certain stage. Instead, Jonathan was left in a playpen for an entire day without toys or human contact. One teacher, appalled by this "punishment," reported it to Doellefeld-Clancy. She quickly moved her son to another center.

There are other problems. In some states and localities, the back-   10
grounds of child-care workers are checked. In Georgia, owners of day-care centers are **vetted** by the Georgia Bureau of Investigation. But in states such as Missouri, church-related day-care centers are exempt from virtually all regulation—as a parent we will call "Dave" discovered to his horror.

Dave thought he had solved the day-care problem when he found   11
a responsible-looking church-affiliated center for his son, then 2. "Then one day when I suggested we go outside and play," Dave recalled, "my son said, 'Are we going to play Pull Your Pants Down?' I said, 'What do you mean?' and he said, 'That's a game we play at school.'"

Dave and his wife sat down with their son and elicited the infor-   12
mation that an adult at the day-care center involved the children in "games" that included taking their pants down and touching them. They reported their findings to state authorities, who questioned their son, found him credible, and said they would investigate.

"They went to the center and asked, 'Is there someone here who   13
abuses children?'" Dave recalled with indignation. "What do you think the answer was? No action was taken against the center."

Dave and his wife have since put their son in another day-care   14
center, and they have taken him to a counselor. "We think we found out in time," Dave said. "We hope that no permanent damage was done."

Most children, of course, probably will never be injured or   15
molested in child care. But, as Barbara Reisman, Executive Director of the Child Care Action Campaign (CCAC), an advocacy group, points out, "Of course you want children to be in a place where they're not in danger, but that's not enough. All children should be cared for in a bright, engaging space by well-trained, well-qualified people who love children."

That kind of child care is not a luxury but a practical necessity   16
for the economy, Reisman argues. Some studies show that early childhood education of the kind provided in quality day-care settings can help keep kids from dropping out of school later.

---

vetted: checked

Advocates argue that good child care can also benefit employers.   17
Richard Stolley, president of CCAC, was instrumental in the
development of a day-care center at Time, Inc., the large media
company where he is editorial director. "It's a productivity issue,"
he explained. "The number of employees who don't show up or
who show up **harried** because child-care arrangements have fallen
through is enormous. Child care is not a women's issue. It has an
effect on productivity of men and women, on the whole working
family."

Angela Roffle, Kathy Doellefeld-Clancy and Dave are three faces   18
of the national problem of child care. Each has struggled to find quality care—each is, somehow, finding a way to solve the problem.

Other countries take a different approach. If Angela Roffle had   19
been born in France, she would have received free pre-natal health
care, been granted maternity leave and her children would have
been eligible for government-sponsored preschools. In more than
100 countries, Dave and Kathy Doellefeld-Clancy would be entitled
to parental leave from their jobs to ensure their children were properly cared for.

In the United States, parents can get a tax credit of up to $1,440   20
annually for child care (which, typically, can cost two times that).
Can our government afford to do more?

"The real question," Reisman argued, "is, 'Can it afford not   21
to?'" One study shows that 25% of mothers on welfare can't take
jobs because they can't find adequate child care. The social costs of
not having good preschool and after-school care, Reisman said, may
be far greater than the expense of providing them.

Some communities and businesses are working to find solutions to   22
the day-care dilemma. The Hilltop Day Care Center in Florissant, Mo.,
was begun a generation ago by the School of Social Work of Washington University. It was designed to provide educationally enriched day
care for low-income children. Today, Hilltop—headquartered in an old
bank building—is a subsidiary of Lutheran Family and Children's
Services and has about 90 children, mostly from low- and middle-
income families, enrolled.

"It's a place where our kids can interact with other children,"   23
Valerie Joyner told me when she and her husband, Thomas, stopped

---

harried: disturbed

by the center. "They prepare kids for reading and learning." Two of the Joyners' three children attended Hilltop, and their 6-year-old is thriving in kindergarten after a year there.

Not far away, in an old public-school building in St. Louis, is   24
McCare, a day-care center for employees of McDonnell Douglas, the aircraft manufacturer. "We are completely self-supporting," Steve Zwolak, the center's director, told me proudly. "We charge from $85 to $145 a week, and we have 61 staff members for 186 kids." At McCare, infants get personal attention; older kids get educational play and parents are encouraged to stop in during their breaks.

When I visited, Ann McMahon Piening was dropping off her two   25
kids. Formerly an engineer, she was laid off by the company, but her husband still works there. She says that McCare has helped her establish herself in a new career. "I couldn't do it without McCare," she said. "I wouldn't be willing to leave my children unless I was sure they were safe and getting the kind of attention I would give them myself. My husband and I can go to work ready to do our best, happy that our children are well taken care of."

HOME DAY CARE PROVIDERS FACE INCREASING DEMAND
Tammy Hansen

Lynne Lyberger drops her twin sons off at the Livermore Laboratory   1
Employee Children's Center on her way to work. Her boys, who have been going to the lab-sponsored day care facility since they were 3 months old, spend their weekdays there at a monthly cost of $900 each.

Across town, Janette Billingsley starts her day by saying goodbye   2
to her husband and two teenage children as they head for work and school.

Parents begin dropping their children at her family home day   3
care, where she is licensed to care for 14 children, ages 2 to 10. A former preschool teacher, Billingsley opened her day care 10 years ago to be more available to her own children. . . .

Nationally, there are more than 50 million working mothers,   4
according to U.S. Census data. Most of these women return to work in her child's first three to five months, according to the National Institute of Child Health and Human Development. Parents across

the country face what First Lady Hillary Rodham Clinton has called the "silent crisis" of finding good, affordable child care.

Providers fear things may get worse in the wake of welfare reform. 5 With an anticipated increase in demand from welfare parents going to work, competition for . . . child care spots . . . will increase. Infant and odd-hours care are especially hard to find.

Only 1 percent of the county's licensed and license-exempt day care 6 homes and centers provide evening, overnight or weekend care. Forty percent offer before- and after-school care. Five percent accept children under the age of two. Yet, 40 percent of calls to the state resource and referral network are about infant care, 14 percent ask about before- and after-school and 5 percent seek weekend or overnight care.

Care providers also worry about an influx of untrained workers 7 because some former welfare recipients may see in-home child care as a source of income. Without training, such new providers could lower the bar for child care. Child care providers in homes and centers must have some schooling, be trained in CPR and first aid and pass a tuberculosis test. But anyone can care for the children of one other family without any such training. . . .

Training, however, is only part of the story, according to child 8 care activist Marcy Whitebook, co-director of the Center for The Child Care Work Force, Berkeley. The center is a nonprofit group lobbying for better wages and training for providers.

"Eighty-five percent of the child care in this country is mediocre 9 or poor," she claimed. Child care providers are some of the nation's lowest paid employees. . . .

HIGH STAFF TURNOVER IMPERILS CHILD CARE, RESEARCHER SAYS
Anastasia Hendrix

UC Berkeley researcher Marcy Whitebook was quietly putting the 1 final touches on her 79-page child care study when another report on the same subject sent academics, parents and care providers into tantrums. While she said she hardly expects her findings—being released today—to stir the same kind of controversy, she hopes they will refocus the debate over child care and its effects.

Many parents were devastated by recent research—funded by 2 the National Institute of Child Health and Human Development—that seemed to conclude the more time preschoolers spent in child care, the more likely they were to be aggressive or defiant. The researchers later said they were divided about the findings and that some data might have been misrepresented. "But the real issue is not whether 14 million kids under 5 are going to be in child care," Whitebook said. "The issue is: How do we make the child care kids are in better?"

The answer, she argues, is in her report, "Then and Now: 3 Changes in Child Care Staffing," which details the staggeringly high turnover rate of teachers and directors at child care centers.

Whitebook, a senior researcher at the Institute of Industrial Rela-   4 tions at the University of California at Berkeley, spent six years, from 1994 to 2000, studying 75 centers in San Mateo, Santa Clara and Santa Cruz—the most extensive and long-term study of its kind. She found "profound instability" in the workforce, with 75 percent of teachers and 40 percent of directors at those centers in 1996 gone four years later. "We had complete turnover of staff in two years—chaos!" one employee is quoted in the report as saying. Staffers were driven out by low pay, unable to survive on the average annual salary of $24,606, said Whitebook, explaining that the majority actually saw their wages decrease by as much as 6 percent after adjusting for inflation.

The study also found that more than half of the centers were unable   5 to fill positions that had been vacated, and those who were hired tended to have less education than their predecessors. "About half of those who had left in 1996 had a bachelor's degree or specialized early childhood training, whereas only a third of those who came in did," she said.

There is simply too much incentive to take other jobs, said Claudia Wayne, spokeswoman for the Washington, D.C.-based Center   6 for the Child Care Workforce, which assisted in the research. "A child care teacher who has an early education degree and is caring for 3- and 4-year-olds can make twice as much if she or he goes across the street and teaches 5- and 6-year-olds, and will get health insur- ance, pension, sick leave and other benefits," she said. "Many of the teachers who might prefer to work with younger kids find it very hard to do that when trying to support a family and make ends meet."

The only way to attract and keep highly trained day care teachers is to pay them more, Whitebook said. But because most parents cannot   7 afford to pay more for care, her solution is to find third-party payers to help support the system. "We have options for primary and secondary education and for college, but we don't have it prior to kindergarten, when even a middle-class family often can't afford the burden of high-quality care," she said. "The equation does not add up."

It's a contradiction, Whitebook said, considering the extensive 8 research that shows improving the first years of a child's education produces enormous benefits. "Science has really shown us that early environments matter and that nurturing relationships are essential to maximize [children's] development," she said.

Perhaps the most unsettling thing about Whitebook's findings is 9 that most of the centers included in the project were of high quality, many boasting nationally accredited enrichment programs. "This is a rosy picture. It paints the best we have to offer," Whitebook said. "And if this is how bad it is in a sample of high-quality programs, imagine what's going on in a sample that's less high quality."

The funding-quality problem has gnawed at Whitebook for three 10 decades—ever since she went to work at a child care center after graduating from college. Incensed by the low wages and equally low status, she has researched the issue ever since, authoring five major studies. Her latest study was funded by the David and Lucile Packard Foundation. "I think we're talking about a major kind of social change, and that takes time," Whitebook said. "I really think it's going to take

Wage trend for child care teachers

All wages reflect dollar value in 2000. Each category reflects average wages for the position.

Staff position	1996 wage	2000 wage	Change
Teachers	$14.95	$14.04	−6%/$0.91 per hour decrease
Assistants	$11.04	$10.80	−3%/$0.24 per hour decrease
Teacher-Directors	$17.48	$19.58	12%/$2.10 per hour increase
All teaching staff	$14.56	$14.01	−4%/$0.55 per hour decrease

Source: "Then and Now: Changes in Child Care Staffing"

parents not looking at this as a personal issue and feeling guilty when hearing these stories," she said, "but really getting angry and seeing it as a political issue instead—and telling elected officials that we need help. It's not just a low-income issue anymore."

AN INTERVIEW WITH MARY S.

The speaker, a 26-year-old woman with two small children, discusses why   1
she chose to return to her job as a county social worker, even though she
didn't have to for financial reasons.

I stayed home with the children for nine months after my youngest   2
was born, and I hated the intellectual **stagnation** and social isolation
I felt. I kept very busy (all young mothers do) taking care of the children and the house, cooking, cleaning, gardening. But it was really
lonely work. An infant and a toddler, as sweet as they were, were not
great conversationalists. And when my husband came home tired
from work, he didn't want to talk about the world outside the house.
He wanted to spend time with the children. Besides, by 6:30 or 7:00
in the evening, I was too physically exhausted to be much of an intellectual companion anyway.

When I decided to return to work at the welfare department,   3
I felt somewhat guilty. Here I was going to a job that I didn't *have* to
have and leaving my children with a babysitter from 7:30 in the
morning until 5:30 or so at night. And, like my husband, I too came
home tired. But also like him, I really wanted to spend time with my
children when I got home.

There's been a lot written about "quality" versus "quantity" time,   4
and a lot of it is rationalizing the less-than-ideal situation of busy parents
who don't spend much time with their children. However, because I got
the intellectual and social stimulation I require from a job outside the
home, I was a much happier person and, as a result, I feel I was a far
better parent than I had been when I was a full-time homemaker.

CANADA TAKES STEPS TOWARD UNIVERSAL CHILD CARE
Colin Nickerson

Imagine dropping your child off at a high-quality day care center   1
where the tuition is $3.40 a day, regardless of family income. That's

---

stagnation: inactivity, failure to progress

not happening in the United States anytime soon—but it is a reality for growing numbers of Canadian families.

In Quebec, an innovative government-sponsored program has won 2 wide praise from child care specialists, educators and parents groups. This week, British Columbia became the second Canadian province to create a publicly funded day care system open to all families—rich, poor and the sprawling majority in between. As in Quebec, day care centers in the western province will charge a minimal fee for care in licensed centers staffed by trained teachers and paraprofessionals.

In the 1960s, Canada carved a defining social policy line 3 between itself and the United States with the adoption of a national health care system, free to all citizens. Now the country appears to be blazing a similar path in day care. "These provinces are taking pioneering steps that could be followed by the rest of the country, as happened with the medical system," said Gillian Doherty, adjunct professor of family relations at Ontario's University of Guelph. "It shows Canadians remain committed to publicly funded social support systems, as opposed to the (American-style) obsession with cutting government expenditures no matter what the social cost."

The sharpest contrast between day care in the United States and 4 the two Canadian provinces shows on the bottom line, with Quebec and British Columbia families paying about $70 a month for the same level of care for which middle-income families in New England shell out $800 to $1200 a month, on average, per child. "We have a long way to go to make child care as affordable for working class families as it is becoming in Canada," said Mark Smith, coordinating director for the Massachusetts-based Parents United for Child Care. . . .

Until now, the best day care in Canada tended to be offered to 5 the poor or the rich, with middle-income families unable to afford top centers and unable to qualify for government-funded programs. "This is what all governments should be doing," said Sharon Gregson, a mother of four in Vancouver, where the provincial Ministry of Social Development has pledged to spend $30 million on a new program open to all families on equal terms. "Parents, some of whom are paying as much as $1,000 a month, are going to be getting a break that is literally going to change lives." Other provinces may follow Quebec and British Columbia, raising the possibility that Canada will join Scandinavia in creating a national network of day care centers staffed by teachers and licensed child care specialists. . . .

"Society is moving quickly toward recognizing that child care is a   6
critical part of a child's development," said Jan Pullinger, British
Columbia's minister of social development. "A publicly funded system makes sure that everyone's children get to benefit." Meanwhile,
Quebec's 2-year-old $1 billion day care program is considered by
some observers to be the most innovative in North America, with
more than 100,000 children enrolled in government-run programs
that cost parents 5 Canadian dollars a day, the equivalent of $3.40 in
the United States.

CHILD CARE SACRED AS FRANCE CUTS BACK
THE WELFARE STATE
Marlise Simons

Martine Susini performs the thankless tasks of any day-care director: 1
picking up tricycles here, cleaning tiny hands there, stopping to
check on milk bottles or the state of the mini toilets. Yet here in
France she is known as Madame la Directrice and her job holds considerable prestige.

Mrs. Susini heads a crèche, a municipal day nursery, in Paris   2
that occupies a spacious modern building on **Rue Edgar Faure.** As
director, she gets an adjacent apartment to insure that she is available for emergencies. And to care for her 88 children she has the
help of 25 trained employees, a ratio approaching that of a luxury
hotel.

"We can manage, but more staff would be even better," said   3
Mrs. Susini, who keeps a neat office with files and charts worthy of
an executive. She may not get additional employees on Rue Edgar
Faure, but elsewhere the numbers of officially approved child-care
workers and nurseries continue to expand.

That expansion, when France has reluctantly begun to trim its   4
swollen and costly **welfare state,** is a barometer of how strongly the
French endorse government-provided child care and how much they
have come to count on it. Strict budgetary rules . . . have forced
the government to make unpopular cuts in medical services and

---

Rue Edgar Faure: Edgar Faure Street;   **welfare state:** a government that
provides its citizens with services such as free medical care, inexpensive
higher education, free old-age care, and free child care

retirement benefits, but the generous subsidies for day care and health services for children up to the age of 3 continue to swell.

In Paris, for instance, a city of two million, there are already 520 5 subsidized nurseries, most of them run by the local government. In the last year, the municipality has opened eight new day-care centers and modernized six others. The city budget for day care rose by 60 percent between 1989 and 1994.

When the conservative government was elected in 1993, the 6 rate of spending on day care slowed, but each year spending levels continue to rise. In 1996, Paris spent $182 million on day care, 9 percent more than in 1994. The day-care network is expanding too in the rest of the country.

A number of other European countries, notably in Scandinavia, 7 continue to provide excellent child care for preschool children at relatively low prices, despite cuts in other aspects of the welfare state.

While American parents are deeply divided over day care for 8 small children and many feel that infants and toddlers are best off at home tended by their parents, the French and many other North Europeans have few **qualms** about such care.

Demand, and even a sense of entitlement, has grown among 9 young parents in recent years as studies showed that children who attended day nurseries and pre-school centers performed better in the first years of elementary school. Parents seem widely convinced, surveys have shown, that group child care makes for more stable, less **rambunctious** teen-agers. On a Paris playground you can hear mothers of toddlers talk of "awakening" and "civilizing" their children.

Hélène Desegrais had to wait four months to get a place for her 10 daughter Diane, who is 2. Since then, a weight has fallen off her. It means she can look for a job and take some courses. As a single, unemployed mother, she pays the $33 minimum monthly fee, although the real cost per child is $800.

"I've been really lucky," Mrs. Desegrais said. "Diane is already 11 more open, she plays more and she is talking more."

One reason French parents feel so comfortable with government 12 child care is that it is generally of high quality. Another reason is that

---

qualms: doubts;   **rambunctious:** disorderly

many Europeans, including the French, who are used to social-democratic traditions, have an attitude toward social spending that fundamentally differs from Americans; further, they are generally more comfortable with government involvement in society, particularly in education.

Outside experts have at times looked to France as a model 13 because of the consistent quality of its system. Day care first grew notably here after World War II when the government sought to protect small children from malnutrition and disease. But expansion has been fastest in the last two decades as more and more women joined the work force. The Paris municipal government, for instance, has increased its budget for day care more than fivefold since 1977.

Paris takes particular pride in its network of public and private 14 nurseries. For its 70,000 children up to the age of 3, there are 24,200 city-sponsored places; some 6,000 infants are on waiting lists. It is not known exactly how many parents decline to send their children to day care because the mother is at home or the child is left with a **nanny** or baby sitter. The city also employs some 2,600 care givers licensed to receive up to three or four children in their home.

Finding a vacancy in Paris, though, can take up to a year. Some- 15 times it takes connections, at the town hall, for instance. Anxious mothers register for a vacancy during pregnancy, call on social workers, visit the local town councilor and pay regular visits to several nursery directors to plead their case.

Paris officials say the capital needs more nurseries than other 16 cities because proportionately more married women here work outside the home and fewer have the support system that relatives offer in the **provinces.**

Rosaria Methenni, 30, is one such Parisian. She picks up her 17 18-month-old son, Kevin, from the Edgar Faure nursery after finishing her shift at the bakery where she works. Her husband, a car mechanic, has dropped Kevin off at 7:30 on his way to work. As is customary, they are charged 10 percent of their joint salary for Kevin's fees, which comes to $175 a month. Fees are also charged on a sliding scale, with poor parents paying as little as $33 and the richest a maximum of

---

nanny: live-in baby sitter;   **provinces:** areas of a country outside its capital

$640 a month. From ages 3 to 6, all children go to preschool, which is free.

"The nursery is marvelous but it's still a lot of money for us,"   18
said Mrs. Methenni, who has another child, age 7. But without this day care, she concedes, she could not keep her bakery job and the family would have to live on the $882 her husband brings home. To pay the nursery fee, the couple does some janitorial work on weekends.

Last year, she sometimes paid a woman to look after Kevin at   19
home. "For all you know, the child gets smacked or ignored," she said. She added that the nursery had made Kevin livelier.

These are exactly the kind of comments Mrs. Susini, the nurs-   20
ery director, loves to hear. "Our aim is to stimulate the children and to make them independent," said Mrs. Susini, who is licensed as a nurse and a teacher. Her nursery looks like a joyful place, with plenty of playrooms, toys, a paddling pool and tiny beds and cradles.

A psychologist calls regularly to discuss possible behavior prob-   21
lems and a pediatrician comes twice a week. "It's a disadvantage of nursery life that when one child gets a cold or diarrhea or an eye infection many get it," Mrs. Susini said. Some parents have withdrawn their children altogether after a particularly unpleasant brush with a nursery-based epidemic.

This being France, even little children get tasty, wholesome   22
meals. Fresh produce is delivered every day and two cooks prepare lunch on the premises. On this day, it was poached fish with carrot mousse and a yogurt.

To reduce noise and create a more intimate mood, the   23
building is divided into four sections, each with its own kitchen and playing and bathing spaces. Age groups are mixed. "It's more natural and calmer," said Françoise Goyard, who tracks when each child slept, ate and had a diaper changed. "If you put only fierce 2-year-olds in a room you get too much biting and scratching."

Besides nurseries, the city organizes other support systems. There   24
are day-care homes, where a supervised and trained baby sitter receives up to three children in her home. And there are licensed play schools where a child may be dropped off just two half-days a week. Two Paris nurseries keep extended hours from 5 A.M. to 10 P.M.

to help parents who work unusual shifts in places like hospitals, theaters or public transport.

One of them is The Magic House, in eastern Paris. "Both parents   25
must work difficult hours," a supervisor said. "Whatever the hours
they keep, the child should stay here only for eight hours. This cannot be the child's home."

Anne Husson said she had to wait more than six months to get   26
her 2-year-old into The Magic House. "But it was definitely worth
it," said Mrs. Husson, who organizes conferences and cultural
events and, like her husband, comes home late once or twice a
week. "It was always a panic and a scramble to have Alma looked
after."

Some care givers see unwanted side effects to the system.   27
Because sick children must stay at home, parents often give them
drugs to cure them, perhaps too quickly, a pediatric nurse said. "All
of our children already had a lot of medicines at their young age,"
the nurse said disapprovingly.

As nurseries have increased in number, some care givers see a   28
shift in attitude toward raising children, an expectation that
the state will provide them with child care, that makes them
uncomfortable.

"Young couples plan on a child and they automatically think   29
nursery," Mrs. Susini said. "Young people now approach us as if it is
our duty to take their child. Some become aggressive when there is
no room. There is a new definition of what it means to be a parent.
I wonder and worry about that."

Post-reading

Write brief summaries of each of the readings above, separating in each
case facts from emotions, feelings, desires, and opinions. Ask yourself the
following questions:

How sympathetic are you to women who don't necessarily have to work
but who want to? What basis do you have for your feelings?

Is the child care "crisis" a real one? Explain in detail why you do or do not
think so.

Do all women have the same problem with child care? If not, note carefully the differences for different women.

Just as women are mothers, men are fathers. Should fathers be playing more of a role in child care, and if so, what should it be?

Does the French system seem to you to represent a model for the United States to follow? Why or why not?

Essay Assignment

Write an essay in which you discuss the issue of who should be primarily responsible for taking care of the children. You may want to take a position on this issue and make a recommendation, acknowledging, of course, that there's no "right" answer for everyone. On the other hand, your essay may simply illuminate this issue without offering a resolution or making a recommendation.

Pre-writing

As you think about organizing your essay, keep these points in mind:

1.   Give your readers enough background to understand the importance and complexity of the issue.
2.   Acknowledge the strengths, as well as the weaknesses, of the arguments you cite—including your own.
3.   Remember that a statement is not an argument; a statement needs to be supported with facts and/or well-founded opinions in order to become an argument.

Also refer to the section "Writing Discussion Essays" (pages 363–365) for ideas on structuring your essay. As you have in previous assignments, jot down a working thesis and outline.

Writing

Although you may feel strongly one way or the other on this issue, remember that there's no right or wrong answer. There are, however, stronger and weaker arguments. In order to compose the strongest one you can, keep an open mind while you write and use the most compelling support you can muster. And be sure to review the Writer's Checklist on pages 435–437.

RATING THE MOVIES

The debate over what is and is not suitable for certain audiences has been going on at least since the fifth century B.C., when Greek dramatists and their critics considered the appropriateness of certain subjects for the stage. With the advent of motion pictures, the debate took on a new dimension. Here was a medium that was widely and easily accessible to children and adolescents. On any given Saturday afternoon, young people could (and did) flock to the movie houses to watch whatever was being projected on the silver screen, and parents had no way of knowing whether those movies were appropriate—in subject matter or its treatment—for their children. As you can guess, sex and violence were (and remain) their primary concerns.

Different societies and cultures have taken widely different approaches to what is acceptable content in films and what isn't, and even within individual societies, what is or isn't acceptable has often changed with time. For instance, in the 1950s and early 1960s in the United States, teenagers were not allowed to see a movie showing bare breasts, but they could watch movies featuring killings and other forms of violence. At the same time in France, violent movies were forbidden to those under 16 years-old while even small children could go to movies with nudity. Some societies have forbidden showing kissing on the screen, while others have no restrictions of any kind on who can see what.

In the United States, feelings about what children and teenagers can and cannot see have gradually been changing. Attempting to inform potential audiences, especially parents, of a film's suitability for children, the Motion Picture Producers and Distributors of America established its first code in 1930. Since then the code has been revised twice—in 1968 and 1984—reflecting changing views about what is acceptable for young people to see. For instance, in 1969 the movie *Midnight Cowboy* was given an X rating; today it simply gets an R. Despite or because of the past revisions, some people continue to call for further changes.

Not surprisingly, these codes have raised serious concerns within the movie industry itself and among the public at large. The movie industry argues that the codes interfere with artistic freedom by limiting what a filmmaker can include in a film in order to get it a "General" rating—one that does not restrict an audience by age—and are therefore a form of censorship that forbids certain people to see a film because of its content. A number of people outside the film industry concur while a number disagree. The following reading assignments reflect much of the confusion and uncertainty over whether or not to rate movies and, if so, how best to do it.

Reading Assignment

Pre-reading

Before you begin reading this assignment, work out for yourself on paper what concerns *you* have about labeling or rating movies. Ask yourself questions like the following:

> Should movies carry ratings or labels of any kind? A basic question involved here is whether in a free society, where the First Amendment to the Constitution protects our freedoms to speak and write, movies should be any more censored than books are.

> Under what circumstances should movies be labeled or rated? Should labels describe a movie's content for the guidance of the audience or act as censors? Or should they do both? Why? What characteristics should be brought to the attention of a potential audience? Sex? Violence? Nudity? Why?
>
> If a rating system should act as a censor, who should be forbidden to see what?

This is a complex topic intellectually and emotionally. Intellectually, it involves our First Amendment rights as American citizens to freedom from censorship. Emotionally, it taps into people's most deeply held beliefs about issues like sex and violence.

Reading

Try to read the following material with as open a mind as possible, and remember to read actively.

THE MOTION PICTURE ASSOCIATION MOVIE RATING SYSTEM
Jack Valenti

How It All Began

When I became president of the Motion Picture Association of   1
America (MPAA) in May 1966, the slippage of Hollywood studio authority over the content of films collided with an avalanching revision of American mores and customs.

By summer of 1966, the national scene was marked by insurrec-   2
tion on the campus, riots in the streets, rise in women's liberation,

protest of the young, doubts about the institution of marriage, aban-
donment of old guiding slogans, and the crumbling of social traditions. It would have been foolish to believe that movies, that most
creative of art forms, could have remained unaffected by the change
and torment in our society.

A New Kind of American Movie

The result of all this was the emergence of a "new kind" of American   3
movie—frank and open, and made by filmmakers subject to very few
self-imposed restraints.

  Almost within weeks in my new duties, I was confronted with   4
controversy, neither amiable nor fixable. The first issue was the film
"Who's Afraid of Virginia Woolf," in which, for the first time on the
screen, the word "screw" and the phrase "hump the hostess" were
heard. In company with the MPAA's general counsel, Louis Nizer,
I met with MGM's chief executive officer because this movie also represented a first—the first time a major distributor was marketing a
film with nudity in it. The Production Code Administration in California had denied the seal of approval.

  I backed the decision, whereupon MGM distributed the film   5
through a subsidiary company, thereby flouting the voluntary agreement of MPAA member companies that none would distribute a film
without a Code seal.

  Finally, in April 1968, the U.S. Supreme Court upheld the consti-   6
tutional power of states and cities to prevent the exposure of children to books and films that could not be denied to adults. . . .

  I knew that the mix of new social currents, the irresistible force of   7
creators determined to make "their" films and the possible intrusion of
government into the movie arena demanded my immediate action.

The Birth of the Ratings

By early fall, I was ready. My colleagues in the National Association   8
of Theatre Owners joined with me in affirming our objective of
creating a new and, at the time, revolutionary approach to how we
would fulfill our obligation to the parents of America. . . .

The Purpose of the Rating System

The basic mission of the rating system is a simple one: to offer to par-   9
ents some advance information about movies so that parents can

decide what movies they want their children to see or not to see. The entire rostrum of the rating program rests on the assumption of responsibility by parents. If parents don't care, or if they are languid in guiding their children's moviegoing, the rating system becomes useless. Indeed, if you are 18 or over, or if you have no children, the rating system has no meaning for you. Ratings are meant for parents, no one else. . . .

The criteria that go into the mix which becomes a Rating Board   10
judgment are theme, violence, language, nudity, sensuality, drug abuse, and other elements. Part of the rating flows from how each of these elements is treated on-screen by the filmmaker. In making their evaluation, the members of the Ratings Board do not look at snippets of film in isolation but consider the film in its entirety. The Rating Board can make its decisions only by what is seen on the screen, not by what is imagined or thought.

There is no special emphasis on any one of these elements. All   11
are considered. All are examined before a rating is applied. Contrary to popular notion, violence is not treated more leniently than any of the other material. Indeed many films rated X in the past and NC-17 now, have at least tentatively been given the "adults only" rating because of depictions of violence. However, most of the directors/producers/distributors involved have chosen, by their decision, to edit intense violent scenes in order to receive an R rating.

How the Ratings Are Decided

The ratings are decided by a full-time Rating Board located in Los   12
Angeles. There are 8–13 members of the Board who serve for periods of varying length. They work for the Classification and Rating Administration, which is funded by fees charged to producers/distributors for the rating of their films. The MPAA President chooses the Chairman of the Rating Board, thereby insulating the Board from industry or other group pressure. No one in the movie industry has the authority or the power to push the Board in any direction or otherwise influence it. . . .

There are no special qualifications for Board membership, except   13
the members must have a shared parenthood experience, must be possessed of an intelligent maturity, and most of all, have the capacity to put themselves in the role of most American parents so they can view a film and apply a rating that most parents would find

suitable and helpful in aiding their decisions about their children's moviegoing. . . .

No one is forced to submit a film to the Board for rating, but the   14
vast majority of producers/distributors do in fact submit their films
for ratings. Any producer/distributor who wants no part of any rating
system is free to go to the market without any rating at all or with
any description or symbol they choose as long as it is not confus-
ingly similar to the G, PG, PG-13, R, and, NC-17. The rating symbols
are federally-registered certification marks of the MPAA and may not
be self-applied.

The Board View on Ratings

The Board views each film. Each member present estimates what most   15
parents would consider to be that film's appropriate rating. After
group discussion, the Board votes on the rating. Each member com-
pletes a rating form spelling out his or her reason for the rating.

Each rating is decided by majority vote.   16

The producer/distributor of a film has the right under the rules to   17
inquire as to the "why" of the rating applied. The producer/distribu-
tor also has the right, based on the reasons for the rating, to edit the
film—if that is the choice of the producer/distributor—and come back
to the Board to try for a less severe rating. The reedited film is brought
back to the Board and the process goes forward again. . . .

What the Ratings Mean

G: "General Audiences-All Ages Admitted."   18

This is a film which contains nothing in theme, language, nudity   19
and sex, violence, etc. which would, in the view of the Rating Board, be
offensive to parents whose younger children view the film. The G rating is not a "certificate of approval," nor does it signify a children's film.

Some snippets of language may go beyond polite conversation   20
but they are common everyday expressions. No stronger words are
present in G-rated films. The violence is at a minimum. Nudity and
sex scenes are not present; nor is there any drug use content.

PG: "Parental Guidance Suggested. Some Material May Not Be Suit-   21
able For Children."

This is a film which clearly needs to be examined or inquired into   22
by parents before they let their children attend. The label PG plainly

states that parents may consider some material unsuitable for their children, but the parent must make the decision.

Parents are warned against sending their children, unseen and   23
without inquiry, to PG-rated movies.

The theme of a PG-rated film may itself call for parental guidance.   24
There may be some profanity in these films. There may be some violence or brief nudity. But these elements are not deemed so intense as
to require that parents be strongly cautioned beyond the suggestion of
parental guidance. There is no drug use content in a PG-rated film. . . .

PG-13: "Parents Strongly Cautioned. Some Material May Be Inap-   25
propriate For Children Under 13."

PG-13 is thus a sterner warning to parents to determine for   26
themselves the attendance in particular of their younger children as
they might consider some material not suited for them. Parents, by
the rating, are alerted to be very careful about the attendance of
their under-teenage children. . . .

If nudity is sexually oriented, the film will generally not be found   27
in the PG-13 category. If violence is too rough or persistent, the film
goes into the R (restricted) rating. A film's single use of one of the
harsher sexually derived words, though only as an expletive, shall
initially require the Rating Board to issue that film at least a PG-13
rating. More than one such expletive must lead the Rating Board to
issue a film an R rating, as must even one of these words used in a
sexual context. These films can be rated less severely, however, if by
a special vote, the Rating Board feels that a lesser rating would more
responsibly reflect the opinion of American parents. . . .

An R-rated film may include hard language, or tough violence,   28
or nudity within sensual scenes, or drug abuse or other elements, or
a combination of some of the above, so that parents are counseled,
in advance, to take this advisory rating very seriously. Parents must
find out more about an R-rated movie before they allow their
teenagers to view it.

NC-17: "No One 17 And Under Admitted."   29

This rating declares that the Rating Board believes that this is a film   30
that most parents will consider patently too adult for their youngsters
under 17. No children will be admitted. NC-17 does not necessarily
mean "obscene or pornographic" in the oft-accepted or legal meaning

of those words. The Board does not and cannot mark films with those words. These are legal terms and for courts to decide. The reasons for the application of an NC-17 rating can be violence or sex or aberrational behavior or drug abuse or any other elements which, when present, most parents would consider too strong and therefore off-limits for viewing by their children. . . .

The Public Reaction

We count it crucial to make regular soundings to find out how the   31
public perceives the rating program, and to measure the approval and disapproval of what we are doing.

Nationwide scientific polls, conducted each year by the Opinion   32
Research Corporation of Princeton, New Jersey, have consistently given the rating program high marks by parents throughout the land. The latest poll results show that 76% of parents with children under 13 found the ratings to be "very useful" to "fairly useful" in helping them make decisions for the moviegoing of their children.

On the evidence of the polls, the rating system would not have   33
survived if it were not providing a useful service to parents.

The rating system isn't perfect but, in an imperfect world, it   34
seems each year to match the expectations of those whom it is designed to serve—parents of America.

THE BIG CHILL
Lois P. Sheinfeld

In the following excerpts from an article published in Film Comment, *the author discusses the ratings of the Motion Picture Association of America in relation to the proposed ratings of the Parents Music Resource Center (PMRC), an organization founded by several politically prominent women who want to label rock music albums regarding their content. The PMRC argues that if labeling is good for movies, then it's good for music. However, Sheinfeld questions whether labeling is good for movies. She asks, "Are ratings good sense—or censorship?"*

Ratings went into effect in 1968, as the result of an agreement   1
between the MPAA, NATO (National Association of Theater Owners), and IFIDA (International Film Importers and Distributors of America). . . .

The MPAA Rating Board, based in Los Angeles, has six full-time   2
members and a part-time chair, Richard Heffner. The members are
chosen by Heffner with the approval of Jack Valenti, MPAA president
and Heffner's boss. We know very little about them. Their names and
backgrounds are closely guarded secrets. . . . These few individuals
are paid to watch movies all day and, according to Valenti, to rate
them "as most parents" would "on each of several categories such
as theme, violence, language, nudity, sex." The MPAA's half-dozen
Supermoms-and-pops are supposed to guess what countless millions
of differing parents think. . . .

An examination of this system in the light of principles that the   3
Supreme Court has recognized as limiting governmental censorship
demonstrates how far the MPAA's rating scheme intrudes upon free
expression. Not only does this system compel the repression of original work, it denies a willing audience access to that work.

First, state regulation of artistic expression has been strictly con-   4
fined to what fits the [Supreme] Court's definition of obscenity.
Restricting speech merely because of its supposed offensiveness has
been unequivocally condemned. . . . "Above all," the Court held in
1972, "the First Amendment means that government has no power
to restrict expression because of its message, its ideas, its subject
matter, or its content." . . .

Second, even where obscenity is concerned, the Court has for-   5
bidden vague and open-ended standards for censorship. . . .

Third, . . . any system for banning movies or other forms of   6
expression as obscene must provide rigorous procedural safeguards
against administrative error and unaccountability. The censor must
bear the burden of proof of obscenity, with prompt judicial review
to follow.

Obviously, the MPAA Rating System is, on all of these accounts,   7
more repressive than any laws that a state could constitutionally
enforce. Nevertheless, industry members suggest that it is the lesser of
two evils: that, but for the Rating System, the states might enact censorship legislation that would be costly to upset in court. . . .

The notion that the Rating System is more benign than any   8
potential state censorship ignores its powerfully prescriptive effects.
Its supposedly "voluntary" character . . . is a gross misrepresenta-
tion. Newspapers, television and radio stations refuse to carry ads
for, reviews of, or stories about X-rated films. Theater owners refuse

to play them, and distributors refuse to handle them. No wonder *Variety* likened an X rating to "a confession of guilt," carrying the punishment of being "shut out . . .from the market." . . . No wonder studios will order films cut, recut, and again recut until the Rating Board is satisfied enough to remove the dreaded X. . . .

Thus is the "voluntary" nature of the Rating System—much 9 emphasized by Heffner and Valenti—exposed for what it is. It amounts to a "voluntary" choice between economic suicide and self-subjection to a scheme of censorship more repressive than any government could get away with. . . .

Finally, the Rating System not only provides precedent and sup- 10 port for those like the PMRC, who would model the censorship of other media on it, but also invites ever-increasing pressure for more drastic forms of artistic content regulation. A September 1985 report of the National Council of Churches (NCC) recommended improvement of the present [rating] system by adding "simple, short phrases" of explanation such as "Brief Frontal Nudity," "Mild Comic Violence," and "Strong Graphic Language," which would "accompany PG, PG-13, R and X ratings, be displayed at the box office and [be] included by theatres in telephone descriptions of the films." This would, according to the NCC, "considerably further the industry's own objective to provide advance information to enable parents to make judgments on movies they wanted their children to see." The NCC also advocates the application of the MPAA ratings to videocassettes and cable TV.

Some have suggested additional movie ratings: V for violence, 11 L for language (profanity), S for sensuality. But the biggest battle took place over a proposed SA (substance abuse) or X rating for films depicting drug use. The Senate Permanent Subcommittee on Investigations held hearings on this subject in November 1985. Said Senator William Roth, subcommittee chair: "We're not holding the threat of censorship. . . . We're looking to encourage those in the movie industry to join us in the fight against drug abuse." Nancy Reagan and Dr. Carlton Turner, President Reagan's policy advisor on drug abuse, have also taken to proclaiming that the favorable portrayal of drug use in films has an adverse effect on children.

"If parental attitudes were strong enough and communicated to 12 us," proposed Richard Heffner [chairman of the MPAA], "a movie that showed pot smoking could be rated X." *Parade Magazine* thereupon polled 55,000 people, finding that 96 percent favored an SA rating and 90 percent favored giving these films an X rating as well. Taking both Heffner and the poll at face value, the X rating would have had to be assigned to films like *Private Benjamin, Nine to Five, Poltergeist, Silkwood, Romancing the Stone, The Big Chill, Trading Places,* and *Desperately Seeking Susan.*

On April 8, 1986, MPAA and NATO (National Association of   13 Theater Owners) disclosed the industry's new rule on drug use portrayal: Any films that depict or refer to the use of drugs will automatically receive a PG-13, R, or X rating. Barbara Dixon, spokesperson for the MPAA, cited John Hughes' and Universal's *Sixteen Candles* (PG) as a film which would have fallen within the new strictures because teenagers were shown "**gratuitously** smoking marijuana."

THE RATING GAME
Paul Attanasio

This essay, written by a movie critic for the Washington Post *and published in the* New Republic, *discusses the whole issue of rating the movies along the usual lines—including sex, violence, and profanity. Despite his humorous tone, he does suggest an alternative to the present labeling system, which he sees as artificial and arbitrary.*

The *Desperately Seeking Susan* you can see at your local **bijou** is not   1 the movie Susan Seidelman originally made. There's a scene, for example, in which Rosanna Arquette clambers out of Aidan Quinn's bed. Look hard, but you still won't see her breasts—they've been "optically darkened" to blend into the shadows. Then there's the scene in which Robert Joy amorously mauls Madonna while she sits atop a pinball machine; the joke is that the crescendo of bells and buzzers comments on their passion. That scene's been edited, too, even though Madonna never really gets undressed. Such is the work of the Motion Picture Association of America's rating board, which occasionally sees nudity even *through* clothes.

For almost 17 years, the MPAA has been rating the suitability of   2 movies for people under the age of 17. . . . The single, generally phrased standard for ratings (taking into account the film's level of

---

gratuitously: unnecessarily, for no purpose;   **bijou:** movie theater

violence, sexuality, nudity, and profanity) is: "Would the average American parent consider this film suitable for children under 17?" A movie is rated G if the average parent would consider it acceptable for children of all ages; PG ("parental guidance") indicates that parents should use their discretion about whether it is suitable for their kids to see on their own; PG-13 if the film contains disturbing material to a degree that it requires a closer look for preteens; R if the film is acceptable for children only with the attendance of the parent; and X for "clearly adult" films. In 1984 roughly 30 percent of the films rated got a PG; 60 percent got an R. . . .

A kind of common law of ratings has evolved, and inevitably, the **parsing** of distinctions gets pretty silly. Nudity can get you a PG as long as it's in a pristine jungle setting with no men around (*Sheena*); if the nudity comes in a sexual setting, it's generally an R. Shots of the drawings of Aubrey Beardsley had to be cut from *Crimes of Passion* before the film could be rated R; the same drawings are available to children in any bookstore. . . . Generally the ratings board seems more tolerant of violence than sex—full frontal nudity is usually an automatic X, while lots of heads have to roll before a film will be rated X for violence. Then again, self-mutilation, like the scene in *The Evil Dead* where a creature bites off his own hand, is an X-rated no-no. *Dogs* got an R because it featured a pack of dogs—"children's favorite household pets"—gone berserk. And according to producer Don Simpson, Paramount's head of production at the time, *Prophecy* initially got an X because of a shot of a bear chewing an automobile tire. . . .

King David had the same decapitations, impalings, and assorted slashings and hewings as *Friday the 13th: Part V,* but it was the Bible, the actors spoke with English accents, and most of all, had the good taste to keep their clothes on while they lost their heads. It got a PG-13. And so forth. . . .

Partisans of the ratings system **couch** their defense in **pseudo-**democratic rhetoric. Because ratings are "advisory," each parent is allowed to decide whether his children should see a movie. The problem is that in this democracy, the kids themselves count not at all; and once you start with this principle, it's hard to limit it. How

───────

parsing: detailed analysis;   **couch:** to phrase, to word;   **pseudo-:** false, fake would we feel if books received ratings, and a 15-year-old had to be accompanied by his parent before he could check *Huckleberry Finn,* or even *Ball Four,* out of the library? And why should movies be different?

The system's primary virtue—that it is a single, simple unified   6
system—is also its downfall. The psychology of children is complex; different kids get nightmares from different things. What's more, in a country as large and varied as ours, the idea of a central organ of taste is preposterous. A parent in the Bible Belt might find the chain saw murder of a woman perfectly appropriate Saturday night fun, while the utterance of a single "goddamn" would call for a gallon of earwash. A feminist in downtown Washington might feel exactly the opposite.

Part of the answer, then, is to return the judgment to the locali-   7
ties, just as the Supreme Court has done in its obscenity rulings. Most local papers, including my own, now include a parents' guide at the end of film reviews, describing the content of the picture in terms of nudity, violence, sex, and profanity. Besides the **salubrious** effect of forcing people to read their local movie critic, the substitution of the parents' guide for a ratings code, both more specific and more attuned to local mores, would allow parents to make better decisions for their children. And because such a system would be truly advisory, it would allow for one of the most time-honored traditions in American movies—a kid sneaking into a theater against his parents' order.

GIVE MOVIE RATERS A PG, FOR PIGHEADEDNESS
It's time to retire a censorship system that stifles artists and doesn't work
Tom Shales

Jack Valenti was not interviewed for this article because I'm not   1
speaking to him. The peppery president of the Motion Picture Association of America no longer sounds like a man who loves the movies—if indeed he ever did—but rather like a man who loves only the movie ratings system he helped foist on America three decades ago.

---

salubrious: healthful, wholesome

And a man who loves the studio bosses who pay his enormous   2
salary.

The MPAA—which lobbies for Big Hollywood, Colossal Holly-   3
wood, Stupendous Hollywood—also assigns the G, PG, PG-13, R and
NC-17 ratings that are supposed to advise parents on the content of
films their children might see. But the already infamous case of Stan-
ley Kubrick's last film, "Eyes Wide Shut," and the way the MPAA handled it, has inspired one of the loudest and most sustained storms of
protest from the filmmaking community since the cockeyed, trou-
ble-prone system was imposed.

In apparently every country but the United States, "Eyes Wide   4
Shut" includes shots of nudity and what the MPAA refers to, with
deep dread, as **"coital motion"** between two adults. This occurs during a bizarre orgy scene that takes place at a country estate. For the
domestic version . . . , 65 seconds have been digitally reconstituted
so that clothed bodies obscure the audience's view and the nude
bodies are thus concealed.

"Eyes Wide Shut" in America is "Eyes Wide Cut."   5

Sources at Warner Bros., which released the film, insist that   6
Kubrick approved the changes before his death in March. A practical
man, he was warned during production that the MPAA would slap
an NC-17 rating on the film if it were submitted with the orgy as
Kubrick shot it. Kubrick knew, as does everyone in the movie business, that an NC-17, successor to the old stigmatic X rating, is the
official commercial kiss of death.

No one under 17 is supposed to be admitted to films thus rated,   7
whether accompanied by a parent or not, and many newspapers
refuse advertising for NC-17 films, thereby helping to keep their
release a secret and dooming them at the box office. Kubrick was an
artist, a genius, a perfectionist—in a league with directors like Alfred
Hitchcock, Federico Fellini and Martin Scorsese—but like them he
worked in the world of commercial filmmaking and knew that a film
hardly anybody sees isn't worth the considerable trouble it takes to
make it.

Valenti has denied it tirelessly and **disingenuously,** but the MPAA   8
ratings are censorship. The threat of an NC-17 has forced innumerable

---

coital motion: motions indicating a sex act;   **disingenuous:** pretending to
be innocent

filmmakers back to the editing room to cut out scenes Valenti and his board of anonymous film raters don't like. They also censor some films at the script stage, cautioning filmmakers to go easy in spots that might prove troublesome later.

If the authors of books were subjected to similar censorship,   9
every writer in America would be screaming bloody murder. Not every movie is a work of art (nor is every book or painting), but the motion picture is an art form. Surely that much has been established by now. The producers of mechanical junk like "Wild Wild West" are not hampered by the ratings system, but serious filmmakers who tackle challenging themes are.

What's surprising in this latest skirmish is how vindictive, reckless   10
and nasty Valenti has been in reacting to criticism. When young film-makers Matt Stone and Trey Parker ("South Park: Bigger, Longer & Uncut") complained about the injustices of the system, Valenti snapped that he wished he could re-rate their R movie NC-17 (what, as punishment for defying His Lordship?) and childishly referred to them as "hair-balls."

When Roger Ebert, perhaps the most influential film critic in   11
America, wrote a column denouncing the absurd **bowdlerization** of "Eyes Wide Shut," and when 35 members of the Los Angeles Film Critics Association also denounced it, Valenti trashed them as "so-called intellectual critics" and dismissed their objections as **piffle**.

Such "Constant Whiners," Valenti wrote in an ill-advised column   12
for *Daily Variety*, "talk to each other, write for each other, opine with each other and view with **lacerating** contempt the rubes who live Out There, west of Manhattan and east of the San Andreas Fault. The CW's think that everyone ought to view an orgy as a **diurnal** event, observing such goings-on with a 'been there, done that' casual yawn."

What on earth is going on in Wacky Jack's brain?! This is how   13
Valenti responds to those who criticize his precious system and who, in their criticisms, have said nothing personally disparaging about Valenti himself? Maybe it is time to say something personal and dis-paraging about Valenti himself, since he sounds like a man who has gone round the bend. . . .

---

bowdlerization: cutting out of sexy parts;   **piffle:** nonsense;   **lacerating:** cutting, wounding;   **diurnal:** daily

A MAJOR STUDIO TESTS THE (SEXY) WATERS OF NC-17
Joel Topcik

On Friday, Fox Searchlight will release Bernardo Bertolucci's new   1
film, "The Dreamers," uncut and with an NC-17 rating—reversing
the studio's original plan to distribute it with an R and signaling
that after a long, troubled adolescence, the NC-17 may have finally
come of age.

"The Dreamers" is the latest in a short list of major studio films   2
to be released with an NC-17—and perhaps the most conspicuous
since 1995, when MGM's "Showgirls" convinced studios that the
controversial adults-only rating was a box-office liability. When the
Motion Picture Association of America introduced it in 1990, the
rating was meant to redeem adult films from the **stigma** of pornog-
raphy. (The first studio film rated NC-17 was Philip Kaufman's
"Henry and June," based on episodes in the life of the writer Henry
Miller.) But since that time, studios have routinely required filmmakers to cut offending images to secure an R rating, and thereby a
wider audience.

Set during the student protests of 1968, "The Dreamers" fol-   3
lows three teenage film buffs who experiment with sex in a Paris
apartment. When the association rated the film NC-17 "for explicit
sexual content," Fox Searchlight, the art house subsidiary of 20th
Century Fox, reminded Mr. Bertolucci that his contract obligated
him to deliver an R-rated film. Independent studios and distributors of foreign films can avoid the NC-17 by releasing films unrated;
major studios like Fox, as members of the association, do not have
that option.

"We were in a **quandary**," said Peter Rice, Fox Searchlight's pres-   4
ident. "We had a film from one of the greatest filmmakers who ever
made films, and we couldn't release it without a rating."

Both Mr. Rice and Stephen Gilula, Fox Searchlight's president   5
of distribution, agreed that NC-17 was the appropriate rating for
the film they submitted to the association. "There's full-frontal
nudity, both sexes," Mr. Gilula said. "There are a number of simu-
lated sex acts but no hard-core sex. It's just the sheer volume of
sexuality."

---

stigma: mark;   **quandary:** state of confusion

Perhaps most provocative are scenes of masturbation and several   6
close-up shots of male and female genitalia, which Mr. Gilula described
as "fairly often and fairly matter-of-fact." They are integral to the film
"in terms of surprising the audience," he said. "Startling, I should say.
There are three I'm thinking of right now that will catch people off-
guard." What's more, the characters are young, and two of them are
brother and sister.

As the studio weighed its options, the film played at the Venice   7
International Film Festival, where Mr. Bertolucci decried the prospect
that it would be "amputated and mutilated" by Fox for American
audiences.

Mr. Gilula said that Mr. Bertolucci's remarks were not the reason   8
Fox Searchlight abandoned its pursuit of an R rating. But he allowed
that Mr. Bertolucci's **preemptive** objections "publicized the fact that
there would be two versions of the movie"—one for American audiences, the other for the rest of the world—if the company altered
"The Dreamers" to earn an R. (Britain's film board gave it an 18 certificate, which bars viewers under 18—a designation often given to
violent films that the M.P.A.A. has rated R.)

Last fall, Fox Searchlight began to study the environment for dis-   9
tributing and marketing adult films. The studio discovered that
national theater chains like Loews and AMC were willing to carry
such a film. A survey of major cities found that only Seattle prohibits
its newspapers from printing advertisements for NC-17 films.

"We found that the conventional wisdom that the rating is a   10
liability is really not the case," said Mr. Gilula. "The issue had become
essentially dormant, so it offered us a fresh start."

Mr. Rice, the company president, said he was inspired by the   11
film culture of the 1970s. "Films made by important, thoughtful filmmakers for discerning adult audiences were not meant to be seen by
children," he said. "Trying to sanitize every film so you can take a
12-year-old to it—why does that have to be?"

Post-reading

The reading selections discuss two approaches to labeling movies: the MPAA's
rating system and Attanasio's parents' guide. In addition, Sheinfeld argues against

---

preemptive: acting before another can act

any form of rating, claiming that ratings are simply censorship in another form. In order to analyze and evaluate the information, look at these approaches again, making notes on the following matters:

1. To what extent does each rating system involve censorship, forbidding some from seeing certain movies, and on what basis? Be sure to consider the economic effect to the moviemaker of having his or her audience reduced.
2. To what extent does each system merely describe movies?
3. What attitudes toward violence, profanity, nudity, sex, or other matters does each system reflect? In other words, if a war story with lots of "blood and guts" is rated PG-13 and a love story in which there is partial nudity is rated R, what does that say about the raters' sense of what teenagers should be able to see? That is, what values underlie each labeling system? Do you agree with these values?

Go back to the notes you took before you read these articles. Have your ideas on this topic changed in any way? If so, how and for what reasons? If not, what specific parts of the articles support your original ideas?

Essay Assignment

Write an essay in which you discuss one or more of the key issues involved in rating movies—the desirability of being able to rate them, the danger of ratings acting as tools of censorship, the key values that seem to underlie current or proposed rating or labeling systems. If you can, come to your own conclusion about what you think should be done in regard to rating movies.

Pre-writing

The first thing you need to do is to isolate the issues surrounding this topic that you are most interested in discussing. Then, using your own experience and the ideas of the writers you have read, try to line up the positive and negative arguments for each issue. For instance, if you want to write about the desirability of using a rating system but also address the dangers of censorship, you will want to consider both sides of each of those questions. If you want to consider the different proposed systems, you will want to line up the advantages and disadvantages of each.

It is extremely important to use concrete instances in your discussion. For example, the person who argues that the First Amendment guarantees that our artistic works will not be censored needs to consider whether children should be allowed to see movies depicting extreme, graphic violence or explicit sexual activities. At the same time, the person who would forbid such movies to children must be prepared to say what is wrong with having children see them. In discussions of these kinds, it is highly desirable to try to base your examples on specific movies and, if possible, specific scenes from them.

In working out your ideas on a controversial issue like this one, a discussion with a person whose views are different from yours can be very helpful, as long as you don't start arguing with each other. Listening to the points of an opponent and writing them down can be an excellent way of developing your own thinking. In any case, you need not come to a firm conclusion on this troublesome question. Your essay may simply discuss what you feel are the main problems.

As you think about organizing your essay, remember these points:

1. Provide enough background so your readers understand the importance and complexity of the issue.

2. Acknowledge both the strengths and the weaknesses of arguments you cite, including your own.

3. Remember that a statement is not an argument. A statement needs support from facts and/or well-founded opinions to become an argument.

For further ideas on structuring your essay, refer to the section "Writing Discussion Essays" (pages 363–365). As in previous assignments, jot down a working thesis and outline.

Writing

Your introduction should very briefly explain what the ratings problem is and the aspects of the problem you think are most important.

In the body of your essay, you will shape your discussion to cover the central issues involved for and against rating systems, or you may decide to discuss the relative merits and failings of different kinds of rating systems.

Your conclusion will either present your recommendations concerning using or not using ratings systems or, if you do not want to come to such a conclusion, restate the problem as you see it, much as you did in your introduction. Review the Writer's Checklist on pages 435–437 while you work on this assignment.

IS HATE SPEECH FREE SPEECH?

In recent years there have been occasional attacks on college campuses by students against other students—not physical attacks but verbal ones, taking the form of signs, pamphlets, handouts, and speech. The worst of these have constituted insults and name-calling based on the victims' being members of ethnic minorities or being homosexual. Some universities have chosen to try to prevent such language assaults by drafting rules forbidding them. At the University of Michigan, the following rule was passed:

> Physical acts or threats or verbal slurs, invectives or epithets, referring to an individual's race, ethnicity, religion, sex, sexual orientation, creed, national origin, ancestry, age, or handicap, made with the purpose of injuring the person to whom the words or actions are directed and that are not made as a part of a discussion or exchange of an idea, ideology, or philosophy, are prohibited.

The university also published guidelines giving the following examples, among others, of prohibited speech:

> Racist graffiti written on a door of an Asian student's study carrel.
>
> A male student makes remarks in class like "Women just aren't as good in this field as men," thus creating a hostile learning atmosphere for female students.
>
> Male students leave pornographic pictures and jokes on the desk of a female graduate student.
>
> You exclude someone from a study group because that person is of a different race, sex, or ethnic origin than you are.
>
> Your student organization sponsors entertainment that includes a comedian who slurs Hispanics.
>
> You laugh at a joke about someone in your class who stutters.

Eventually the guidelines were withdrawn and, under threat of legal action, the rules were rescinded.

Similar rules were drawn up at the University of Connecticut, and under these a student named Nina Wu was expelled for hanging a poster on the outside of her door listing "homos," among others, as unwelcome. She sued and was reinstated, and the university has changed its rules.

While most people will agree that none of us should use insulting speech based on race, sex, sexual orientation, and so on, it can become very difficult to decide what kinds of speech constitute insults. If a white student calls a black student a nigger, is that an insult? If the black student calls the white student a honkey, is that an insult? Should they both be kicked out of school? If a male student, because of his background, genuinely thinks that females are inferior, are the females insulted? Should the male student be expelled from school for thinking that?

The following readings include the text of the First Amendment to the Constitution, our guarantee of freedom of speech, and four views on the issue of hate speech and free speech on university campuses.

Reading Assignment

Pre-reading

It is easy to think of kinds of speech, insults and so on, that one might want to prohibit if possible. Nobody wants to be called names or in any way belittled because of something one has no control over, such as one's ethnicity or sex or sexual orientation or some disability. But think now about other kinds of situations. Are students hurt or insulted if they are left out of social situations or professional groupings because of sex, sexual orientation, or ethnicity? Is there an objective way to tell whether speech or actions are insulting or offensive? Is there an objective way to tell whether speech or actions are *intended* to be offensive? Is it possible to offend someone without intending to do so? Have you ever told an ethnic joke or slurred someone in some way? Have you ever muttered, "That's a woman for you," or "That's just like a man"? Are these examples of insensitivity?

What kinds of actions, aside from expulsion, might universities consider in an attempt to reduce or eliminate offensive speech and actions from campuses?

Reading

THE FIRST AMENDMENT TO THE U.S. CONSTITUTION

Congress shall make no law respecting an establishment of religion, or prohibiting the free exercise thereof; or abridging the freedom of speech, or of the press; or the right of the people peaceably to assemble, and to petition the Government for a redress of grievances.

Note: While the First Amendment specifically limits only Congress, later amendments and rulings extended the prohibitions of the First Amendment both to the federal government as a whole and to state governments. You should also note that the First Amendment extends to other forms of expression aside from speech. For instance, the Supreme Court has held that burning the American flag in protest of government policies is a form of protected "speech."

THE DEBATE OVER PLACING LIMITS ON RACIST SPEECH MUST NOT IGNORE THE DAMAGE IT DOES TO ITS VICTIMS
Charles R. Lawrence III

Charles R. Lawrence III is a professor of law at Georgetown University. His article, which appeared in the October 25, 1989, Chronicle of Higher Education, *is adapted from a speech to a conference of the American Civil Liberties Union.*

I have spent the better part of my life as a dissenter. As a high school   1
student, I was threatened with suspension for my refusal to participate in a civil-defense drill, and I have been a conspicuous consumer
of my First Amendment liberties ever since. There are very strong reasons for protecting even racist speech. Perhaps the most important of
these is that such protection reinforces our society's commitment to
tolerance as a value, and that by protecting bad speech from government regulation, we will be forced to combat it as a community.

But I also have a deeply felt apprehension about the resurgence   2
of racial violence and the corresponding rise in the incidence of
verbal and symbolic assault and harassment to which blacks and
other traditionally subjugated and excluded groups are subjected.
I am troubled by the way the debate has been framed in response to
the recent surge of racist incidents on college and university
campuses and in response to some universities' attempts to regulate
harassing speech. The problem has been framed as one in which the
liberty of free speech is in conflict with the elimination of racism.
I believe this has placed the bigot on the moral high ground and
fanned the rising flames of racism.

Above all, I am troubled that we have not listened to the real   3
victims, that we have shown so little understanding of their injury,
and that we have abandoned those whose race, gender, or sexual
preference continues to make them second-class citizens. It seems to
me a very sad irony that the first instinct of civil libertarians has been
to challenge even the smallest, most narrowly framed efforts by
universities to provide black and other minority students with the
protection the Constitution guarantees them.

The landmark case of *Brown v. Board of Education* is not a case   4
that we normally think of as a case about speech. But *Brown* can be
broadly read as articulating the principle of equal citizenship. *Brown*
held that segregated schools were inherently unequal because of the
message that segregation conveyed—that black children were an
untouchable caste, unfit to go to school with white children. If we
understand the necessity of eliminating the system of signs and
symbols that signal the inferiority of blacks, then we should hesitate
before proclaiming that all racist speech that stops short of physical
violence must be defended.

University officials who have formulated policies to respond to   5
incidents of racial harassment have been characterized in the press
as "thought police," but such policies generally do nothing more
than impose **sanctions** against intentional face-to-face insults. When
racist speech takes the form of face-to-face insults, catcalls, or other
assaultive speech aimed at an individual or small group of persons, it
falls directly within the "fighting words" exception to First Amendment protection. The Supreme Court has held that words which "by
their very utterance inflict injury or tend to incite an immediate
breach of the peace" are not protected by the First Amendment.

If the purpose of the First Amendment is to foster the greatest   6
amount of speech, racial insults disserve that purpose. Assaultive
racist speech functions as a **preemptive strike**. The invective is
experienced as a blow, not as a proffered idea, and once the blow is
struck, it is unlikely that a dialogue will follow. Racial insults are particularly undeserving of First Amendment protection because the
perpetuator's intention is not to discover truth or initiate dialogue
but to injure the victim. In most situations, members of minority
groups realize that they are likely to lose if they respond to epithets
by fighting and are forced to remain silent and submissive.

Courts have held that offensive speech may not be regulated in   7
public forums such as streets where the listener may avoid the
speech by moving on, but the regulation of otherwise protected
speech has been permitted when the speech invades the privacy of
the unwilling listener's home or when the unwilling listener cannot
avoid the speech. Racist posters, fliers, and graffiti in dormitories,

---

sanctions: penalties;   **preemptive strike:** in warfare, an attack to prevent
one from being attacked

bathrooms, and other common living spaces would seem to clearly fall within the reasoning of these cases. Minority students should not be required to remain in their rooms in order to avoid racial assault. Minimally, they should find a safe haven in their dorms and in all other common rooms that are a part of their daily routine.

I would also argue that the university's responsibility for ensuring   8
that these students receive an equal educational opportunity provides a compelling justification for regulations that ensure them safe passage in all common areas. A minority student should not have to risk becoming the target of racially assaulting speech every time he or she chooses to walk across campus. Regulating vilifying speech that cannot be anticipated or avoided would not **preclude** announced speeches and rallies—situations that would give minority-group members and their allies the chance to organize counterdemonstrations or avoid the speech altogether.

The most commonly advanced argument against the regulation   9
of racist speech proceeds something like this: We recognize that minority groups suffer pain and injury as the result of racist speech, but we must allow this **hate mongering** for the benefit of society as a whole. Freedom of speech is the lifeblood of our democratic system. It is especially important for minorities because often it is their only vehicle for rallying support for the **redress** of their grievances. It will be impossible to formulate a prohibition so precise that it will prevent the racist speech you want to suppress without catching in the same net all kinds of speech that it would be **unconscionable** for a democratic society to suppress.

Whenever we make such arguments, we are striking a balance   10
on the one hand between our concern for the continued free flow of ideas and the democratic process dependent on that flow, and, on the other, our desire to further the cause of equality. There can be no meaningful discussion of how we should reconcile our commitment to equality and our commitment to free speech until it is acknowledged that there is real harm inflicted by racist speech and that this harm is far from trivial.

To engage in a debate about the First Amendment and racist   11
speech without a full understanding of the nature and extent of

---

preclude: prevent;   **hate mongering:** spreading hate;   **redress:** remedy;
unconscionable: excessive, not restrained by conscience

that harm is to risk making the First Amendment an instrument of domination rather than a vehicle of liberation. We have not all known the experience of victimization by racist, **misogynist,** and **homophobic** speech, nor do we equally share the burden of the societal harm it inflicts. We are often quick to say that we have heard the cry of the victims when we have not.

The *Brown* case is again instructive because it speaks directly to   12 the **psychic** injury inflicted by racist speech by noting that the symbolic message of segregation affected "the hearts and minds" of negro children "in a way unlikely ever to be undone." Racial epithets and harassment often cause deep emotional scarring and feelings of anxiety and fear that pervade every aspect of a victim's life.

Brown also recognized that black children did not have an equal   13 opportunity to learn and participate in the school community if they bore the additional burden of being subjected to the humiliation and psychic assault contained in the message of segregation. University students bear an **analogous** burden when they are forced to live and work in an environment where at any moment they may be subjected to denigrating verbal harassment and assault. The same injury was addressed by the Supreme Court when it held that sexual harassment that creates a hostile or abusive work environment violates the ban on sex discrimination in employment of Title VII of the Civil Rights Act of 1964.

Carefully drafted university regulations would bar the use of   14 words as assault weapons and leave unregulated even the most **heinous** of ideas when those ideas are presented at times and places and in manners that provide an opportunity for reasoned rebuttal or escape from immediate injury. The history of the development of the right to free speech has been one of carefully evaluating the importance of free expression and its effects on other important societal interests. We have drawn the line between protected and unprotected speech before without dire results. (Courts have, for example, exempted from the protection of the First Amendment obscene speech and speech that **disseminates** official secrets, that defames or libels another person, or that is used to form a conspiracy or monopoly.)

---

misogynist: women-hating;   **homophobic:** fear or hatred of homosexuality; **psychic:** mental;   **analogous:** similar;   **heinous:** terrible, awful;   **disseminates:** spreads around

Blacks and other people of color are skeptical about the argument   15
that even the most injurious speech must remain unregulated because,
in an unregulated marketplace of ideas, the best ones will rise to the top
and gain acceptance. Our experience tells us quite the opposite. We
have seen too many **demagogues** elected by appealing to America's
racism. We have seen too many good liberal politicians shy away from
the issues that might brand them as being too closely allied with us.

Whenever we decide that racist speech must be tolerated because   16
of the importance of maintaining societal tolerance for all unpopular
speech, we are asking blacks and other subordinated groups to bear
the burden for the good of all. We must be careful that the ease with
which we strike the balance against the regulation of racist speech is
in no way influenced by the fact that the cost will be borne by others.
We must be certain that those who will pay that price are fairly represented in our deliberations and that they are heard.

At the core of the argument that we should resist all govern-   17
ment regulation of speech is the ideal that the best cure for bad
speech is good, that ideas that affirm equality and the worth of all
individuals will ultimately prevail. This is an empty ideal unless those
of us who would fight racism are vigilant and **unequivocal** in that
fight. We must look for ways to offer assistance and support to
students whose speech and political participation are chilled in a
climate of racial harassment.

Civil-rights lawyers might consider suing on behalf of blacks whose   18
right to an equal education is denied by a university's failure to ensure
a nondiscriminatory educational climate or conditions of employment.
We must embark upon the development of a First Amendment
jurisprudence grounded in the reality of our history and our contemporary experience. We must think hard about how best to launch legal
attacks against the most indefensible forms of hate speech. Good
lawyers can create exceptions and narrow interpretations that limit the
harm of hate speech without opening the floodgates of censorship.

Everyone concerned with these issues must find ways to engage   19
actively in actions that resist and counter the racist ideas that we would
have the First Amendment protect. If we fail in this, the victims of hate
speech must rightly assume that we are on the oppressors' side.

---

demagogues: leaders who appeal to passions and emotions;   **unequivocal:**
firm;   **jurisprudence:** philosophy of law

FREE SPEECH ON THE CAMPUS
Nat Hentoff

Nat Hentoff is the author of The First Freedom *and was an editor for the* Village Voice.

A flier distributed at the University of Michigan some months ago   1
proclaimed that blacks "don't belong in classrooms, they belong hanging from trees."

At other campuses around the country, manifestations of racism   2
are becoming commonplace. At Yale, a swastika and the words WHITE POWER were painted on the building housing the University's Afro-American Cultural Center. At Temple University, a White Students Union has been formed with some 130 members.

Swastikas are not directed only at black students. The Nazi sym-   3
bol has been spray-painted on the Jewish Student Union at Memphis State University. And on a number of campuses, women have been singled out as targets of wounding and sometimes frightening speech. At the law school of the State University of New York at Buffalo, several women students have received anonymous letters characterized by one professor as **venomously** sexist.

These and many more such signs of the resurgence of bigotry   4
and know-nothingism throughout the society—as well as on campus—have to do solely with speech, including symbolic speech. There have also been physical assaults on black students and on black, white, and Asian women students, but the way to deal with physical attacks is clear: Call the police and file a criminal complaint. What is to be done, however, about speech alone—however disgusting, inflammatory, and rawly divisive that speech may be?

At more and more colleges, administrators—with the enthusiastic   5
support of black students, women students, and liberal students—have been answering that question by preventing or punishing speech. In public universities, this is a clear violation of the First Amendment. In private colleges and universities, suppression of speech mocks the secular religion of academic freedom and free inquiry.

The Student Press Law Center in Washington, D.C.—a vital source   6
of legal support for student editors around the country—reports, for

---

venomously: poisonously

example, that at the University of Kansas, the student host and producer of a radio news program was forbidden by school officials from
interviewing a leader of the Ku Klux Klan. So much for free inquiry on
that campus.

In Madison, Wisconsin, *The Capital Times* ran a story in January   7
about Chancellor Sheila Kaplan of the University of Wisconsin branch
at Parkside, who ordered her campus to be scoured of "some anony-
mously placed white-supremacist hate literature." Sounding like the
legendary Mayor Frank ("I am the law") Hague of Jersey City, who
booted "bad speech" out of town, Chancellor Kaplan said, "This
institution is not a lamppost standing on the street corner. It doesn't
belong to everyone."

Who decides what speech can be heard or read by everyone?   8
Why, the chancellor, of course. That's what **George III** used to
say, too.

University of Wisconsin political science professor Carol Tebben   9
thinks otherwise. She believes university administrators "are getting
confused when they are acting as censors and trying to protect students from bad ideas. I don't think students need to be protected
from bad ideas. I think they can determine for themselves what ideas
are bad."

After all, if students are to be "protected" from bad ideas, how   10
are they going to learn to identify and cope with them? Sending
such ideas underground simply makes them stronger and more
dangerous.

Professor Tebben's conviction that free speech means just that   11
has become a decidedly minority view on many campuses. At the
University of Buffalo Law School, the faculty unanimously adopted a
"Statement Regarding Intellectual Freedom, Tolerance, and Political
Harassment." Its title implies support of intellectual freedom, but the
statement warned students that once they enter "this legal community," their right to free speech must become tempered "by the
responsibility to promote equality and justice."

Accordingly, swift condemnation will befall anyone who engages   12
in "remarks directed at another's race, sex, religion, national origin,
age, or sex preference." Also forbidden are "other remarks based on
prejudice and group stereotype."

George III: king of England during the American Revolution

This **ukase** is so broad that enforcement has to be alarmingly subjective. Yet the University of Buffalo Law School provides no due-process procedures for a student booked for making any of these prohibited remarks. Conceivably, a student caught playing a Lenny Bruce, Richard Pryor, or Sam Kinison album in his room could be tried for aggravated insensitivity by association.

13

When I looked into this wholesale cleansing of bad speech at Buffalo, I found it had encountered scant opposition. One protester was David Gerald Jay, a graduate of the law school and a cooperating attorney for the New York Civil Liberties Union. Said the appalled graduate: "Content-based prohibitions constitute prior restraint and should not be tolerated."

14

You would think that the law professors and administration at this public university might have known that. But hardly any professors dissented, and among the students only members of the conservative Federalist Society spoke up for free speech. The fifty-strong chapter of the National Lawyers Guild was on the other side. After all, it was more important to go on record as vigorously opposing racism and sexism than to expose oneself to charges of insensitivity to these **malignancies.**

15

The pressures to have the "right" attitude—as proved by having the "right" language in and out of class—can be stifling. A student who opposes affirmative action, for instance, can be branded a racist.

16

At the University of California at Los Angeles, the student newspaper ran an editorial cartoon satirizing affirmative action. (A student stops a rooster on campus and asks how the rooster got into UCLA. "Affirmative action," is the answer.) After outraged complaints from various minority groups, the editor was suspended for violating a publications policy against running "articles that perpetuate derogatory or cultural stereotypes." The art director was also suspended.

17

When the opinion editor of the student newspaper at California State University at Northridge wrote an article asserting that the sanctions against the editor and art director at UCLA amounted to censorship, he was suspended too.

18

At New York University Law School, a student was so disturbed by the **pall of orthodoxy** at that prestigious institution that he wrote

19

---

ukase: dictatorial order (Russian); **malignancies:** evils; **pall of ortho-doxy:** atmosphere of restriction

to the school newspaper even though, as he said, he expected his letter to make him a **pariah** among his fellow students.

Barry Endick described the atmosphere at NYU created by "a host   20 of watchdog committees and a generally hostile classroom reception regarding any student comment right of center." This "can be arguably viewed as symptomatic of a prevailing spirit of academic and social intolerance of . . . any idea which is not 'politically correct.'"

He went on to say something that might well be posted on cam-   21 pus bulletin boards around the country, though it would probably be torn down at many of them:

> We ought to examine why students, so anxious to wield the Fourteenth Amendment, give short shrift to the First. Yes, Virginia, there are racist assholes. And you know what, the Constitution protects them, too.

Not when they engage in violence or vandalism. But when they   22 speak or write, racist assholes fall right into this Oliver Wendell Holmes definition—highly unpopular among bigots, liberals, radicals, feminists, sexists, and college administrators:

> If there is any principle of the Constitution that more imperatively calls for attachment than any other, it is the principle of free thought—not free only for those who agree with us, but freedom for the thought we hate.

The language sounds like a **pietistic** Sunday sermon, but if it   23 ever falls wholly into disuse, neither this publication nor any other journal of opinion—Right or Left—will survive.

Sometimes, college presidents and administrators sound as   24 if they fully understand what Holmes was saying. Last year, for example, when *The Daily Pennsylvanian*—speaking for many at the University of Pennsylvania—urged that a speaking invitation to **Louis Farrakhan** be withdrawn, University President Sheldon Hackney disagreed.

"Open expression," said Hackney, "is the fundamental principle   25 of a university." Yet consider what the same Sheldon Hackney did to

---

pariah: outcast;   pietistic: overly reverent;   **Louis Farrakhan:** African-American leader known for anti-Jewish statements

the free-speech rights of a teacher at his own university. If any story distills the essence of the current decline of free speech on college campuses, it is the Ballad of Murray Dolfman.

For twenty-two years, Dolfman, a practicing lawyer in Philadel- 26 phia, had been a part-time lecturer in the Legal Studies Department of the University of Pennsylvania's Wharton School. For twenty-two years, no complaint had ever been made against him; indeed, his student course-evaluations had been outstanding. Each year students competed to get into his class.

On a November afternoon in 1984, Dolfman was lecturing 27 about personal-service contracts. His style somewhat resembles that of Professor Charles Kingsfield in *The Paper Chase.* Dolfman insists that students he calls on be prepared—or suffer the consequences. He treats all students this way—regardless of race, creed, or sex.

This day, Dolfman was pointing out that no one can be forced 28 to work against his or her will—even if a contract has been signed. A court may prevent the resister from working for someone else so long as the contract is in effect but, Dolfman said, there can "be nothing that smacks of involuntary servitude."

Where does this concept come from? Dolfman looked around 29 the room. Finally, a cautious hand was raised: "The Constitution?"

"Where in the Constitution?" No hands. "The Thirteenth 30 Amendment," said the teacher. So, what does *it* say? The students were looking everywhere but at Dolfman.

"We will lose our liberties," Dolfman often told his classes, "if we 31 don't know what they are."

On this occasion, he told them that he and other Jews, as 32 ex-slaves, spoke at Passover of the time when they were slaves under the Pharaohs so that they would remember every year what it was like not to be free.

"We have ex-slaves here," Dolfman continued, "who should 33 know about the Thirteenth Amendment." He asked black students in the class if they could tell him what was in that amendment.

"I wanted them to really think about it," Dolfman told me 34 recently, "and know its history. You're better equipped to fight racism if you know all about those post–Civil War amendments and civil-rights laws."

The Paper Chase: movie about law students

The Thirteenth Amendment provides that "neither slavery nor   35
involuntary servitude . . . shall exist within the United States."

The black students in his class did not know what was in that   36
amendment, and Dolfman had them read it aloud. Later, they complained to university officials that they had been hurt and humiliated
by having been referred to as ex-slaves. Moreover, they said, they had
no reason to be grateful for a constitutional amendment which gave
them rights which should never have been denied them—and gave
them precious little else. They had not made these points in class,
although Dolfman—unlike Professor Kingsfield—encourages rebuttal.

Informed of the complaint, Dolfman told the black students he   37
had intended no offense, and he apologized if they had been offended.

That would not do—either for the black students or for the   38
administration. Furthermore, there were mounting black-Jewish tensions on campus, and someone had to be sacrificed. Who better than
a part-time Jewish teacher with no contract and no union? He was
sentenced by—**George Orwell** would have loved this—the Committee on Academic Freedom and Responsibility.

On his way to the **stocks,** Dolfman told President Sheldon Hack-   39
ney that if a part-time instructor "can be punished on this kind of
charge, a tenured professor can eventually be booted out, then a
dean, and then a president."

Hackney was unmoved. Dolfman was banished from the cam-   40
pus for what came to be a year. But first he was forced to make a
public apology to the entire university and then he was compelled
to attend a "sensitivity and racial awareness" session. Sort of like a
Vietnamese reeducation camp.

A few conservative professors objected to the **stigmatization** of   41
Murray Dolfman. I know of no student dissent. Indeed, those
students most concerned with making the campus more "sensitive"
to diversity exulted in Dolfman's humiliation. So did most liberals on
the faculty.

If my children were still of college age and wanted to attend the   42
University of Pennsylvania, I would tell them this story. But where
else could I encourage them to go?

George Orwell: author of the novel *1984,* depicting a future in which lies
are considered truth;   **stocks:** an ancient form of punishment;
stigmatization: being disgraced

HATE SPEECH ON CAMPUS
Joseph S. Tuman

Joseph Tuman is the Director of Forensics and teaches argumentation, debate, and constitutional law in the Speech and Communication Studies Department at San Francisco State University.

Recent efforts by large public universities and colleges aimed at stem-   1
ming the tide of hate speech on campus have caused all of us in the academic community to carefully assess our position on this issue. Hate speech refers to written or spoken words directed towards a particular group (typically although not exclusively a minority group) with the purpose or effect of verbally harassing and harming them. In the educational setting, this can refer to language used both in and outside the classroom, by teacher or student, while still within the campus.

Schools such as the University of Michigan, the University of   2
Wisconsin, and the University of California have already written new regulations to restrict this form of speech, declaring that it disrupts the educational process and retards progress made in bringing equal opportunity and access to education for all.

Does hate speech harm the individual to whom it is addressed?   3
I can speak to this myself. My parents came to this country nearly four decades ago from the Middle East. I was born in Texas and later grew up in California's Central Valley. My early years were spent constantly trying to conform and avoid the appearance of being different. As a young person in public schools, I often heard comments, jokes and insults about my ethnicity and the place my parents had once called home. I can assure you that these comments hurt—and in a different way than they might if reversed against those in more populous numbers. If they caused me some pain as a white male, I can only imagine what they must feel like when they are directed to those already burdened with discrimination in our society.

As an adult and an educator, however, today I see this from a   4
different point of view, standing before the class instead of seated within the class. Consequently, I now find myself internally conflicted over this issue. I have always tried in my class to avoid promoting my own social and political agenda, believing instead that classroom

discussions, within reasonable limits, should be open and accessible for all. This promotes participation from the broadest number of students, and enhances the learning process.

As a teacher, I thus look with unease at regulations which might   5
restrict what can be said in the classroom. My discomfort is grounded in the fact that I am not certain that clear regulations prohibiting hate speech can be designed without also entangling other forms of speech—speech that may otherwise be protected by the First Amendment.

A wise undergraduate student in my own Free Speech class   6
debated me on this point last year, declaring that those rules aren't so difficult. People know what kind of words and insults we're talking about, she said—and to illustrate her point, she promptly recited three different types of racist, sexist and homophobic slurs.

For me, however, her examples were the obvious ones. Yes,   7
most people do know about bigoted, hurtful insults and slurs—but should we draft a rule that prohibits only the obvious choices? Many forms of racist and sexist speech, for example, are oftentimes far more subtle, although their impact is no less devastating. How do we define rules prohibiting these? I assume we do this by making our restriction broader, but when we do so, how do we avoid prohibiting other speech which may not necessarily be hate speech?

This was the problem for Michigan, when a graduate student   8
teacher challenged the University of Michigan's rules, arguing they were so broad that they forced him to remove parts of his lecture material for fear of offending some unknown members of his class. He didn't in fact know if the material would offend anyone or not— but the rule was so broad that he feared the risk of penalty if he guessed wrong. The federal court hearing the case declared Michigan's rules unconstitutional.

In spite of the pain of my own past experience, I find I cannot   9
endorse rules such as these, either. Hate speech is the expression of bigotry and prejudice—and these in turn are the products of ignorance. I know no better place to address ignorance than in our schools, and no better way to do so than in exposing all of our ideas, good and bad, ugly and beautiful, to the light of scrutiny within our classes.

RETHINKING CAMPUS SPEECH CODES
Ben Wildavsky

Just a few years after rules banning offensive words began cropping   1
up at colleges and universities across America, the brief reign of these
controversial campus speech codes appears to be drawing to a close.

A ruling earlier this week declaring Stanford University's hate-   2
speech ban unconstitutional is the latest in a string of legal setbacks
for speech codes and anti-harassment rules.

The court decisions—and **derisive** attacks by critics of campus   3
"thought police"—are spurring colleges coast to coast to scrap or
retool rules that may run afoul of the First Amendment.

The Stanford decision "is the final nail in the coffin of speech   4
codes," said Sheldon Steinbach, general counsel for the American
Council on Education, which represents 1700 colleges and universities.

"It sends a lasting **shot across the bow** of institutions that think   5
speech codes, as constructed in the late '80s and early '90s are the
appropriate way of dealing with interpersonal conflict."

To be sure, campus wars over race and gender have hardly died   6
down. Indeed, such issues as affirmative action are more contentious
than ever.

But speech codes have done little to ease campus tensions, leav-   7
ing other students fearful of making a race or gender **faux-pax**.
Speech and harassment rules may instead have fanned the flames of
intolerance.

"If you're fearful that somehow you will misspeak," Steinbach   8
said, "you wind up avoiding the very people you need to get to
know."

With its speech code now on hold, and no decision yet on   9
whether to mount a costly appeal, Stanford joins several major institutions whose campus rules have been held unconstitutional:

- In 1989, a federal judge overturned parts of the University of
  Michigan's speech code after a biopsychology graduate student
  said he feared the rules would prevent him from discussing
  controversial theories about biological differences among the
  sexes and races.

---

derisive: mocking;   **shot across the bow:** warning—from the old naval
custom of firing a cannon ball across the bow of a ship to warn it to stop;
faux-pax: mistake—French for false step (pronounced foe-pah)

- In 1991, the University of Wisconsin's speech code was struck down as overly broad and "unduly vague." The university, one of the first to ban racial and sexual slurs, redrew its code more narrowly before scrapping it entirely in 1992.

- In 1993, a fraternity successfully sued Virginia's George Mason University after its members were disciplined for parodying an African American woman as part of an "ugly woman" contest. "Even as low-grade entertainment," the judge ruled, the skit "was inherently expressive and thus entitled to First Amendment protection."

Cross-Burning Decision

A major impetus behind the move away from speech codes was a 1992 Supreme Court ruling that struck down a hate-crime ordinance in St. Paul, Minn., and held that cross-burning could be considered protected speech under the First Amendment.   10

In some cases, colleges have abandoned anti-harassment and speech codes after public outcry rather than legal action.   11

In one widely publicized incident, the University of Pennsylvania disciplined a white male student for calling a group of five black sorority sisters "water buffalo" when they made noise outside his dorm room late one night.   12

The Hebrew-speaking student insisted the phrase was not racist but simply a literal translation of an Israeli expression for noisy, disruptive people. The university dropped the charges and later withdrew its speech code.   13

The Stanford code, adopted in 1990, grew out of an incident two years earlier in which two first-year students defaced a poster of Beethoven with racial caricatures.   14

"Fighting Words"

Unlike other broadly written rules, the Stanford code was carefully crafted to avoid any "chilling effect" on debate of sensitive topics. It forbade only "fighting words" linked to sex and race.   15

"It's about as narrow as you can get. All it prohibits is the face-to-face use of racial **epithets**," said the code's architect, Stanford law professor Thomas Grey.   16

---

epithets: insulting names

Yet Santa Clara County Superior Court Judge Peter Stone still   17
found the rules a barrier to free expression.

"The Speech Code prohibits words which will not only cause peo-   18
ple to react violently, but also cause them to feel insulted or **stigmatized**," he wrote in his 43-page opinion. "(Stanford) cannot proscribe
speech that merely hurts the feelings of those who hear it."

Stone's ruling hinged on a 1992 state law extending free-speech   19
protections to private universities, which historically have not been
covered by the First Amendment.

Stanford Is Significant

Even though no other state has such a law, Stanford's prestige and   20
visibility mean this week's court decision is likely to send a national
message about speech codes.

"They're going out the door," said Robert Rosenzweig, former   21
president of the Association of American Universities. "I would be
surprised to see any significant number of institutions now adopting
codes, and where they exist they will be increasingly dead letters—
unenforced law."

Rosenzweig and others said the Stanford decision is particularly   22
significant because Stanford's rules were carefully drawn to pass constitutional muster.

"This ruling says that with the best of intentions and the best of   23
lawyers, it still is not possible to craft a speech code that doesn't vio-
late the Constitution," said Paul McMasters, executive director of the
Freedom Forum First Amendment Center at Vanderbilt University.

"In a place where free-flowing dialogue and debate should be   24
revered," said McMasters, "speech codes put restrictions on that very
ideal."

A survey of 384 public colleges and universities conducted by   25
the center last year found that 36 percent had rules punishing "hate
speech." Many of the rules, the center concluded, are probably
unconstitutional.

The University of California, which adopted a system-wide   26
speech code in 1989 prohibiting "fighting words" that create a "hostile and intimidating environment," is studying the Stanford ruling,
said UC deputy general counsel Gary Morrison.

---

stigmatized: labeled as inferior

"The issue, it seems to me, is whether at some point words lose   27
their essentially protected, expressive nature," he said, "and become
simply tools for purposes of angering and intimidating someone, just
like a slap in the face."

As speech codes fall by the wayside, some colleges are turning   28
instead to other rules of conduct to punish student behavior considered offensive.

"Now they have sexual harassment codes and racial harassment   29
codes so broadly drawn that they include a lot of speech," said
attorney John Howard of the individual rights foundation in Los
Angeles, one of several conservative groups that have helped
students bring legal challenges to campus harassment rules.

"Instead of using them as a tool to fight harassment," he said,   30
"they use them as a political weapon to silence people with whom
they disagree."

Post-reading

The article by Hentoff presents a pretty straightforward argument—speech
should not be censored—and Hentoff tries to show us why it shouldn't by
showing us what can happen when it is censored in one way or another. You
will need to decide whether the examples he gives represent sufficiently serious
offenses against our freedom of speech so that what is lost in freedom to speak
outweighs what is gained by the censorship.

Lawrence's article requires very careful reading. In it, he notes that the
courts have, in fact, put limitations on the First Amendment in the past, and
you will need to note carefully what those limitations are. Specifically, while
speech in public places is protected, speech on private property is not. If you
don't like what someone is saying in your house, you can throw him or her out.
If you run a private university, you can make up whatever rules you want concerning expression on campus. The Supreme Court has also established what is
called the "clear and present danger" test. That is, advocacy of *immediate*
violence or lawlessness is not protected.

Lawrence also cites as being applicable here the landmark Supreme Court case
Brown v. Board of Education. Prior to this decision, many states had set up what
they called "separate but equal" schools and colleges for black and white students.
Of course, the schools weren't equal at all, though they were certainly separate.
The *Brown* decision abolished racially segregated educational systems. Look back
at the fourth, twelfth, and thirteenth paragraphs in Lawrence's essay to understand

how he sees this decision as being relevant to the hate-speech issue. (Of course, although Lawrence speaks primarily about hate speech against African-Americans, his argument extends to other kinds of racism as well as to sexism, homophobic speech, and slurs based on age and on disabilities.)

Tuman's article is a carefully thought-out consideration of the issue from someone who has found himself on both sides of it, a person who suffered slurs because of his background and ethnicity and who is now responsible for being an effective teacher trying to promote a free exchange of ideas.

Essay Assignment

Write an essay in which you discuss the issue of free speech versus hate speech on college campuses. You may come to the conclusion that some form of censorship (you should specify the form it should take) or some form of punishment (you should specify the kinds of punishment and what the punishments would be given for) should be instituted to prevent the abuses of hate speech, or, conversely, you may wish to argue that we will have to accept abuses of free speech in order to protect free speech. In discussion essays, another option is simply to discuss, to try to shed light on the issue rather than trying to resolve it.

Pre-writing

As you think about organizing your essay, remember these points:

1. Present adequate background to enable your readers to understand the importance and complexity of the issue.

2. Be sure to acknowledge the strengths, as well as the weaknesses, of the arguments you cite, including your own.

3. Remember that a statement is not an argument; a statement needs to be supported with facts and/or well-founded opinions in order to become an argument.

The section "Writing Discussion Essays" (pages 363–365) contains further ideas on structuring your essay. As you have in previous assignments, jot down a working thesis and outline.

Writing

Although you may feel strongly about this issue, remember that even the United States Supreme Court has had difficulty deciding the question of what speech is protected and what isn't. In fact, the Court has changed its mind on this issue several times over the years. The issue is complex and difficult. Accordingly, you may simply wish to discuss the issue, showing its complications, rather than coming down on one side or the other. If, however, you do want to argue for one position or the other, keep an open mind and acknowledge the arguments on the other side. Review the Writer's Checklist on pages 435–437 while you work on this assignment.

SHOULD COLLEGE ATHLETICS BE REFORMED?

As universities and colleges with major athletic programs continue to compete with one another for the best high school athletes and for the championships that bring to them literally millions of dollars, the argument continues to rage as to whether such schools should continue their current emphasis on big-time sports. Those who favor the current situation point to the huge amount of income such sports generate, at least at the most successful schools, and argue that many otherwise disadvantaged young men and women may get college educations because of their athletic talents, whereas otherwise they would not. Opponents claim that universities should be in the business of teaching academic subjects, not providing a training ground for professional basketball and football leagues.

Part of the problem is that although the organization governing college athletics, the National Collegiate Athletic Association (NCAA), has issued firm rules on recruiting and scholarships for athletes, cheating among major institutions has continued. Another difficulty is that at many schools with big-time programs, athletes are isolated from the rest of the student body, living in special dorms, being given make-work jobs created especially for them, and taking many (if not most) of their classes in programs designed by athletic departments. As a result, a large percentage of them never graduate, never earn a college degree, and are, ironically, incapable of competing professionally in the "real world" outside the college walls.

Reading Assignment

Pre-reading

As a way of beginning to think about this topic, ask yourself questions like the following: What are the problems surrounding college athletics? How are the athletes treated? Is the athletic program fair to them? Why or why not? Is it fair to the other students? Why or why not? What should be the role of athletics in a college?

Discuss this issue with your classmates, friends, and any college athletes you know. How do the athletes you know feel about this issue? You may wish to talk to coaches or others involved with your college's athletic program. Remember to take notes so you won't forget their arguments when it's time to write your essay.

Reading

The following articles address the role of athletics in colleges and thereby raise the fundamental question about what a university should be. They also illustrate that in this case, as with any complex issue involving individuals and institutions, what is best for the individual is not necessarily best for the institution and vice versa. Remember to read actively, taking notes, as you explore this issue.

In reading these articles, you will run across two references you may not be familiar with, the Knight Commission and the Bowl Championship Series (BCS). The John S. and James L. Knight Foundation, established in 1950, is "dedicated to furthering their ideas of service to community, to the highest standards of journalistic excellence and to the defence of a free press." The foundation formed a Commission to look into the workings and ethics of big-time college athletics and issued its first report in 1991. Subsequent reports have been issued annually. The members of the Commission are primarily current and former university presidents, and they have been highly critical of the ways in which major college athletic programs are run. To see the Commission's "Statement of Principles" and to read their reports, log on to knightfdn.org.

The Bowl Championship Series was established by the four major college football bowl games and the six major college football conferences, plus Notre Dame. The stated aim of the BCS was to determine a national champion in major college football at the end of every season. The real reason, however, was to make sure the bowls and major conferences shared the millions in revenue generated by the bowls and to make equally sure that teams belonging to other conferences were shut out of this revenue stream, which amounts to many millions of dollars.

HELPING TOP ATHLETES MEET MINIMUM STANDARDS
Kate Zernike

The 200 students gathered in makeshift classrooms at the hotel here   1
today are among the country's best high school basketball players, and almost all are being offered the chance to attend some of the country's most elite schools. All they have to do is raise their College

Board test scores to a total of 820 out of a possible 1600 points. That is almost 200 points below the national average, and far beneath the average at some of the schools interested in them. For most of the players, getting 820 will be difficult.

The young athletes are playing basketball at the weeklong ABCD   2
camp run by Adidas, the athletic goods company, and are sitting through classes on "life skills" and academics to help them succeed in college. This year, for the first time, the ABCD camp is offering the players a prep course taught by the Princeton Review, which more typically gives its expensive beat-the-test courses to **affluent** students trying to raise their scores from above-average to **Ivy League.** "We're trying to let these kids know, these are the rules and you have to play by the rules," said Richard Kosik, a New York public school teacher who directs the academic component of the camp. "Stop complaining and learn how to beat your opponent—in this case, the test."

[In June, 2001], the Knight Commission, a panel largely com-   3
posed of college presidents, concluded that the academic standards of college sports were **"abysmal"** and "disgraceful" and recommended that coaches be instructed that their job is "primarily to educate young people" and that athletes should meet the same academic requirements as other students. The courses offered here serve as a reminder that at least for now, athletes are still different from the average college student. Camp officials readily say that the test preparation is focused on getting these athletes to the bare minimum so they can play. The admission standards of many schools are different for the best athletes, and so is daily life at those schools, where there are often weaker courses and people to help the athletes get through them. "They don't live the regular college life," said Daniel Feigin, a codirector of the camp. Besides, he added, many of the students are more interested in playing professionally. "The colleges are a little steppingstone for them," he said. "The **blue-chip** kids are going to stay two or three years, just to get their bodies bigger."

The real reason most of the athletes are here is to be scouted by   4
coaches from Division I colleges, places like Stanford, Duke and Georgetown. There are 700 coaches and 200 players, all of them

---

affluent: wealthy;   **Ivy League:** athletic conference in which schools such as Harvard, Yale, and Princeton play;   **abysmal:** rock bottom;   **blue-chip:** star young men. As happens in any market whenever demand exceeds supply, the players are a hot commodity. Their athletic accomplishments are such that camp officials said that they were all but assured admission into some Division I schools, and that most will get free tuition, room and board.

There are rules, set by the National Collegiate Athletic Association: the players have at least a year to get their scores up to 820 on the College Board tests and a 2.5 high school grade point average. (Those numbers may vary, if one is significantly above the minimum.) On practice tests taken here, most scored about 700 combined on the verbal and math tests. In one classroom, just 4 out of 39 had reached the 820 minimum.

The Princeton Review specializes in teaching tactics to outwit the test, especially fitting here, where the goal is a quick fix. The tutor begins by explaining the minimum score and telling students how many questions they have to answer to reach that goal. They get 200 points for simply filling in their names, the tutors point out, and have to answer only 55 percent of the questions to score 1100 points. Several students say they are nervous. Others have a hard time focusing on the tips for success. "With athletes, there's a tendency for people, under the guise of helping, to say 'Don't worry, we'll do it for you,'" Mr. Kosik said. As the humidity floods in through the open doors in one classroom, students slump in their chairs, slipping off the bright, white slip-on shoes Adidas has provided. An hour later, several have put their heads on the tables, and when Mr. Kosik drops in, he has to tell one student, who has stretched his lanky frame over three chairs, to sit up and listen. With a cheerleader's pitch and persistent cheer, the tutor, Adi Opochinski, offers advice: don't read the full passages on the reading sections, spend your time on the questions instead, then make an educated guess about the most politically correct answer. "Why don't you do it for us?" one athlete asked, when the class was struck on an analogy requiring them to know the meaning of "desolate." Later, Ms. Opochinski asked, "What do you do if you don't know the answer?" "Ask the teacher?" one replied.

Some students insisted that they would be fine. "I'm good at test-taking," said Brandon Jenkins, a high school junior from Detroit. Others are aware that standards are lowered for athletes and say such treatment encourages laziness. "It's making them not work that hard; they just do it to get it done," said Allan Ray, 17, a junior at St. Raymond's High School in the Bronx, who said he had already scored above the minimum. "They should at least have to be average. You're just going to have to leave college early if you fail a class." Mr. Feigin, who teaches at Trevor Day School, a private school on the Upper West Side of Manhattan, said his school advised college-bound students not to go to a school where they will be over their heads academically. Meanwhile, he said, some schools know that athletes are in far over their heads. "The colleges know who they are admitting," he said. "They know these kids are going to help make so much revenue that to hire an academic adviser for them, or have four different classes to accommodate them, is nothing."

GRADUATION RATES AT TOP-TIER FOOTBALL PROGRAMS POOR
Steve Wieberg

At what price athletic success?   1

Three months after a strong rebuke of college athletics from the   2
Knight Commission, the latest study of players' graduation rates rekindles the issue, revealing a sharp division between the richer, more powerful programs and those of more modest scope.

Schools in the six top-tier conferences that form the cornerstone   3
of the Bowl Championship Series do a much poorer job of graduating athletes at the same rate as their non-athletes—the NCAA's benchmark for effectiveness. Using 4-year averages, 50 of the 63 schools show a lower rate for football players than for all men in the student body at those same schools. At nearly half of those major programs, from Michigan to Georgia Tech and 28 more, the football rate is 10 or more points beneath the school's overall rate. Non-BCS schools fare better. Almost two-thirds, or 33 of the 51 for which figures are available, graduate their football players at the same rate or better than the rate for all men. That's the case at nine of the 10 schools in the Western Athletic Conference, for example.

The disparity extends beyond football. Graduation rates in men's   4
basketball lag throughout major colleges but most of all in the BCS big leagues. There, in three of every four cases, it falls at least 10 points behind the rate for men overall. Twelve of those schools failed to graduate a black player who came in on scholarship from 1991–94, and 11 more graduated fewer than 20%. . . .

The Knight Commission pulled no punches in June when it   5
decried low graduation rates in football and basketball and concluded after nearly a year of study that "big-time athletics departments seem to operate with little interest in scholastic matters
beyond the narrow issue of individual eligibility." It recommended
holding athletes to the same admissions criteria as schools do all students, reducing the length of playing seasons "to afford athletes a
realistic opportunity to complete their degrees" and, by 2007, barring programs that graduate fewer than 50% of their athletes from
conference championships and postseason play. . . .

2003 NCAA TOURNAMENT: ACADEMICS; STUDY FINDS
TOP TEAMS FAILING IN THE CLASSROOM
Frank Litsky

A study released yesterday of how college athletes performed in the   1
classroom showed that the academic achievements of many of the
16 men's basketball teams remaining in the NCAA tournament [in
2003] did not match their accomplishments on the court. At many
of the 16 universities, basketball players graduated at a rate significantly lower than for all male athletes on athletic scholarships, and
the rates were even more striking for African-American male basketball players.

Five of the 16 remaining men's teams had graduation rates that   2
were a third to a half lower than the university's overall graduation
rate for all male athletes, the study showed. In 6 of the 16 universities, the graduation rate for African-American basketball players
was a third to three-quarters lower than the rate for all male athletes. At only three of the universities—Kansas, Duke and Butler—
did at least two-thirds of African-American male basketball players
graduate. At seven of the colleges, 30 percent or fewer of all
African-American players graduated. In the time frame that was
studied, no African-American players graduated at two universities
in the Round of 16: Syracuse and Oklahoma. In fact, no male players of any race graduated from Oklahoma. The data for the study
were furnished by the National Collegiate Athletic Association,
which measured whether basketball players who entered college
between 1992 and 1995 had graduated within six years of beginning college.

The study was overseen by Richard Lapchick, the director of the   3
Institute for Diversity and Ethics in Sport at the University of Central
Florida in Orlando, who has analyzed athletes' graduation rates for
two decades. "Men's basketball is the scandalous problem in college
sports, with the worst graduation rates," Lapchick said. "There are
328 colleges that play Division I men's basketball, and 58 of those
that had African-American players did not graduate even one during
this last six-year period. . . .

BIG SPENDERS ON CAMPUS SPENDING YOUR MONEY
Selena Roberts

There are public schools on the **plains** closing up as easily as pop-up   1
books, but there is a window in the dusty gloom, and, with a little
Windex, the elite can watch Nebraska's own Huskers play from that
skybox perched in the heavens. There are hardworking taxpayers
boarding up storefronts in shrinking towns that are down to their
last stoplight, but the Mayor of Husker Nation, Steve Pederson,
recently handed nearly $800,000 to the state employee Frank Solich
to make him disappear after a 9-3 season.

As Timothy Egan reported last week in the *New York Times*,   2
Nebraska has 7 of the nation's 12 poorest counties, but Pederson,
also known as Nebraska's athletic director, will soon lure a replacement coach into his department's deep pockets with a salary in the
$1 million range, maybe even more. "At no point do taxpayers pay
for the athletic department," said Nancy Kenny, Nebraska's associate athletic director, when reached last week. "We are 100 percent
self-supporting."

For a moment, ignore how this fiscal isolation has left   3
Nebraska's frothy football lords disconnected from reality, and take
Kenny at her good word. As the only game in the state, where a
Husker jersey's closest competition might be a John Deere cap,
Nebraska athletics may well have a claim on independence. Other
Division I shopoholics, from Ohio State to Florida State, rely on state
bonds or student fees or taxes on tickets—or all of the above—to
finance their $100 million-plus in facility upgrades, each college

---

plains: an area east of the Rocky Mountains ranging from Texas north to
Montana and the Dakotas

desperate to create the "wow" factor for a 17-year-old blue-chip recruit, who, no doubt, could be wowed by a double cheeseburger.

To woo celebrity coaches, public universities offer cars, special 4 housing options and low-interest loans that do not register in the salaries of these state employees. To secure the sideline rock stars, there are lucrative buyouts that are the envy of every faculty member with a worn elbow patch and a broken bicycle spoke. "It's appalling" said Andrew Zimbalist, an economics professor at Smith College, who wrote "Unpaid Professionals: Commercialism and Conflict in Big-Time College Sports" (Princeton University Press, 1999). "There are coaches walking away with **golden handshakes,** something you might think taxpayers would complain about."

Other Division I big spenders, like Oregon, turn to wealthy alumni, 5 like Nike's Phil Knight, for capital improvements, eager to replace the stench and monotony of a weight room with climate-controlled features and plasma-screen televisions. Can't pay an athlete? Then, make their stay a spa experience.

"I think we have engaged in an ungodly arms race," Vanderbilt's 6 chancellor, E. Gordon Gee, said in a telephone interview on Thursday. "I leapt off first." In September, Gee boldly decided to end the athletic department's separate kingdom, reintegrating it into the institution. The restructuring is intended to end athletic segregation, underscored when universities offer coaches their own salary scale and hand athletes separate cafeterias, workout facilities, dorms, classrooms and, in many cases, educational expectations. Easy for Vanderbilt, right? After all, the SAT stat leaders are the first to hand over their milk money as the Southeastern Conference's pushover. As Gee has said, he would "be pumping gas" if he had tried this at one of his previous stops, like Ohio State. . . .

NCAA BOARD OF DIRECTORS ADOPTS LANDMARK ACADEMIC REFORM PACKAGE

Indianapolis—A landmark academic reform package aimed at dramati- 1 cally strengthening the educational success of student-athletes and holding universities and teams accountable was unanimously approved (on April 29, 2004) by the NCAA Division I Board of Directors. . . .

---

golden handshakes: money paid to an employee to get him or her to quit

The comprehensive, three-year effort to improve the academic   2
progress, retention and graduation rates of student-athletes is the most
far-reaching effort of its kind in the history of the association, said
NCAA President Myles Brand. "This landmark legislation marks the beginning of a sea change in college sports," Brand said. "These are
strong and well-thought-out reforms that are critically necessary to ensuring that student-athletes are academically successful. For the first
time ever, the NCAA will have the ability to hold institutions and teams
accountable for the academic progress of their student-athletes." . . .
Brand praised Division I college and university chancellors and
presidents for their leadership in spearheading the groundbreaking
academic reform package, which sets out two types of penalties.

First, contemporaneous penalties, such as the loss of a scholar-   3
ship for one year if a student-athlete on scholarship leaves school in
poor academic standing, are expected to begin in 2005–06. The
Board of Directors will review in two years whether the contemporaneous penalties need to be more stringent. Second, historical penalties associated with academic failure over time may include
scholarship reductions; recruiting limitations; ineligibility for NCAA
team postseason or preseason competition, including bowl games
and NCAA championships; and, in the most extreme cases, restricted
membership status for the institution in the NCAA. These penalties
would begin in three years, rather than four as originally proposed.

An academic-progress rate, or APR, will be calculated by the   4
NCAA and include all scholarship student-athletes entering an institution. The package also will establish a graduation-success rate
based on a six-year timeframe for graduation and including all scholarship student-athletes entering the institution. The . . . program will
require that institutions submit to the NCAA annual documentation
showing compliance with the academic-progress rate.

The "cut rate" that will establish acceptable program and grad-   5
uation standards will be calculated after the collection of data this
year. While holding institutions accountable for academic progress,
the program will take into account institutional differences in
mission, sport, culture and gender. . . . Brand stressed that the new
academic accountability requirements for institutions and teams
build on new academic standards established last fall for student-
athletes to ensure steady progress toward degree completion. Those
measures include requiring student-athletes to complete 40 percent

of degree requirements by the end of their second year of college, 60 percent by the end of their third year and 80 percent by the end of year four. . . .

PLAN CREATES LOOPHOLES, NOT EDUCATED ATHLETES
Marc Isenberg

Last week, the National Collegiate Athletic Association passed legis-   1
lation it described as historic to hold institutions and sports programs accountable for educating student-athletes.

The legislation, which is known as the incentive/disincentive   2
plan, will penalize Division I teams whose graduation rates fall below a certain percentage. Progress of current athletes toward a degree will also be part of the formula, or metric, as the NCAA calls it. Penalties will include a reduction in the scholarships a team can award and, in extreme and persistent cases, ineligibility for bowl games and the NCAA basketball tournament. (The proposal theoretically refers to all sports; in practice, graduation rates are low primarily in football and basketball.)

The desire of the NCAA and its members to improve graduation   3
rates is positive. But there must be no graduation without education. Will adoption of this new metric cause those universities not now dedicated to educating their football and basketball players to alter course? I think not. Instead, those universities will produce higher graduation rates through more special courses for athletes, more pressure on professors to grant athletes unearned good grades and more academic work performed for athletes under the guise of tutoring. Current practices that can easily be abused, like athletic department employees' administering tests to athletes while they travel to games, will be expanded. New gimmicks will be developed. If the past is any guide, a few athletic programs will get caught, but most will get away with it.

In fact, a loophole in the legislation could make the **chicanery**   4
unnecessary. Any player who leaves the institution "in good academic standing" will not count against the institution's graduation rate. Fair and reasonable, right? In reality, every athlete in the NCAA tournament or in a bowl game must be in good academic standing; otherwise, he

---

chicanery: cheating

would be ineligible to compete. To have a 100 percent graduation rate, a university would have to graduate only one scholarship player per team per year and encourage the others to leave without their degrees while "in good academic standing."

Based on high school grades and test scores, Division I football   5
players and men's basketball players, on the average, arrive at college less prepared academically than the general student population. Then, instead of being assisted in catching up academically, they are immediately plunged into about 40 hours a week of practice, meetings and games. The NCAA's words tell athletes that classwork comes first and that graduation is the most important objective. But when athletic events are scheduled on class days, the NCAA's actions tell athletes that sports come first. The only meaningful way to improve graduation rates—by educating athletes—is to enable them to compete in the classroom. While the incentive/disincentive plan opens the door for increased abuse, the NCAA has overlooked the obvious: a return to freshman ineligibility and the banning of midweek football and midweek basketball games requiring day-before travel.

Freshman Residency Playing on a freshman team with limited   6
practice time, limited travel and a relatively short season would encourage athletes who have no interest in higher education to seek pathways to pro sports other than college, freeing up scarce athletic scholarships for actual student-athletes. It would also enable athletes to devote their first year in college—a year of difficult adjustment for most students—to developing the skills and habits necessary to performing college-level academic work.

Banning Most Midweek Games Class attendance is a vital part   7
of belonging to the college community. Before the insatiable demand of television for college games at every hour of every day, athletes could, if they chose to, attend almost every class during the regular season. Now, football and basketball players are required by the demands of midweek games to miss many of their classes.

These two simple policies would send a clear message to all   8
athletic administrators, coaches and athletes—that class attendance and academic performance are the first priority.

Although it is possible to schedule games to avoid all or almost   9
all missed classes, there is a strong current of thought in NCAA circles that it cannot be done. We know it can be done. Genuine change will come only if the NCAA stops bowing to every demand of its television

partners and makes rules that put athletes in the classroom. Athletic competition that requires athletes to miss class should be banned (or at least severely limited). Most sports could institute such a ban immediately. The television contracts for men's basketball would make it difficult to effect a total ban, but we could eliminate 70 percent to 80 percent of the current missed class time if we made that our priority.

The 13-year NBA veteran Elden Campbell, when asked if he   10
earned a college degree, replied, "No, but they gave me one anyway." Campbell faced the truth squarely. The NCAA's new graduation metric, with or without the in-good-academic-standing loophole, will only disguise continued failure to educate student-athletes.

THE IVY LEAGUE AT 30: A MODEL FOR COLLEGE ATHLETICS OR AN OUTMODED ANTIQUE?
Douglas Lederman

The Ivy League was officially born 30 years ago this fall [1986], the   1
product of a protest movement by eight college presidents who were dismayed by the growing professionalism of intercollegiate athletics. To ensure the amateurism of their athletic programs, the league's members agreed to forbid athletic scholarships and admissions breaks for athletes, oppose freshman eligibility, shorten athletic seasons, and ban off-season practice.

Many scoffed at the arrangement then, and many cynics still do   2
today. But even its critics admit that the Ivy League has, with minor adjustments, stayed its original course and, in most cases, held true to its ideas.

That course, however, has led the Ivy League away from the   3
mainstream of big-time intercollegiate athletics, where its members once competed. Four years ago, the Ivy institutions were forced out of the National Collegiate Athletic Association's top level of play by new standards governing stadium size and minimum attendance.

Such a demotion may have been inevitable, since even Ivy   4
officials admit that the league's ability to compete successfully at a national level in the major revenue sports is a thing of the past. Beyond the issue of competitiveness, however, observers both inside and outside the conference raise questions about what may

lie ahead as the Ivy League . . . continues to march somewhat out of step with other college sports programs. Has the league's adherence to its principles—ideals shared by few other colleges that compete seriously in sports—isolated its members? Can the Ivy League be a model for the way intercollegiate athletics should be run, or is it just an **antiquated** reminder of the way things once were? Will other colleges eventually follow the Ivy League's lead, or will the competitive gap that already exists simply continue to widen?

In the late 1940s and early 1950s, gambling scandals rocked college basketball, and a case of academic fraud **decimated** the football team at the U.S. Military Academy. Commentators, citing escalating competition and rapidly expanding stadiums, bemoaned the burgeoning professionalism of major college sports. In response, the NCAA adopted sweeping rules governing recruiting and financial aid that became known as the "sanity code." The name suggested measures of desperation; the rules were abandoned as unworkable in a vote by NCAA members. 5

Eight prestigious Northeastern institutions—Brown, Columbia, Cornell, Harvard, Princeton, and Yale Universities, Dartmouth College, and the University of Pennsylvania—formulated their own response: a new confederation designed to make sure that intercollegiate sports remained in their proper place. Although the colleges had been playing each other in football for decades, the 1954 Ivy Group accord brought them together formally in all sports. In the agreement, the presidents of the eight institutions insisted that "players shall be truly representative of the student body and not composed of specially recruited athletes. . . . In the total life of the campus, emphasis upon intercollegiate competition must be kept in harmony with the essential educational purposes of the institution." 6

The league adopted two major **tenets:** athletes would be admitted under the same criteria as the rest of its students, and the colleges would provide financial aid based only on need. 7

There has been some tinkering over 30 years: the restoration of freshman eligibility in most sports, the lengthening of the football season from 9 to 10 games, and a stricter system for monitoring admissions 8

---

antiquated: too old to be useful;   **decimated:** destroyed;   **tenets:** principles, doctrines

standards, in response to what Brown's president Howard Swearer calls "some slippage" in such standards within the league in the 1970s.

Recruiting has also changed. The Ivy colleges have intensified their recruiting in an effort to keep pace with their peers in the league and with other top colleges that offer athletic scholarships. "I think we've been caught up in recruiting more than the founders would have hoped," says Al Paul, the athletic director at Columbia, "but we do it within our predetermined rules and regulations."

Some observers have questioned the purity of Ivy motives on other issues, such as playing major powers like Penn State and the firing of coaches who don't win enough games. But despite some adaptations to keep up with the times, the Ivy League has clung **tenaciously** to its guiding ideals, its officials say.

"The league's underlying principles from 30 years ago are still our underlying principles today," says Columbia's Al Paul, "and we've stuck to them even though we've been alone much of the time."

Recent examples of national prominence by Ivy teams have been rare. Penn made the final four in men's basketball in 1979, Columbia was national runner-up in men's soccer in 1982, and Harvard was runner-up in the men's hockey championships in 1983 and 1986. But Ivy teams have lost substantial ground in football and basketball. "Our ability to compete in the major sports has surely gone down," says Mr. Paul. "Recruiting outside the league has gotten too intense." "In the so-called major sports we found ourselves playing opponents who were simply outclassing us on a regular basis," adds Joan S. Girgus, dean of the college at Princeton and an Ivy League policy committee member. The Ivy teams have thus altered their goals. "We're very happy shooting for the Ivy title."

Officials at the institutions most frequently compared to the Ivy colleges in terms of balance between sports and academics—Duke, Northwestern, Rice, Stanford, and Vanderbilt Universities, for example—admire the league but suggest that its situation is unique. Roy Kramer, athletic director at Vanderbilt, says the Ivies' lack of dependence on income from sports is the single biggest difference between Vanderbilt and the Ivy colleges. "Because of the Ivy set-up, those schools are in the enviable position of not having to worry

---

tenaciously: persistently, stubbornly

about gate receipts to pay for athletics," he says. "But because of
the region we're in and the people we play, we couldn't do that
unless the entire mold of intercollegiate athletics changed."

Post-reading

As a way of beginning to examine this issue, return to the reading selections
and list the following:

- The benefits of college athletic programs for (1) students and (2) the institution
- The negative aspects of college athletic programs for (1) students and (2) the institution

Additionally, think about the role of higher education and answer the following
questions and explain the reasons for your responses:

- Should colleges focus solely on academics?
- Are universities appropriate training grounds for professional athletes?
- Should college athletes be forced to compete academically with other students or should they be on a separate track?
- Do separate academic tracks—one for athletes and one for other students—diminish the value of a college's degree?

Essay Assignment

Write an essay in which you discuss the role of athletics in colleges.
You may conclude that certain reforms should be made and wish to
recommend some. Or you may prefer to discuss the issue in general
in order not to recommend reform but to shed light on this heated
debate.

Pre-writing

As you think about organizing your essay, remember these points:

1. Present adequate background to enable your readers to understand the importance and complexity of the issue.

2. Be sure to acknowledge the strengths, as well as the weaknesses, of the arguments you cite, including your own.

3. Remember that a statement is not an argument; a statement needs to be supported with facts and/or well-founded opinions in order to become an argument.

The section "Writing Discussion Essays" (pages 363–365) contains further ideas on structuring your essay. As you have in previous assignments, jot down a working thesis and outline.

Writing

Although you may feel strongly one way or the other on this issue, remember that there's no right or wrong answer. There are, however, stronger and weaker arguments. To compose the strongest one you can, keep an open mind while you write and use the most compelling support you can generate.

THE WRITER'S CHECKLIST

The Idea Draft

1. Does your idea draft *respond fully* to the assignment?
2. Are your ideas *organized* in the way you want?
3. Does your *introduction* explain what the essay will be about and what its purpose is?
4. Do you have a *thesis* that states your point or indicates the issue the essay will address?
5. Do the *body paragraphs* each have a *topic sentence?* Do they develop the main points by giving *specifics and examples* to support those points?
6. Does your *conclusion* state your belief about the issue, make a recommendation for change, or summarize your main points?
7. Have you *collaborated* with at least one trusted friend or fellow student who has read your draft *critically,* looking for lapses in logic or other weaknesses in content?

Sentence Combining

In revising your idea draft, keep in mind the possibility of using verbal phrases in a few of your sentences. Use your sentence-combining exercises and the sentences below as models for how you can use these structures:

- In "High School Papers Grow Up," notice how Jerry Carroll uses an end-of-sentence verbal phrase to tie together two points instead of making two sentences of them:

  Written by Kathryn Pallokoff, 17, the article is a careful and responsible account of the problem, *giving figures on the spread of the disease and warning of the importance of "safe sex."*

- In "Censorship: A Fact of Life Students Are Forced to Face," Jonathan Yardley writes a similar sentence and then one in which he puts a verbal between the subject and verb of his sentence; in the latter case, many writers would have started the sentence with the verbal phrase instead:

  The majority quite specifically reaffirmed that broad principle, *qualifying it only by the observation . . . that a school need not tolerate student speech that is inconsistent with its "basic educational mission." . . .*

  The principal of Hazelwood High School, in restricting the contents of an issue of *Spectrum,* was attempting among other things to teach his journalism students a lesson about what is and is not a responsible exercise of journalistic freedom.

- In "The Ivy League at 30," Douglas Lederman shows a common use of *to* verbal phrases:

  To ensure the amateurism of their athletic programs, the league's members agreed to forbid athletic scholarships and admissions breaks for athletes, oppose freshman eligibility, shorten athletic seasons, and ban off-season practice.

Later Drafts

1. Taking into account the constructive criticism you have received, have you *revised* accordingly—that is, reorganized, if organization was a problem, or given additional support, if support was?
2. Have you read your essay *aloud,* listening closely to what it *actually says,* not just what you think it says? (This is another good place to work with a trusted fellow student or friend. Have him or her read your essay aloud; both of you should listen closely to what it says.)

3. Have you *revised your sentences* if they seemed unclear or awkward as you read them aloud?
4. Have you checked for those *mechanical difficulties* that you know you sometimes have? Have you used the dictionary to check words that you think may be *misspelled?*

Final Draft

If you have followed this assignment step by step, you have worked exceedingly hard on this essay. Therefore, make sure your final draft reflects your care and effort; make it as professional looking as possible.

1. Type it neatly, using the format your instructor has assigned.
2. Proofread slowly and carefully, word by word, line by line. (One last time, ask a trusted friend to proofread it *after* you have, or exchange your essay with another student and proof each other's.)

*S*entence Combining

SHAPING SENTENCES TO SHOW RELATIONSHIPS: VERBAL PHRASES

You have already used two verb forms—*ing* and *have*—as noun modifiers. These same kinds of words plus one other verb form, the *base* form, are frequently used to combine ideas.

From your dictionary work and previous sentence-combining practice, you remember, of course, that all verbs have *base, -ing,* and *have* forms such as these:

base	**-ing**	**have**
walk	walking	walked
laugh	laughing	laughed
think	thinking	thought
take	taking	taken

You may also recall that the base form is often preceded by the word *to* (to walk, to laugh, and so on), and so we will call these *to* forms from now on. We use these *to* forms in many ways, as in the following example:

The road to take was supposed to be the one on the left.

But we use the *to* form in these ways automatically, without thinking about it. However, all three verb forms—*have, -ing,* and *to*—have a function that students do not automatically use them for, at least not as much as experienced writers do, and that is to join into one efficient sentence ideas that would otherwise be in two sentences. Here are examples using each of the three verb forms; the phrases made from these three verb forms, by the way, are called *verbal phrases.*

> **Two sentences:** The police were watching a drug dealer from the window of a second-floor apartment. They photographed him making a sale.
> **One sentence:** Watching a drug dealer from the window of a second-floor apartment, the police photographed him making a sale.
> **Two sentences:** The children were enchanted by the Christmas play. They shrieked and laughed throughout.
> **One sentence:** Enchanted by the Christmas play, the children shrieked and laughed throughout.
> **Two sentences:** I wanted to help my roommate get an A on a crucial midterm. I stayed up half the night working with her on her math.
> **One sentence:** To help my roommate get an A on a crucial midterm, I stayed up half the night working with her on her math.

The *to* form of the verb used this way can also be preceded by the words *in order.* Whether or not you use *in order* makes no difference to the meaning of the *to* phrase or of the sentence; the use of *in order* is purely a stylistic option open to the writer. The following two sentences mean exactly the same thing:

> To get the car started, you have to turn the key and smack the dashboard simultaneously.
> In order to get the car started, you have to turn the key and smack the dashboard simultaneously.

One other option you need to be aware of is that you can also end sentences with these kinds of verbal phrases. There is no law that says they always have to come at the beginning. In fact, it has been shown statistically that published writers use them at the ends of sentences more than they do at the beginnings.

Finally, it is important to remember that although these verbal phrases don't actually have subjects, there must be in the sentence a word that tells the reader what you mean their subjects to be and that word is usually the subject of the sentence. Look at this example:

> Singing loudly, John walked into the side of a truck.

Who is singing loudly? John, of course, the subject of the sentence. Now look at this example:

Singing loudly, a truck ran over John.

This doesn't work because we know that trucks can't sing. The same rule holds when the verbal phrase comes at the end of the sentence, as here:

I walked through the forest, observing the birds and the bees. (This works because I, the subject, am doing the observing.)
The forest was a pleasure to stroll through, observing the birds and the bees. (This doesn't work very well because there is no word in the sentence to tell who is doing the observing, and the subject, *forest,* cannot be the observer.)

EXERCISE

In the exercise below, make the second sentence in each pair into a verbal phrase attached to either the beginning or the end of the first sentence. In deciding where to place the phrase, test the sound of the sentence first; sometimes a phrase will work equally well at the beginning or the end, and sometimes it will not. In the first five exercises, the verbal phrases are underlined to help you. Example:

Mary saved her money.
She wanted to buy a new guitar.

Solution: To buy a new guitar, Mary saved her money.

Or:

Mary saved her money <u>to buy a new guitar.</u>

A note on punctuation: We normally set off all three of the verbal phrases with a comma when they come at the beginning of the sentence, and we normally set off the *-ing* and *have* forms with a comma when they come at the end of the sentence. But, for no particular reason, writers usually do not set off sentence-ending *to* phrases. As always, the rule is, when in doubt about whether to use a comma, don't.

A Day in the Country

1. John and Mary planned to leave at 8:30 in the morning.
   They hoped <u>to get a good spot at the picnic grounds.</u>
2. They made trip after trip from the house to the car.
   They were <u>loaded down with things they simply couldn't leave behind.</u>

3. They finally had to leave behind their bicycles and Schnoz, their pet anteater. They wanted <u>to get the car doors closed.</u>

4. The car developed a flat tire. The car was <u>packed to the ceiling with every manner</u> of picnic and camping gear.

5. Mary unloaded some of the supplies. She was <u>muttering some phrases she should not have muttered.</u>

6. John finally got the tire replaced. He was burdened with a great ignorance about spare tires.

7. They decided to take a shortcut down a back road. They wanted to save some time.

8. They saw no identifiable landmarks. They were pausing finally to get their bearings.

9. The ants at the picnic grounds were getting edgy and irritable. They were waiting for John and Mary to show up.

10. Schnoz had given them some crumbs of information about the picnic. He wanted to get even for having been left at home.

EXERCISE

In the following exercise, you will practice two new aspects of verbal phrase use. One is placement. Verbal phrases may introduce sentences or they may end sentences. Normally, we use them to introduce sentences when they provide background to the main idea of the sentence:

Mary had decided to throw a big party. (background)
She began to make a list of possible guests. (main idea)

Having decided to throw a big party, Mary began to make a list of possible guests.

On the other hand, when the verbal phrase *develops* the idea of the main sentence, we usually put it at the end. This is where you will find most verbal phrases in the work of professional writers.

Mary began to make a list of possible guests. (main idea)
She first wrote down the names of her closest friends. (development)

Mary began to make a list of possible guests, first writing down the names of her closest friends.

The second aspect of verbal phrase use you will practice here is using more than one verbal at the ends of sentences in order to develop the idea as completely as possible:

Mary began to make a list of possible guests. (main idea)
She first wrote down the names of her closest friends.
She next noted people she couldn't stand.
She finally considered the borderline group.

Mary began to make a list of possible guests, first writing down the names of her closest friends, next noting people she couldn't stand, and finally considering the borderline group.

In these exercises, the main-idea sentence is always the first one. In the first five, the sentences to be turned into verbal phrases have been identified as background or development.

The Movie Critic

1. John decided to become a movie critic.
   He was watching two movie critics on a television show one night. (background)

2. He began to go to the movies four or five times a week.
   He wanted to polish up his critical skills. (background)

3. He invited Mary to come with him.
   He thought she would be a good audience for his criticism. (development)

4. She was happy to go to the movies with him.
   She thought John was really getting interested in her. (background)

5. She began to grow tired of these dates.
   She was seeing movies she hated. (development)
   She was listening to John's stupid comments about them. (development)
   She was losing a lot of study time. (development)

6. She began to turn down John's movie invitations.
   She pretended she had a headache.
   Or she said she had too much work to do.

7. She wondered why he didn't want to do anything but see movies.
   She was thinking about John's peculiar new dating pattern.

8. She began quizzing him about all these movie dates.
   She wanted to find out what he was up to.

9. When she found out that he just wanted an audience for his dopey practice criticism, she hit the ceiling.
   She realized that he was just taking advantage of their friendship.

10. Then she gave him a good lesson in constructive criticism.
    She told him what an insensitive clod he was.
    She made him understand how she felt.

EXERCISE

One last point having to do with verbal phrases. Frequently, we will put prepositions in front of -ing verbals in order to make our intended meaning clearer. For instance, instead of writing this:

Having considered all the pros and cons, John decided to buy a new car rather than a used one.

we could write this:

After having considered all the pros and cons, John decided to buy a new car rather than a used one.

Similarly, this:

Working out every day, I feel a lot better.

could become this:

By working out every day, I feel a lot better.

Or this:

John grew sleepy doing his homework.

could become one of these:

John grew sleepy while doing his homework.
John grew sleepy when doing his homework.

Try adding prepositions in as many of the following sentences as you can, but don't feel that you have to add a preposition in every case. Some phrases will sound better without one. Remember that you can add a preposition only if you are working with an *-ing* verb form.

Be sure to consider carefully whether the verbal phrases are background or development so you know whether to put them at the beginning or the end of the sentences. In each of these sentences, *the main idea is in the first sentence.*

The Concept of Tribute

1. Glenisha discovered some interesting new ways to make money.
   Glenisha took a course in ancient history.

2. She discovered the concept of tribute.
   She pored over her history texts.

3. She considered how to produce sufficient gratitude.
   She realized that her boyfriend, Raymont, wasn't sufficiently grateful to her to pay tribute.

4. She decided not to see him for three weeks.
   She wanted to produce some gratitude.

5. Raymont tried everything to get in touch with her.
   He called.
   He rang her doorbell.
   He sent messages via her roommate.
   He slid notes under the door.
   He sent a telegram.

6. Glenisha called him up.
   She began to note a certain desperation in his messages.
   She felt he was achieving the proper state of gratitude.

7. She told him that she now required one movie and one dinner each week in exchange for the pleasure of her company.
   She explained the concept of tribute.

8. Raymont began to study ancient history.
   He wanted to learn how to handle the tribute problem.

9. He called up Glenisha right away.
   He discovered that ancient peoples avoided tribute by developing new allies.

10. He told her that he had developed a new ally, Joanne.

    He explained that the concept of shortness of funds was more powerful than the concept of tribute.

REVIEW

In the following exercises, you will practice using everything you have studied so far by combining each group of sentences into a single sentence.

The Original Olympics

1. The citizens of Elis decided to add contests to their celebrations.

   They wanted to honor Zeus.

   Zeus was the foremost of the gods of ancient Greece.

   Elis was a small Greek city-state.

   The contests were athletic.

   The celebrations were religious.

2. These celebrations were held in a place and were run by the citizens of that city.

   The place was called Olympia.

   Olympia was a holy site near Elis.

   It was dedicated to Zeus.

   The citizens served as judges of the contests.

3. The Olympic games lasted for more than a thousand years.

   They began in 776 BC.

   They were held every four years.

   They ended when a Christian ruler stamped them out.

4. The games began as part of a celebration.

   The celebration was small.

   The celebration was local.

       [join]

   They soon grew into the most important sports event of ancient times.

   They attracted athletes.

   They attracted spectators.

   The athletes were the greatest.

   The athletes were from the whole Mediterranean area.

   The spectators were numerous.

5. Spectators had to endure poor living conditions.

   Spectators wished to attend the games.

   The living conditions were no housing.

   They were little water.

   They were no sanitation facilities.

   The water was for drinking or bathing.

   　[join]

   The men were willing to make almost any sacrifice to attend.

   The men were the wealthiest.

   The men were of that time.

6. The games were open only to men, and the ranks of spectators were closed to women.

   The men competed naked.

   The women were married.

   The women could be executed if caught there.

7. Chariot races usually opened the games.

   The races were violent affairs.

   They were filled with accidents and injuries.

   They attracted the attention of the spectators.

8. Besides chariot and horse racing, the contests included wrestling and boxing, the pancratium, and the pentathlon.

   The pentathlon was a mixture of five sports.

   The five sports were the long jump.

   They were the discus throw.

   They were the javelin throw.

   They were a foot race.

   They were wrestling.

9. Today we think of the Greeks as a people.

   They loved philosophy.

   They loved poetry.

   They loved science.

   　[join]

   The pancratium was a fight.

   The pancratium was the favorite event of the spectators.

   The pancratium was the bloodiest of the Olympic contests.

The fight was to the finish.

The fight was between two contestants.

The two contestants were punching.

They were kicking.

They were wrestling.

They were strangling.

They were biting.

They were gouging each other.

They did these things until one gave up, was knocked out, or died.

10. Contestants sometimes resorted to bribery, for all honors went to the winners, and nothing went to the losers.

The contestants wanted to win in the Olympics.

The contestants were desperate.

The winners were glorious.

The winners were often given great sums of money and even lifetime pensions by the citizens of their cities.

The losers were miserable.

The losers were jeered and treated with scorn, even by their own families.

Hobbyists

1. We tend to associate people mostly with their jobs.

    [join]

An aspect of human behavior is the ways.

The aspect is fascinating.

People choose to entertain themselves in these ways.

They entertain themselves in their spare time.

2. Of course, most people do things.

The things are obvious.

The things are watching television.

The things are going to the movies.

The things are reading.

    [join]

Some choose other forms of entertainment.

These forms are more active.

This entertainment is some hobby to get involved in.

3. Interestingly, women tend to find ways of amusing themselves.
   These ways can be seen as useful.
   They are tending a garden.
   They are knitting.
   They are working for organizations.
   The organizations help needy people.

4. Men most often get involved in hobbies.
   They want to entertain themselves in their odd hours.
   The hobbies are much more like play.
   They are collecting stamps.
   They are building model ships or trains.
   They are playing golf.
   They are making pointless improvements on their cars.

5. Most men get a large part of their self-esteem from their work.
   [join]
   Many men can't wait to get home.
   They are bored with jobs.
   The jobs are dreary.
   The jobs keep them locked in offices all day.
   There they can escape into worlds of their own creation.

6. The model railroader might spend an entire evening.
   The model railroader is dedicated.
   He is trying to get effects on a boxcar.
   The boxcar is miniature.
   The effects are just the right ones.
   The effects are of rust, dust, and mud.

7. The model shipbuilder will happily put in hours.
   He is fascinated by the beauty of rigging and sails.
   He will be studying ships-of-the-line of the mid-eighteenth century.
   The ships are British.

8. A group of people are the ones.
   The group is particularly interesting.
   They play war games.
   The games are usually recreations of famous battles of the past.

9. The wargamers will spend hours or even weeks.
   They are slurping their beer or their soft drinks.
   They are refighting a battle.
   The battle is between the French and the Austrians in 1797.
   Or the battle is between the North and the South in 1864.

10. The hobbyist might seem to be wasting time.
    The hobbyist is busy.
    The hobbyist is living in his fantasy world.
    The time is valuable.
    [join]
    The hobbyist is a man or a woman.
    The man or woman is happy.
    The man or woman is bothering no one.

SHAPING SENTENCES TO SHOW RELATIONSHIPS: PARALLELISM

Three of the FANBOYS words, the coordinators, can join parts of sentences: *and, or,* and *but.* The one we use most frequently is *and.* When we use one of these words to join sentence parts, we have to make sure that the parts they join are alike, that they are grammatically similar. Here are some common examples; the sentence parts being joined have been underlined:

John and Mary didn't know what to do on their day off.
They liked to walk but didn't feel like hiking.
They considered going to a movie or driving out of town.

Because the sentence parts being joined are like one another, they are said to be in parallel with each other, and the joining of such structures with *and, or,* or *but* is called parallelism.

In the exercises below, you will be given pairs of sentences. In each case, you should find the parallel structures within each pair of sentences and join them using *and, or,* or *but.* You can tell what the parallel structures are by eliminating repetition of words in the sentence pairs, as in these examples:

She bought a dog.
~~She bought~~ a cat.

Solution: She bought a dog and a cat.

He rowed his boat up the creek.
~~He~~ tied it to a tree.

Solution: He rowed his boat up the creek and tied it to a tree.

John hates television.
Mary ~~hates television~~.

Solution: John and Mary hate television.

She bought her house with her savings.
~~She bought her house with~~ money she made on her book.

Solution: She bought her house with her savings and money she made on her book.

Notice that in these examples, no comma has been used before the coordinators. Normally, we use the comma only when the coordinator joins two complete sentences, rather than parts of sentences.

EXERCISE

In the following pairs of sentences, the word and, or, *or* but *in parentheses follows the first sentence to tell you which word to use in creating the parallel structures.*

Maria Makes a Decision

1. Maria was looking for part-time work as a secretary. (or)
   She was looking for part-time work as a receptionist.

2. She hoped for a good job. (but)
   She found a bad one.

3. She worked for a fast-food outlet serving gristly hamburgers. (and)
   She worked for a fast-food outlet serving greasy fries.

4. The hamburgers were tasteless. (but)
   The hamburgers were cheap.

5. The employees were overworked. (and)
   They were underpaid.

6. All of them were fed up with the low pay. (and)
   They were fed up with the poor working conditions.

7. Maria disliked the work. (but)
   She made several friends on that job.

8. One of her friends, Martha, was saving to go to college. (and)
   She was saving to buy a used car.

9. Martha hoped to get a scholarship. (or)
   She hoped to get a student loan.

10. Discouraged by her job, Maria decided to return to school. (and)
    She decided to pursue a major in engineering.

Parallelism in Series

As you know, we often join three or more elements in sentences with coordinators, particularly with *and*. In these cases, the basic rule of parallelism still holds: All of the elements being joined should usually be *similar* grammatically, as in these examples:

> I took French, history, math, and psychology.
> Mary, John, and I went to see a play.
> She got a loan, a scholarship, and a cash award from a large company.

You will notice that in the first example, the elements in the series are all the same, all nouns naming a school subject. In the second example, the elements are not quite the same; they all indicate people, which is the main thing, but one is a pronoun rather than a noun. In the third example, the first two elements are simple nouns without modifiers, but the third noun has a lot of modifiers.

There is no problem with that. The only important thing is that all of the elements are nouns; the nouns may or may not have modifiers, as you wish. The same is true for verbs in parallel; it makes no difference what the forms of the different verbs are or what kinds of words follow them so long as all the verbs will work with the same subject. Here is a sentence with a string of nouns that are parallel despite the differences in how the nouns are modified:

> Under the Christmas tree, the children found
>> three books for each of them,
>> a tricycle,
>> an incredible new doll with a vocabulary of 200 words,
>> and a train that made sounds like the real thing.

Here is a sentence with a string of verbs that are parallel despite the different forms of the verbs and the different kinds of structures following them:

By the end of the day, John
had seen his car destroyed,
had been taken to the hospital for X-rays, which turned out negative,
was two hundred dollars poorer,
and wished he had stayed in bed.

You should notice also that when we join three or more elements in a parallel series, we put commas between all of them, including one before the coordinator.

EXERCISE

Combine the following groups of sentences to make parallel series of two, three, or four elements. In some cases, you will also have to join complete sentences with coordinators or subordinators.

A Day at the Mall

1. John went to a shopping mall.
   Mary went to a shopping mall. (and)
   Uncle Fred went to a shopping mall.

2. They hoped to buy a few clothes.
   They hoped to have a good lunch. (and)
   They hoped to see what was what.

3. John was looking for a light sweater. (or)
   He was looking for a new shirt in the latest style.

4. Mary wanted a silk blouse. (and)
   She wanted some earrings.

5. Uncle Fred hoped to find a rich widow.
   He hoped to find a wealthy divorcee. (or)
   He hoped to find a pretty woman looking for a good time.

6. John did not like the sweaters he saw. (and)
   He did not like the shirts he saw.
   He was tempted to spend a lot of money on some shoes he didn't need.

7. Mary looked at a lot of blouses. (but)
   She didn't like any of them.
   None were cut in the style she wanted.

8. Uncle Fred approached widows.
   He stopped divorcees. (and)
   He accosted pretty women who seemed to be looking for a good time.
   None would have anything to do with him.
   Several threatened to call the police.

9. By the end of the day, John had not found a sweater he liked. (or)
   He had not found a shirt he liked.
   Someone had stolen his shoes.
   He was trying on the ones he didn't need.

10. Mary had had enough of the mall.
    She had had enough of John. (and)
    She had had enough of looking at silk blouses.
    She had absolutely had enough of Uncle Fred.

11. Uncle Fred was marching off to the car unhappy. (and)
    He was marching off to the car displeased with the day.

12. Instead of a pretty widow, he had a sheriff's deputy on one arm. (and)
    Instead of an attractive divorcee, he had a city police officer on the other.
    Instead of a pretty woman, a state police officer was following him with a stern look on his face.

REVIEW

In the following exercises, you will practice using all the sentence-combining skills you have studied so far.

The Story of Pepper

1. Pepper originally came from Malabar.
   It also came from Sumatra.
   Pepper is the fruit of a vine.
   The fruit is dried.
   The vine is called *Piper nigrum.*
   Malabar is a coastal region of India.
   Sumatra is the second largest island of Indonesia.

2. Now it comes from five nations.
   It comes from India.
   It comes from Indonesia.
   It comes from Malaysia.
   It comes from Sri Lanka.
   It comes from Brazil.
   These nations have joined to form the International Pepper Community.

3. Pepper is made by picking peppercorns.
   The pepper is black.
   The peppercorns are green.
   It is made by leaving them in the sun to dry.
   Pepper is made by letting the peppercorns dry even longer.
   The pepper is white.
   It is made by washing the husks from the peppercorns.
   The husks are dried.
   The peppercorns are black.

4. We take pepper for granted now.
   It used to be a commodity.
   It was one of the rarest commodities.
   It was one of the most expensive commodities.
   It was one of the most prized commodities.
   The commodities were in the Western world.

5. The ancient Greeks loved pepper.
   The Romans loved pepper.
   The Romans learned where it came from.
   They established trade routes.
   The routes were between the Red Sea and the Malabar Coast.

6. They were interested in pepper.
   They were also interested in other goods.
   The goods were rare.
   The goods were from the East.
   The goods were cloves.
   The goods were nutmeg.
   The goods were cinnamon.
   The goods were pearls.
   The goods were ivory.

7. Alaric captured Rome in 408 AD.
   Alaric was king of the Visigoths.
   He demanded a ransom.
   The ransom consisted partly of gold.
   The ransom consisted partly of silver.
   The ransom consisted partly of three thousand pounds of pepper.

8. In 1101 the army of Genoa won a great victory.
   Genoa is an Italian city.
   Each soldier was rewarded with two pounds of pepper.
   Around this time, peppercorns were even used as currency.
   The currency was between individuals and cities.

9. The explorers were seeking pepper.
   The explorers were seeking the other spices.
   The explorers undertook voyages into uncharted seas.
   The explorers undertook voyages to unknown lands.
   The explorers were great Europeans.
   They were men like Columbus, Magellan, da Gama, and Cabot.

10. Explorers discovered plants.
    The discovery was in the New World.
    The plants produce effects.
    The effects are pepperish.
    The plants are paprika.
    The plants are cayenne.
    The plants are jalapeño peppers.
    These are unrelated to true pepper.
    They were considered inferior by the Europeans.

11. Pepper is so common now.
    We scarcely think of it.
    It was once almost as valuable as gold.

Language of the Eyes

1. Humans communicate through speech.
   They also communicate through writing.
   They also communicate in other ways.
   The other ways are nonverbal.

The nonverbal ways are through posture.

They are through gestures.

They are through facial expressions.

They are through clothing.

2. One of our most important means of communication is governed by a set of rules.

The means is the language of the eyes.

The rules are fairly complex.

We learn the rules without realizing it.

3. "Eye language" varies according to a number of criteria.

One criterion is sex.

Another is social class.

Another is ethnic or national background.

Another is even regions within countries.

4. Most Americans are looking at other people.

They are governed by one basic rule.

That rule is we stare at objects.

We do not stare at people.

5. Americans want to be polite when meeting a new person.

They practice the "look-and-look-away" stare.

This stare says that we recognize the existence of the person.

We do not consider him or her an object.

6. An American male stares at another American male.

The one will usually interpret the look.

The one is being stared at.

The look is the starer's.

He will interpret it as being hostile or sexual.

He sees himself as being turned into an object.

7. A male stares at an American female.

She may also resent the stare.

She will do so for the same reason.

8. But it is not considered rude for a man to look closely at the parts of a woman's body.

This is in France.

It is in Italy.

It is in Mexico.
It is in many other countries also.
The parts of her body are her shoulders.
They are her arms.
They are her breasts.
They are her hips.
They are her legs.

9. American women are usually embarrassed by this kind of examination.
They are new to such countries.
The examination is close.
The examination is of their bodies.
French, Italian, and Mexican women are accustomed to it.
They expect it.

10. Americans like to be looked at.
It shows that we are interesting or attractive.
Most of us don't like to be looked at too much.

CHAPTER *7*

Writing the In-Class Essay

Rarely, if ever, in "real" life will you be asked to write an extended piece of prose on the spur of the moment, especially on a topic you haven't had time to think about at some length. True, your boss may want you to whip out a last-minute report, so you may have to write feverishly for a few hours to meet her deadline. But, because it is the "stuff" of your job, you will have thought about the material you are dealing with and therefore have plenty to say in a report. Consequently, organization will be your first concern, then revision, and finally proofreading.

In college, however, you are occasionally presented with in-class writing assignments. This chapter will focus on the two most common ones—the essay exam and the writing test.

THE ESSAY EXAM

Frequently, an instructor will assign an in-class essay exam in order to test your knowledge and understanding of the subject matter of the course. The following assignments might sound familiar: "Write an essay in which you discuss the major causes of the Revolutionary War," or "Based on what we have discussed about the major theories of gender role development, write an essay in which you make predictions about the personality traits of children raised by a single father."

As in "real" life, these assignments ought not to hit you cold, since you will have spent class and study time discussing, thinking, and reading about the topics. Therefore, as long as you have studied the material, your job should be fairly straightforward although made somewhat stressful given the time constraints.

Don't, however, let those constraints panic you. Approach in-class essay assignments as you do any other writing task.

1. Read the question *carefully,* noting what *exactly* the instructor is asking for. If the question asks for the main causes of the Revolutionary War, then what are they? (Do not get sidetracked by the minor causes, although you may want to mention them in passing—in your introduction, for example.) If your instructor wants you to exhibit your knowledge of the major theories of gender role development and how they relate to the development of certain characteristics in a particular situation, focus on those two aspects of the course work. *Whatever the assignment, make sure you understand what the instructor is asking you to write about.*

2. Jot down on scrap paper or in your examination book the main points your essay will address: the several main causes of the war or the major theories and the personality characteristics of children raised by a single father, to continue with our examples.

3. Decide in what order you are going to discuss the points and number them. You may, for example, want to give the most important cause of the war first or start with the most important theory.

4. Look at what you've written down and compose a thesis that states your points and indicates the problem (the assignment) your essay will address.

What you've got now is a rough idea draft, and that's probably all you'll have time to do with the in-class idea draft. However, ask yourself the same kinds of questions you do when you're writing an essay outside of class; use the same kind of Writer's Checklist.

- Does this idea draft *respond fully* to the assignment?
- Are the ideas *organized* in a way that makes sense?
- Does the *thesis* point clearly to the direction the essay will take?

When you have adequately addressed these questions, it's time to write a working draft.

1. Using your rough idea draft as a guide, write your essay, making sure you cite examples and specifics from your textbook, lectures, and discussion notes to support your points. When you have written all that you want to say, **stop**. Don't fret about a rhetorically brilliant conclusion at this point. (One small piece of advice that you will appreciate when you begin to revise: Write on every other line, unless the instructions say you should not.)

2. After you've finished your essay, go back and read over it slowly and carefully, thinking about the ideas it presents and noting any places where the writing makes you stop or is confusing. (Because you have to write exam essays without benefit of other readers, you have to become "another reader," as best you can, and read your essay with as much distance as possible, as though it were someone else's essay.)

3. When you've finished reading the whole thing, go back and revise, fixing up confusing sentences, adding words that got left out, crossing out a part that may not belong, and so on.

4. Now is the time to double-check your conclusion. You've got a "working" draft just about ready to submit, so does it need a more complete conclusion? Would a brief restatement of the main causes of the war wrap it up more effectively? If so, go ahead and write a short, concluding paragraph. However, if you think the essay has done its job in responding to the assignment and ends appropriately, write no more.

5. One last task, if you have time: Read the essay once more, looking for spelling and mechanical errors that you know you sometimes make. This is the proofreading part of the process. When you've done this, turn the essay in.

THE WRITING TEST

Sometimes in-class essay assignments are designed not to test your knowledge of course material but to test your ability to write, period. Sometimes these serve as "exit exams" from particular writing courses (Freshman English, for example) or, more alarmingly, as a graduation requirement; both have to be dealt with successfully.

The only way they differ from the essay exam discussed above is that frequently the question asks you to write about a topic you've given no thought to. You have to think about the topic, then, on the spur of the moment.

Again, do not panic. Just take a piece of notepaper and start thinking—*in words, on paper*—about the assignment. Here's an example of the kind of question used often in such an exam.

Write an essay in response to the following question:
Who is an historical figure you admire and why?

Okay, think historical figures and jot down a few names such as Marie Curie, Martin Luther King, Jr., Eleanor Roosevelt, Babe Ruth, Julius Caesar, and so on. The very fact that these names enter your mind suggests that the people have meaning for you, and, consequently, you probably have something to say about why they do. Then quickly ask yourself which one you admire most (which one you have the most ideas about) and jot those ideas down. Now that you've got a topic and a few ideas about it, go back to the section in this chapter on the idea draft and follow the steps outlined.

One last word about the writing test: These questions are usually designed so that many students with different backgrounds and experiences can respond to the topic. They tend to be, therefore, quite broad. Your job is to find a specific topic you know something about as quickly as possible and write an essay. Do not worry about a "right" answer. Just respond as thoughtfully as possible—and be relieved that this exercise is unlikely to be repeated in your professional life. But, in case it is, you know how to approach the writing test.

PLANNING YOUR TIME

In both writing tests and essay exams, part of what is being tested is your ability to plan your time. Here's a possible formula, but one to be modified as appropriate.

- One-quarter of your time for planning your idea draft and writing a thesis.
- Half of your allotted time for writing the essay.
- A quarter of the time for revising and proofreading.

Remember what you have learned about beginning to write any essay. *Do not just leap in and start writing.* Calmly think about the topic; jot down ideas, examples, and thoughts. Ask yourself questions about the topic. Thoughtfully organize your idea draft as you would if it were an assignment to write outside of class, and then start writing the draft. If you schedule your time wisely, you will have plenty of time to reread your essay and make whatever revision or editing is necessary.

Despite its added pressure, the in-class essay exam is still just an essay assignment, so the effective writing habits you have learned from this text will work for you in this situation, too.

III

Proofreading Skills Workbook

There are three rules for writing well. Unfortunately, no one knows what they are.

W. Somerset Maugham

INTRODUCTION

Grammar versus Usage

This part of your book contains rules, explanations, and exercises in many common matters of English usage. Usage is not the same as grammar. While every native speaker of English has a full command of its grammar, many of us are a little shakier when it comes to usage. Usage covers, for the most part, rules that apply only to *written* English—not to the spoken language: spelling words correctly, for instance, or using apostrophes. Fortunately, we don't have to worry about spelling or apostrophes when we speak.

What, Me Worry?

Many students size up usage issues in the following ways:

1. They are a pain in the neck—no more, no less.
2. They are the picky stuff that only English teachers care about.
3. They will drive you crazy if you worry about them (so it's better not to worry about them).
4. Finally, they have nothing to do with expressing your ideas.

Point 4 is correct, and point 1 is mostly correct, but the other two points are mistakes, and they can cost you.

Suppose you are the manager of a large business and you are planning to hire someone to an executive position. One of the application letters you get is full of spelling errors and other kinds of obvious mistakes in English. Are you going to hire that person?

Most English teachers know that usage issues have nothing to do with how well you express yourself, but they also know that to everyone else, usage errors are the most important part of writing. A letter or a memo full of errors in usage says to most of the world that the writer is sloppy, incapable, or, even worse—stupid. The moral is that usage may drive you crazy, but you'd better worry about it anyway.

Because people differ quite a bit from one another in which rules of written usage they know and which ones they don't, the first thing you will find in this section is a little quiz designed to help you and your teacher find out whether you have any weaknesses in common matters of usage and, if so, what they are. Then you can work on just your problems without having to plod through exercises on matters you already know.

In most cases, the following materials are designed so that you can work on them on your own outside of class. When you have worked through a particular usage lesson, you will then know the rules governing it, and when you have done the exercises correctly, you will have shown that you know how to apply the rules. But—and this is a big "but"—reading rules and doing exercises do not automatically translate into handling these usage issues correctly forever more.

Learning versus Doing

When you find out that you have a particular usage problem—say, your subjects and verbs don't agree often enough or you tend to leave -*ed* endings off verbs—you can be sure of one thing: You've been practicing doing it the wrong way for years. Every time you've made the mistake, whether you've had the mistake pointed out to you or not, you've gotten more practice in doing it wrong. That probably adds up to a lot of practice. Doing a couple of sets of exercises in which you do it the right way can't compare with all that previous practice in doing it wrong. So even when you learn the right way, you'll still do it the wrong way unless you make a big effort to overcome all that negative practice.

When to Worry—and When Not to Worry

But make the effort when you're proofreading, not when you're writing. If you get all hung up on questions of usage when you try to write, it really will drive you crazy, and you won't write well. Remember what you learned about writing in drafts, and proofread for your own usage problems in your final draft. Keep handy a list of just those usage errors you are likely to make, and proofread for each one of them separately (or two at a time, at the most). Gradually, you will get to the point where your positive practice will start to outweigh your negative practice, and then you'll start handling most of your usage issues almost automatically.

PROOFREADING QUIZ

Part I

Correct any punctuation errors you find in the following sentences. If any of your punctuation changes require that you change a capital letter to a small one or vice versa, make those changes also. Some of the sentences may be correct.

1. Joanne bought an expensive car. Although she had recently quit her job.

2. When her husband found out about it, he was furious.

3. She reminded him of the extravagant stereo he had bought recently, it was much more powerful than they needed or could use.

4. He replied that they could both enjoy the stereo. While only she could enjoy her car.

5. He didn't know that she hated the stereo. A fact he was soon to find out.

6. When the dust finally settled, he had returned the stereo, Joanne still had the car.

7. Their marriage was saved, even though they still had a car they couldn't afford.

8. There are only a few problems I can't handle, thus I don't worry much.

9. Money comes into my life in small quantities, however it leaves in large ones.

10. There seems to be nothing I can do about this, it just seems to be a characteristic of mine.

11. I took a course entitled "Love Your Money." Thinking that if I loved it more, I'd hang on to it longer.

12. That helped for a little while, then I just returned to my old habits.

13. I'd like to get this problem under control. Because it is getting me into serious financial difficulties.

14. I might be in trouble right now, I just got a bank statement today and it looks pretty bad. My savings having fallen to an all-time low.

15. The situation looks pretty serious, therefore I think I'd better do something about it.

Part II

Each of the sentences below contains one verb, together with its subject. If the verb is correct, write C in the blank at the end of the sentence. If the verb is incorrect, write the correct verb form in the blank.

Example:

John bit the cow.	**C**
There are a tavern in the town.	**is**

1. There is only a few places in the country we haven't visited. _____

2. A study of several thousand very experienced travelers show some interesting results. _____

3. There's a great many wealthy people among them.   ———————

4. But the wealthiest ones in the study has not always traveled more than the others.   ———————

5. The results of the study were of value to the travel industry.

6. The good athlete keep to a regular training schedule.   ———————

7. The basis of many of our problems, especially the big ones, are our ways of approaching them.   ———————

8. There is, in fact, three things anyone can do about their problems.   ———————

9. My aunt like to make a big Thanksgiving dinner every year.

10. Sheila and Mary hates to be late to parties.   ———————

11. A person I knew in high school have won a scholarship to college.   ———————

12. Working short hours and earning a good salary are my main requirement in life.   ———————

Part III

Carefully proofread the following sentences, correcting the mistakes. Some sentences may contain more than one error.

1. Its a bad idea to go grocery shopping when your hungry.

2. The cat stuck its claws into my leg, and it was to painful for words.

3. There are many things people can do to make there lives worse than they have to be, and to often these are exactly the things that they do.

4. When you know who's seat you have taken, you will know who's going to be on you're case.

5. The dog took it's time getting into there truck; it was to lazy to hurry.

6. We know that your doing someone elses work and who's it is.

7. I can't stand the mess in my two sisters rooms.

8. The new father hated to change his babies diaper, so he was glad his wife didn't have twins.

9. In north america we mostly speak english, but central americas dominant language is spanish.

10. I had planned to take history 301, but since I had already signed up for another history class, I decided to take calculus instead.

11. The president of the united states is also the commander-in-chief of the armed forces, though, of course, he isn't actually a general.

12. I am use to getting good grades, but I know that college is a lot harder than valley view high school.

13. When I was in high school, I knew I was suppose to study, but I often didn't.

14. When they were juniors, several friends of mine drop out because they hate to do the assign work.

15. They had never realize the importance of school to one's future.

16. Of all those in my group, only me and John Williams graduated.

17. Me and Jane had a great time at the costume party, and the hosts gave her and me first prize for best costumes.

18. A person who drops out won't be able to compete in the job market; they will have to turn to crime or just stay poor.

19. High school didn't mean much to John and I, but we stuck with it.

20. I knew she running for president, but her boyfriend planning to vote for someone else.

1. IDENTIFYING SUBJECTS AND VERBS

Fundamental to doing almost any kind of work with sentences is being able to identify subjects and verbs. Every sentence, as you know, has to have a subject and a verb; otherwise, it isn't a sentence. Although the subject usually comes before the verb in English sentences, it is easier to start by finding the verb.

You may have learned that verbs are words that express actions. That is true, but it isn't helpful, for while most verbs do express actions, many verbs don't and lots of words that are not verbs do. Look at this sentence:

Swimming is my favorite sport.

What is the action word? Obviously, it is *swimming*, but *swimming* isn't the verb. One could even say that *sport* is an action word, in a sense, because sports are, by definition, active. But *sport* isn't the verb either. As you probably have realized, *is* is the verb. Look at the same sentence rewritten slightly:

> Swimming was my favorite sport.

Which word has been changed? How has the meaning of the sentence changed? The verb *is* has been changed to its past-tense form *was* and so the meaning of the sentence has changed slightly. It now describes how I used to feel about it. We could also write the sentence this way:

> Swimming will be my favorite sport.

Now the sentence tells how I think I will feel about swimming in the future. The question now is, So what? And the answer is that since all English sentences have to be in some tense or time—present, past, or future—and because the verbs in our sentences tell what that tense or time is, we can easily find the verbs in our sentences by changing the time of them and seeing what word changes. Look at the following examples.

What is the verb in this sentence?

> The student in the back row sleeps through the lectures.

If we change the sentence to put the action in the past—last week, say—what changes?

> The student in the back row slept through the lectures.

What is the verb?

> sleeps/slept

Let's change the following sentence so that its action takes place in the future:

> The people downtown threw paper out their windows.
> The people downtown will throw paper out their windows.

What is the verb?

> threw/will throw

Some verb forms, as you probably know, consist of more than one word. The future form is one example. Here are some others:

> She is throwing a party.
> She has thrown a party.
> She used to throw parties.

EXERCISE 1.A

The sentences below are all in the present tense; locate the verbs in them by rewriting them twice, first in the past and second in the future (using will*). It might help you to imagine the sentence beginning with the word* Yesterday *when you want to change it to past tense and* Tomorrow *when you want to change it to the future. Underline the verbs in your rewritten sentences.*

Example:
John buys too many records.
(Yesterday) John bought too many records. (past)
(Tomorrow) John will buy too many records. (future)

Sentences followed by (2) have two verbs; be sure to change the tense of both of them and underline both in your rewrites.

1. Mary takes business courses.

   _____

2. She plans to own her own corporation.

   _____

3. A huge corporation is a desirable thing to own.

   _____

4. Mary also studies English and mathematics.

   _____

5. Corporations run on letters and numbers.

   _____

6. Executives need solid writing skills.

   _____

7. They require a good command of math.

_____

8. The Brand-X Corporation is failing because its president uses his fingers to count. (2)

_____

_____

9. Executives of the Brand-Y Corporation study writing, and so they write superior letters. (2)

_____

_____

10. Brand-Y Corporation, which makes ballpoint pens, earns an excellent profit. (2)

_____

_____

EXERCISE 1.B

The following short paragraph is written in the present tense. Change the verbs in it to the future tense by drawing a line through each verb and writing the future form above it.

The party is a huge success. Almost all of the invited guests accept the invitations. They all arrive on time. No one who is not invited tries to come. Everyone is happy. The guests enjoy the food and drink. They like the music and dance enthusiastically. No one argues, breaks anything, or drinks too much. The hosts and the guests are all delighted.

EXERCISE 1.C

Through an amazing oversight, a friend wrote the following paragraph the other day in the present tense, only realizing afterward that the events described there had actually taken place the week before. In short, she should have written it in past tense. Revise it by drawing a line through each present-tense verb and writing the past-tense form above it.

I go to a bookstore that also sells picture frames, for I wish to price their frames. The reason I do that is that earlier in the week I visit a print shop and see many attractive prints that I want to buy. But in frames they are very expensive. I decide to buy the prints inexpensively and to frame them myself. At the bookstore I discover where to find such frames, and so I buy two prints from the print shop and two frames from the bookstore, and then my living room looks more attractive.

Locating Subjects: The First-Noun Rule

Once you can locate the verbs in a sentence, it is easy to find their subjects. The subject is the word in front of the verb that answers the question *who* or *what* in relation to the verb.

> Storms rage in California.
> (What rages? Storms.)
>
> George is beating on the door.
> (Who is beating on the door? George.)
>
> The car in the garage is mine.
> (What is mine? The car.)
>
> The cat and the dog belong to Julia.
> (What belongs to Julia? The cat and the dog.)

You will notice that in these sentences, the subject is the first noun in the sentence (or, in the case of the last one, the first noun and the noun joined to it with *and*). This rule—the first-noun rule—will hold true in perhaps 90 percent of the sentences you or anyone else ever writes. You can't count on it every time, but when in doubt, look to the very first noun.

To practice identifying subjects, return to Exercise 1.A and draw two lines under the subjects in each sentence.

Subjects Separated from Verbs

The only tricky part about identifying subjects and verbs comes when there is more than one noun in front of the verb.

> The sweater in the drawer is made of wool.

Usually the *who* or *what* question will solve the problem. Who or what is made of wool, the sweater or the drawer? In this case, it's obvious. But sometimes the *who* or *what* question won't solve the problem or will even be misleading:

The hole in the sweater will have to be fixed.

Who or what will have to be fixed—the hole or the sweater? In this situation, remember the first-noun rule; the first of the nouns will be the subject—in this case *hole*. *Sweater* is not the subject of the sentence even though it makes sense to say that the sweater will have to be fixed.

Most exceptions to the first-noun rule occur when the sentence begins with a word or group of words followed by a comma, as in these cases:

Tomorrow, she will buy the parachute. In the afternoon, she will use it.

In these circumstances, the subject is the first noun following the comma.

The only other exception to be careful of is nouns in the possessive form, that is, ending in an apostrophe (my *sisters'* boyfriends) or an apostrophe and *s* (my *sister's* boyfriend). Possessive nouns cannot normally be the subjects of sentences.

EXERCISE 1.D

Locate the verbs in the following sentences and underline them once. Then look for the subjects and underline them twice.

1. The peaches on the trees are ripe now.

2. The blue of the sky is extremely beautiful.

3. The people in that neighborhood litter their streets with trash.

4. Flowers and weeds grow in Juanita's garden.

5. Up in the sky, the birds from the north are flying south.

6. The argument of the president makes no sense.

7. The basis of this plan is a good one.

8. My sister's friend hangs out with some dangerous people.

9. My best friend's father takes English classes in the evening.

10. At the end of the street, two houses and an old warehouse are falling down.

There Sentences

There is a special kind of sentence in English that does not begin with a noun, and you have just read one of them. It is the *there* sentence:

There is a tavern in the town.
There are two taverns in the town.

In this type of sentence, the subject is the noun that *follows* the verb. Notice that in the first example above, the verb is *is*—that is, it is singular—while in the second example, the verb is *are*, the plural. Notice also that the noun following the first verb is singular and the noun following the second is plural. They are the subjects of the sentences and the reason for the difference in the verbs.

EXERCISE 1.E

Identify the subjects in the following there sentences and underline them.

1. There are many people in the woods.

2. There are animals around here also.

3. There will be a problem soon.

4. There were troubles in that part of town yesterday.

5. There was a loud clap of thunder last night.

6. There was a bunch of strange people in here yesterday.

7. There is too much water in that lake.

8. There are three newspapers published in this town.

9. There are frequently loud noises in that deserted house.

10. There used to be a barrel of rainwater at the corner of the house.

2. AGREEMENT BETWEEN SUBJECTS AND VERBS

Imagine that you are an alien who has just landed in a spaceship from the planet Blog, and you are studying a strange Earthling language called English. The person you are studying with shows you how English verbs work in the present tense by writing them down this way, using the verb *walk*:

Singular		**Plural**	
I	walk	we	walk
You	walk	you	walk
he/she/it	walks	they	walk

You examine this for a moment and then say, in your native Blogese, "Wait a minute. You made a mistake here. One of these verbs is wrong." Look at them yourself. Which verb would seem illogical to a creature from another planet? Which one doesn't fit with the rest?

Of course, the *he/she/it* form of the singular doesn't fit with the rest because it is the only one with an *s* ending. Every other one is *walk* and it is *walks*. It's totally illogical, and it's even useless, but there it is.

It is true that in some forms of spoken English people say "he walk" or "she walk" or (in the case of an alien from Blog) "it walk." That makes sense logically, but it still isn't the correct form in writing.

By the way, agreement between subject and verb almost exclusively involves this present-tense form. The only time it's a concern in the past tense is when we use the verb *be,* and then we get these changes:

I was	we were
you were	you were
he/she/it was	they were

In the present tense, the verb *be* has these endings:

I am	we are
you are	you are
he/she/it is	they are

If you can keep *was* and *were* straight, which most people do, you only have to watch for verbs following *he/she/it* nouns when you're writing in the present tense.

What's a *he/she/it* noun? Here are a few examples. Note that they all refer to one person or thing.

he = George, Juan, my father, the man in the car, the outfielder who won the batting title, a zoologist (Any of these nouns or phrases could be replaced by *he.*)

she = Michelle, your sister, the woman over there, the little girl playing in the sand, your attorney (Any of these nouns or phrases could be replaced by *she.*)

it = your pen, my paper, our class, discovering gold, excitement, a gigantic mess on the floor (Any of these nouns or phrases could be replaced by *it.*)

All of these words or phrases appearing as the subject of a sentence in the present tense would need a verb ending in *s:*

George likes Michelle.

The outfielder who won the batting title comes from Puerto Rico.

Michelle thinks George is a dope.

The little girl playing in the sand looks very happy.

Your pen is writing on my paper.

The gigantic mess on the floor needs to be swept under the sofa.

Basic Subject-Verb Agreement

The basic subject-verb agreement problem is simply to remember that in the *he/she/it* form of the present tense, the verb has to end in *s*. All the other present-tense verb forms end with their normal letter.

Here is a small complication to the basic rule. If your verb has two or more subjects joined by an *and,* the subjects become *they,* plural instead of singular, and the verb doesn't get an *s:*

Carlos and Lois feel like taking a walk.

But if two subjects are joined by *or,* the subjects become singular and the verb does get an *s:*

Carlos or Lois thinks I'm wrong.

(Note that only *one* of them thinks it.)

EXERCISE 2.A

In the following sentences, do the following things:

- Identify the subject of the verb, which is in parentheses.
- Decide whether the subject can be replaced by *he, she, it,* or *they.*
- Write *he, she, it,* or *they,* whichever is correct, and the correct form of the verb in the blank below the verb.

Warning: Keep the verbs in the present tense. Do not change them to past. For instance, in sentence 1, the verbs should **not** be changed to *thought* and *looked.*

Example:

Maylene (write) her aunt the latest news.

_____she writes_____

Thirty people (think) I'm wrong.

_____**they think**_____

John and Willie (know) about the problem.

_____**they know**_____

1. Lois (think) Carlos (look) down on the alien from Blog.

_____   _____

2. The alien (hate) being called an alien.

_____

3. The alien (prefer) being called a Blogite.

_____

4. Carlos (feel) that if people from China (be) called Chinese, the alien

_____   _____

   should be a Blogese.

5. Actually the alien (have) a name, Dork.

_____

6. Most people (dislike) aliens from outer space, but Lois and Carlos (find)

_____   _____

   Dork a pleasant companion, once one (get) over his complexion.

_____

7. His skin (have) a texture similar to library paste coated with egg white.

_____

8. Most of his legs (be) covered with green bristles, but the left front one (be)

_____   _____

   smooth and brown, while the right front one (look) bumpy and orange.

_____

9. The planet Blog (circle) a sun twenty light-years from us.

   _____

10. Its atmosphere (be) a mixture of hydrogen, oxygen, and bug spray.

    _____

11. Lois or Carlos (want) to visit there someday.

    _____

12. Lois (feel) sorry for Dork because the poor alien (long) to return to his

   _____   _____

   native planet.

13. Here, he (have) to squirt himself with bug spray every hour or die.

    _____

14. His breathing organs (require) the atmosphere of his home.

     _____

15. The bug spray (make) him smell bad, and his popularity (suffer) as a result.

    _____

EXERCISE 2.B

We often use nouns that don't indicate people or physical things as the subjects of our sentences. Words such as agreement, conflict, entertainment, gardening, history, and maturity are examples. These, of course, are it *subjects, and it is important to remember that when two of them are joined by* and *in the subject spot, they take a plural verb:*

Analysis [it] of these documents reveals that illegal activities [they] are still occurring.
The discovery and publication [they] of these documents have embarrassed the government.

Write the correct verb form on the line beneath the verbs in the following sentences:

1. The history of the United States (affect) us today.

   _____

2. Conflict between opposing points of view often (make) our government

   _____

   inefficient, but the framers of the Constitution designed it that way.

3. Fear of a tyrant and distrust of the masses (be) why they set up a system

   _____

   based on conflict.

4. Other European and Asian democracies (employ) a parliamentary system

   _____

   in which the ruling party (have) all the power.

   _____

5. Conflicts of the past, such as the Civil War, still (affect) us today.

   _____

6. Distrust of government and fear of big business, the results of nineteenth-century labor strife, still (influence) labor relations today.

   _____

7. Past African slavery and discrimination against Chinese immigrants still (play) negative roles in our society.

   _____

8. Getting rid of some of these old influences (be) necessary for us to grow

   _____

   productively in the future.

9. At the same time, retaining the best of the past (help) us keep our

   _____

   unique national identity.

10. A positive American characteristic (have) always been a willingness to

    _____

    recognize and try to correct our own failures.

EXERCISE 2.C

Write the correct verb form on the line beneath the verbs in the following sentences:

1. The issue of whether women should pursue careers in the world of work (involve) many genuine issues as well as many old prejudices.

   _____

2. Probably almost nobody now (believe) in the old saying "Women's place is

   _____

   in the home."

3. Most people (accept) that most women who can will at least find jobs, if

   _____

   not careers.

4. But many of those who seem to accept this fact really (act) as though

   _____

   they (be) opposed to women working.

   _____

5. The person who (say) he or she (be) for women in the workforce but at the

   _____

   same time (oppose) maternity leave (be) not in favor of women working.

   _____   _____

6. For regardless of whether a woman (work) or not, she (be) still the only

   _____   _____

   one who can have children.

7. And to have children, one (need) to be able to have time off to give birth

   _____

   and to care for the infant during its early years.

8. Other countries, particularly in Europe, (have) made practical provisions

   _____

   for women to be able to work.

9. France, for instance, (have) established "écoles maternelles" or preschools

_____

that (provide) care for the children of working parents.

_____

10. Since most women now (want) satisfying careers of their own, and since

_____

in most families the wife (have) to work for the family to make ends meet,

_____

it (seem) only right that government (set) up licensed, properly staffed

_____   _____

pre-schools to meet this need.

Subject-Verb Agreement in *There* Sentences

One kind of sentence begins with the word *there*, and this *there* does not refer to the location of anything. Here are some examples:

There is a tavern in the town.
There was some ice cream in the house yesterday.
There's going to be a big party tonight.
There are three buttons missing from my shirt.

Although *there* is the first word of these sentences and comes right in front of the verb, it isn't the subject. Read the following short passage, in which the verbs in the *there* sentences are underlined, and see whether you can figure out why some of the verbs are singular (*is*) and some plural (*are*):

There is an old saying. It goes, "There are more ways than one to skin a cat."
There is a great truth in this saying. It means that usually there are several possible solutions to any problem.

Why is the verb singular in the first sentence below? Why is it plural in the second sentence?

There is a problem here.
There are two problems here.

What are the subjects of these sentences? Where do we find the subject of *there* sentences? Write here the rule for subject-verb agreement in *there* sentences:

_____

_____

_____

_____

EXERCISE 2.D

Write the correct form of the verb **be** *in the blank in the following sentences and underline the verb's subject. When the word past appears after the verb slot, use* **was** *or* **were;** *when the word present appears, use* **is** *or* **are.**

Example:

There _____ (present) a coat in the closet.

There _____is_____ a coat in the closet.

There _____ (past) two coats in the closet.

There _____were_____ two coats in the closet.

1. There _____ (present) 50,000 books in our library.

2. Of them, there _____ (present) one that I am anxious to read.

3. There _____ (present) an excellent chance that it won't be there when I try to find it.

4. There _____ (past) three days last week when I felt unwell.

5. There _____ (past) one in particular when I was quite sick.

6. There _____ (present) no feeling worse than some physical illness unless it's being unprepared for an exam.

7. We learned that though there _____ (past) a lot of rules on one in high school, there _____ (present) a lot of responsibilities on one in college.

8. There _____ (present) a major project waiting for me at home, but there _____ (present) little I can do about it now.

9. There _____ (present) several reasons why I need to get at least a B in this course, but there _____ (present) one major obstacle in my way.

10. There _____ (past) quite a few people at the party, but there _____ (past) only one I was hoping to meet.

3. PAST TENSE AND PAST PARTICIPLES

Past Tense

Every sentence you write will indicate the time of the sentence—that is, whether it expresses present time, future time, or past time. Like most other Western European languages but unlike most Eastern languages, English shows its sentence-time through its verbs. Present tense generally uses the base form of the verb, future tense uses *will* plus the base form, and past tense adds *-ed* (most of the time) to the base form, as in these cases:

Today, I walk to the store.
Tomorrow I will walk to the store.
Yesterday I walked to the store.

There are two little complications to this otherwise fairly simple system. One of them, covered in Chapter 1, is that not all past-tense verbs end in *-ed,* as in these cases:

Present	**Past**
I think	I thought
I sink	I sank
I eat	I ate

For a review of these verbs, see Chapter 1 ("Recognizing Verb Forms," page 48 in the Sentence Combining section).

The other complication applies only to the *-ed* verb endings; when we speak, we don't pronounce all *-ed* endings. Read the following sentence aloud in your normal voice, as though you were speaking it; listen to see whether you hear the *-ed* endings on the verbs *walk* and *talk:*

Yesterday I walked to the record store and talked to my friend there.

Most people either will not pronounce the verb endings at all or will pronounce them only as a very slight, almost inaudible *t* sound. Other *-ed* endings most of us do pronounce quite noticeably:

> I conducted an experiment to see whether anyone would return a borrowed book.

But the fact that we don't pronounce many *-ed* endings distinctly means that when we write, we may not hear them in our minds and so leave them off. But whether pronounced or not, they must always be there in writing. So if you're having trouble getting the *-ed* endings on your verbs, you'll need to work on it, but at least you know that there's a logical explanation for your problem.

Correcting an *-ed* problem is a pretty easy proofreading task. All you have to do is remember three things:

1. When you proofread, check each of your paragraphs to see what time you are expressing. If you are talking about the past, check each verb in each sentence to make sure it has a needed *-ed* ending. (But remember that even a passage in the past tense may legitimately have some present-tense sentences or parts of sentences in it.)

2. There are two common words that *always* have *-ed* endings: *supposed* and *used*. It's best to get used to (see that?) writing these words the way they're supposed to (and that?) be written in the first place.

3. Any verb form that has the word *to* in front of it *never* takes an *-ed* ending: She wanted to talk to her friend on the phone, but her mother needed to use it for business.

EXERCISE 3.A

Rewrite the following sentences, changing the verbs in each from present tense to past tense:

1. In the high school cafeteria, Suzanne looks at Ramon and her heart stops beating.

———————————————————————————————

2. She walks up to him and tries to start a conversation.

———————————————————————————————

3. But she learns that only baseball interests him.

_____

4. Getting no response in person, she finally mails him a letter inviting him to a party.

_____

5. She believes this might do the trick.

_____

6. In a few days, she walks to her mailbox and notices a letter for her from Ramon.

_____

7. She hurries to open it.

_____

8. Ramon invites her to a baseball game he is playing in.

_____

9. In the high school cafeteria, Suzanne gazes at Glenn and her heart stops beating.

_____

10. She strolls up to him and asks, "Do you play baseball?"

_____

EXERCISE 3.B

The following passage is in the past tense. Proofread it for past-tense verbs that are missing their -ed endings, and look for any misspelled instances of used to _or_ supposed to.

In the 1920s and '30s, some European military theorists believe that in the future, wars could be won simply by airplanes bombing civilian populations. They argue that the people being bombed would be driven mad, and they convince most airmen of the time that their planes would be able to destroy totally a nation's industry. In 1941, Germany attempt to put this theory into practice by bombing England night and day.

But the English, who were suppose to be driven mad, hardly let themselves be affected by it. They quickly got use to hiding in shelters when the bombers drop their bombs, and at the same time, the Royal Air Force destroy huge numbers of the German bombers. American and British bombers devastate much of Germany, but they were unable to destroy German industry. Aerial bombardment during World War II never accomplish what its proponents believe it would—until the atomic bomb was invented near the end of the war.

Past Participles

Frequently when we write, we use verbs that have more than one part, for instance:

She *might have walked* to school yesterday, but she *will take* the bus tomorrow.
Or:
He *wants to be considered* a serious person, but no one *wants to think* of him that way.

There is something a little curious about some of the verb words in these two sentences. In the first sentence, there are two verbs, *walk* and *take*. But one ends in *-ed* and the other one doesn't. Why is that? Similarly, in the second sentence, there are also two verbs, *consider* and *think;* again, one of them ends with an *-ed* and the other one doesn't.

The reason for these differences is that English has a distinctive pattern involving verbs using more than one word:

If the main verb is preceded by some form of the verb *be, have, become,* or *get,* the verb itself has to end in *-ed* (unless it takes an irregular form like *thrown* or *bought* or *taken*).

This pattern would not present problems for most of us if it weren't that we generally don't pronounce these *-ed* endings when we say them, and so it can be hard to remember to put them on when we write. This is another one of the many cases in which English pronunciation and spelling are different.

EXERCISE 3.C

In the following sentences, forms of the verbs be, have, become, *and* get *are underlined; rewrite each sentence, correcting the verb following* be, have, become, *and* get *by writing it in its* -ed *ending version.*

Example:

Pak <u>was</u> not prepare for class.

 Change to:

Pak was not prepared for class.

1. Mai <u>had</u> always expect Pak to buy her something romantic for Valentine's Day.

2. But Pak preferred <u>to be</u> instruct in the kind of present Mai might like <u>to have</u> purchase for her.

3. He <u>was</u> also too embarrass to buy her lingerie; he <u>became</u> totally fluster when he saw bras and panties.

4. As a result, Mai usually <u>got</u> irritate as February 14th neared, and Pak was apt <u>to get</u> depress.

5. Pak felt he <u>had been</u> badly use in the past when he <u>had</u> purchase Mai some nice present, like the chain saw.

6. Mai <u>was</u> use to these kinds of presents, but she <u>became</u> determine to make Pak see the light.

7. Pak <u>might have</u> never pick up on the sort of thing Mai <u>was</u> interest in except that she had gotten an idea.

8. She <u>had</u> order for Pak a nice assortment of catalogues.

9. He <u>was</u> suppose to look at them and <u>be</u> inspire to buy her some perfume or sexy underwear.

10. Unfortunately, he <u>got</u> turn on by the Victoria's Secret catalogue, <u>was</u> particularly fascinate by page 10, <u>became</u> totally infatuate with a bra model there, and ran off to New York to find her.

EXERCISE 3.D

Rewrite the following sentences, underlining the verbs be, have, become, *and* get *and changing the verbs following them to their -ed form. (Note that not every appearance of these four verbs is necessarily followed by another verb that has to be changed.)*

1. In the history of first dates in the world, for the most part disaster has follow disaster.

2. To be sure, there have been times when couples have encounter their life-long soul mates, but more often, one or both of the persons have been seriously disillusion.

3. Abelard became enamor of Eloise at first sight, and Romeo got snare by Juliet's beauty when he first saw her, but on many first dates, the couples are overwhelm with disinterest for each other.

4. Oftentimes, one person is fascinate by the other, but the other is bore by the first.

5. In my dating lifetime, I have encounter both situations.

6. Once I was totally enchant by a lovely young woman, but she got bore with me on sight.

7. She became so tire of my witty conversation, she fell asleep.

8. A friend of mine tried to be prepare for a first date by reading two newspapers and three news magazines, but his date was totally uninterest in anything but rock stars.

9. When the person who is thrill by politics meets the person who is turn on only by basketball, disaster results.

10. Many people have return from first dates swearing that they will never get involve with the opposite sex for the rest of their lives.

EXERCISE 3.E

The following passage is in the past tense. Proofread it for both *past-tense verbs that are missing their -ed endings and* verbs *after* be, have, become, *and* get *that need -ed endings.*

People became interest in building a transcontinental railroad across the United States only after the California Gold Rush, which happen in 1849. The population of California had suddenly expand, and the state contain great wealth. California had been admit to the Union, but it was cut off from the rest of the United States. Only Native Americans live between Omaha, Nebraska, and California, over a thousand miles away. Most people going to California travel by ship, but that require a trip all the way around the tip of South America. Some wagon trains attempt to cross the continent, and many manage to succeed, but the way was difficult and dangerous. Many such travelers were kill by the difficulties of the trip itself. Some trains were wipe out by Native American raiders. And the terrible ordeal of the Donner Party, most of whom were kill by the terrible Sierra winter, show what could happen when a group happen to make a few mistakes. As a result, many efforts got start to begin building a railroad. In Washington, the government became involve when Congress pass the Pacific Railroad Act of 1862, and out west, a man named T. D. Judah went into the mountains and survey a route across the Sierra Nevada. A group of entrepreneurs in Sacramento who became call the Big Four got interest, and while the Civil War was still raging, the effort to build a railroad had start.

4. THE PAST-TO-PRESENT TENSE (PRESENT PERFECT)

In addition to the regular past tense, which English uses to express actions completed in the past, we have another tense—the past-to-present, or present perfect, tense.

The past tense, of course, is simply the standard *-ed* form or one of its irregular cousins (like *bought, ate,* or *sank*). The past-to-present tense includes the words *has/have* or *has/have been* in front of the verb:

I have enjoyed baseball for many years.
She has found her new life satisfying.
We have been poor now for much too long.
He has been a sailor for twelve years.

While we use the past tense mostly for events that took place entirely in the past, we use the past-to-present tense for two other purposes. Look at the following two sentences; what is the difference in meaning between them?

George attended college for two years.
George has attended college for two years.

In the first instance, which involves the regular past tense, George attended college at some time in the past but is no longer doing so. The action of attending college started and ended in the past. In the second instance, which involves the past-to-present tense, George is still attending college. The action of attending college started in the past and is continuing into the present.

There is a second difference between the past tense and the past-to-present tense. Look at the following two sentences; what is the difference between them?

Teresa bought her textbooks yesterday.
Teresa has bought her textbooks.

In the first case, in which the regular past is involved, we know when the action took place. But in the second case, we don't know exactly when it took place.

And so we can see that there are two main differences between the regular past tense and the past-to-present tense.

Regular past

Expresses an action completed in the past.

Expresses an action that took place at a specific time in the past.

Past-to-present

Expresses an action begun in the past but continuing to the present.

Expresses an action that took place at some unspecific time in the past.

Finally, it is important to note that situations in which either the regular past or the past-to-present may be used are quite common in English.

In trying to remember whether to use the past tense or the past-to-present tense, it can be helpful to note that there are words and phrases in English other than verbs that also indicate the time of the sentence and typically go with either the past tense or the past-to-present tense.

Words and phrases that indicate the past tense are ones that point to specific times in the past such as these:

yesterday	last year
in the morning	on Wednesday
the other day	two weeks ago
at three o'clock	after dinner
then	next
soon	later

Words and phrases that indicate past-to-present actions or situations are ones like these:

since	since yesterday
recently	up to now
so far	for the time being
	for (plus any time word or phrase)

EXERCISE 4.A

Rewrite the following sentences to use either the regular past or the past-to-present tense. If there is a word or phrase in any sentence that helps you know which tense to use, underline it.

1. Last week I (buy) a new pair of shoes.

   _____

2. Up to now I (enjoy) them greatly.

   _____

3. Early in the fall, Joanne (decide) to study harder.

   _____

4. Since making that decision, she (get) much better grades.

   _____

5. I (cook) for only three years now.

   _____

6. It (take) me that long to learn the rudiments of that art.

   _____

7. I (start) to learn when I first (live) on my own.

   _____

8. It (be) a struggle at first, but it (be) a pleasure since then.

   _____

9. The world (experience) increasing problems in recent years.

   _____

10. The Cold War between the United States and the Soviet Union (last) about forty years, but since then, animosities between the two countries (diminish).

_____

_____

EXERCISE 4.B

Rewrite the following sentences to use either the regular past or the past-to-present tense. If there is a word or phrase in any sentence that helps you know which tense to use, underline it.

1. Not long ago, Josefa (decide) that she (want) a pet to keep her company.
2. She (consider) getting a dog but (decide) that although dogs are good company, they are too fawning and undignified.
3. She (consider) getting a cat but (decide) that although cats are independent and dignified, they are not good company.
4. So she (decide) to buy an elephant.
5. Since she (purchase) last Thursday a medium-sized Indian elephant at the local pet store, Josefa (discover) some advantages and disadvantages to owning a pet elephant.
6. Max, the elephant, (prove) to be loyal, faithful, and affectionate.
7. Ever since Josefa got him, he (accompany) her on her morning jog, (sleep) at the foot of her bed at night, and (do) all the heavy lifting around the house.
8. Unfortunately, there (be) some problems too.
9. When Max (try) to jump into the car to go shopping with Josefa, he (flatten) the car.
10. When he (try) to curl up on her lap in the evening, he (squash) her.
11. Also, the bills for hay (be) awfully high since Max (be) around.
12. So fond of Max though she is, Josefa recently (consider) getting a somewhat smaller pet.
13. The other day in a pet store window, she (see) a particularly attractive black widow spider.

EXERCISE 4.C

Write the correct verb form, either past tense or past-to-present tense, in the blanks in the following paragraph.

Providing adequate medical care to all our citizens is a problem the United States

_____ (be) more avoiding than dealing with over the past forty or

fifty years. Shortly after World War II, every European country _____

(adopt) some form of "socialized medicine" to take care of their citizens. When I

_____ (live) in France in the 1950s, the government _____

(pay) for most doctors' and dentists' fees and medicines for every citizen. Since then,

these coverages _____ (be) expanded, and citizens of European countries

_____ (be) secure about being able to afford health care. Canada also

_____ (adopt) a system of government control over the costs of medical

care. Over the same period of time, the United States _____ (have) not

been able to bring itself to adopt a system like either the European or Canadian ones.

"Socialized medicine" _____ (become) almost a four-letter word here.

As a result, since World War II millions of Americans _____ (suffer) the

effects of ill health, including premature death. We _____ (show) that

we value our principles more than we value human life.

5. THE PAST-BEFORE-PAST TENSE (PAST PERFECT)

English uses a third form of past tense besides the other two—the regular past and the past-to-present. The third form is underlined in the following sentence:

We <u>had given up</u> on seeing them when they suddenly arrived.

As this sentence indicates, the past-before-past tense indicates a time further in the past than the regular past, a past *before* the normal past. This past-tense form, also called the past perfect, uses the word *had* before the base form of the verb. In the example above, the action "they suddenly arrived" takes place in the regular past while the action "we had given up on seeing them" takes place in the time before the regular past. Here are three other examples of the past tense and the past-before-past tense:

The War of 1812 had already ended when the Battle of New Orleans was fought. (The battle was fought after the war was over.)

Marcus got a C on the final exam, but he had previously gotten A's on all the quizzes.

They had eaten dinner and cleaned up the dishes by the time their guests finally arrived.

Note that we do not use the *had* form of the past for any reason other than comparing two past times; we do *not* use it to sound more formal.

When we use the words *before* and *after* to show time relationships, we can use either the regular past tense or the past-before-past tense.

She had tried four different models before she decided to buy the least expensive one.

She tried four different models before she decided to buy the least expensive one.

After she had tried four different models, she decided to buy the least expensive one.

After she tried four different models, she decided to buy the least expensive one.

EXERCISE 5.A

Rewrite the following sentences, using either the regular past tense or the past-before-past tense. When you have a choice between the two in sentences using before *or* after, *use the regular past.*

1. Alisha (work) as a waitress and a dancer before she (go) to law school.

   _____

2. She (become) sick of being poor by the time she (graduate).

   _____

3. When I (see) her for the first time in years, she (change) her style completely.

   _____

4. She (begin) to wear expensive, stylish clothes.

   _____

5. She (look) much better and (seem) happier than she (have) in the days when she (work) for low wages.

   _____

   _____

6. When Eric (buy) a used car, the man who (own) it previously (tell) him he (take) good care of it.

_____

_____

7. By the time the new pitcher (come) to our team, he (play) for three other teams in his career.

_____

_____

8. When I (go) to the bookstore to get my texts, the clerk (say) they (not come in) yet, but they (be) on order for at least a month.

_____

_____

9. After Juanita (eat) at that restaurant, she (feel) ill.

_____

10. I (make) the mistake of betting on a team that (lose) its past thirteen games.

_____

EXERCISE 5.B

Rewrite the following sentences, using either the regular past tense or the past-before-past tense. When you have a choice between the two in sentences using before *or* after, *use the regular past.*

1. When she (graduate) from high school, Eva Martinez was not interested in going to college.

2. She (feel) she (study) enough in high school.

3. By the time she (graduate) she (read) about history, (learn) about science, (study) math, and (write) papers, and that was enough.

4. The time (arrive) to get a good job.

5. She (want) to start a career and make a lot of money.

6. When she (be) 14, she (decide) to be a TV newscaster.

7. She (be) attractive and (speak) well, and she (look) somewhat older than her age.

8. Before she (go) job hunting, she (prepare) by reading the newspaper to her reflection in the mirror.

9. When she (do) that several times, she (feel) she was ready.

10. The TV executive she (speak) to (ask) if she (have) any experience.

11. He (ask) if she (have) any training.

12. He (ask) if she (graduate) from college.

13. He (look) at her as though she (drop) in on him from Mars.

14. He (say) they didn't need anyone like her just at this time.

15. After three more experiences like that one, Eva (decide) she would go to college after all.

EXERCISE 5.C

Fill in the correct verb form—past or past-before-past—in the following paragraph.

In 1863, Abraham Lincoln _____ (be) faced with a serious problem. The American Civil War _____ (be) going on for two years, but the North still _____ (not make) significant progress against the South in Virginia. In the preceding two years, President Lincoln _____ (appoint) general after general to lead the Union's Army of the Potomac, but Robert E. Lee, the Confederate general in Virginia, _____ (defeat) every one of them. In the western theater, however, the Union _____ (be) successful. In particular, an unknown Union general named Ulysses S. Grant _____ (defeat) the Confederates every time he _____ (fight) them. Noticing Grant's success, Lincoln finally _____ (decide) to make him commander of all the Union's armies. He _____ (put) him in charge of the whole war. Grant immediately _____ (formulate) a plan for defeating the Confederacy and _____ (put) it into effect. The result _____ (be) a Union victory. Until Grant's appointment, the Union _____ (struggle) to defeat an opponent with only half its strength, but when he _____ (take) charge, victory _____ (become) inevitable.

EXERCISE 5.D

In the following exercise, fill in the correct verb form—present tense, past tense, past-to-present tense, or past-before-past tense.

Before doing this exercise, briefly review the instructions for using past-to-present and past-before-past tenses. Then carefully work out in the case of each verb whether its action is in the present, the regular past, the past-to-present, or the past-before-past. Don't guess.

Roughly between 1953 and 1957, an automotive revolution _____ (hit) the United States. It _____ (be) during that period that the famous Volkswagen Beetle, or "Bug," _____ (arrive) on the American automobile market, the first imported car to reach a mass market in the United States. The history of this car before the 1950s _____ (be) rather strange.

By the mid-1930s, Germany _____ (be) in the grip of a severe economic depression for over a decade. Up to that time, people _____ (have) a hard time getting work, and German industry _____ (stagnate). Before he took power, the new German leader, Adolf Hitler, _____ (develop) many new schemes to get the country back on its feet, and one of them _____ (be) to develop a new, low-priced automobile that everyone could afford. So when he became Chancellor, he _____ (commission) the great automotive designer, Ferdinand Porsche, to design a new "people's car." (*Volks* in German _____ (mean) *people's* and *wagen* _____ (mean) *vehicle*.) Porsche _____ (be) also famous for designing sports cars and military tanks.

The Second World War _____ (put) an end to the Volkswagen, but after the war manufacture of them _____ (begin), and starting in 1949, a few of them _____ (begin) to trickle into the United States. The original design _____ (be) hardly changed at all, and the early VWs _____ (show) it. For instance, they _____ (have) no fuel gauges, totally inadequate rear windows and windshield wipers, and only six-volt batteries.

German production of the Beetle _____ (be) discontinued in 1979, but the love affair of Americans now in their 40s and 50s with the car _____ (have not) died. A friend of mine _____ (own) one since the mid-80s. Eric Hansen, author of *Motoring with Mohammed*, _____ (travel) all over looking for Beetles, and in 1972, he _____ (find) one in the mountains of Pakistan. Recently, a restored Beetle _____ (be) on sale at a rare car dealer in San Francisco for $12,900. The Beetle _____ (have) not died and gone to automobile heaven yet.

Now the Volkswagen company _____ (build) a new, modern version of the old Beetle. It remains to be seen whether it will ever achieve the original Beetle's popularity.

6. COMMA-SPLICE ERRORS

Comma splices occur when the writer joins two complete sentences with a comma only:

My elephant was a lot of fun, I liked her enormously.

Note that if you put a period after *fun*, where the comma is, you would have two correctly punctuated sentences. *Remember that commas do not, by themselves, connect sentences.*

While comma splices are errors, they are in some ways a good sign. One of the marks of immaturity in writing is long strings of short sentences, with no indications by the writer of the relationships among them. Comma splices at least tell the reader that the writer saw a close connection between the ideas in the two sentences joined by the comma. It is better, of course, to tell the reader the same thing in a more precise way or in a way that the reader is used to seeing.

Finding Comma-Splice Errors

The best way of finding comma-splice errors is to start by asking your teacher not to mark them but only to indicate in some way that you have made the mistake in a particular line or lines in your paper. Then you should read the sentence in that line, starting in a preceding line if that's where your sentence starts. Read the sentence aloud in your normal voice, as though you were reading it to someone else. When we read aloud, we do two things when we come to the ends of sentences. Our voice drops slightly on the last word, and we pause. Read listening to your own voice and when you pause, check for a comma splice. Your teacher may be able to help you do this the first time or two, making sure you don't skip past the pauses too quickly.

Correcting Comma Splices

The best way to correct them is to try to see what logical relationship there is between the two sentences and find a word that expresses that relationship. In many cases words like *but, although, while, because,* or *and so* will work well.

Another way to show that sentences are closely related to one another is to use a semicolon. You might think of this punctuation mark as a *semiperiod,* since it is half period and half comma, working like the period to show the reader that a sentence has ended but also working like the comma to show that more of the same idea is coming.

Therefore and *However*

Please notice that we did not suggest joining sentences with *however, thus,* or *therefore.* These words do *not* join sentences. They may introduce sentences, but they do not join them, and so the following sentences contain comma-splice errors despite the presence of *however* and *therefore:*

> Shortly after World War II, the American dollar was one of the world's strongest currencies, however now it is one of the weakest.
>
> Most people know nothing about economics, therefore they can be easily fooled in this area by politicians.

For those sentences to be correct, there would have to be a period or a semicolon after the first sentence in each pair. In any case, use *however* and *therefore* very sparingly. You will find them used rarely in good writing, and it is not wise to rely upon them much, for they are heavy words that call attention to themselves. Good writers use conjunctions (*and, but, so,* and the rest of the FANBOYS) much more frequently than these words.

These Words Join Sentences	**These Words Don't Join Sentences**
for, and, nor, but, or, yet, so	therefore, thus, consequently, however
because, since	for example, for instance
although, though, while	now, then
even though, whereas	

EXERCISE 6.A

Read the following exercises aloud in your normal voice, trying to notice when you pause. When you've identified a comma splice, correct it by using a conjunction such as but, although, while, because, *or* and so *if you can; otherwise use a semicolon. Some of the sentences are correct.*

1. Our football team finished in the bottom ten again last year, they are pretty untalented.

2. The offense averaged only 3.6 points a game, the defense was worse.

3. When they scored their first touchdown, the coach fainted.

4. The heaviest player on the team weighed 240 pounds, he was the quarterback.

5. The team needs new blood, most of their old blood is on the football field.

6. They had one momentous triumph, they won their last game of the season.

7. Our opponents were favored by 39 points, they were probably a little overconfident.

8. It was the greatest upset of the year, nobody ever expected anything like it.

9. The team tried to carry the coach around the field on their shoulders, they couldn't lift him.

10. It is true that he's a little heavy, he weighs about 300 pounds, more or less.

11. He once played guard for the Sacramento Poltroons, a minor-league football team.

12. The effort to lift him injured three players, who had to be hospitalized afterward.

13. The team we beat, our arch-rivals, went into shock after the game, they had to see therapists to cure their depression.

14. Many became suicidal, they had lost to the worst team in the state.

15. Thus we can see the value of athletics, they are good for the pocketbooks of psychologists.

EXERCISE 6.B

The following passage contains some comma-splice errors. Rewrite the passage, making no changes except to correct those errors.

My history as a cook is very spotty, it contains a lot more failures than successes. When I was in college, my earliest cooking efforts consisted largely of putting cheese spread on crackers, although making bologna sandwiches was also an early triumph. In the army, cooking consisted of getting cans open, sometimes a problem with the can openers they gave you. Advanced cooking was heating the food in the cans, a task mostly beyond my abilities. Later in life, I began to specialize, the cheese sandwich became my first area of concentration. The cheese sandwich is a delicate dish, requiring great care in the preparation, sloppiness can easily ruin it. First, it is important to choose the right cheese, not all cheeses make good sandwiches. Second, the bread must be chosen carefully, it must complement the cheese. Dark, strongly flavored breads like pumpernickel are best with strong cheeses, light cheeses taste best on sourdough or other light white breads. For the gourmet cheese sandwich, butter on the bread is a must, lettuce and mustard are also desirable. Having mastered the cheese sandwich, I am now thinking of getting into hot foods.

7. SENTENCE FRAGMENTS

Any group of words that isn't a complete sentence but is punctuated like one is a sentence fragment—or fragment for short. If you read magazines, you will find many sentence fragments used on purpose, usually for emphasis. Advertisements are often written in virtually nothing but fragments. Does that mean it's all right to have them in your essays or other school writing? Generally, no. You may find occasion to use a fragment once in a great while in a formal paper, but both academic and business writing do not favor them.

While an intentionally written fragment may be effective, fragments written accidentally almost never are. They just look wrong and may even confuse the reader momentarily. There are three causes of accidental fragments, and if you write them, you should be aware of these causes, for normally one of them—and only one—will be the reason for your fragments. After you read over this section, then, you should analyze your own fragments, with the help of your teacher if necessary, to see what kind they are and why you seem to be writing them. In that way, you can study this section selectively, concentrating on the part of it relevant to you.

Three Kinds of Fragments and Their Causes

The most common sentence fragment is actually not so much a fragment as a punctuation error. We will call it the *punctuation fragment*. The punctuation fragment looks like this:

> The legislature passed a mandatory seat-belt law. An attempt to protect drivers from their own recklessness.
>
> She became one of the most successful lawyers in the firm. Simply because she was willing to work night and day.

The underlined groups of words are not sentences, but they could easily be part of the sentences preceding them; all that is necessary is to change the periods after the sentences to commas and the capital letters of the fragments to lowercase letters.

Why do we sometimes write fragments like these? No one can be sure, but it is easy to make mistakes in areas where we know better when we are concentrating mainly on what we want to say.

A second kind of sentence fragment is the *knowledge fragment*. This fragment may look like the punctuation fragment and will often be correctable in the same way—that is, by simply attaching it to the sentence preceding it. But the knowledge fragment is the fragment that the writer really thinks is a complete sentence. Here is a common knowledge fragment:

> The North began the Civil War confident of a quick victory. Whereas it took four years of hard fighting before the South was finally defeated.

Many people don't realize that *whereas* is like *because* and that a group of words beginning with *whereas* can't stand alone any more than a group of words beginning with *because* can.

The least common kind of sentence fragment, fortunately, is the *process fragment*. This is what a process fragment looks like:

> Women born in the first three or four decades of the twentieth century, who, despite intelligence and education, were rarely able to enter the professional worlds of business, medicine, and the law.

Here, the word *who* prevents this from being a complete sentence, just as in the following simpler example:

> Women who were rarely able to become doctors.

The simplest correction is simply to delete the *who*, which would make both examples above correct, complete sentences. But why does anyone write a sentence like the first one? Because the writer lost track of the sentence as he or she was writing and simply didn't notice that the *who,* which is all right in itself, made the finished "sentence" into a fragment. In other words, the writer got lost in the writing process.

Correcting Fragments

Because most fragments are not knowledge fragments, it is best to start the study of fragments with a review of the kinds of nonsentence structures that are most likely to be written as fragments and with exercises to help distinguish them from complete sentences.

Punctuation Fragments

The following kinds of structures are the ones most often accidentally punctuated as sentences:

She just stared at her food. A soggy unappetizing mess.
> *This is just a noun phrase describing the food; it has no subject and verb.*

She just stared at her food. Although she hadn't eaten for two days.
> *This group of words has a subject and verb, but the word although makes it into a dependent clause that must be attached to a complete sentence.*

She just stared at her food. Thinking about all the problems she'd had.
> *There is a subject and verb buried in this phrase, but the phrase, beginning as it does with an* -ing *verb, is just a verbal phrase and not a sentence.*

Knowledge Fragments

The following kinds of structures are the ones people most often think of as sentences, although they are not:

She just stared at her food. Whereas John began eating right away.
> She just stared at her food. While John dug into his.
>> *Whereas* and *while are subordinating conjunctions, making otherwise complete sentences into dependent clauses that cannot stand alone and must be attached to complete sentences.*

She just stared at her food. Which was a silly thing to do.

> Which *cannot introduce complete sentences unless they are questions* ("Which *hat is yours?"). To correct, either join the* which *structure to the preceding sentence with a comma or change* which *to* that *or* this.

She just stared at her food. The reason being that she had eaten only an hour before.

> *The phrase* the reason being, *which is a carryover from speech, is not a complete sentence because* being *is not a verb but a verbal. To make this phrase a complete sentence,* being *would have to be changed to* was *(or, in a present-tense sentence,* is*). You can also attach it to the sentence preceding it by changing the period after* food *into a comma. But the best thing to do is change* the reason being that *to* because *and change the period to a comma.*

The band went crazy on the stage. The lead guitarist smashing his instrument. The drummer jumping onto the drums. Other band members tearing off their clothes.

> *These structures are exactly like* the reason being. *Each is like a sentence except that following the subject is an* -ing *verb instead of a regular verb. As in the case of* the reason being, *the best correction is simply to make all of these structures into one sentence by replacing the periods with commas. The other alternative would be to change the* -ing *verb forms into regular verbs.*

EXERCISE 7.A

Recognizing Punctuation Fragments

In the following series of short passages, there are punctuation fragments. Correct all fragments by rewriting the whole passage as a complete sentence.

1. My Lien's high school was gearing up for its big event of the year. A turtle race.

_____

2. My Lien planned to enter. Although she did not own a turtle.

_____

3. She went to the lake. Hoping to find one there.

_____

4. At the lake, she found sand, rocks, and water. But no turtles.

_____

5. At pet stores and the aquarium, she heard the same words. "No turtles."

_____

6. As the day of the race neared, My Lien grew despondent. Fearing she had no chance.

_____

7. Her parents remained cheerful. Because her father had a secret.

_____

8. He had a business acquaintance with an odd hobby. Breeding turtles.

_____

9. On the day before the race, her father came home with a big surprise. A brand-new, five-speed racing turtle.

_____

10. My Lien's turtle swept the field. Leaving the others in the dust.

_____

EXERCISE 7.B

Following is a series of short passages in which there are one or more punctuation fragments. Copy each passage carefully. Correct each punctuation fragment by attaching it to the sentence preceding it.

1. The people of Smeltsburg elected Ronald Muffin mayor for a second term. Thinking he would once again do a good job. They did not realize that he planned to sell City Hall, a building of great historical importance.

_____

_____

2. City Hall had been built in 1864 to house wounded Civil War veterans, but it was used for that purpose only one month. The time it took for the one wounded veteran to get better.

_____

_____

3. Historians have discovered that of the 105 Smeltsburg men who went into
   the army, few ever saw combat. Even though all were fit for duty.

   _____

   _____

4. Most of the Smeltsburg Company hid behind trees during the battles. A
   fact that came out after the war when it was found that they were the only
   company in both armies with no casualties.

   _____

   _____

5. The one wounded Smeltsburg man was hurt when a chicken attacked him.
   Giving him severe pecks on his hands and face, wounds that sent him
   home to Smeltsburg.

   _____

   _____

6. After he was healed, the Smeltsburg Veterans Hospital was made the City
   Hall. A place where the returning veterans could gather and lie about the
   war. Their favorite form of entertainment.

   _____

   _____

7. Since the town's population has dropped to thirty-four, Mayor Muffin
   believes a city hall is no longer necessary, thus making possible the sale of
   the building. While perhaps acquiring a new business or employer for the
   town.

   _____

   _____

EXERCISE 7.C

Recognizing Knowledge Fragments

*Following are several short passages in which nonsentence constructions are
punctuated as sentences. Copy the passages, correcting the errors either by making
the nonsentence part of the sentence preceding it or by changing it into a sentence.*

1. Most fast food is tasteless. Whereas most good food is expensive.

   _____

2. Most people are happy with tasteless food. Which is why fast-food places make money.

   _____

3. I prefer food with taste. While Glen doesn't care what he eats.

   _____

4. I got a hamburger the other day. Its bun bursting with lettuce, tomato, pickles, and who knows what.

   _____

5. I couldn't taste the meat. The reason being there wasn't any. [Revise using *because*.]

   _____

6. The greasy meat in most fast-food places isn't nutritious. Whereas all the salad piled onto it is.

   _____

7. Glen loves it all. Which mystifies me.

   _____

8. He won't accept fake money or listen to manufactured music. While he will eat fake food.

   _____

8. PRONOUNS

Pronouns as Subjects and Objects

As you know, pronouns (*I, you, he, she, we, they, it*) can be subjects of sentences or other structures with verbs in them:

> I ordered the books that you and she ordered, but they didn't come, and it was the mailman's fault.

As you also know—whether you know you know it or not—other pronouns (*me, you, him, her, us, them, it*) can be objects:

> We sent them an order, but they lost it, and for me and him, that created difficulties.

Subject pronouns come in front of verbs, just as noun subjects do:

> She found the problem.
> He lost his wallet.
> Mary found the problem.
> John lost his wallet.

Object pronouns follow verbs or prepositions, just as noun objects do:

> Mary found it.
> Mary likes him.
> John went with them.
> Mary found the problem.
> Mary likes George.
> John went with George and Tom.

People run into a problem sometimes when they have two pronouns joined by an *and* in a subject spot. Have you ever heard anyone say a sentence like one of these?

> Me went to a movie last night.
> Me worked on the car all day.

Probably not. But how about one of these?

> Me and her went to a movie last night.
> Me and John worked on the car all day. (Or, John and me worked on the car.)

The "me and her went" or "me and John worked" are just as wrong as the "me went" and the "me worked" and for the same reason: The words *me, her,* and *him* are all object pronouns, but in these sentences they've been used as subjects.

Here is a list of the subject and object pronouns; just skim it:

Subject	Object
I	me
you	you
he	him
she	her
we	us
they	them
it	it

Normally, we don't put an object pronoun in a subject spot unless we pair it with another noun or pronoun. When we use pronouns as subjects all by themselves, we always use them correctly. So to check whether you've used a pair or one of a pair correctly, ask yourself which pronoun you would use if you were using it by itself. For instance, look at the following sentence with pronouns used as subjects:

Me and her left the party early.

To check the *me* pronoun, ask yourself whether you would say, "Me left the party early." To check the *her* pronoun, ask yourself whether you would say, "Her left the party early." You know you wouldn't say either of those things, so you also know how the sentence should be written:

She and I left the party early.

EXERCISE 8.A

For practice, check the subject pronouns in the following sentences; not every one is incorrect. Write in the correct pronoun where needed.

1. Mary and me took out John's garbage.

2. He and the cat brought it back in, bits at a time.

3. Me and the cat had a fight over some fish bones.

4. Him and John had similar tastes in food.

5. It occurred to Mary and me that we were quite different.

6. Mary felt that she and I should leave them to themselves.

7. She said that her and the cat could never get along.

8. I secretly hoped that me and her could sneak off together.

9. We agreed that John and her could never share the same kitchen.

10. The cat and John thought that Mary and me were lacking in taste.

Pronoun Order

There may be some activities in which "me first" is a good motto, but not in writing. In writing, *me* always comes second. So the following sentence is incorrect:

They gave the tickets to me and Susan.

It should, of course, be

They gave the tickets to Susan and me.

Uses and Misuses of *They*

The word *they,* of course, is a plural pronoun. It refers to both people and things:

The people on the corner were angry. They were waving their arms and shouting.
I spilled the whole box of nails on the floor. They were scattered everywhere.

Informally, in speech, we often use *they* when it doesn't actually refer to anything at all, as in these examples:

They say that lightning never strikes twice in the same place. (Who says it?)
I'd hate working in a department store. They have to put up with too many irritating people. (Who does?)
The Dropsocket Corporation is making news again. They have come out with an internal combustion pencil sharpener. (Note that while the company gets the singular verb *is* in the first sentence, it's referred to by the plural pronoun *they* instead of the singular *it.*)

Unfortunately, in writing, all our pronouns (except indefinite ones, which we don't need to worry about) are supposed to refer to some specific noun. We would do better to write the sentences above like this:

People say that lightning never strikes twice in the same place.
I'd hate working in a department store. Clerks have to put up with too many irritating people.
The Dropsocket Corporation is making news again. It has come out with an internal combustion pencil sharpener.

EXERCISE 8.B

In the following practice sentences, locate the instances in which they is misused and correct the sentences in whatever way seems to you best. Be sure not to change any *they* that is correctly used.

1. They say that there is nothing new under the sun, but the Snidely Wingnut Company has proven this saying wrong.

2. They have developed a whole new line of self-cleaning dog food dishes.

3. People are always complaining about their dog food dishes. After the dog uses them three or four times, they get disgusting.

4. The advantage of this new dish is that they will never get dirty again.

5. When the dog has eaten, the dish dissolves all the leftover particles of food in acid so that they won't stick to the dish.

6. Down at the Snidely Wingnut Company they do admit that there is one little bug they have to work out yet.

7. That's the acid solution left in the dish, which kills the dog the next time they try to eat out of the dish.

Pronoun Reference

Other pronouns besides *they* must, of course, be used correctly too. As we write, concentrating on what we're trying to say, it's very easy to forget precisely *how* we've said what we've previously said. This sort of forgetting, which is natural in writing, can lead to many technical problems in the finished product, and that's why revising and proofreading are so important. One of the easiest problems to spot and fix is mixed-up pronoun references—that is, having a pronoun that refers to no noun at all or having a pronoun that is in the wrong number for the noun it refers to, for example, a singular pronoun referring to a plural noun.

You can use this table as a reminder, if you want one, of how pronouns work:

he, she:	refers to one male or one female
his, her:	possessive form of *he, she*
they:	refers to more than one male, more than one female, or more than one thing
their:	possessive form of *they*
we:	refers to more than one person, including the writer; also refers to today's society or world
our:	possessive form of *we*

EXERCISE 8.C

In the following passage, fill in the correct pronouns from the list above. In addition, underline the noun each pronoun refers to.

The relationship between New England parents in the seventeenth century and

(   ) children was very different from what we see now. Then as now, parents

often had to deal with sons and daughters who became somewhat rebellious when
(   ) reached their teen years. One of (   ) solutions to this problem, particularly in the case of a boy, was to send (   ) away to be an apprentice to a
skilled artisan or a businessman. (   ) would have to live apart from (   )
parents for most of the year, learning from a master how to be a blacksmith or a
shoemaker. Girls could also be sent to live with another family where (   )
would have to learn the arts of cooking and making cloth from someone other than
(   ) mother. A woman who was raising a girl other than (   ) own daughter would tend to be more strict with (   ) charge than with (   ) own
child. In our time, parents no longer send (   ) children off to be apprentices
to others, but many parents, faced with difficult teenagers in the house, often wish
(   ) could.

Pronouns with Indefinite Nouns

Sometimes when we write, we don't want to refer to particular people but
to people in general. At these times, we may find ourselves using words or
phrases like the following:

people	people in seventeenth-century New England
a person	a person looking for a job
students	Japanese students
a student	a student who is falling behind in class
one	anybody

English does not make life easy for us when we are using these *indefinite* nouns
and phrases. In particular, there is one little awkward situation that bothers
many people. It is this: When you want to refer to men or women, or people
in general, or even things, there is one handy all-purpose pronoun for you to
use: *they* or *them.* But when you want to refer to a single person or thing, you
have to make up your mind whether you want to use the masculine pronoun,
he, or the feminine pronoun, *she,* or the neuter pronoun, *it.* There's nothing so
bad about this except that sometimes your pronoun follows an *indefinite*
noun—that is, a noun that although singular refers to people in general. Here
is an example:

A child should never be left unattended in a parked car.

The word *child* is clearly singular, but at the same time it clearly refers to any child or all children. Singular nouns that perform this kind of function are called indefinite nouns, or indefinites. Now, since this indefinite noun is singular, would you follow this sentence with the word *He* referring to *child* or the word *She?* How about the next sentence?

> A person who attends school and works will have quite a few problems.

Would you want your next sentence to begin with *He* or *She?*

Traditionally, the rules of English usage have always said that we use the masculine form to refer to indefinite nouns like *child, person, student, worker,* and so on. But in recent years, many people, women in particular, have argued that it is inappropriate always to use a masculine pronoun when referring to both men and women. In speech there has never been a problem because people have been in the habit for centuries of just using *they* to refer to indefinite nouns and pronouns. But in writing that is still considered incorrect because *they* is plural and most indefinite nouns are singular. What to do? Writers tackle this situation in different ways.

The His/Her Option

In this option, one uses "he or she" or "him or her" or "his or hers" when referring to indefinites:

> A person who attends school and works will have quite a few problems. He or she will have to budget his or her time carefully so that the demands of neither school nor work will overwhelm him or her.

You can see how quickly this gets out of hand, and the trouble is, once you start doing it, you have to keep doing it. It's not usually a great option.

The Plural Option

In this option, the writer avoids singular indefinites whenever possible, using plurals instead:

> People who attend school and work will have quite a few problems. They will have to budget their time carefully so that the demands of neither school nor work will overwhelm them.

The Alternating Option

In this one, the writer uses masculine pronouns sometimes and feminine pronouns other times. This is all right as long as it doesn't confuse the reader.

The Whatever-You-Want Option

In this one, women may use feminine pronouns and men masculine pronouns.

Pronouns with Indefinite Pronouns

Just as English has indefinite nouns, so it also has indefinite pronouns, and they too cause a lot of trouble. The most common indefinite pronouns are these:

anyone   anybody
someone   somebody
no one   nobody
everyone   everybody
each (whether followed by a noun or not)

Although all these words clearly refer to more than one person, they are still grammatically singular, at least most of the time. Notice that one group of them has the word *one* in it, a help in remembering that they are supposed to be singular, and notice that the other group has the singular word *body* in it. The following examples all illustrate correct pronoun usage with these indefinites (remember that the masculine/feminine problem exists with indefinite pronouns just as it does with indefinite nouns):

Anyone can get good grades if he (she) just studies hard enough.
I would like to find someone to do my work for me. She (he) could take as long as she (he) wanted.
Each of us will have to make up his (her) mind for himself (herself).

There are several exceptions to this rule, but the most common and important one is that when the indefinites *no one/nobody* or *everyone/everybody* refer to specific groups of people, they take plural pronouns, as in these cases:

No one at the party wanted to leave. They were all having too good a time.
Everybody was extremely happy with the concert. They all applauded and cheered at the end.

In summary, when one of the indefinite words, either noun or pronoun, is used to refer to people or a group of people in general, it is followed by a *singular* pronoun: *he/she, him/her*. When *no one/nobody* or *everyone/everybody* refers to a specific group rather than a general group, it is followed by a *plural* pronoun: *they/them*.

EXERCISE 8.D

In the following sentences, fill in the blanks with the correct pronouns. In the case of indefinite nouns, you may change the noun according to the "plural option" listed above.

1. A student who tries to work too many hours will pay the price.

   _____ social life will be a disaster.

2. Anyone who wants to live a happy life should find a balance between

   _____ need for rest and recreation and _____ need to work.

3. Everyone who wants _____ community to work effectively

   must contribute some of _____ own time to it. Each person

   must do _____ share. Each must contribute some of

   _____ own time and talent.

4. Society is greatly concerned about the abused child. The problem is that

   when _____ becomes a parent, _____ is likely

   to abuse _____ own children.

5. Everyone in the class was angry; _____ all complained to the department.

EXERCISE 8.E

For more practice in pronoun use, write sentences as directed here.

1. Write a sentence in which you use *anyone* followed by the correct pronoun.

   _____

2. Write a sentence in which you use *someone* followed by the correct pronoun.

_____

3. Write a sentence in which you use *everyone* followed by the correct pronoun.

_____

4. Write a sentence in which you use *everyone* to refer to a specific group followed by the correct pronoun.

_____

5. Write a sentence in which you use *each* followed by the correct pronoun.

_____

6. Write a sentence in which you use *a person* as subject, followed by the correct pronoun.

_____

7. Write a sentence in which you use *a student* as subject, followed by the correct pronoun.

_____

One and *You*

Sometimes students get somewhat confused about whether to use *one* or *you* or the plural *they* in situations in which they are writing about people in general, as in the following passage from a student paper; note the underlined words:

> From this report a person will find out what is expected in certain positions and what kind of job one can expect. Most jobs fall into the following four main categories: jobs requiring the person to have experience; jobs requiring one to have some education; jobs requiring them to be a college graduate; and jobs aimed at particular age groups. One must keep all these questions in mind when looking for a job.
>
> Most employers' first question is whether you have had any experience relating to the type of job. With experience one can find better pay, more benefits, and you may even start your own business.

Because the idea is to be as consistent as possible in the pronouns we use, we should not switch back and forth between singular and plural without some logical reason for doing so. Otherwise we just confuse the reader. In the same way, we should not switch between *one* and *you,* unless we really want to refer to *anyone* with *one* and to the reader with *you.*

Because this writer switches constantly, he has a big problem. He has started with the indefinite noun *person* followed by the indefinite pronoun *one,* which is all right. Both of them are singular and both mean "anyone." But then he has gone on to use the plural *them* to refer to *person* and shifted from *one* to *you* and *your.*

If you want to start with a singular indefinite noun like *person,* stick to the pronouns *one* and the combination *he* or *she.* Don't switch to the plural *them,* and don't switch from *one* to *you.* If, as you go along, you find that the way you've started is awkward and uncomfortable—that you can't easily be consistent because of the way you started—*go back to the beginning and change that;* don't just change in midstream.

Remember:

one: means anyone in general
you: means *your reader* specifically

EXERCISE 8.F

For practice, rewrite the student passage above in two versions:

1. Rewrite it as the original writer did, starting with *a person* in the first line; after that, be sure to use singular pronouns; use *one* where the original writer did.

2. Rewrite it using *people* instead of *person* in the first line; after that, be sure to use plural pronouns throughout, including where the original writer used *one.*

9. USING *A* AND *AN*

While in speech it doesn't generally matter much whether we use the word *a* or the word *an* in front of a noun, using the wrong one in writing is, to most readers, a really glaring mistake.

The rule for using these two words is pretty simple. Most of the time, we use *an* in front of a word beginning with one of the five vowel letters:

a, e, i, o, u

And, of course, we use *a* in front of words beginning with all the rest of the letters. So normal usage works like this:

an *a*rmadillo	a toad
an *e*lephant	a giraffe
an *i*llness	a sickness
an *o*rphan	a child
an *u*mbrella	a raincoat

Naturally, there are exceptions, but at least they are sensible ones. Regardless of the actual spelling of a word, if its first letter *sounds* like a consonant, we will use *a* in front of it, as in this case. This happens fairly frequently with words beginning with *u*.

a united organization

a U.S. army unit

Notice that the *u* in these two cases is pronounced like *y*.

Similarly, if a consonant *sounds* like a vowel, we will usually put *an* in front of it. This happens in San Francisco all the time when the city's name gets abbreviated to S.F., because the letter *s* all by itself is pronounced *ess*:

an S.F. restaurant guide

EXERCISE 9.A

In the following sentences, write in the correct word, a *or* an.

1. _____ major problem for our basketball team is that no player is more than 5 feet 10 inches tall.

2. Even _____ average referee tends to look down on this team.

3. It takes _____ awfully clever coach to devise plays that they can use.

4. And it takes _____ unusually bad team to lose to them.

5. They will have _____ occasional scoring spurt when some-one gets hot, but _____ event like that is rare in their lives.

6. They have _____ talented guard but not _____ active front line.

7. But the guard is _____ undersized 5 feet 2 inches.

8. _____ slam dunk is out of the question for this team, and

   even _____ layup is pretty rare.

9. _____ equally talented team can always beat them, and it is
   terrible to watch what happens when _____ really good team
   comes to town.

10. They always present _____ interesting spectacle on the court,
    since they look _____ lot like children who have wandered into
    the wrong place.

10. NOUN PLURALS

Most nouns in English have both singular and plural forms, and in most
cases, their plurals take an *s* ending—as in the words you have just been reading: *nouns, forms, cases, plurals,* and *words.* Everyone knows this.

But because we don't always pronounce those *s* endings when we speak, some
of us find it difficult to remember to put them on plural nouns when we write.

An added complication for some of us is that our particular speech patterns
have a rule that says we don't need to add *s* endings when it is obvious that the
noun is plural—in other words, when the *s* would simply be redundant. For
instance, if we use the word *two* in front of the noun *car,* then we know that we
are talking about more than one car without adding an *s* on it. So what's the point
of adding it? There is no particular point except that in written English it has to
have an *s* or your reader will think that you've made a simple mistake and that
you're a dope.

Notice too that English has an interesting pattern when the word *one*
appears in front of a noun. Normally, of course, the word *one* means just that
and so a noun following it would not be a plural:

one paper
one basketball

But if we write *one of,* then the noun following will be a plural:

one of the papers
one of the basketballs

The idea is that this means one out of several papers or many basketballs.

EXERCISE 10.A

In the following exercises, find the word indicating a plural noun (for example, a number, a word like several *or* many, *or the words like* one of*), then find the noun that should have a plural s ending and add that ending.*

Sometimes making a plural noun near the beginning of a sentence will mean that other nouns further along will have to be changed to plurals too. *Underline all nouns you change into plurals.*

1. The high school prom was being looked forward to by almost all of the student.

2. Raquel was one of the person most anticipating the event.

3. She and three of her friend were on the planning committee.

4. Many of the prom in the past year had been failure, so they were determined to make this one of the rare success.

5. Several difficulty presented themselves, however.

6. One was a group of boy who had disrupted two dance earlier in the year.

7. Another was a bunch of girl who had bad attitude and caused trouble.

8. A third was they couldn't agree on which of several band to hire.

9. Raquel, many of whose family member were diplomat, came up with a solution to these problem.

10. She hired a band led by the older brother of one of the trouble some boy.

11. She told two of the other boy that some of the difficult girl really liked them and hoped they would take them to the prom.

12. The prom turned out to be the most successful dance in several year, but Raquel missed it because she was hired by the United Nation to solve some difficult problem in Asia and Africa.

EXERCISE 10.B

Do the following exercises to practice using noun plurals:

1. Write three sentences in which you use numbers before nouns (for instance, *three cats*).

2. Write three sentences in which you use the words *many of.*

3. Write three sentences in which you see the words *one of.*

4. Write a sentence in which you use the words *a family of.*

5. Write a sentence in which you use the word *several* in front of a noun.

6. Write a sentence in which you use the word *some* in front of a noun.

7. Write a sentence in which you use the words *a group of.*

11. NONCOUNTABLE NOUNS

Some nouns do not take plural forms. These are called *noncountable* nouns. English has the very curious practice of dividing up its nouns into two types— those representing things that can be counted and those representing things that can't be counted. The *countable* nouns are the ones that take *s* plurals. We can, for instance, count:

> *grains* of sand
> *drops* of water
> *pieces* of aluminum
> *kinds* of beauty

But we can't count:

> sand
> water
> aluminum
> beauty

So we don't put *s* endings on those nouns.

Noncountable nouns fall into two large categories: mass nouns and abstract nouns. Mass nouns, which indicate things in their generic or undivided forms, are such words as these:

> *foods:* meat, fish, chicken, coffee, tea, milk
> *elements, minerals, and gases:* aluminum, iron, neon, hydrogen, sand, water, air

Abstract nouns include words such as these, which do not have *s* plural forms:

information	clothing
research	weather
advertising	luggage
homework	money
housework	advice

experience   equipment
knowledge   music

Sometimes it doesn't seem logical to think of some of these abstract nouns as representing things one can't count. For instance, we talk about counting our money all the time, and one could certainly count the number of homework items one had to do. But the language insists that we are actually counting not money but dollars and cents (note the *s* endings on these words) and the items of homework we have to do. When a noun refers to a concept rather than a thing itself, it is a noncountable noun and usually doesn't take a plural form.

To confuse things even more, some nouns can be used to indicate concepts or abstractions some of the time, in which case they don't have *s* endings, and at other times they can refer to specific things, in which case they do. For instance, we can say:

The dorm serves chicken all the time.

But we can also say:

George is raising chickens in his backyard.

The first use of *chicken* refers to the meat as an abstraction while the second use refers to the specific birds.
Similarly, we say:

I have been studying philosophy for years.

And in this case, we would mean that we have studied the specific *philosophies* of numerous philosophers.

In still other cases, some nouns will take an *s* ending whether they are being used to refer to generic forms or not. For instance, the following uses are correct:

The dorm serves carrots all the time.
The dorm serves beets all the time.
The dorm serves peas all the time.

On the other hand, the words *corn, broccoli,* and *spinach* never take an *s* form. It's a wonder that anyone ever learns English.

Often the best policy is simply to try to memorize common noncountable nouns. Start with the thirteen abstract nouns listed above, and if you make the mistake of adding an *s* ending to other noncountable nouns, memorize those words, too.

12. DROPPED CONTRACTIONS OF *IS* AND *ARE*

Some spoken forms of English offer three alternative ways of using forms of the verb *be* in the present tense. In these forms, you can say any of the following:

She is going.   They are going.
She's going.   They're going.
She going.   They going.

We are going.   You are going.
We're going.   You're going.
We going.   You going.

While these are all equally correct in speech, unfortunately only two of the forms are correct in writing: the one using the full verb *is* or *are* and the one using the contracted form *'s* or *'re*. The third form, in which *is* and *are* are deleted, is not considered correct in written English.

EXERCISE 12.A

In the following sentences, write both *correct forms of subject and verb in the blanks, as in this example:*

This morning (John) _____John's_____ / _____John is_____ walking
to school.

1. (Lorene) _____ / _____ considering marriage.

2. She has had three dates with Ricky, and now (she) _____ /

    _____ thinking of marrying the man.

3. Her friends keep telling her (she) _____ / _____
    making a big mistake.

4. (They) _____ / _____ taking these ideas of hers very
    seriously.

5. Several of (them) _____ / _____ thinking of talking
    to her parents about her plans.

6. Some of the (others) _____ / _____ actually consid-
    ering kidnapping her to let her get over her passion.

7. Meanwhile, (Ricky) _____ / _____ going about his
    business.

8. (He) _____ / _____ not even sure he wants to date
    Lorene again.

9. Actually, (he) _____ / _____ sort of thinking of
    asking Valerie for a date.

10. (Lorene) _____ / _____ going to be somewhat sur-
    prised when she learns that her (wedding) _____ /
    _____ being postponed.

EXERCISE 12.B

In the following passage, locate the places where the verbs is *and* are *are missing,
and write them in.*

George trying to get together a group of friends to participate in historical

reenactments. He has gotten them interested in the 9th and 10th U.S. Cavalry,

the two black regiments of the old post–Civil War army, the famous "Buffalo

Soldiers." They increasingly busy acquiring or having made uniforms and

equipment of the period. They subscribing to magazines devoted to historical

reenactments, and they planning to attend events with other men and women

who interested in the same period. George spending amazing amounts of time

in the library. He doing research on the U.S. Cavalry of the last half of the

nineteenth century. His wife being kept so busy making blue cavalry uniforms

she starting to think of either going into the uniform business or divorcing

George.

13. FORMING DIRECT QUESTIONS

Questions Beginning with Who, What, Why, Where, When, *and* How

In written English, unlike in some forms of spoken English, questions beginning with the *wh* words (plus *how*) have to flip-flop the normal subject-verb word order:

normal: He likes her.
             He likes it. (or He does like it.)

question: Who does he like?
             What does he like?

With a verb other than the verb *be,* we don't simply switch the order of the subject and verb; rather, we put a form of the verb *do* in front of the subject and then use the regular base form of the main verb after the subject:

normal: She misses her cat.
question: Who *does* she miss?

normal: They miss their mother.
question: Who *do* they miss?

normal: He found his money.
question: What *did* he find?

Notice that in the present tense, the verb *do* has to agree in number with the subject following it.

When a form of the verb *be* is the main verb, it just moves in front of its subject in the question form:

normal: She is there.
question: Where is she?

normal: They were unhappy.
question: Why were they unhappy?

normal: She is leaving.
question: When is she leaving?
             How is she leaving?

In the case of questions in the future tense, it is the word *will* that moves in front of the subject:

　　normal:　　She will leave.
　　question:　When will she leave?

REVIEW

　　In questions, when do we use a form of the verb *do* in front of the subject? When do we use the original verb rather than *do*?
How do we handle the future tense in questions?

EXERCISE 13.A

　　In the exercises below, change the sentence into a question beginning with the word indicated:

1. Calbert lost his wallet.
   How _____

2. He is very absent-minded.
   Why _____

3. He lost it yesterday.
   When _____

4. He lost it in the gym.
   Where _____

5. He will eventually find it.
   How _____

6. He will then be happy.
   When _____

7. He will need it on Saturday.
   What _____

8. He is improving as a student.
   How _____

9. He is getting better in English.
   Why _____

10. His teachers like him.
    Why _____

EXERCISE 13.B

Write three questions beginning with where, what, *and* when *in which you use a form of the verb be:*

Example:
Where are my shoes?

Write three questions beginning with where, what, *and* when *in which you use a verb other than the verb be:*

Example:
Where have my shoes gone?

Write three questions beginning with why, how, *and* what *in which you use a verb in the future tense:*

Example:
Why will we have rain?
How will the game end?

Yes-No Questions

Questions that require only yes-no answers work in pretty much the same way as *wh* questions. If the verb has more than one part, the *first* part goes in front of the subject:

She *should* get a good grade.
Should she get a good grade?
He *will* be successful.
Will he be successful?
We *haven't* completed the work.
Haven't we completed the work?
He *could* have been the best.
Could he have been the best?

If the verb has only one part, then a form of the verb *do* has to be used in front of the subject:

She got a good grade.
Did she get a good grade?

He succeeded in business.
Did he succeed in business?
We completed the work.
Did we complete the work?

But if the verb is a form of the verb *be*, it just flip-flops with the subject:

He is successful.
Is he successful?
They were out of town.
Were they out of town?

REVIEW

What is the rule for yes-no questions in which the verb has more than one part?
What is the rule for yes-no questions in which the verb has only one part?
What is the rule for yes-no questions when the verb is a form of *be?*

EXERCISE 13.C

Change the following sentences into questions:

1. George could have gone to college.

   _____

2. George went to college.

   _____

3. Tanya should have studied hard.

   _____

4. Tanya studied hard.

   _____

5. George was an outstanding student.

   _____

6. The supplies will arrive tomorrow.

   _____

7. The supplies arrived today.

_____

8. These supplies are totally inadequate.

_____

9. The game was lost through bad luck.

_____

10. We lost the game through lousy talent.

_____

EXERCISE 13.D

1. Write three questions using verbs that have more than one part (for instance, verbs beginning with *should, could, will,* or *have*).
2. Write three questions using one-part verbs. These sentences will have to start with a form of the verb *do.*
3. Write three questions based on one-part forms of the verb *be* (that is, *am, is, are, was, were*).

14. FORMING INDIRECT QUESTIONS

In addition to direct questions, all forms of English, both spoken and written, allow us to use what are called indirect questions. Here are two examples of direct questions and their indirect counterparts:

direct: What can I do?   indirect: I wonder what I can do.
direct: Can I do it?   indirect: I wonder whether (if) I can do it.

As you know, in direct questions we change the order, or flip-flop, the subject and verb, putting the verb in front of the subject. But in indirect questions, we don't; we continue to use the standard nonquestion word order of subject first and verb second. This is contrary to some forms of spoken English in which the subject and verb are flip-flopped in indirect questions.

An indirect question always appears in the second half of a sentence that starts out not being a question, like these:

I asked her . . .
I wonder . . .

In fact, the verbs *ask* and *wonder* are very common signs that an indirect question is coming up. The other signs are whether certain words follow them, specifically the question words beginning with *wh* (plus the word *how*) and the words *whether* and *if*. Here are some typical indirect question sentences:

I asked her *what* she wanted.
I asked her *why* she did it.
I asked her *where* she was going.
I wonder *whether* you'll like the concert.
I wonder *if* the plane will be on time.
I wonder *when* it will get here.

In these kinds of sentences, be sure to use the normal order of first subject, and then verb following the *wh* word or the words *if* and *whether.*

EXERCISE 14.A

Complete the following sentences:

1. I wonder whether _____

2. I wonder if _____

3. I wonder where _____

4. I wonder why _____

5. I wonder when _____

6. I asked him whether _____

7. I asked him if _____

8. I asked him what _____

9. I asked him why _____

10. I asked him when _____

15. APOSTROPHES TO SHOW POSSESSION

In English, we can show that someone possesses something in several ways. We can say, "The book belongs to Mary," or we can say, "Look out for the tail of the cat," but, of course, we would normally refer to "Mary's book" and "the cat's tail." Here are three sentences with possessives in them:

I love John's limousine.
The boy's eyes got wider.
The dancer's dreams were shattered.

First rule: When a noun does not end in s (John, boy, dancer), we make it into a possessive by adding 's.

Here are three more sentences with possessives in them; they are slightly different from the first three:

I love Charles' limousine.
The two boys' eyes got wider.
The three dancers' dreams were shattered.

Second rule: When a noun does end in s (Charles, boys, dancers), we make it into a possessive by adding only '(although many writers prefer to add 's, as in *Charles's*, for singular nouns ending in s).

These two rules can be summed up in the following rule:

When you have a noun that should be a possessive, first write it the way you normally would *and then* add the apostrophe or the apostrophe + s.

There are a few more rules covering special cases, but this is the one you will use 90 percent of the time. Practice it in the following exercises.

EXERCISE 15.A

Rewrite each underlined group of words using apostrophes to show possession.

Example:
He washed the socks of his girlfriend.
his girlfriend's socks
He remembered the addresses of all his girlfriends.
all his girlfriends' addresses

1. She found the treasure of the pirate.

_____

2. She found the treasure of the pirates.

_____

3. We ate the apple of the farmer.

_____

4. We ate the apples of the farmers.

_____

5. George kept track of the homeruns of his favorite player.

_____

6. He did not keep track of the birthday of his girlfriend.

_____

7. She wanted to know why he was more interested in the statistics of baseball players than he was in her.

_____

8. He said it wasn't interest; it was that the home runs of ballplayers come more frequently than her birthdays.

_____

9. Try as we might, the important days of people are hard for many of us to remember.

_____

10. It would help if I could get the government to make national holidays of the birthdays of my best friends.

_____

Two special situations come up occasionally in apostrophe use. One involves what are called *compound nouns*—that is, nouns made up of more than one word:

    mother-in-law   someone else

To these words, we simply add the *'s* at the end:

    mother-in-law's   someone else's

The other situation involves the possession of something jointly by two (or more) people:

    Fred and John own a boat
    Fred and John's boat

But if we want to show that Fred and John each own separate boats, we would write:

Fred's and John's boats

EXERCISE 15.B

Rewrite each underlined group of words using apostrophes to show possession.

1. I loved the house of John and Marsha.

   _____

2. The house of my sister-in-law was right next door.

   _____

3. The house of the air force commander-in-chief was across the street.

   _____

4. At the stadium, the city refurbished the restrooms of the men and the women.

   _____

5. The foreign policies of Presidents Reagan and Carter were quite different.

   _____

6. But the basic tasks of their secretaries of state remained the same.

   _____

7. One of the famous events in American history is the journey west of Lewis and Clark.

   _____

8. The shoes of Mary and Charles are exactly the same color—yellow.

   _____

9. The interests of my stepfather are very broad.

   _____

10. The jointly owned Mercedes of Marie, Sue, and Ellen is starting to fall apart.

    _____

You now know practically everything there is to know about using apostrophes to show possession. People often get anxious about this simple matter and start using apostrophes all over the place, even when they aren't correct. Along a country road have you ever seen a sign like this?

FRESH EGG'S

Or a student will write

I thought it was hers.

and then say, "Wait a minute. *Hers* is possessive. I better use an apostrophe," and change it to

I thought it was her's.

The farmer is wrong and the student is wrong. All the farmer means is that he has more than one egg for sale; the eggs don't own anything. And we never use apostrophes with pronouns to show possession—never ever—only with nouns. So don't overdo it. Remember the following three guidelines.

1. When a noun that shows possession does not end in *s*, we add to it *'s*.
   The artist's skill was obvious.
   But when a noun that shows possession does end in *s*, we add to it either *'* or *'s*.
   The clowns' antics were very funny.
2. In the case of compound nouns, we add the *'s* or the *'* to the last word.
   The Secretary of the Interior's plan was bad.
   The two mother-in-laws' (or mother-in-laws's) disagreement was obvious.
3. When two or more nouns indicate joint possession of something, we add the *'s* or the *'* only to the last noun.
   Joan and Mary's airplane crashed.
   John and Charles' boat sank.
   But when two or more nouns possess the same kind of thing but possess it separately, we add the *'s* or the *'* to each of the nouns.
   Joan's and Mary's airplanes both won prizes.
   John's and Charles' boats both sank.

Don't worry about plurals and possessive pronouns.

1. We *never ever* use an apostrophe with an *s* when the *s* just indicates a plural.

    The eggs of the farmer are not as fresh as the farmer's sons.

2. We *never ever* use an apostrophe with a pronoun that shows possession.

    Now that they got theirs, I want mine.

    If she flaunts hers, he intends to flaunt his.

    If it flaunts its, you can flaunt yours.

EXERCISE 15.C

Rewrite each underlined group of words using apostrophes to show possession.

1. The marriage of Edgardo and Flora was a modern one in that they both worked.

    _____

2. The job of Flora was as a junior executive for a meatball company.

    _____

3. The job of Edgardo was inspecting feathers in a pillow company.

    _____

4. The jobs of Edgardo and Flora were both very tiring.

    _____

5. The demands of their bosses were heavy and frequent.

    _____

6. The tendency of the boss of Flora was to give her reports to work on over the weekend.

    _____

7. The boss of Edgardo often gave him extra bushels of feathers to inspect at the very end of the day.

    _____

8. They complained to each other that the jobs of their parents hadn't been as difficult as theirs were.

    _____

9. Edgardo noticed that the supervisor of his brother-in-law was considerate and kindly.

_____

10. The policy of this supervisor was to treat his employees fairly.

_____

11. As a result, the loyalty to the firm of the employees was outstanding.

_____

12. Theirs was a faithfulness that was comparable only to the faithfulness to its master of a dog.

_____

13. The grumblings of the workers at the company of Edgardo indicated a lot of unhappiness there.

_____

14. Flora finally talked to her boss about the morale of her and her co-workers.

_____

15. Now the morale of everyone is very high, and the meatballs are coming out rounder than ever.

_____

16. HOMOPHONES

Homophones are words that sound alike but are spelled differently and mean different things. For example, in this sentence, "Only a few hours ago, that house was ours," the words *hours* and *ours* sound the same to most people and so are considered homophones. While very few students have trouble with words like those, some do get confused in other cases, particularly those in which one word is a contraction and the other is a possessive.

You're/Your

Read the following passage and underline *you're* and *your* every time you find them.

If your coat isn't ready at the cleaners, you're going to have nothing warm to wear

this evening, and your mother will probably have a fit. If you're really planning on going to the party, you'd better make plans to borrow a coat just in case, or your

goose will be cooked.

Which shows possession? _____

Which is a contraction of *you are?* _____

EXERCISE 16.A

In the blanks below, write your *or* you're:

1. Now that _____ in college, _____ high school
   probably seems a million miles away.

2. When _____ ready to leave, it's irritating to be held up.

3. If _____ parents are understanding during _____
   teen years, that time can be a good one.

4. If _____ always fighting with them, it isn't so pleasant.

5. When _____ all fired up during a basketball game, the adrena-

   line in _____ body is flowing.

Write three sentences using the word *your:*

6. _____

7. _____

8. _____

Write three sentences using the word *you're:*

9. _____

10. _____

11. _____

It's/Its

Read the following passage and underline *it's* and *its* every time you find them.

It's time to take the cat to the veterinarian again. It's gotten some scratches on

its nose and ears, probably from a fight, and I'm pretty sure it's time for its shots as well. In some ways, it's kind of a nuisance to own a cat, but I find its company very pleasant.

Which shows possession?_____
Which is a contraction of *it is* or *it has?*_____

EXERCISE 16.B

In the blanks below, write it's *or* its:

1. When _____ time to be fed, the dog heads straight for _____ dish.

2. Now that _____ been decided who will wash the car, _____ time to get started on it.

3. When the cat got _____ tail caught in the refrigerator door, it yowled _____ head off.

4. Let's try to find out whether _____ too late to get the tickets.

5. I'm sure the table is expensive; _____ made of rosewood, and _____ surface is in beautiful condition.

Write three sentences using the word *its:*

6. _____

7. _____

8. _____

Write three sentences using the word *it's:*

9. _____

10. _____

11. _____

Who's/Whose

Read the following passage and draw a line under *who's* and *whose* every time you find them.

I don't know who's going to pay for the band at the party tonight, and I don't know whose problem it is, but it's not mine. The committee whose decision it was to hire the group should also decide who's to follow through on it, including who's going to have to come up with the money. The people whose actions have produced this mess should now clean it up.

Which shows possession?_____
Which is a contraction of *who is?*_____

EXERCISE 16.C

In the blanks below, write whose *or* who's:

1. When I found out _____ job you were taking, I wondered _____ I would get.

2. _____ responsible for this mess we're in?

3. I know _____ responsible, but I don't know _____ going to get us out of it.

4. Try to find out _____ going on the picnic and _____ car we'll be taking.

5. I think I know _____ woods these are.

Write three sentences using the word *whose:*

6. _____

7. _____

8. _____

Write three sentences using the word *who's:*

9. _____

10. _____

11. _____

The three pairs of homophones covered above—*you're/your, it's/its,* and *who's/whose*—have something in common. Notice that in each case, the word with the apostrophe is a contraction, a combination of two words:

you're = you are
it's   = _____ it is or it has
who's = who is or who has

Notice also that in each case, the word without the apostrophe is a possessive pronoun:

your = your hat (Pick up your hat.)
its   = _____ its fur (The cat is licking its fur.)
whose = whose coat (Whose coat is this?)

While nouns in their possessive forms always use apostrophes, pronouns in their possessive forms *never* use apostrophes.

There/Their

Read the following passage and underline *there* and *their* every time you find them.

There are three main kinds of pests at movie theaters. The worst are the ones who

insist on talking to their friends throughout the whole film. About as bad are the

mothers who bring their little children, who sit there not understanding anything

and either ask questions all the time or cry. Then there are the ones crunching

their way through a monster vat of popcorn. Unfortunately, there seems to be

little one can do about most of these nuisances.

Which is a way of introducing a thought or indicates a location? _____
Which shows possession?_____

EXERCISE 16.D

In the blanks below, write there *or* their:

1. _____ are several ways of messing up a date.

2. One standard one is to plan to go to a concert but not get _____ on time.

3. Then _____ are the people who don't write down _____ dates and appointments and just plain fail to show up.

4. _____ dating histories tend to be short and sad ones.

5. People who are considerate of _____ dates and get _____ acts together ahead of time generally have a happier time.

Write three sentences using the word *there* to introduce an idea.

6. _____

7. _____

8. _____

Write three sentences using the word *their* to indicate possession.

9. _____

10. _____

11. _____

To/Too

Read the following paragraph and underline the words *to* and *too* every time you find them.

> A friend of mine has made a list of movies he wants to see, but it's much too long. He must have four or five hundred titles on the list, and it would simply take too many hours to try to watch them. He not only wrote down all those titles, but he even added comments to each one, too, writing things such as "not to be missed." I went to the video store to try to rent a few things on his list but couldn't find any of them. They were too rare for my local store to handle. I thought I might make a similar list too, but mine would be a great deal shorter.

Which form means either *also* or *very?* _____

EXERCISE 16.E

Write either to *or* too *in the blanks in the following passage. If the word* also *or* very *would fit, write* too. *Otherwise, write* to.

> Chung set out _____ buy a CD player, but he was thinking of getting a new tape recorder _____. The tape recorder he owned was _____ old to function well anymore. The first CD player he looked at had _____ many frills and was far _____ expensive. He was somewhat drawn to another machine, but that one was rather expensive _____. He examined every machine carefully, and an attractive saleswoman tried to help him out. Finally, he found some equipment that seemed _____ do

about what he wanted, and he decided _____ buy it. Unfortunately, he owed _____

much on his credit card, and so the store told him _____ hit the road. The

saleswoman was not _____ interested in his proposal _____ go on a date either.

17. CAPITALIZATION

Rules for capitalizing nouns are particularly hard to remember because they are so arbitrary. They are even completely different from one language to another. Here are the most common ones in English:

1. The first word of every sentence must be capitalized.
    My cat ate the doughnuts.

2. People's names and initials and the names of animals are capitalized.
    George F. Handel
    P. D. Q. Bach
    Black Beauty (but not *horse*)
    Fido (but not *dog*)

3. Titles and abbreviated titles are all capitalized.
    Doctor Mary Jones
    Mary Jones, M.D.
    J. W. Birdwalk, Ph.D.
    President Lincoln
    Senator Wilson
    John Jones, Coordinator of Special Programs
    Mother (when used as a name)

4. When title words are not used as actual titles, they are not capitalized.
    She took her mother to the doctor, and they ran into one of their senators along the way.

5. Names of specific places with formal names are capitalized.
    Great Britain
    Thailand
    the Grand Canyon
    Arizona

Cleveland

the Algonquin Hotel

Main Street

6. Words referring to places without naming them are not capitalized.
    We walked down the street, past several hotels. Being in a strange city, we
    weren't sure which one to choose.

The following passage illustrates rules 1 through 6:

My mother went to see Doctor Jones yesterday, but the doctor was not in. She

stopped by City Hall on Franklin Street to visit with her old school friend, Mayor

Jane Wilson, but the street was blocked off by the police. One of the police, Officer

Johnson, told her that a big movie company was making a film in the building.

7. Names of languages and nationalities are always capitalized.
    English
    Chinese
    Mexican
    Canadian

8. But not when they don't refer to the language or the country.
    french fries
    canadian bacon
    russian roulette
    chinese checkers

9. In school, course titles are capitalized but not the names of subjects, except
    when the subject is a language (see rule 7 above).

Capitalize	**Do Not Capitalize**
Sociology 110	My best subject is sociology.
History of English	I am taking a course in the history of English.

Following is a passage that illustrates rules 7 through 9:

My friend Bo Ericksson, a Swedish exchange student, put another round of

spanish onion on his hamburger and talked about his schedule. "I'm taking

four courses, history, physics, math, and English. I'd like to take French too, but

I don't have the time. My best course so far is History 230, Early American

Colonies."

10. The names of religions are capitalized and so are the names of organizations.
    Judaism (and Jewish)
    Buddhism (and Buddhist)
    Catholic Church
    Democratic Party
    Ford Motor Company
    Business Students Association

11. The titles of stories, books, poems, movies, television shows, magazines,
    newspapers, and the like are capitalized, except for short words like *a, the,
    of, and,* and so on. These words are capitalized only if they are the first
    word of the title.
    The New Yorker
    The Atlanta Constitution
    A Hazard of New Fortunes
    The Lord of the Rings
    Cat on a Hot Tin Roof

12. Periods or events in history are capitalized and so are organized current
    events that have names.
    the Wars of the Roses
    the Reformation
    the Boxer Rebellion
    the Senior Prom
    the Boston Marathon

The following passage illustrates rules 10 through 12:

In an excellent book entitled *A Fall of Fortresses*, Elmer Bendiner describes the lives

and experiences of the men who flew the bombers of the U.S. Army Air Force

over Europe during World War II. The book is particularly valuable in its treat-

ment of the disastrous Battle of Schweinfurt.

13. Days, months, and holidays are capitalized but not seasons.
    Monday
    January

Martin Luther King's Birthday

fall

winter

14. Capitalize directions when they refer to specific geographical areas but not otherwise.

The following passage illustrates this rule and also rule 13.

Joanne is going to drive south this summer because she comes from the

South and wants to revisit her hometown. She plans to leave on a Monday

early in May.

EXERCISE 17.A

The following exercises cover rules 1 through 6. In every instance in which there should be a capital letter, write the capital over the small printed letter.

1. on their trip to europe, my father and mother planned to visit ireland and scotland, where they had relatives, and then cross the english channel to spend some time in paris, where their best friend, a dentist, was planning to be.

2. as it turned out, the dentist, doctor sam jones, had to change his plans and was still in london, staying in a hotel on a street made famous in the 1960s, carnaby street.

3. i stayed home and took care of ping and pong, our two cats, and tried to flirt with professor fludge, the unmarried mathematics professor who lives next door.

The following exercises cover rules 7 through 14. Write in capital letters where they belong.

4. my roommate at the college of california is a spanish student named Rosa, who is in the united states for the first time.

5. her english is excellent, and she has done very well in english 100 and english 200 as well as all the classes in her major, political science.

6. although she is catholic and I am protestant, we get along extremely well, even when discussing religion.

7. for one thing, our tastes are quite similar; we both enjoy reading the new york times book review as well as the american edition of the french magazine elle, and we are both fans of the rock group slimy potato.

8. the biggest difference between Rosa and me is that she is very conservative by american standards; I am a republican from the midwest but I'm not nearly as conservative as she is.

9. one saturday last fall, we both went to the annual fall mixer, a big dance sponsored by the humanities students association, a dance where you didn't bring dates.

10. Rosa had a wonderful time, but her conservative spanish heritage really came to the fore when the boy she met tried to give her a french kiss, and she slapped him hard enough that you could hear it back in barcelona.

EXERCISE 17.B

The following exercises cover all fourteen of the capitalization rules.

1. Write a short sentence about the president of the United States in which you use the word *president* twice, once in its capitalized form and once in its ordinary form.

   _____

2. Write a short sentence in which you use the name of the town or city in which you live and tell about a place in another state or country you would like to visit.

   _____

3. Write a short sentence about a language you have studied or are studying or would like to study.

   _____

4. Write a short sentence in which you name all the subjects you are taking this term and the name of one course.

   _____

5. Write a short sentence in which you name your religion or an organization you have belonged to or have worked for.

   _____

6. Write a short sentence in which you name three out of the following four things: a television show, a book you have read, a newspaper, a movie.

   _____

7. Write a short sentence about a specific period of history that you know about or a well-known historical event.

   _____

8. Write a short sentence in which you mention a favorite holiday and also the region of the country you live in.

   _____

EXERCISE 17.C

The following exercises cover all fourteen capitalization rules. Write the capital letter in over the lowercase letter where a capital is appropriate.

1. When marvin drizzle decided to go to the west coast on a vacation beginning the july fourth weekend, he decided to visit an old friend of his in san francisco.

2. His friend, marlene snips, was now president of a small company manufacturing tourist items to be sold in shops in chinatown.

3. Her firm, *it ain't what it seems, inc.,* also made fake plants, such as bushes, trees, weeds, and even spanish moss, for film studios.

4. Marvin had read in the newspaper and in newsweek that san francisco had a large hispanic, as well as asian, population, and because his mother was mexican-american, he was interested to see the mission district, the center of the city's hispanic population.

5. Marlene, who had taken a course in the history of san francisco at san francisco state university, told him that during world war ii, the city's population had been largely irish, italian, and chinese.

6. While many black workers and their families had come west during the second world war to work in the shipyards, the biggest influx of new groups had taken place in the sixties, seventies, and eighties.

7. Marvin said, "I came out to this city for a vacation, and I feel as though I've enrolled in a sociology class."

8. He admitted that he found it quite interesting to hear english, chinese, and spanish all being spoken on the same street.

9. Marlene took him to all the standard tourist sites, such as the golden gate bridge, and introduced him to her business friends, the president of the chamber of commerce, a few lawyers, and others.

10. When marvin returned to the east coast, he spent a week resting up from his vacation before going back to his job as a publisher.

CREDITS

This page constitutes an extension of the copyright page. We have made every effort to trace the ownership of all copyrighted material and to secure permission from copyright holders. In the event of any question arising as to the use of any material, we will be pleased to make the necessary corrections in future printings. Thanks are due to the following authors, publishers, and agents for permission to use the material indicated.

Chapter 1

6: Joyce Maynard, "Looking Back: A Chronicle of Growing Up Old in the Sixties,"

8: Michael Barrier and Martin Williams, " 'Introduction' to A Smithsonian Book of Comic-Book Comics"

Paul R. Erlich, "The Population Bomb,"

9: John J. Macionis, "Aging and the Elderly," *Sociology,* 5th edition (Englewood Cliffs, NJ: Prentice-Hall, 1995).

11: Marya Mannes, "But Will It Sell?"

16: Jane Brody, "Fatigue: The Cause is Usually Emotional," the *New York Times,* January 23, 1980. Copyright © 1980 by The New York Times Co. Reprinted by permission.

20: Roger D. McGrath, *Gunfighters, Highwaymen, and Vigilantes: Violence on the Frontier.* Copyright © 1984 The Regents of the University of California. Reprinted by permission of The University of California Press.

23: Robert L. Heilbroner, "Don't Let Stereotypes Warp Your Judgment," *Reader's Digest,* January 1962. Copyright © 1961 by International Business Machines Corp. Reprinted by permission of William Morris Agency, Inc., on behalf of the author.

30: Joyce Maynard, "His Talk, Her Talk," in *Viewpoints: Readings Worth Thinking and Writing About*, W. Royce Adams, ed., D. C. Heath & Co., 1988. Reprinted by permission of Robert Cornfield Literary Agency.

32: Mark A. Sherman and Adelaide Haas, "Man to Man, Woman to Woman," *Psychology Today*, June 1984. Copyright © 1984 (PT Partners, L.P.). Reprinted with permission from *Psychology Today* Magazine.

Chapter 2

62: Tom Wolfe, "King of the Status Dropouts" from *THE PUMP HOUSE GANG.* © 1965 by Farrar, Straus and Giroux.

63: Joan Didion, "On Morality" from *SLOUCHING TOWARD BETHLEHEM.* © 1965 by Joan Didion. © 1968 by Farrar, Straus and Giroux.

64: Joyce Maynard, "His Talk, Her Talk," in *Viewpoints: Readings Worth Thinking and Writing About,* W. Royce Adams, ed., D. C. Heath & Co., 1988. Reprinted by permission of Robert Cornfield Literary Agency.

64: Mark A. Sherman and Adelaide Haas, "Man to Man, Woman to Woman," *Psychology Today,* June 1984. Copyright © 1984 (PT Partners, L.P.). Reprinted with permission from *Psychology Today* Magazine.

66: Vanessa Thai, "Student,"

74: Jerrold Gor, "Student,"

76: Peggy Van

78: Jane Brody, "Fatigue: The Cause is Usually Emotional," the *New York Times,* January 23, 1980. Copyright © 1980 by The New York Times Co. Reprinted by permission.

79: Roger D. McGrath, *Gunfighters, Highwaymen, and Vigilantes: Violence on the Frontier.* Copyright © 1984 The Regents of the University of California.

Reprinted by permission of The University of California Press.

79: Robert L. Heilbroner, "Don't Let Stereotypes Warp Your Judgment," *Reader's Digest,* January 1962. Copyright © 1961 by International Business Machines Corp. Reprinted by permission of William Morris Agency, Inc., on behalf of the author.

Chapter 3

93: John J. O'Connor, "What Are TV Ads Selling to Children?" the *New York Times,* June 6, 1989. Copyright © 1989 by The New York Times Co. Reprinted by permission.

95: Daniel Riffe, Helen Goldson, Kelly Saxton, and Yang-Chou Yu, "Females and Minorities in TV Ads in 1987 Saturday Children's Programs," *Journalism Quarterly,* 66(1), September 1989. Reprinted by permission of *Journalism Quarterly.*

102: Robert B. Reich, "Why the Rich Are Getting Rich and the Poor Poorer," *New Republic,* May 1, 1989. Copyright 1989 New Republic. Reprinted by permission.

109: Adapted from Bureau of Labor Statistics, U.S. Department of Labor, "Tomorrow's Jobs," *Occupational Outlook Handbook,* 2004.

121: Mary Kay Blakely, "Help or Hindrance?" *Sacramento Bee,* January 20, 1987. Reprinted with permission of the author.

124: Larkin, *Confessions of a Former Women's Magazine Writer,* from quackwatch.org. Reprinted by permission of Stephen Barrett, M.D.

129: Susan Dudash, "We've Come a Long Way, But Magazines Stayed Behind," the *Daily Collegian.* © 1989 Collegian, Inc. Used with permission.

136: Jib Fowles, "Advertising's 15 Basic Appeals," ETC: *A Review of General Semantics,* Volume 39, Number 3, Fall

1982. Reprinted by permission of International Society for General Semantics.

Chapter 4

174: From Integrations (015509955) by William Robinson © 2003 Thomson-Heinle.

183: Edmund S. Morgan, *The Puritan Family: Religion and Domestic Relations in Seventeenth-Century New England* (New York: Harper & Row, 1966). Reprinted with permission of the author.

185: Louis B. Wright, "Everyday Life in Colonial America,"

188: Tamar Lewin, "Women Working More and Parenting More," the *New York Times,* Oct. 17, 2006. © 1998 The New York Times Co. Reprinted by permission.

190: : Eric Schmitt, "For First Time, Nuclear Families Drop Below 25% of Households," the *New York Times,* May 15, 2001. © 2001 by The New York Times Co. Reprinted by permission.

195: William S. Robinson, "New Math-Science Study Rates U.S. Students Mediocre at Best"

196: Barbara Vobejda, "Why Are U.S. Kids Poor in Math?" *Honolulu Star-Bulletin and Advertiser,* January 11, 1987. Copyright 1987 The Washington Post. Reprinted by permission.

197: Cynthia G. Hicks, "Failing Schools Try Longer Day".

198: Kie Ho, "We Should Cherish Our Children's Freedom to Think," *Los Angeles Times,* 1983. Reprinted by permission of the author.

200: James Fallows, "Strengths, Weaknesses, and Lessons of Japanese Education," *Educational Research Service* (1990). Used with permission.

207: Student essay entitled, "School Here in the United States and There in Vietnam"

208: Richard Morin, "Some Public Schools Don't Make the Grade," *Washington Post* National Weekly Edition, January 18, 1999, p. 34. Copyright 1999, The Washington Post. Reprinted with permission.

218: Lauran Neergard, "U.S. Spends Most on Health, but France No. 1 in Treatment," *Associated Press,* June 20, 2000. © 2000 Associated Press. All rights reserved. Dist. by Valeo IP. Reprinted with permission.

219: Dutton, "Health Care in France and the United States: Learning from Each Other".

224: Sara R. Collins, Ph.D., "Health Care Costs and Instability of Insurance: Impact on Patients' Experiences with Care and Medical Bills," Testimony before the Subcommittee on Oversight and Investigations, Committee on Energy and Commerce, U.S. House of Representatives, June 24, 2004.

227: Marc Kaufman and Bill Brubaker, "Study: Drug Prices Outpace Inflation; Price Increases Undermine Medicare Discount Card," from "Higher Prices Erode Value of Medicare Cards," the *Washington Post,* May 26, 2004. Copyright 2004, The Washington Post. Reprinted with permission.

228: Micah L. Sifry and Nancy Watzman, "The Incredible Shrinking Health Care Debate," *Is That a Politician in Your Pocket?* Copyright © 2004. Reprinted with permission of John Wiley & Sons, Inc.

233: Robert Pear, "Drug Companies Increase Spending on Efforts to Lobby Congress and Governments," the *New York Times,* June 1, 2003, p. 33. Copyright © 2003 by The New York Times Co. Reprinted with permission.

234: David U. Himmelstein, M.D. and Steffie Woolhander, M.D., "Why the U.S. Needs a Single Payer Health System." From Physicians for a National Health Program, Internet site, accessed on October 2, 2001. Used with permission.

Chapter 5

269: Dennis McLellan, "Part-Time Work Ethic: Should Teens Go For It?" *Los Angeles Times,* November 7, 1986. Copyright 1986 Los Angeles Times. Reprinted by permission.

274: Ben Wildavsky, "McJobs: Inside America's Largest Youth Training Program," *Policy Review,* Summer 1989. Reprinted by permission of The Heritage Foundation, 214 Massachusetts Avenue, N.E., Washington, DC 20002.

279: Amitai Etzioni, "Why Fast-Food Joints Don't Serve up Good Jobs for Kids," the *Washington Post,* August 24, 1986. Reprinted by permission of the author.

283: Katherine Cress, "Why Not Ask the Students? Urban Teenagers Make the Case for Working," *Phi Delta Kappan* (October 1992). Used with permission.

294: E. G. Krug, K. E. Powell, and L. L. Dahlberg, "Firearm-Related Deaths in the United States and Thirty-Five Other High- and Upper-Middle-Income Countries," *International Journal of Epidemiology* 27 (1998): 214-221. Copyright © 1998 by International Epidemiological Association. Reprinted by permission of the International Epidemiological Association.

297: From E. G. Krug, K. E. Powell, and L. L. Dahlberg, "Firearm-Related Deaths in the United States and Thirty-Five Other High- and Upper-Middle-Income Countries," *International Journal of Epidemiology* 27 (1998): 214–221. Copyright © 1998 by International Epidemiological Association. Reprinted by permission of the International Epidemiological Association.

298: From E. G. Krug, K. E. Powell, and L. L. Dahlberg, "Firearm-Related Deaths in the United States and Thirty-Five Other High- and Upper-Middle-Income Countries," *International Journal of Epidemiology* 27 (1998): 214–221. Copyright © 1998 by International Epidemiological Association. Reprinted by permission of the International Epidemiological Association.

299: From E. G. Krug, K. E. Powell, and L. L. Dahlberg, "Firearm-Related Deaths in the United States and Thirty-Five Other High- and Upper-Middle-Income Countries," *International Journal of Epidemiology* 27 (1998): 214–221. Copyright © 1998 by International Epidemiological Association. Reprinted by permission of the International Epidemiological Association.

302: J. H. Sloan, A. L. Kellermann, D. T. Reay, J. A. Ferris, T. Koepsell, F. P. Rivara, C. Rice, L. Gray, and J. LoGerfo, "Handgun Regulations, Crime, Assaults, and Homicide: A Tale of Two Cities," the *New England Journal of Medicine,* 39 (1988), 1256–1262. Reprinted by permission of the *New England Journal of Medicine.*

308: Wayne LaPierre, "Crime is the Basic Problem, Not Guns," *Ithaca Journal,* March 21, 1989. Reprinted with permission of the publisher.

310: Kristen Wyatt, "Do Gun Laws Work? Study is Inconclusive," *Associated Press/San Francisco Chronicle,* October 3, 2003, p. A5. Copyright 2003 Associated Press. All rights reserved. Distributed by Valeo IP. Reprinted with permission.

311: Micah Sifry and Nancy Watzman, "Of Killer Pens and AK-47s," *Is That a Politician in Your Pocket?* Copyright © 2004. Reprinted with permission of John Wiley & Sons, Inc.

314: Gail Buchalter, "Why I Bought a Gun," *Parade,* February 21, 1988. Reprinted by permission of the author.

317: Cynthia G. Hicks, "Firearm Deaths of Children and Teens in United States".

318: Wm. Robinson, "A Teacher Considers Gun Violence on Campus"

320: Anonymous.

324: Christine de Hass, "Pregnancy at Hazelwood High," *Hazelwood High School Spectrum,* May 13, 1983. Reprinted with permission.

326: Shari Gordon, "Divorce's Impact on Kids May Have Lifelong Effects," *Hazelwood High School Spectrum,* May 13, 1983. Reprinted with permission.

327: Jean Seligmann and Tessa Namuth, "A Limit on the Student Press," *Newsweek,* January 25, 1988. Copyright © 1988 Newsweek, Inc. All rights reserved. Reprinted with permission.

329: Jerry Carroll, "High School Papers Grow Up," *San Francisco Chronicle,* January 21, 1988. © San Francisco Chronicle. Reprinted by permission.

332: Fred M. Hechinger, "High Court Gives a Civics Lesson," the *New York Times,* January 17, 1988. Copyright © 1988 by the New York Times Co. Reprinted by permission.

334: Jonathan Yardley, "Censorship: A Fact of Life Students Are Forced to Face," the *Washington Post,* January 18, 1988. Copyright 1988 the Washington Post. Reprinted by permission.

Chapter 6

366: Michael Ryan, "Who's Taking Care of the Children?" Copyright © 1992 by Michael Ryan. Initially published in *Parade* magazine. All rights reserved. Reprinted by permission of *Parade* and the author's agents, Scovil Chichak Galen Literary Agency, Inc.

370: Tammy Hansen, "Home Day Care Providers Face Increasing Demand," *Oakland Tribune,* January 11, 1998, pp. D1-D5. Reprinted with permission of the *Oakland Tribune.*

371: Anastasia Hendrix, "High Staff Turnover Imperils Child Care, Researcher Says," *San Francisco Chronicle,* April 29, 2001. © San Francisco Chronicle. Reprinted with permission.

373: Source: "Then and Now: Changes in Child Care Staffing."

374: Colin Nickerson, "Canada Blazes Trail on Day Care," *Boston Globe,* June 8, 2000. © Boston Globe. Reprinted with permission.

376: Marlise Simons, "Child Care Sacred as France Cuts Back the Welfare State," the *New York Times,* December 31, 1997, p. A1. Copyright © 1997 by the New York Times Co. Reprinted by permission.

383: Jack Valenti, Motion Picture Association of America, "Voluntary Movie Rating System," accessed at http://www.mpaa.org/movieratings/about/index.htm on August 25, 2004. Courtesy of MPAA.

388: Lois P. Sheinfeld, "Ratings: The Big Chill," first appeared in *Film Comment,* June 1986. Reprinted by permission of the author.

391: Paul Attanasio, "The Rating Game," the *New Republic,* June 17, 1985. Reprinted with permission of the *New Republic.*

393: Tom Shales, "Give Movie Raters a PG, for Pigheadedness," the *Washington Post,* National Weekly Edition, August 16, 1999, p. 21. Copyright 1999, The Washington Post. Reprinted with permission.

396: Joel Topcik, "A Major Studio Tests the (Sexy) Waters of NC-17," the *New York Times,* February 1, 2004, p. 26. Copyright © 2004 by the New York Times Co. Reprinted with permission.

402: Charles R. Lawrence III, "The Debate Over Placing Limits on Racist Speech Must Not Ignore the Damage It Does to Its Victims," *Chronicle of Higher Education,* October 25, 1989. Reprinted by permission of the author.

407: Nat Hentoff, "Free Speech on Campus," *Progressive,* May 1989. Reprinted by permission of the publisher.

413: Joseph S. Tuman, "Hate Speech on Campus," *Inside,* San Francisco State University. Reprinted by permission of the author. Joseph Tuman is an assistant professor in the Department of Speech and Communication Studies at San Francisco State University.

415: Ben Wildavsky, "Rethinking Campus Speech Codes," *San Francisco Chronicle,* March 3, 1995, pp. 1, 15. Copyright 1995 San Francisco Chronicle. Used by permission.

421: Kate Zernike, "Education Helping Top Athletes Meet Minimum Standards," the *New York Times,* July 11, 2001. Copyright © 2001 by the New York Times Co. Reprinted by permission.

424: Steve Wieberg, "Graduation Rates at Top-Tier Football Programs Poor," *USA Today,* September 19, 2001, p. C7. Reprinted with permission.

425: Frank Litsky, "2003 NCAA Tournament: Academics; Study Finds Top Teams Failing in the Classroom," the *New York Times,* March 25, 2003. Copyright © 2003 by The New York Times Co. Reprinted with permission.

426: Selena Roberts, "Big Spenders on Campus Spending Your Money," the *New York Times,* December 7, 2003. Copyright © 2003 by the New York Times Co. Reprinted with permission.

427: NCAA, "NCAA Board of Directors Adopts Landmark Academic Reform Package," Press Release, April 29, 2004.

429: Marc Isenberg, "Plan Creates Loopholes, Not Educated Athletes," the *New York Times,* May 2, 2004. Copyright © 2004 by the New York Times Co. Reprinted with permission.

430: Douglas Lederman, "The Ivy League at 30: A Model for College Athletics or an Outmoded Antique?" *Chronicle of Higher Education,* November 19, 1986. Copyright 1986 The Chronicle of Higher Education. Reprinted with permission.

INDEX

INDEX OF AUTHORS AND TITLES